The Jewish Metropolis

New York City from the 17th to the 21st Century

The Lands and Ages of the Jewish People

Series Editor: Ira Robinson (Concordia University, Montreal)

The Jewish Metropolis

New York City from the 17th to the 21st Century

Edited by
Daniel Soyer

BOSTON
2021

2012

BP53

Library of Congress Cataloging-in-Publication Data

Names: Soyer, Daniel, editor.
Title: The Jewish metropolis : New York from the 17th to the 21st century / edited by Daniel Soyer.
Other titles: New York from the 17th to the 21st century
Description: Boston : Academic Studies Press, 2021. | Series: The lands and ages of the Jewish people
Identifiers: LCCN 2020046615 (print) | LCCN 2020046616 (ebook) | ISBN 9781644694886 (hardback) | ISBN 9781644694893 (paperback) | ISBN 9781644694909 (adobe pdf) | ISBN 9781644694916 (epub)
Subjects: LCSH: Jews--New York (State)--New York--History. | Jews--New York (State)--New York--Social life and customs. | New York (State)-- New York--Ethnic relations. | New York (N.Y.)--Social life and customs.
Classification: LCC F128.9.J5 J578 2021 (print) | LCC F128.9.J5 (ebook) | DDC 974.7/004924--dc23
LC record available at https://lccn.loc.gov/2020046615
LC ebook record available at https://lccn.loc.gov/2020046616

ISBN 9781644694886 (hardback)
ISBN 9781644694893 (paperback)
ISBN 9781644694909 (adobe pdf)
ISBN 9781644694916 (ePub)

Book design by Lapiz Digital Services.
Cover design by Ivan Grave.
Published by Academic Studies Press.
1577 Beacon Street
Brookline, MA 02446, USA
press@academicstudiespress.com
www.academicstudiespress.com

1/31/22

Contents

Introduction:
New York as a Jewish City

Daniel Soyer

American culture makes a close association between Jews and New York City. The popular imagination associates Jews with New York foodways (deli, bagels), speech (Yiddish vocabulary), attitudes and manner (speed, brusqueness, irony, sarcasm), industries (garments, banking, entertainment), politics (liberalism, neo-conservatism), high culture (visual arts, literature, music, social criticism), and popular culture (theater, advertising, music). Some, like the comedian Lenny Bruce, have seen the Jewish and New York essences as virtually identical. "To me," Bruce remarked, "if you live in New York or any other big city, you are Jewish. It doesn't matter even if you're Catholic; if you live in New York you're Jewish." American Jews, conversely, have often emphasized the links between New York Jews and Jews in other parts of the country. Indeed, Jews in other places sometimes defined themselves in relation to New York, their own communities having emerged as colonies of the New York metropole.[1]

---

1   See Ted Merwin, *Pastrami on Rye: An Overstuffed History of the Jewish Deli* (New York: NYU Press, 2015); H. L. Mencken, *The American Language: An Inquiry into the Development of English in the United States* (New York: Alfred A. Knopf, 1946), 216–18, 368, and Supplement I (New York: Knopf, 1945), 433–35; Hana Wirth-Nesher, "The Accented imagination: Speaking and Writing Jewish America," in *Imagining the American Jewish Community*, ed. Jack Wertheimer (Hannover/Waltham: University Press of New England / Brandeis University Press, 2007), 287–88; Lenny Bruce, *How to Talk Dirty and Influence People* (1962; New York: Fireside / Simon and Schuster, 1992), 5 (Google Books, accessed December 25, 2017); Deborah Dash Moore, *To the Golden Cities: Pursuing the American Jewish Dream in Miami and L.A.* (New York: Free Press, 1994), 1–6, 32, 37, 47, 49–50, 59, 62, 63–64, 70, 85–86, 208, 260, 275.

Among scholars, the tendency to identify New York with Jewish America is evident even in the titles of such classic works as Moses Rischin's *Promised City* (New York as the New Jerusalem) and Deborah Dash Moore's *At Home in America* (New York as America itself). More recently, despite a growing body of literature on the history of Jews elsewhere or more self-consciously on the creation of the New York image, historians frequently make the easy assumption that New York was somehow a "Jewish city."[2]

In fact, both scholars and lay people have good reason to think of New York as a Jewish city. Since the end of the nineteenth century, there have been more Jews in the Big Apple than in any other single municipality— more than there ever were in Warsaw, Vilna, Tel Aviv, or Jerusalem. For much of the period, the city's Jewish population could only be compared to those of other *countries*. In 1930, for example, the five boroughs' 1.8 million Jews about equaled those of Romania, Lithuania, Latvia, Germany, and Palestine put together. In 1950, the city's 2 million Jews were twice those of Israel, and about same in number as those of the Soviet Union. Even after fifty years of decline, at the beginning of the twenty-first century, 972,000 New York Jews outnumbered those of Tel Aviv and Jerusalem combined. Looking at it another way, for a time in the mid-twentieth century, Jews were the largest single ethnic group in the city, at about 30% of the population.[3] Moreover, the significance of New York goes beyond numbers. As Stephen Whitfield put it, "The culture of American Jewry was born in Eastern Europe and was then transplanted and refashioned in cities such as

---

2   Moses Rischin, *The Promised City: New York's Jews, 1870–1914* (Cambridge, MA: Harvard University Press, 1962); Deborah Dash Moore, *At Home in America: Second Generation New York Jews* (New York: Columbia University Press, 1981). See also Hasia Diner, *Lower East Side Memories: A Jewish Place in America* (Princeton: Princeton University Press, 2000); Hasia Diner, Jeffrey Shandler, and Beth Wenger, *Remembering the Lower East Side: American Jewish Reflections* (Bloomington: Indiana University Press, 2000). The author observed historians making the assumption that New York was a "Jewish city" at a recent working group on New York City Jewish history at the Center for Jewish History, New York.

3   Moore, *At Home in America*, 23; H. S. Linfield, "Statistics of the Jews," *American Jewish Yearbook* 32 (1930/1931): 227, 229; Evyatar Friesel, *Atlas of Modern Jewish History* (New York: Oxford University Press, 1990), 17; "Jewish Population Estimates of Selected Cities," 73, and Leon Shapiro and Boris Sapir, "World Jewish Population," 247, 249, both in *American Jewish Yearbook* 51 (1950); *Jewish Community Study of New York, 2002* (New York: UJA-Federation, 2004), 30; Central Bureau of Statistics, "Localities and Population, by Type of Locality and Population Group," https://www.cbs.gov.il/he/publications/doclib/2002/2.%20shnaton%20population/st02_12x.pdf, accessed September 10, 2020.

New York."[4] No wonder that Academic Studies Press commissioned a book on New York City Jewry for its Lands and Ages of the Jewish People series, alongside volumes on Germany, Canada, and Medieval Iberia.

But is New York really a Jewish city? Jews were never a majority of the population, as they were in Salonica or Bialystok, or in many East European *shtetlekh*. Neither were Jews the largest *religious* group, which from the mid-nineteenth century were Catholics. Indeed, it is possible to write the histories of many crucial aspects of the city's overall history and hardly mention Jews at all.[5]

New York Jews knew this. There were many neighborhoods in the city where they did not feel at home, and memoirists such as Alfred Kazin and Vivian Gornick comment on the foreignness and exoticism of the city's Manhattan core. Even at their demographic peak, then, Jews felt more at home in some parts of New York than others.[6]

It probably makes more sense to think about when, how and where New York has been a Jewish city. Indeed, it is not even so obvious what "Jewish" has meant in New York. The city has been home to a wide range of Jews and Jewishness: Sephardi, Mizrahi, and Ashkenazi; German and East European; poor garment workers and wealthy financiers; English, Yiddish, German, Ladino, Arabic, and Hebrew speakers; women and men; Orthodox, Reform, and secular; leftwing and rightwing; immigrant and native-born; gay and straight; Manhattan sophisticates and "outer borough" middle-Americans, and so on. The New York Jewish experience has been so diverse that it would take, indeed has taken, multiple volumes to cover adequately.[7] This book thus only provides an entrée to the topic.

---

4   Stephen Whitfield, *In Search of American Jewish Culture* (Hannover/Waltham: University Press of New England / Brandeis University Press, 1999), 1.

5   T. J. Shelley, "Catholics," in *Encyclopedia of New York City* (New Haven: Yale University Press, 1995), 192; James T. Fisher, *On the Irish Waterfront: The Crusader, the Movie, and the Soul of the Port of New York* (Ithaca: Cornell University Press, 2009).

6   Beth Wenger, *New York Jews and the Great Depression: Uncertain Promise* (New Haven: Yale University Press, 1996), 81; Moore, *At Home in America*, 86.

7   For a treatment of the history in three volumes, see Howard Rock, *Haven of Liberty: New York Jews in the New World, 1654–1865,* Annie Polland and Daniel Soyer, *Emerging Metropolis: New York Jews in the Age of Immigration, 1840–1920,* and Jeffrey S. Gurock, *Jews in Gotham: New York Jews in a Changing City, 1920–2010,* all parts of *City of Promises: A History of the Jews of New York,* ed. Deborah Dash Moore (New York: New York University Press, 2012). A one-volume version is Deborah Dash Moore et al., *New York Jews: A History* (New York: New York University Press, 2017).

Periodization and Jewish Diversity in New York

The customary periodization of New York Jewish history only obscures the diversity of the city's Jewish life since the seventeenth century. During the "Sephardic Period" from 1654 to 1825, for example, the single congregation served as the center of all aspects of Jewish communal life. Shearith Israel used the Sephardic rite, but as early as 1720, the majority of local Jews, and thus of synagogue members, were Ashkenazim. In any case, their numbers remained small—400 in 1775, about 1.6% of the city's population. No one yet saw any particular connection between New York and Jews.

It was during the "German Period" (1825–1880) that New York became a significant Jewish population center. By 1880, there were some 80,000 Jews in the city.[8] But not all of them were "German," whatever that may have meant at the time. The descendants of colonial Jewry—Sephardic and Ashkenazi—remained, of course. But the new immigrants, too, actually came from a range of places in Central Europe: the German states, Posen (western Poland, under the control of Prussia), Alsace, Bohemia, Moravia, Hungary, Lithuania, and so forth. Moreover, they now created a diverse Jewish communal structure, pioneering new modes of expressing Jewish identity and formal affiliation. Not only were there many new congregations organized according to old-world origin and tradition, but some congregations began to innovate new styles of worship that coalesced into the Reform movement in Judaism. As importantly, some began to experiment with new forms of secular Jewish expression, including fraternal orders such as B'nai B'rith, and philanthropic endeavors like Jews' Hospital (later Mt. Sinai).

In popular culture, the Jewish image sometimes merged with that of the Germans, but although they were still less than ten percent of the city's population, for the first time an association of Jews with New York, or at least parts of it, began to emerge. The Chatham Street old-clothes market, notably, was said to be populated by "natty, blackbearded, fiercely mustached" Jewish merchants out to cheat unwary shoppers, many of them simple country folk.[9] They were the first "New York Jews."

It was in the "East European" period (ca. 1880–1924), when New York absorbed the majority of the nearly two and a half million Jews, mainly from Eastern Europe—the Russian and Austro-Hungarian empires, and

---

8   Polland and Soyer, *The Emerging Metropolis,* 7, 13.
9   Polland and Soyer, *The Emerging Metropolis,* 10–11.

Romania—who arrived in the United States, that the city emerged as the greatest Jewish metropolis of all time. New York became a major world center of Yiddish culture—especially in the areas of journalism, theater, and poetry. But even then, New York Jewry was diverse. New York Jewry ranged from right to left, from ultra-traditional to ultra-modern. Besides Yiddish, New York Jews also published in Hebrew, Russian, and other languages.

An additional stream of Jewish immigration came from the Ottoman Empire, Greece, the Middle East, and North Africa. Some 30,000 Sephardic Jews, many of them Ladino-speaking, established their own mutual aid associations, synagogues, and newspapers. Often ill-treated by the much more numerous Ashkenazim, who doubted their Jewishness, they also took part in the major communal and political movements of the day, sometimes serving as a bridge between the Jewish and emerging Latinx communities.

In this period, and in that of the "second generation" (ca. 1920–ca. 1970), New York's Jewish geography became more complicated, as the population spread outward from the original main area of settlement in what from about 1905 was called the Lower East Side. By 1916, the Jewish population had dispersed over bridges and via transportation lines to neighborhoods in upper Manhattan, Brooklyn, and the Bronx. [10] Identifiable as Jewish not only by names on the census registers, but by the school rolls, languages spoken, and the stores, synagogues, and other organizations that catered to their residents, these neighborhoods were differentiated by class, politics, and religious inclination.

By this time, Jews made their livings as factory workers, shopkeepers, professionals, and bankers. But the New York industry most closely associated with Jews was, of course, the ready-made garment industry, especially in women's wear. Jews entered the industry just as it was taking off at the end of the nineteenth century, and for a long time they dominated its workforce. Clothing production also offered an avenue of upward mobility for some who became contractors and even manufacturers. At the same time, Jews led the garment unions, which pioneered a form of social unionism. Even after the presence of Jews as workers in the shops began to fade, many remained as employers or union officials.

---

10   Moses Rischin, "Toward the Onomastics of the Great New York Ghetto: How the Lower East Side Got Its Name," in Diner et al., *Remembering the Lower East Side*, 13–24; Moses Rischin, *The Promised City: New York Jews, 1870–1914* (Cambridge, MA: Harvard University Press, 1962), 93.

The Fall and Rise of Jewish New York

As New York underwent dramatic economic and demographic shifts in the decades after World War II, many Jews moved to the suburbs or the sunbelt, and the Jewish population began to fall. By the end of the twentieth century, there were fewer than a million Jews in the five boroughs, the lowest number in nearly a hundred years. Some neighborhoods, such as Brownsville in Brooklyn, and much of the Bronx, that had been heavily Jewish now had virtually no Jews living in them.[11]

Those who remained experienced the city in paradoxical ways. On the one hand, Jews were at the height of their political, economic and cultural influence. Especially in Manhattan and certain neighborhoods of Brooklyn and Queens, Jews remained in the forefront of the liberal establishment, radical insurgencies, and cosmopolitan cultural circles. At the same time, however, many Jews felt increasingly ill at ease in the city. Turf battles in transitional neighborhoods, and racialized conflicts like the 1968 conflict between the heavily Jewish teachers' union and the minority-led Ocean Hill-Brownsville school board alienated many from their traditional liberalism. This was especially true of lower-middle-class Jews in the outer boroughs, and of the Orthodox, who joined the "white backlash" against insurgent minorities.

In the midst of its travails, New York City began to recover. After half a century of decline, New York Jewry also began to grow, once again topping one million. New York's Jewish population had been shored up by waves of Soviet immigrants in the 1970s and 1990s, but its renewed growth was mainly due to the natural increase of the Orthodox, and especially the Haredi ("ultra-Orthodox") sector. Indeed, in 2011 some 61% of Jewish children lived in orthodox households, giving some indication of the future direction of the community.

Nevertheless, as the city itself, twenty-first-century New York Jewry was more diverse than ever before. Sephardim and Mizrahim—primarily Bukharan, Syrian, Kavkazi, and Georgian, as well as some percentage of Israelis—now constitute a much greater percentage of the Jewish population than they did in the early twentieth century. Tens of thousands of Jews live in LGBTQ households, or households with nonwhite or multiracial members. And despite the growth of the Orthodox community, for example, there has also been an increase in the number of Jews with little Jewish

---

11 *Jewish Community Study of New York, 2002,* 30, 33.

identification or practice. Moreover, New York Jewry differs from the rest of American Jewry in significant respects – poorer, more likely to be foreign born, and more Orthodox.[12]

An Unusual Caveat

There have been many New Yorks, and there have been many Jewish New Yorks. Large sections of the city were never "Jewish" and Jews did not always feel at home there. Even where and when Jews did predominate or play a central role, they were a diverse lot. New York Jews have pioneered religious reform and led the resurgence of traditionalist orthodoxy; they have spoken English, German, Yiddish, Ladino, Hebrew, Russian, Arabic, and English again; they have been among the richest financiers and poorest shop workers; they have provided the base for political radicalism and liberalism, and the intellectual power behind resurgent conservatism. This book covers some aspects of the history of New York Jewry from the seventeenth to the twenty-first century. Essays deal with economic, social, political, and cultural influences of Jews on the city and the city on its Jews. But the history of New York Jews is so complex that there are many areas left uncovered: The book touches on Jews as builders but not as garment manufacturers. It has chapters on the visual arts and literature, but not dance or theater. It discusses Yiddish and Ladino New York in the early twentieth century, but not the Bukharan, Syrian, Russian, or Israeli communities of the turn of the twenty-first. It lacks chapters on philanthropy, family life, and transnational links. So for those wanting a comprehensive picture of Jewish New York, it is just the beginning. There is more reading to do.

Acknowledgements

Thank you to Ira Robinson, editor of the Lands and Ages of the Jewish People series, and to the editors at Academic Studies Press, for conceiving of this book, and to the contributors for agreeing to participate and coming through with their chapters. Thanks to Kaitlin Shine for helping to compile the "further reading" lists. And thanks to all for their patience.

---

12   For these and other insights, see *Jewish Community Study of New York: 2011* (New York: UJA-Federation of New York, 2011).

For Further Reading

Diner, Hasia. *Lower East Side Memories: A Jewish Place in America.* Princeton: Princeton University Press, 2000.

Diner, Hasia, Jeffrey Shandler, and Beth Wenger. *Remembering the Lower East Side: American Jewish Reflections.* Bloomington: Indiana University Press, 2000.

Fisher, James T. *On the Irish Waterfront: The Crusader, the Movie, and the Soul of the Port of New York.* Ithaca: Cornell University, 2009.

Friesel, Evyatar. *Atlas of Modern Jewish History.* New York: Oxford University Press, 1990.

Gurock, Jeffrey S. *Jews in Gotham: New York Jews in a Changing City, 1920–2010.* New York: New York University Press, 2012.

Jewish Community Study of New York, 2002. New York: UJA-Federation, 2004. http://www.cbs.gov.il/statistical/populationeng.htm.

Jewish Community Study of New York: 2011. New York: UJA-Federation of New York, 2011.

Mencken, H. L. *The American Language: An Inquiry into the Development of English in the United States.* New York: Alfred A. Knopf, 1946.

Merwin, Ted. *Pastrami on Rye: An Overstuffed History of the Jewish Deli.* New York: NYU Press, 2015.

Moore, Deborah Dash. *At Home in America: Second Generation New York Jews.* New York: Columbia University Press, 1981.

———. *To the Golden Cities: Pursuing the American Jewish Dream in Miami and L.A.* New York: Free Press, 1994.

Moore, Deborah Dash et al. *Jewish New York: A History.* New York: New York University Press, 2017.

Polland, Annie, and Daniel Soyer. *Emerging Metropolis: New York Jews in the Age of Immigration, 1840–1920.* New York: New York University Press, 2012.

Rischin, Moses. "Toward the Onomastics of the Great New York Ghetto: How the Lower East Side Got Its Name." In *Remembering the Lower East Side: American Jewish Reflections*, edited by Hasia Diner, Jeffrey Shandler, and Beth Wenger, 13–24. Bloomington: Indiana University Press, 2000.

Rischin, Moses. *The Promised City: New York's Jews, 1870–1914.* Cambridge, MA: Harvard University Press, 1962.

Rock, Howard. *Haven of Liberty: New York Jews in the New World, 1654–1865.* New York: New York University Press, 2012.

Shelley, T. J. "Catholics." In *Encyclopedia of New York City*, 190–93. New Haven: Yale University Press, 1995.

Wenger, Beth. *New York Jews and the Great Depression: Uncertain Promise* New Haven: Yale University Press, 1996.

Whitfield, Stephen. *In Search of American Jewish Culture.* Hannover/ Waltham: University Press of New England / Brandeis University Press, 1999.

Wirth-Nesher, Hana. "The Accented Imagination: Speaking and Writing Jewish America." In *Imagining the American Jewish Community,* edited by Jack Wertheimer, 296–303. Hannover/Waltham: University Press of New England / Brandeis University Press, 2007.

Important Note

After he was invited to write for this volume, and after his chapter was submitted and accepted, one contributor—the demographer Steven M. Cohen—was revealed to have engaged in a long pattern of sexual harassment of female colleagues, students, and subordinates. He subsequently admitted the truth of the charges and resigned from his academic and communal positions. There is no doubt that Cohen's egregious actions merit his ouster from all positions that would bring him into contact with, let alone give him power over, undergraduates, graduate students, or indeed any colleagues. He should not control money and institutions that he might use to block people's careers or projects. Despite Cohen's personal behavior, the editor has decided to go ahead and include his chapter in the book because it provides useful information on New York Jewry in the 21st century, and on the principle that his obnoxious and unprofessional personal behavior does not necessarily negate the value of his work. It is true that some question the direction of his scholarship – particularly in its concern for "Jewish continuity," birthrates and in-marriage – but his positions on these matters are at least arguable.[1] In any case, they barely figure in the chapter presented here. Whatever their positions on these issues, readers should understand that the decision to include Cohen's work rested with the editor, Daniel Soyer, and not with any of the other contributors, whose work should be judged on its own individual merits.

---

1   For a discussion of the issues involved in this matter, see the roundtable based on Lila Corwin Berman, Kate Rosenblatt and Ronit Stahl, "Continuity Crisis: The History and Sexual Politics of an American Jewish Communal Project," *American Jewish History* 104, no. 2/3 (2020): 167–194.

Chapter 1

Colonial Jews in New Amsterdam, New York, and the Atlantic World

John M. Dixon

Introduction

Surveying the early history of the United States from the vantage point of the late 1830s, American scholar George Bancroft identified New York as "always a city of the world." He explained that this mid-Atlantic port, founded by the Dutch as New Amsterdam in the early seventeenth century, grew quickly to contain a diverse mix of Europeans and Africans. Bancroft stated that religious refugees comprised a sizeable portion of the colonial population of New Amsterdam/New York City. They arrived, he wrote, by the 1650s with the full support of the Holland-based directors of the Dutch West India Company (WIC) who controlled Dutch New Netherland prior to the English conquest of that North American territory in 1664. The religious migrants included Jews. As Bancroft stated with typical elaboration, "children of the bondmen that broke from slavery in Egypt, the posterity of those who had wandered in Arabia, and worshipped near Calvary, found a home, liberty, and a burial-place on the Island of Manhattan."[1]

---

1   George Bancroft, *History of the United States, From the Discovery of the American Continent,* vol. 2 (Boston: Charles Bowen, 1837), 301.

Recent scholarship partly upholds Bancroft's nineteenth-century characterization of early New York as a diverse and tolerant port-town with an important Jewish population. Historians today generally agree that colonial New Amsterdam/New York was a bustling, biracial, multi-ethnic, and polyglot entrepôt that operated as a crucial point of exchange between the North American continent and the Atlantic Ocean. British, Dutch, and French whites lived on the island of Manhattan alongside free and enslaved Blacks. Separate Anglican, Calvinist, Presbyterian, Huguenot, Lutheran, Quaker, Baptist, Methodist, and Jewish congregations catered to people's spiritual needs. Nevertheless, disharmony accompanied this diversity. Political factionalism, religious friction, slave riots, and social unrest blighted early New York life.[2]

One important caveat to Bancroft's statement is that New York, at least as far as it looked eastward, was a city of the Atlantic world more than of the world *in toto* during the seventeenth and eighteenth centuries. The vast majority of colonial New York sailings arrived from or departed to seaports in North America, the Caribbean, Europe, and Africa.[3] This attachment to the wider Atlantic basin fundamentally shaped the early history of Jews in New York City. The first group of Jewish immigrants came from Brazil in 1654. Other Jews subsequently arrived from Europe, the Caribbean, or elsewhere in North America. Many were itinerant and familiar with multiple parts of the Atlantic littoral. Individually and collectively, they maintained strong cultural, kinship, and commercial ties to Jewish and non-Jewish communities in Amsterdam, London, and the Caribbean. Moreover, they linked New York to an early modern trading diaspora known as the Portuguese Nation or *Nação*. One of several mercantile nations that helped to join distant Atlantic port-towns, this dispersed community was comprised largely but not exclusively of Sephardic Jews and *conversos* (descendants of Jewish converts to

---

2   Patricia U. Bonomi, *A Factious People: Politics and Society in Colonial New York* (New York: Columbia University Press, 1971); Joyce D. Goodfriend, *Before the Melting Pot: Society and Culture in Colonial New York City, 1664–1730* (Princeton, NJ: Princeton University Press, 1992); Joyce D. Goodfriend, *Who Should Rule at Home?: Confronting the Elite in British New York City* (Ithaca, NY: Cornell University Press, 2017).

3   It should be noted that a lucrative Indo-Atlantic trade enriched some New York merchants during the last few decades of the seventeenth century. See Kevin P. McDonald, *Pirates, Merchants, Settlers, and Slaves: Colonial America and the Indo-Atlantic World* (Oakland, CA: University of California Press, 2015), esp. chap. 2.

Christianity). It sustained networks of trust that facilitated the circulation of goods and capital across geographic and political spaces.[4]

During much of the twentieth century, historians of early American Jewry understated these Atlantic ties and stuck loyally to the North American geography of traditional United States history. They embedded Jews in a national narrative by emphasizing the longevity of the North American Jewish community and highlighting Jewish contributions to United States history. Unfortunately, they simultaneously isolated North America from the rest of the Atlantic World in an ahistorical manner. For decades, scholars accepted that cost. In a landmark three-volume 1970 study, *Colonial American Jew*, Jacob Rader Marcus focused on the Jewish communities of "the North American mainland colonies," but also conceded that "the seventeenth century Dutch and English dependencies in Brazil, Surinam, and the West Indies were far more noteworthy."[5]

Recently, the rise of Atlantic history—a field that emerged in the 1970s and gained heightened prominence in the 1990s—has encouraged historians of early American Jews and Judaism to pursue more expansive approaches that include the largest Caribbean Jewish communities and the transatlantic networks and pathways that linked North American Jews to ports across the Atlantic World. Consistent with this trend, the early history of Jews in New York City has now been resituated in Atlantic as well as North American contexts. Although more work needs to be completed, a new framework for early New York and early American Jewish history is beginning to emerge.[6]

---

4   Jonathan I. Israel, *Diasporas within a Diaspora: Jews, Crypto-Jews and the World Maritime Empires, 1540-1740* (Leiden: Brill, 2002); Daviken Studnicki-Gizbert, *A Nation upon the Ocean Sea: Portugal's Atlantic Diaspora and the Crisis of the Spanish Empire, 1492-1640* (Oxford: Oxford University Press, 2007).

5   Jacob Rader Marcus, *The Colonial American Jew, 1492-1776*, 3 vols. (Detroit, MI: Wayne State University Press, 1970), vol. 1, xxv.

6   Noah L. Gelfand, "A Transatlantic Approach to Understanding the Formation of a Jewish Community in New Netherland and New York," *New York History* 89, no. 4 (2008): 375-95; Eli Faber, "The Borders of Early American Jewish History," in *The Jews in the Caribbean*, ed. Jane S. Gerber (Oxford and Portland, OR: Littman Library of Jewish Civilization, 2014), 281-88; Barry L. Stiefel, *Jewish Sanctuary in the Atlantic World: A Social and Architectural History* (Columbia, SC: University of South Carolina Press, 2014).

Portuguese Jews and the Dutch Atlantic

It is surprising how few Jews settled in New Amsterdam given that they were a core constituent of the early modern Dutch Atlantic.[7] The historic importance of twenty-three Sephardic refugees from Brazil who arrived in New Amsterdam in 1654 is overstated. Not one of these twenty-three migrants remained long on Manhattan Island and so their collective reputation as the founders of North America's first permanent Jewish settlement is inflated.[8] Rather than extol their arrival as the starting point for American Jewish history, it is more appropriate to ask why they and other Jews failed to create a permanent religious community in Dutch New Amsterdam at a time when Jewish settler communities existed in Dutch Curaçao and the Guianas, as well as in the English and French Caribbean.

As in other Dutch American colonies, most of the Jews who travelled to New Amsterdam between 1654 and 1664 were part of a western Sephardic diaspora heavily involved in the mercantile and imperial ventures of the Dutch Atlantic.[9] The origins of this diaspora date back to the expulsion of Jews from Spain in 1492. Thousands of exiled Jews travelled southward and eastward from Spain at the end of the fifteenth century to North Africa, or to the Italian cities of Ferrara, Venice, and Livorno, or to the Ottoman Empire, where the Aegean port town of Salonica became a major Sephardic center. Thousands more headed westward by land or sea to Portugal. Tragically, their relief from Catholic persecution proved only temporary. In 1497, the Portuguese king succumbed to Spanish pressure and ordered the expulsion from Portugal of all Jewish adults unwilling to convert to Christianity, as well as the compulsory baptism of Jewish children.

These events created a large Portuguese *converso* population that included an unknown number of *crypto-Jews* who practiced Judaism in secret. The flourishing Flemish city of Antwerp became a favored destination for Portuguese *conversos* in the mid-sixteenth century until

---

7   On the Dutch Atlantic, see Pieter C. Emmer and Wim Klooster, "The Dutch Atlantic, 1600–1800: Expansion without Empire," *Itinerario* 23, no. 2 (1999), 48–69; Benjamin Schmidt, "The Dutch Atlantic: From Provincialism to Globalism," in *Atlantic History: A Critical Appraisal*, ed. Jack P. Greene and Philip D. Morgan (New York: Oxford University Press, 2009), 163–87; Wim Klooster, *The Dutch Moment: War, Trade, and Settlement in the Seventeenth-Century Atlantic World* (Ithaca, NY: Cornell University Press, 2016).

8   Arthur Kiron, "Mythologizing 1654," *Jewish Quarterly Review* 94, no. 4 (2004): 583–94.

9   Jane S. Gerber, *The Jews of Spain: A History of the Sephardic Experience* (New York: Free Press, 1992); Israel, *Diasporas within a Diaspora*.

parts of the Netherlands initiated a long revolt against Spanish rule—known as the Eighty-Years War—that eventuated in Dutch independence in 1648. When Antwerp came under Dutch siege in 1585, many of its Portuguese residents relocated to Hamburg and Amsterdam. By the 1590s the latter city had supplanted Antwerp as the major commercial and shipping center in the region, becoming a focal point for the processing and distributing of colonial goods such as sugar, spices, tobacco, gold, silver, and diamonds. As a thriving Protestant stronghold offering ample economic opportunity and a safe refuge from the Inquisition, Amsterdam appealed to Portuguese exiles, many of whom felt safe enough there to practice Judaism openly. By the 1630s the Dutch city contained in excess of 1,000 Jews. That number increased even further as Ashkenazi Jews fled west from Poland and the Ukraine to escape the pogroms of 1648–1649. By the time Amsterdam's famous synagogue, the Esnoga, was completed in 1675, supplementing an earlier synagogue built in 1636–1639, the city's Jewish population numbered around 2,500. Along with London's Bevis Marks Synagogue (built in 1699–1701), the Esnoga provided a model for eighteenth- and early nineteenth-century synagogue construction around the Atlantic World.[10]

Amsterdam's influence on the Atlantic, and vice versa, increased dramatically during the seventeenth century as the Dutch ambitiously challenged Spanish territorial and commercial dominance of the Americas. Soon after a twelve-year Spanish-Dutch truce ended in 1621, the Dutch organized the WIC with the intention of expanding Dutch transatlantic trade and developing colonial settlements in the Americas. New Netherland already existed, but the WIC took over its management and established New Amsterdam as a commercial and administrative hub for the colony in the mid-1620s. For the most part, however, the WIC had its eyes on a more glittering prize: Portugal's highly profitable sugar region in northeastern Brazil.[11] Because the crowns of Spain and Portugal were unified between 1580 and 1640, Portuguese Brazil was drawn into the Dutch war of independence. In 1630 Dutch forces captured Pernambuco and commenced a twenty-four-year Dutch occupation of that part of Brazil.

---

10   Miriam Bodian, *Hebrews of the Portuguese Nation: Conversos and Community in Early Modern Amsterdam* (Bloomington, IN: Indiana University Press, 1999), 2, 28; Stiefel, *Jewish Sanctuary in the Atlantic World*, 3, 219–21, 225–29.

11   Wim Klooster, "The Place of New Netherland in the West India Company's Grand Scheme," in *Revisiting New Netherland: Perspectives on Early Dutch America*, ed. Joyce D. Goodfriend (Leiden: Brill, 2005), 57–70.

The rise and fall of Dutch Brazil profoundly shaped the course of Jewish settlement in the Americas. A large number of Portuguese Jews left Amsterdam to find wealth and religious freedom in Pernambuco in the 1630s. Their arrival convinced Iberian *conversos* already present in that Brazilian region to revert to Judaism, and Jewish communities swiftly formed. America's first purpose-built synagogue was constructed in the town of Recife by 1640 as Jews there enjoyed an unusually tolerant and open society. Sadly, Pernambuco fell into crisis in the mid-1640s when Portuguese planters indebted to Dutch financiers rebelled against Dutch rule. Violence and the destruction of plantations ensued before Portuguese forces retook the territory in 1654. Hundreds of Sephardic Jews fled to other parts of the Atlantic World during this upheaval. Most went to Amsterdam, but many resettled in the Americas. The twenty-three who ended up in New Amsterdam were but a tiny portion of this number.

Although it was short-lived, Dutch Brazil inspired hope among Jews that another religiously tolerant and economically prosperous colony would eventually be created in the Americas.[12] The Jews who fled Dutch Brazil for other parts of the Atlantic World were skilled and experienced in sugar production and therefore of great value to Dutch and English authorities seeking to establish sugar plantations in the Caribbean. Jewish settlement in the Caribbean and North America became entwined in an escalating power struggle between these two Protestant powers. Once Spanish-Dutch conflict ended in 1648, English-Dutch imperial and mercantile rivalry took priority. New Netherland assumed more geo-political importance during and after the First Anglo-Dutch War (1652–1654).[13]

The Jews who came to New Netherland initially migrated in three phases and attempted to form a religious community. The earliest known arrivals—Ashkenazic merchants Jacob Barsimson, Solomon Pietersen, and Asser Levy—disembarked at Manhattan in August 1654 having sailed from Holland as individuals, possibly on a single Dutch ship, the *Peereboom* [*Peartree*]. Shortly afterwards, in early September 1654, another vessel, the *St. Catrina*, brought the famous group of twenty-three Sephardic-Brazilian

---

12 Evan Haefeli, "Breaking the Christian Atlantic: The Legacy of Dutch Tolerance in Brazil," in *The Legacy of Dutch Brazil*, ed. Michiel van Groesen (New York: Cambridge University Press, 2014), 124–45, esp. 140–45; Stuart B. Schwartz, "Looking for a New Brazil: Crisis and Rebirth in the Atlantic World after the Fall of Pernambuco," in *The Legacy of Dutch Brazil*, ed. Groesen, 41–58.

13 Klooster, "The Place of New Netherland in the West India Company's Grand Scheme," esp. 68–69.

refugees from Jamaica or Cuba. Finally, several Sephardic merchants, some of whom had also lived in Dutch Brazil, reached New Amsterdam from the Netherlands in late 1654 or early 1655. This last group included successful merchants and WIC shareholders. One brought a Torah scroll "of parchment with its green veil and cloak and band of India damask of dark purple" borrowed from the Sephardic community of Amsterdam.[14]

These earliest of New York Jews encountered hostility as their number grew. Most notably, Petrus Stuyvesant, the local Director-General who governed New Netherland from 1647 until 1664, requested permission from the WIC to expel all Jews from New Amsterdam. Stuyvesant, a pious Calvinist, wanted to impose the Dutch Reformed religion on his colony, but his plan met with transatlantic resistance. Presumably at the urging of their colonial coreligionists, Jewish leaders in Holland convinced the WIC to permit Jews to remain in New Netherland. Stuyvesant and other local government officials thereafter had to accept some Jewish presence on Manhattan, but they sought to minimize it by implementing regulations that inhibited Jews from making New Amsterdam their permanent home.[15] Paradoxically, New Amsterdam residents distrusted Jews because of their itinerancy even though local officials obstructed Jewish settlement.[16]

In the face of considerable hostility, and with great determination, the Jews of New Amsterdam established a fledgling religious community. They privately practiced their religion together, and rumors circulated as

---

14 Quote from Howard B. Rock, *Haven of Liberty: New York Jews in the New World, 1654–1865* (New York: New York University Press, 2012), 17. Torah scrolls from Amsterdam also arrived in Barbados, Dutch Guiana, Curaçao, Cayenne, and Martinique during the seventeenth century (Gérard Nahon, "Amsterdam and the Portuguese *Nação* of the Caribbean in the Eighteenth Century," in Gerber, *The Jews in the Caribbean*, 67–83, esp. 74).

15 James Homer Williams, "An Atlantic Perspective on the Jewish Struggle for Rights and Opportunities in Brazil, New Netherland, and New York," in *The Jews and the Expansion of Europe to the West, 1450–1800*, ed. Paolo Bernardini and Norman Fiering (New York: Berghahn Books, 2001), 369–93, esp. 377–85; Jaap Jacobs, *The Colony of New Netherland: A Dutch Settlement in Seventeenth-Century America* (Ithaca, NY: Cornell University Press, 2009), 198–202; Joyce D. Goodfriend, "Practicing Toleration in Dutch New Netherland," in *The First Prejudice: Religious Toleration and Intolerance in Early America*, ed. Chris Beneke and Christopher S. Grenda (Philadelphia: University of Pennsylvania Press, 2011), 98–122.

16 On attitudes towards sojourners in New Amsterdam, see Dennis J. Maika, "Securing the Burgher Right in New Amsterdam: The Struggle for Municipal Citizenship in the Seventeenth-Century Atlantic World," in Goodfriend, *Revisiting New Netherland*, 93–128, especially 111–12, 121–23.

early as 1655 that they planned to construct a synagogue in the city. Any such designs were thwarted within a year when Stuyvesant forbade Jews from worshipping publicly in New Netherland despite the fact that purpose-built synagogues had previously been permitted in Amsterdam and Dutch Brazil. In June 1656 the WIC directors ordered Stuyvesant to let Jews trade throughout New Netherland and practice religion in private. Even so, the WIC approved Stuyvesant's ban on Jewish public worship, fearing complete religious freedom might destabilize New Netherland.

Despite this setback, New Amsterdam Jews continued to campaign—albeit individually more than collectively—for religious and economic rights. They won approval for a Jewish cemetery in 1656 after initially being denied permission for a burial ground. When two Jewish merchants, Jacob Barsimson and Asser Levy, formally complained about being excluded from the militia and forced to pay a tax in lieu of serving guard duty, the city government recommended they "depart whenever and whither it pleases them."[17] Levy nevertheless persevered and gained membership in the militia in 1657.

Pressure from Amsterdam brought further change. The WIC feared discriminatory colonial legislation would drive Sephardic merchants with transatlantic connections and experience of Brazilian sugar production away from Dutch America and toward more-accommodating English or French territories. WIC directives prompted Stuyvesant to moderate his enmity toward Jews, some of whom went on to achieve notable wealth and status in New Amsterdam. Several were listed among the 237 New Amsterdam men and women recognized as burghers in 1657, a privilege that bestowed trade and other rights, and that in the recent opinion of one historian provided colonial elites "with a sense of order, stability, and security in the ever-changing Atlantic world."[18] As a further concession, New Amsterdam Jews received the right to buy real estate by 1660. In addition, they encountered fair treatment in New Amsterdam's municipal court, and managed to overturn or circumvent bans from trading along the Hudson and Delaware rivers, engaging in retail trade, and purchasing real estate. Yet, discrimination persisted. Specifically, Jews sometimes paid disproportionate taxes, and, as already noted, public Jewish worship was also prohibited under Dutch rule.[19]

17 Rock, *Haven of Liberty*, 18.
18 Maika, "Securing the Burgher Right in New Amsterdam," 95.
19 Marcus, *The Colonial American Jew*, vol. 1, 215–43; Eli Faber, *A Time for Planting: The First Migration, 1654–1820* (Baltimore, MD: Johns Hopkins University Press, 1992),

These restrictions posed a barrier to Jewish settlement. New Amsterdam's Jewish community probably never exceeded fifty persons (or 0.5% of the town's population) and went into decline by the early 1660s. Its collapse was confirmed in 1663 when New Amsterdam's Torah scroll was returned to the Netherlands.[20] At the time of the English conquest of 1664, very few Jews lived in New Amsterdam. Asser Levy, a Dutch-speaking Ashkenazi, was one, and it is possible that he only stayed because he had fewer alternative opportunities elsewhere in the Americas than the Sephardim who departed. The fact that non-Jewish Dutch firms dominated trade between Holland and New Netherland probably hindered Jewish migration to New Amsterdam.[21] Equally, the development of Sephardic trade networks in the Caribbean in the mid-seventeenth century served to redirect Jewish migration away from North America.[22] In both of these ways, it could be said, the same Atlantic World that brought Jews to New Amsterdam kept them away.

New York Jews and the English Atlantic

With the fall of Dutch Brazil in 1654 and England's conquest of New Netherland in 1664, the Dutch Atlantic collapsed. An empire that had once promised to supersede Spanish dominance of the Americas was now reduced to a few Caribbean territories. Moreover, the first WIC, which had struggled financially since the 1640s, dissolved in 1674; a second WIC created that year lacked the ambition and power that its predecessor had once held. To be sure, the Dutch islands of Curaçao and, later, St. Eustatius maintained successful ports during the eighteenth century. Yet, for the most part, England's superior naval strength and a division of transatlantic trade along

---

29–36; Goodfriend, "Practicing Toleration in Dutch New Netherland," 106, 109; Rock, *Haven of Liberty*, 16–19.

20 Marcus, *The Colonial American Jew*, vol. 1, 238, 244; Leo Hershkowitz, "A Flourishing City: Jews in New Amsterdam, 1654," in *Opening Statements: Law, Jurisprudence, and the Legacy of Dutch New York*, ed. Albert M. Rosenblatt and Julia C. Rosenblatt (Albany, NY: State University of New York Press, 2013), 149–162.

21 Faber, "The Borders of Early American Jewish History," 283.

22 Christian J. Koot, *Empire at the Periphery: British Colonists, Anglo-Dutch Trade, and the Development of the British Atlantic, 1621–1713* (New York: New York University Press, 2011), 78–82, 174–77.

national lines undermined Dutch influence in the Atlantic. From 1675, the English and not the Dutch led transatlantic imperial expansion.[23]

The rise of the English Atlantic coincided with the emergence of an open Jewish community in England. The Navigation Acts passed in the 1650s and 1660s required English colonial goods to be shipped directly to and from England. In so doing, they undermined trade via Amsterdam and encouraged Jews to settle in London. Oliver Cromwell, a republican imperialist who ruled England as Lord Protector from 1653 until 1658, as well as the Stuart monarchs restored to the English throne in 1660, wanted experienced Jewish merchants with strong mercantile connections and knowledge of sugar production to assist English colonial and commercial expansion. Consequently, Jews were informally allowed to re-enter England from 1656, having previously been expelled from that country at the end of the thirteenth century. As many as eighty Jewish families lived in England by 1689.[24]

Jewish settlement in England's North American and Caribbean colonies similarly expanded during the last quarter of the seventeenth century, although the Second (1665–1667) and Third (1672–1674) Anglo-Dutch Wars complicated this process. In 1667 the Dutch captured English Suriname, a colony in the Guianas with a sizeable Jewish population to whom English authorities had granted substantial freedoms. Six years and another war later, the Dutch briefly retook New York. By 1675 most of the English had departed Suriname, leaving behind a Jewish population that was proportionally larger and therefore of greater economic, political, and military influence. The Dutch kept the liberal English policies in place in Suriname in order to prevent a Jewish as well as English exodus.[25]

Meanwhile, England regained control of New York in 1674 without radically altering the status of the few Jews who lived in the city. Although England's Catholic-leaning Stuart monarchy favored religious toleration, many New York merchants viewed Jews as unwelcome commercial rivals rather than good neighbors. An uncertain period ensued. Jews engaged in retail trade and established a kosher slaughterhouse in New York in the 1670s, but then the colony's 1683 Charter of Liberties prohibited public Jewish worship and a 1685 law forbade work, travel, and leisure on the

---

23   Emmer and Klooster, "The Dutch Atlantic 1600–1800"; Klooster, *The Dutch Moment.*

24   Williams, "An Atlantic Perspective on the Jewish Struggle," 386.

25   Alison Games, "Cohabitation, Suriname-Style: English Inhabitants in Dutch Suriname after 1667," *William and Mary Quarterly* 72, no. 2 (2015): 195–242.

Christian Sabbath.[26] After royal intervention nullified that Charter in 1686, the turmoil of the Glorious Revolution (1688–1689) curtailed public Jewish worship in New York once again. The arrival of a new royal governor in 1692 reversed that policy, and Jewish religious services were held in a rented building on Mill Street (now South William Street in Lower Manhattan) from the mid-1690s. During the first half of the eighteenth century, the Jews of New York won further concessions. In particular, they secured citizenship and the ability to vote and hold public office. These gains paved the way for New York State in 1777 to become, in the words of historian William Pencak, "the first state to adopt a constitution granting Jews full political equality with Christians, and the first government in the modern world to do so."[27]

Connections to the Caribbean remained a feature of the New York Jewish community throughout the colonial period. In the extant customs records, around one third of the entries for 1715–1716 that involved Jewish merchants related to trade with Curaçao. These records also show that New York's Jewish merchants traded regularly with Barbados, Curaçao, Jamaica, Saint Christopher, Saint Thomas, and other Caribbean islands during the mid-eighteenth century.[28] Commerce with the Caribbean required less capital investment than transatlantic trade and so suited most New York Jewish merchants. Moreover, it utilized their Portuguese, Dutch, and Spanish language skills and their Sephardic connections. As one historian notes, "New York's Jews enjoyed vital cross-national networks that extended around the Atlantic world and enabled their community to survive and prosper even as the city became increasingly English."[29]

Caribbean links were not just commercial in nature but also familial and religious. Marriages, kinship ties, and shared religious commitments bound North American and Caribbean Jewish communities together.[30] To construct North America's first purpose-built synagogue (the Shearith Israel Synagogue) on Mill Street between 1729 and 1730, funds were sought from Jews in Barbados, Curaçao, Jamaica, and London. Prior to the hiring

---

26 William Pencak, *Jews and Gentiles in Early America, 1654–1800* (Ann Arbor, MI: University of Michigan Press, 2005), 33–34.

27 Pencak, *Jews and Gentiles in Early America*, 19.

28 Leo Hershkowitz, "Some Aspects of the New York Jewish Merchant and Community, 1654–1820," *American Jewish Historical Quarterly* 66, no. 1 (1976): 10–34; Faber, *Time for Planting*, 34–35.

29 Koot, *Empire at the Periphery*, 175–6.

30 Faber, *Time for Planting*, 47–49.

in 1768 of a locally born *hazan*, Gershom Mendes Seixas, all the *hazanim* who led synagogue services in New York were imported from London or elsewhere. New York Jews lent Torah scrolls to Newport and Philadelphia in the 1750s and 1760s, and sent certified kosher meat to the Caribbean in sealed and branded barrels. The Jewish community of Manhattan took its religious role seriously and carefully ensured that the Jewish dietary laws of *kashrut* were observed. When Jews in Curaçao and Jamaica complained about the arrival from New York of improperly butchered beef in 1757, New York elders vigorously defended the purity of the exported kosher meat.[31]

The Shearith Israel Synagogue added a new degree of stability and permanence to a colonial Jewish population that was heavily mercantile and mobile. Around 300 Jews lived in New York in the mid-eighteenth century, and their number expanded to approximately 400 by 1776. New York City had the largest Jewish community in British North America, but its size was unremarkable compared to other parts of the Americas. The Jewish communities of Jamaica, Suriname, and Curaçao were each two or three times larger than that of Manhattan in 1775. Moreover, the islands of Barbados and St. Eustatius separately possessed Jewish communities roughly equal in size to that of New York City.

The relatively small size of Jewish populations in New York and other parts of British North America perhaps explains the striking degree of cooperation and intermarriage between Sephardim and Ashkenazim in colonial North America compared to Europe and parts of the Caribbean.[32] Both groups attended the Shearith Israel synagogue, which continued to use the Portuguese language and to adhere to the Sephardic rite even after Ashkenazim started to outnumber Sephardim in New York, a shift that occurred around 1720. Ashkenazic Jews assumed leadership roles in the community with apparent ease.[33]

---

31 Faber, *Time for Planting*, 49–51; Eli Faber, "Preservation and Innovation: Judaism in America, 1654–1800," in *The Cambridge Companion to American Judaism*, ed. Dana Evan Kaplan (New York: Cambridge University Press, 2005), 23–41, esp. 26–28; Rock, *Haven of Liberty*, 48–50.

32 Gordon M. Weiner, "Sephardic Philo- and Anti-Semitism in the Early Modern Era: The Jewish Adoption of Christian Attitudes," in *Jewish Christians and Christian Jews: From the Renaissance to the Enlightenment*, ed. Richard H. Popkin and Gordon M. Weiner (Dordrecht: Kluwer Academic Publishers, 1994), 189–214; Gerber, *Jews of Spain*, 209; Faber, "Preservation and Innovation," 25.

33 Eli Faber has calculated that Ashkenazim held 54% of the synagogue offices between 1728 and 1760. See Faber, *Time for Planting*, 64.

New York Jews came under considerable pressure to Anglicize and some sought out English or British citizenship in order to escape the prohibitions placed on aliens trading between Great Britain and its colonies. Endenization—a form of partial citizenship granted to hundreds of Jews by the English Crown and Crown-appointed colonial governors from the mid-seventeenth century—allowed Jewish merchants to circumvent the restrictive Navigation Acts. At least six New York Jews (including Asser Levy in 1664) received letters of endenization in the colony, while others became denizens in England. Full naturalization was preferable to endenization, but required legislation. In 1715 New York's colonial assembly allowed for the naturalization of some foreigners who owned real estate. Subsequently, a Plantation Act passed by the British Parliament in 1740 imposed colonial uniformity by making persons, including Jews, who had lived for seven years in a British colony eligible for naturalization. Dozens of New York Jews were naturalized under the terms of the 1715 or 1740 Acts. Additionally, between 1688 and 1770, almost sixty Jews became freemen of New York City, a status that allowed them to vote in municipal and colonial elections, hold public office, and conduct retail trade. Jews were briefly disqualified from voting in New York in 1737, but that incident stemmed from a particular political maneuver and appears to have been anomalous. Ironically, antisemitism may be more evident in the fact that Jews, having won the right to hold public office, were given onerous public duties unwanted by elite Christian New Yorkers.[34]

Historian Joyce Goodfriend has argued that New Yorkers became religious consumers in the mid-eighteenth century. Religious buildings proliferated and New Yorkers, who were growing increasingly accustomed to shopping around for goods, shifted their allegiances between different congregations.[35] Within this context, New York Jews grappled with the problems of conversion, cultural preservation, and religious voluntarism. Evidence of how Jews handled these challenges is largely anecdotal. One well-known case is that of Phila Franks, who in 1742 married Oliver Delancy, the Anglican brother of New York's chief justice. The following year, Phila's brother, David, married a Quaker woman. A sister, Richa, also married a Christian. Whereas these Franks siblings and other New York Jews married outside of their religion, a surprisingly large proportion of

---

34 Hershkowitz, "Some Aspects of the New York Jewish Merchant and and Community"; Faber, *A Time for Planting*, 100–101; Pencak, *Jews and Gentiles in Early America*, 41–46.
35 Goodfriend, *Who Should Rule at Home?*, chap. 4.

adult Jews in New York (45% of men and 41% of women under the age of fifty) chose not to marry at all.[36] Considering these circumstances, as well as the fact that Jews comprised only one or two percent of colonial New York's total population, the steady growth of a Jewish religious community in eighteenth-century British Manhattan was a substantial achievement.

Conclusion: Toward a New Nation

By the end of the colonial period, New York Jews had turned a sojourner community of the Portuguese Nation into a British synagogue community well connected to London and other parts of the Atlantic World. The outbreak of the American Revolution brought a great deal of disruption to this community. Even though Jewish New York merchants directly suffered the burden of colonial regulations and tariffs, few of them embraced political radicalism prior to 1776. Late colonial Jews were politically moderate or conservative on the whole. According to Jacob Rader Marcus, most "grumbled at the Stamp Act and the import duties, but they were not willing to go to war to decide whether the colonies were to be part of a loosely federated or a well-integrated empire."[37] Once the Revolution commenced, however, the Jewish community split evenly along Loyalist and Patriot lines. British occupation of New York City forced Jewish patriots, including Hazan Gershom Mendes Seixas, to take shelter in Philadelphia until 1783. Postwar, Seixas and other exiles returned to Manhattan and New York's Jewish community reunited.

New York's synagogue community was rebuilt after the Revolution in the image of the new country of which it was now part. In 1790 Shearith Israel adopted a constitution and "bill of Rights" that recognized "in free States all Power Originates and is derived from the People."[38] The Jewish community of New York embraced the republican and democratic ideals of

---

36   Pencak, *Jews and Gentiles in Early America*, 46–48.
37   Jacob Rader Marcus, "Introduction," *American Jewish Archives Journal* 27, no. 2 (1975): *Jews and the American Revolution: A Bicentennial Documentary*, ed. Jacob Rader Marcus, 105.
38   Quoted in Pencak, *Jews and Gentiles in Early America*, 71. See also David and Tamar de Sola Pool, *An Old Faith in the New World: Portrait of Shearith Israel, 1654–1954* (New York: Columbia University Press, 1955), 260–62; Jonathan D. Sarna, "The Impact of the American Revolution on American Jews," *Modern Judaism* 1, no.2 (1981): 149–160; Faber, *A Time for Planting*, 116–118; Alan Mittleman, "Judaism and Democracy in America," in Kaplan, *Cambridge Companion to American Judaism*, 299–313.

the newly forged United States, and the country as a whole committed itself constitutionally and culturally to a future of religious tolerance.

It has become something of a commonplace that the Jews of colonial New York, much like the Jews of early modern Amsterdam, advanced Western and Jewish modernity.[39] Such claims need to be treated with caution as the concept of modernity is slippery and value-laden. Still, it remains broadly true that colonial New York Jews grappled with a set of historically new challenges. Surrounded by non-Jews, detached from traditional Jewish authorities and customs, and removed from the fiercest forms of contemporary antisemitism, they experimented with acculturation, republicanism, democracy, religious voluntarism, and the intellectual novelties of the Enlightenment. If these experiences rendered colonial New York Jews modern, then so be it. Regardless, there can be no disputing that they were valuable constituents of a politically, economically, and culturally dynamic Atlantic World.

---

39 See, for instance, de Sola Pool, *An Old Faith in the New World*, 36; Faber, *A Time for Planting*, 1–3; Rock, *Haven of Liberty*, 257–59. On the characterization of Amsterdam Jews as modern, see Daniel M. Swetschinski, *Reluctant Cosmopolitans: The Portuguese Jews of Seventeenth-Century Amsterdam* (Oxford and Portland, OR: Littman Library of Jewish Civilization, 2000), 2–3.

For Further Reading

Bodian, Miriam. *Hebrews of the Portuguese Nation: Conversos and Community in Early Modern Amsterdam*. Bloomington: Indiana University Press, 1997.

Bonomi, Patricia U. *A Factious People: Politics and Society in Colonial New York*. New York: Columbia University Press, 1971.

de Sola Pool, David, and Tamar de Sola Pool. *An Old Faith in the New World: Portrait of Shearith Israel, 1654–1954*. New York: Columbia University Press, 1955.

Emmer, Pieter C., and Wim Klooster. "The Dutch Atlantic, 1600–1800: Expansion without Empire." *Itinerario* 23, no. 2 (1999): 48–69.

Faber, Eli. *A Time for Planting: The First Migration, 1654–1820*. Baltimore: Johns Hopkins University Press, 1992.

———. "Preservation and Innovation: Judaism in America, 1654–1800." In *The Cambridge Companion to American Judaism*, edited by Dana Evan Kaplan, 23–41. New York: Cambridge University Press, 2005.

———. "The Borders of Early American Jewish History." In *The Jews in the Caribbean*, edited by Jane S. Gerber, 281–88. Oxford and Portland, OR: Littman Library of Jewish Civilization, 2014.

Games, Alison. "Cohabitation, Suriname-Style: English Inhabitants in Dutch Suriname after 1667." *William and Mary Quarterly* 72, no. 2 (2015): 195–242.

Gelfand, Noah L. "A Transatlantic Approach to Understanding the Formation of a Jewish Community in New Netherland and New York." *New York History* 89, no. 4 (2008): 375–95.

Gerber, Jane S. *The Jews of Spain: A History of the Sephardic Experience*. New York: Free Press, 1992.

Goodfriend, Joyce D. *Before the Melting Pot: Society and Culture in Colonial New York City, 1664–1730*. Princeton: Princeton University Press, 1992.

———. "Practicing Toleration in Dutch New Netherland." In *The First Prejudice: Religious Toleration and Intolerance in Early America*, edited by Chris Beneke and Christopher S. Grenda, 98–122. Philadelphia: University of Pennsylvania Press, 2011.

———. *Who Should Rule at Home?: Confronting the Elite in British New York City*. Ithaca, NY: Cornell University Press, 2017.

Haefeli, Evan. "Breaking the Christian Atlantic: The Legacy of Dutch Tolerance in Brazil." In *The Legacy of Dutch Brazil*, edited by Michiel van Groesen, 124–45. New York: Cambridge University Press, 2014.

Hershkowitz, Leo. "A Flourishing City: Jews in New Amsterdam, 1654." In *Opening Statements: Law, Jurisprudence, and the Legacy of Dutch New York*, edited by Albert M. Rosenblatt and Julia C. Rosenblatt, 149–62. Albany: State University of New York Press, 2013.

———. "Some Aspects of the New York Jewish Merchant and Community, 1654-1820." *American Jewish Historical Quarterly* 66, no. 1 (1976): 10–34.

Israel, Jonathan I. *Diasporas within a Diaspora: Jews, Crypto-Jews and the World Maritime Empires, 1540-1740*. Leiden: Brill, 2002.

Jacobs, Jaap. *The Colony of New Netherland: A Dutch Settlement in Seventeenth-Century America*. Ithaca, NY: Cornell University Press, 2009.

Kiron, Arthur. "Mythologizing 1654." *Jewish Quarterly Review* 94, no. 4 (2004): 583–94.

Klooster, Wim. *The Dutch Moment: War, Trade, and Settlement in the Seventeenth-Century Atlantic World*. Ithaca, NY: Cornell University Press, 2016.

———. "The Place of New Netherland in the West India Company's Grand Scheme." In *Revisiting New Netherland: Perspectives on Early Dutch America*, edited by Joyce D. Goodfriend, 57–70. Leiden: Brill, 2005.

Koot, Christian J. *Empire at the Periphery: British Colonists, Anglo-Dutch Trade, and the Development of the British Atlantic, 1621–1713*. New York: New York University Press, 2011.

Maika, Dennis J. "Securing the Burgher Right in New Amsterdam: The Struggle for Municipal Citizenship in the Seventeenth-Century Atlantic World." In *Revisiting New Netherland: Perspectives on Early Dutch America*, edited by Joyce D. Goodfriend, 93–128. Leiden: Brill, 2005.

Marcus, Jacob Rader. "Introduction." *American Jewish Archives Journal* 27, no. 2 (1975): *Jews and the American Revolution: A Bicentennial Documentary*, edited by Jacob Rader Marcus, 103–116.

———. *The Colonial American Jew, 1492-1776*, 3 vols. Detroit, MI: Wayne State University Press, 1970.

McDonald, Kevin P. *Pirates, Merchants, Settlers, and Slaves: Colonial America and the Indo-Atlantic World*. Oakland, CA: University of California Press, 2015.

Mittleman, Alan. "Judaism and Democracy in America." In *The Cambridge Companion to American Judaism*, edited by Dana Evan Kaplan, 299–313. New York: Cambridge University Press, 2005.

Nahon, Gérard. "Amsterdam and the Portuguese *Nação* of the Caribbean in the Eighteenth Century." In *The Jews in the Caribbean*, edited by Jane S. Gerber, 67–83. Oxford and Portland, OR: Littman Library of Jewish Civilization, 2014.

Pencak, William. *Jews and Gentiles in Early America, 1654–1800.* Ann Arbor: University of Michigan Press, 2005.

Rock, Howard B. *Haven of Liberty: New York Jews in the New World, 1654–1865.* New York: New York University Press, 2012.

Sarna, Jonathan D. "The Impact of the American Revolution on American Jews." *Modern Judaism* 1, no.2 (1981): 149–60.

Schmidt, Benjamin. "The Dutch Atlantic: From Provincialism to Globalism." In *Atlantic History: A Critical Appraisal*, edited by Jack P. Greene and Philip D. Morgan, 163–87. New York: Oxford University Press, 2009.

Schwartz, Stuart B. "Looking for a New Brazil: Crisis and Rebirth in the Atlantic World after the Fall of Pernambuco." In *The Legacy of Dutch Brazil*, edited by Michiel van Groesen, 41–58. New York: Cambridge University Press, 2014.

Stiefel, Barry L. *Jewish Sanctuary in the Atlantic World: A Social and Architectural History.* Columbia, SC: University of South Carolina Press, 2014.

Studnicki-Gizbert, Daviken. *A Nation upon the Ocean Sea: Portugal's Atlantic Diaspora and the Crisis of the Spanish Empire, 1492–1640.* Oxford: Oxford University Press, 2007.

Swetschinski, Daniel M. *Reluctant Cosmopolitans: The Portuguese Jews of Seventeenth-Century Amsterdam.* Oxford and Portland, OR: Littman Library of Jewish Civilization, 2000.

Weiner, Gordon M. "Sephardic Philo- and Anti-Semitism in the Early Modern Era: The Jewish Adoption of Christian Attitudes." In *Jewish Christians and Christian Jews: From the Renaissance to the Enlightenment*, edited by Richard H. Popkin and Gordon M. Weiner, 189–214. Dordrecht: Kluwer Academic Publishers, 1994.

Williams, James Homer. "An Atlantic Perspective on the Jewish Struggle for Rights and Opportunities in Brazil, New Netherland, and New York." In *The Jews and the Expansion of Europe to the West, 1450–1800*, edited by Paolo Bernardini and Norman Fiering, 369–93. New York: Berghahn Books, 2001.

Chapter 2

New York Jews and the Early Republic

Howard B. Rock

The era of the new republic (1789–1825) was, despite the small size of the Jewish community, a momentous period in the history of the Jews of Gotham. The rise of American republicanism both allowed and encouraged Jews to move into the mainstream of New York life beyond the marketplace: into the social, cultural and political realms. It permitted them to run for high office, increased economic horizons, and provided a degree of social equality that, in the late eighteenth century, very few Jews in the world enjoyed. Moreover, from the beginning of the Revolution, Jews supported republicanism and continued to do so because of the possibilities a new egalitarian society would offer. Within the synagogue, republicanism became part and parcel of religious life as well.

Prior to the American Revolution the Jewish community of colonial New York was a small synagogue community of about sixty families, or about 300 individuals, in a city of 23,000 (1.3%). Its life centered around Shearith Israel, the first synagogue (1730) constructed in the thirteen colonies. While Jews intermixed with the general population commercially—largely as either craftsmen or small, and occasionally prominent, merchants—dietary laws and the laws of the Sabbath and holidays limited their social interaction with the general population.[1]

---

1   For population figures see Edwin Burrows and Mike Wallace, *Gotham: A History of New York City to 1898* (New York: Oxford University Press, 1999), 194; Howard B. Rock,

The quiet inner-directed routine of Gotham's Jewish community was harshly interrupted by Britain's moves in the 1760s to tax the colonies to pay for the costs of the Seven Years' War. Americans regarded parliamentary taxes, both on sugar (Townshend Act) and then on retail sales of all kinds (Stamp Act) as a stroke against liberty and a first move toward enslavement of the colonists. In the cities, merchants were on the front line and Jewish merchants joined in protests though petitions, meetings and boycotts. Ultimately, the result of this conflict was to both remove the Jews from their semi-isolated place in New York society and to infuse their community with republican zeal.

It was one thing to protest and another to commit treason by taking up arms against the King. Every American had to make a decision, including each of the city's Jews. Would they remain loyal to the crown or to the movement for independence?

In the end, the majority of New York's Jewish community chose to join the fight for independence. The city's Jewish merchants, who in tandem with European Jewish merchants inspired the Enlightenment-driven quest for freedom, respect for human dignity, and economic opportunity, aligned their interests with those of the patriot leaders. In Britain, Jews remained second-class citizens, while New York offered political equality, a standing that was soon ratified in New York's 1777 constitution that gave Jews equal standing with other New Yorkers, more equality than any place in the western world.[2]

The American Revolution gave birth to a spirit of republicanism that is critical to understanding the life of the Jewish community in the early republic. Republicanism's origins are found in the political debates and economic sacrifices of the decade before the war began, in which the idea of self-government rose from a political structure (democracy) which current political thought believed doomed to inevitably deteriorate to mob rule. The new Revolutionary ideology melded two strains of thought: the contract ideology of John Locke that stressed individual freedom, and the Scottish common-sense school that stressed the collective pursuit of happiness and a virtuous citizenry. American republicanism also incorporated the millennialism of New England, whose founders sought to create a

---

Haven of Liberty: New York Jews in the New World, 1654–1865 (New York: NYU Press, 2012), chaps. 2–3.

2 William Pencak, *Jews and Gentiles in Early America, 1654-1800* (Ann Arbor: University of Michigan Press, 2005), 68–69; Rock, *Haven of Liberty*, 73–79.

"city upon a hill," an example to the world; and the need to give meaning to seven long years of wartime hardship, including death, exile, illness, impoverishment and fear. What was the purpose of it all? Americans were certain that their new republic was nothing less than a watershed event in human history. Its success or failure was far more important than any individual's life or accomplishments.[3]

That Jews shared ownership of this ideal is apparent in a letter from Shearith Israel to President Washington following his inauguration. The members of the city's congregation declared that the "wonders . . . the Lord of Hosts worked" in ancient Israel were visible in the "late glorious revolution," and in the Federal Constitution, a compact that sealed "in peace what you had achieved in war." Washington replied that "the liberality of sentiment toward each other, which marks every political and religious denomination of men . . . stands unparalleled in the history of Nations." Agreeing that "the power and goodness of the Almighty" were visible in "our late glorious revolution" and the "establishment of our present equal government," he wished America's Jewish congregations "the same temporal and eternal blessings which you implore for me." The Jewish community was to be a full partner in the republican experiment.[4]

The promise of American republicanism included unfettered economic opportunity for all classes other than slaves. Nowhere was this spirit more apparent than in New York City. Although crippled by years of occupation and disrepair, the metropolis rapidly recovered. The entrepreneurial energies unleashed by the republican spirit of the Revolution were apparent throughout the nation, but nowhere better than New York. Spurred by merchants such as John Jacob Astor, New Yorkers became expert at financial speculation, insurance, and manufacturing, transforming the city into the nation's financial center. With the opening of the Erie Canal in 1825, New York began its journey to a world-class metropolis, becoming the entry point for immigrants, and the choice entrepôt for exports from the western

---

3   The literature on republicanism is vast. Among the important works are J. G. A. Pocock, *The Machiavellian Moment: Florentine Political Thought and the Atlantic Republican Tradition* (Princeton: Princeton University Press, 1975); Gary Wills, *Inventing America: Jefferson's Declaration of Independence* (New York: Doubleday, 1978); Pauline Maier, *American Scripture: Making the Declaration of Independence* (New York: Knopf, 1997); and Joyce Appleby, *Capitalism and a New Social Order: The Republican Vision of the 1790s* (New York: NYU Press, 1984).

4   Lewis Abraham, "Correspondence between Washington and Jewish Citizens," *Proceedings of the American Jewish Historical Society (PAJHS)*, no. 3 (1895): 93–95.

states and imports from the rest of the world. No city could match the skill and financial acumen of its merchants, artisans or manufacturers.[5]

The Jews of Gotham shared the Republic's entrepreneurial spirit, freely venturing into all areas of the marketplace. A few, such as copper manufacturer Harmon Hendricks, business partner of Paul Revere, became prominent. Of the twenty merchants who formed the New York Stock Exchange under the famed buttonwood tree, four were Jewish. Simon Nathan was one of four Jewish merchants who built the Park Theater, while Solomon Simson gained renown for his swift clipper ships that sailed to the Far East.[6]

Most Jewish merchants worked on a smaller level. Many bought goods at auction and sold them in retail stores. Jacques Ruden, for example, an immigrant from Suriname, supplied lumber for the building of the new city hall. In addition to retailers and wholesalers, Jewish craftsmen labored in a variety of trades, ranging from the highly successful David Seixas, a manufacturer of sealing wax, ink and crockery, to shoemaker Isaac Moses, so poor he was given a synagogue seat at no charge. Jewish bakers, chair makers, butchers, clockmakers, shoemakers, carpenters, and sail makers were listed in city directories, as were tailors (the most popular trade), goldsmiths, silversmiths, coppersmiths, and blacksmiths. Asher Myers soldered the copper roof of the old city hall and sold two bells to the city for its new city hall and jail. Printers achieved high standing. Benjamin Gomez published more than twenty books, including *Robinson Crusoe, Tom Jones* and works by deist John Priestly. Naphtali Judah printed the radical tracts of Thomas Paine. He also advertised imports, including forty "boxes of playing cards," and gave "the highest prices" for "clean linen and Cotton Rags, old Sail Cloth and Junk."[7]

Jews entered the professions. Samson Simson, scion of a prominent Jewish family, graduated from Columbia College and studied law. Six Jewish physicians are found either in city directories or the records of Shearith Israel. One, Walter Jonas Judah, a graduate of Columbia, including its

---

5   Burrows and Wallace, *Gotham*, chap. 22.

6   Rock, *Haven of Liberty*, 94–98; Samuel Sokobin, "The Simson-Hirsch Letter to the Chinese Jews, 1795," *PAJHS* 49, no.1 (1959): 39; Hyman B. Grinstein, *The Rise of the Jewish Community of New York, 1654-1860* (Philadelphia: Jewish Publication Society, 1947), 416–19.

7   Jacob R. Marcus, *United States Jewry, 1776–1985,* 4 vols. (Detroit: Wayne State University Press, 1989), vol. 1, 191–96; Rita Susswein Gottesman, *The Arts and Crafts in New York, 1800-1804* (New York: New-York Historical Society, 1965), 108, 117, 125, 237, 380; Rock, *Haven of Liberty*, 96–97.

medical school, refused to leave the city during the yellow fever epidemic of 1798 and died in service to the people of Gotham.[8]

As Jews became more prominent in the city's economic life, so too they entered the metropolis's fraternal life—an important sign of Jewish emergence into the broader world. Jewish New Yorkers such as Naphtali Judah and Mordecai M. Noah were Sachems of the Tammany Society. Jews could be found within the ranks of the Mechanics Society, the St. George Society, the New York Gold and Silversmiths Society (Myer Myers assumed the presidency after the Revolution), the Chamber of Commerce, the Mineralogical Society, the New York Medical Society, and the Manumission Society.[9]

The most popular organization was the politically and socially progressive Masonic Order, which accepted all men who believed in a "supreme being," and pledged to perform good deeds and pursue knowledge. Jewish masons, numbering more than fifty, included leading figures in the community. Joel Hart, for example, became Deputy Grand High Priest of the Grand Chapter, Royal Arch Masons. Jewish Masons established a Jerusalem chapter and a special prayer that pleaded with God that they not be numbered "among those that know not thy statutes, nor the divine mysteries of thy secret Cabala," and that their "ruler" be "possessed of knowledge" to explain mysteries as Moses did "in his Lodge to Aaron and other elders of Israel." That so many prominent Jews joined with Christian Masons speaks to their integration into the fraternal life of republican New York.[10]

Republican Politics

New York's Jews took part in one of the greatest contests in American political history: the battle over the legacy of the American Revolution. With the nation deeply divided over the meaning of 1776, the 1790s became one of the most passionate political decades in American history. The Hamiltonians, soon to become the Federalist Party, sought a strong

---

8   Theodore Cohen, "Walter Jonas Judah and New York's 1798 Yellow Fever Epidemic," *American Jewish Archives Journal (AJA)* 48, no. 1 (1996): 23–34.

9   "Sachem" was the title used by leaders of the Tammany Society, at first a fraternal and then a Jeffersonian society whose name was based on pseudo-Indian lore. "Miscellaneous Items Relating to Jews in New York," *PAJHS* 27 (1920): 396–400.

10 Samuel Oppenheim, "The Jews and Masonry in the United States before 1810," *PAJHS* 19 (1910): 1–16; Edmund R. Sadowski, "A Jewish Masonic Prayer," *PAJHS* 48, no. 2 (1958–1959): 134–35; Morris U. Schappes, *A Documentary History of the Jews of the United States, 1654–1875* (New York: Citadel, 1950), 112.

central government. They passed legislation creating a national bank similar to the Bank of England, encouraged the growth of manufacturing, and were staunch supporters of Britain and fierce opponents of the French Revolution. Federalist ideology embraced deference: the less well-educated and well-off were to follow the lead of the nation's educated and wealthy merchants and professionals. Centered in the North, with limited southern support, Federalism was generally uncomfortable with slavery. Its backers and were likely to be strict Christians.

Jeffersonians, when confronted with Hamilton's economic plan, formed the Democratic-Republican Party, the nation's first political party. Supporters of an agriculturally based society with weak central and stronger state governments, they were hostile to financial speculation, regarding banks with fear and suspicion. They supported the French Revolution and still saw Britain as a foe of American independence. Advocates of political egalitarianism for whites, they argued that a shoemaker could make as wise a political choice as a learned attorney. Defenders of civil liberties and a free press, Jeffersonian leaders tended to deist theology. Centered in the South, the party sympathized with slave owners.

New Yorkers could not have been closer to the dispute, as Hamilton formulated his controversial economic program, including federalizing state debts and chartering a national bank, in New York. Even after it lost its standing as capital in 1791, the city remained a key factor in the partisan struggle. In contest after contest, Federalists accused Democratic-Republicans of standing for godlessness and anarchy, while Democratic-Republicans charged that Federalists stood for the British aristocracy that they defeated in '76. Nothing less than the definition of American republicanism was at stake.[11]

No longer the reticent colonial synagogue community, Jews entered the political fray, an important sign of their integration into the society of the new republic. In the 1790s, the majority were Jeffersonians. Prominent Jews were members of the Democratic Society formed to support the French Revolution. Solomon Simson was vice president, chairing a meeting that drafted an address calling on Congress "to take effectual measures to

---

11 Burrows and Wallace, *Gotham*, chap. 21. The literature on the Hamiltonian-Jeffersonian debate is vast. Good starting points would be Stanley Elkins and Eric McKitrick, *The Age of Federalism: The Early American Republic, 1788–1800* (New York: Oxford University Press, 1995); and Sean Wilentz, *The Rise of American Democracy: The Crisis of the New Order, 1787–1815* (New York: W. W. Norton, 2007).

prevent further depredations upon American commerce by the British Government, or any other nation."[12]

1798 was time of fear and frenzy. Federalists had used French seizures of American ships, in the midst of its war with Britain, as an excuse to implement their draconian Alien and Sedition Acts, closing newspapers and jailing editors and even congressmen for criticizing the government's policies. Unlike most of New York City's divines, who supported the Federalists and their measures, Shearith Israel's spiritual leader, Hazan Gershom Seixas delivered a sermon that recalled France's friendship with America "when we were oppressed by the ravages and devastations of an enraged enemy." Resisting Federalist attempts to destroy the opposition, he beseeched the Lord to remove the "spirit of envy and jealousy" from the nation's leaders, producing a society "united in the bonds of brotherly and social love." Naphtali Judah printed the sermon and advertised it from May 30 through June 18. He then ceased dissemination of the pamphlet out of fear of arrest.[13]

The memoir of Mordecai Myers, a New Yorker politically active in the 1790s, reveals the opportunity for Jewish grass-roots political involvement. In the election of 1800, when he was twenty-four, Myers described Aaron Burr telling fellow Democratic-Republicans that "we must, at the next election, put a period to the [Federalist] 'reign of terror.'" Burr mounted a winning campaign by sponsoring "inspiring speeches by some of our most active and patriotic Democrats, young and old" in each ward. Burr chose Myers as one these ward spokesmen, and the Democratic-Republicans carried New York, providing the electoral votes that made Jefferson President.[14]

A number of New York Jews held political offices such as that of tax assessor. Two achieved high political and military office. Mordecai M. Noah served as Sheriff of New York County; Ephraim Hart, father of Joel, was Consul in Scotland. Dr. Jacob La Motta was surgeon and three New York

---

12   Pencak, *Jews and Gentiles in Early America*, 74; Lawrence H. Fuchs, *The Political Behavior of American Jews* (Glencoe, IL: Free Press, 1956), 26–28.

13   Gershom Seixas, *A Discourse Delivered . . . the Ninth of May, 1798* (New York, 1798), 6, 14–15; 1799 sermon, 28–29, 1803 sermon, 19–20, both in Lyons Collection, American Jewish Historical Society; Morris U. Schappes, "Anti-Semitism and Reaction, 1795–1800" *PAJHS* 38, no. 2 (1948): 122–26.

14   Jacob R. Marcus, *Memoirs of American Jews 1775–1865* (Philadelphia: Jewish Publication Society, 1955), 52–61.

Jews were officers in the New York State Militia. Mordecai Myers became an army captain and fought in the War of 1812.[15]

Mordecai M. Noah

After 1800, the Democratic-Republicans controlled New York politics, and Mordecai M. Noah, after he moved to New York in 1817, became New York's most prominent Jewish politician. Born in the city and attracted to the stage (he was a regular at the John Street Theater), he wrote plays throughout his life. His most successful drama was *She Would Be a Soldier* (1819), a tale of a wife who cross-dressed to join her spouse in the army. Noah entered politics as an ardent Jeffersonian journalist in Charleston. In 1813 he was appointed consul in Tunis only to be recalled in 1816. His ambition unshaken, he moved to New York as editor of the *National Advocate,* a newspaper that supported, with Tammany Hall, the Madison and Monroe administrations against the "forbiddingly aristocratic" DeWitt Clinton. Noah soon became the most prominent Jewish representative of Jeffersonian republicanism in New York. [16]

Noah championed his republicanism in orations before the Tammany and Mechanics Societies. He extolled revolutionary patriots, exposed in "rags and tatters" to the "chilling blasts of winter," who understood that they were endowing "millions yet unborn" with the treasure of "rational liberty." They could rest assured that with the help of immigrants and artisans, exchanging "cramped and uncultivated" minds" for "study and reflection," America would "prove false the axiom of tyrants, that man cannot govern himself."[17]

Noah's journalism espoused secular republican thought. He promoted universal (white male) suffrage for New York's 1820 Constitution, and championed an improved water supply, a modern police force, reform of the penal code, and manual labor classes for youths. In the Jeffersonian spirit, Noah declared "no occupation is more useful, more valuable to a country, than that of agriculture." While criticizing ladies' luxury, he advocated public support

---

15   Gustavus Hart, "A Biographical Account of Ephraim Hart and his Son, Dr. Joel Hart, of New York, *PAJHS* 4 (1896): 215–19; Rock, *Haven of Liberty*, 100–102.

16   Jonathan Sarna, *Jacksonian Jew: The Two Worlds of Mordecai Noah* (New York: Holmes and Meier, 1981), 1–13 and chap.3, esp. 35–44.

17   Mordecai M. Noah, *Oration before the Tammany Society* . . . (New York, 1817); *Address Delivered before the General Society of Mechanics and Tradesmen* . . . (New York, 1822).

for female education. A woman could be "accomplished" without being a "pedant," possessing both a "strong mind" and "soft manners." Though he later became an outspokenly racist champion of the institution of slavery, during the early republic he was critical of human bondage. He declared the owners of an illegal slave ship deserving of "solitary confinement." Nothing justified this practice among "men whose birthright is liberty, whose eminent peculiarity is freedom." Acknowledging "repeated instances that the intellect of the blacks is capable of high cultivation," he "deplored" slavery in America as a "domestic evil"; the trade in human chattel was "cursed."[18]

Noah delivered the consecration address at the newly rebuilt Shearith Israel in 1818, enunciating a Jewish version of Jeffersonian republicanism. Describing how Jews for centuries were "the objects of hatred and persecution," he declared that only in "OUR COUNTRY, the bright example of universal tolerance, of liberality, true religion and good faith," did they find acceptance. Only in a nation where justice is administered "impartially," where "dignity is blended with equality" and where "merit only has a fixed value," did this troubled people find peace and safety. Noah's oration contained no references to revelation, salvation, punishment of sin, or repentance. Rather, it asserted that Judaism, "the religion of nature—the religion of reason and philosophy," would flourish in a republican society.[19]

Noah sent Thomas Jefferson a copy of this speech. Jefferson replied that Noah's historical summary offered "remarkable proof" that every religious sect "in power" practiced intolerance, in opposition to "the moral basis, on which all our religions rest." Jefferson endorsed Noah's hope that the Jewish community would place "its members on the equal and common benches of science. . . ."[20]

---

18 Sarna, *Jacksonian Jew*, 51–53; Michael Schuldiner and Daniel J. Kleinfeld, eds., *The Selected Writings of Mordecai Noah* (Westport, CT: Praeger, 1999), 79–81, 84–89, 92–94, 100–104. Jews owned slaves in about the same proportion as Christians. However, during this era New York in 1799 passed a gradual manumission act that ended slavery by 1827. As the institution dwindled in New York, slavery was soon not an internal but a national political issue. Nevertheless, prejudice against Blacks remained strong, with nearly total social separation, and Jews shared these feelings with the white population. See Eli Faber, *Jews, Slaves and the Slave Trade: Setting the Record Straight* (New York: NYU Press, 1999).

19 Mordecai Manuel Noah, *Discourse, Delivered at the Consecration of the Synagogue Shearith Israel* (New York, 1818), 1–19, 23–27.

20 Lewis Abraham, "Correspondence between Washington and Jewish Citizens, *PAJHS* 3 (1895): 94-96. Madison also replied that he observed "with pleasure" that Noah's "sect" shared the "common blessings afforded by our Government and laws." Jefferson had

Jewish republicanism reached its height in Noah's belief that republican America could serve as the homeland for the Jewish people. Noah doubted that Jews would ever immigrate to a "backward Palestine." A return to Jerusalem to rebuild the Temple was no longer central to Jewish civilization. The "restoration of the Jewish nation to their ancient rights and dominion" ought to be in the United States; the most enlightened country of an enlightened age could provide Jewish immigrants with equality and opportunity.[21]

After the New York State legislature declined his request to set aside land for a colony for world Jewry, Noah decided to take on the project himself. Purchasing a few acres on Grand Island on the Niagara River, he staged an elaborate dedication ceremony in September 1825. To the music of Handel's *Judas Maccabeus*, Noah, dressed in robes "of crimson silk, trimmed with ermine" and accompanied by Seneca Chief Red Jacket, began the ingathering of world Jewry. Following a procession to St. Paul's Episcopal Church, where the new colony's cornerstone inscribed with the *Sh'ma* lay on the communion table, Noah "under the auspices and protection of the Constitution and laws of the United States of America," and "by the Grace of God, Governor and Judge of Israel," did "revive, renew and *reestablish* the government of the Jewish Nation." All Jews would find "asylum" in this "free and powerful country," where, living in peace in the colony of Ararat (the resting place of Noah's ark), they would learn the "science of government," the tools of "learning and civilization," and the "arts of agriculture."[22]

Noah urged all Jews to come to Ararat and "unite with their brethren, the chosen people." All prayer would be in Hebrew, though sermons could be "in the language of the country." World Jewry would pay the colony's expenses.[23]

---

mixed attitudes toward the Jews. He championed the rights of Jews but also attacked the Old Testament theology that preached ideas of God that were "degrading and injurious," and termed their ethics "often irreconcilable with the sound dictates of reason & morality." Frederic Cople Jaher, *A Scapegoat in the Wilderness: The Origin and Rise of Anti-Semitism in America* (Cambridge, MA: Harvard University Press, 1994), 130.

21   Sarna, *Jacksonian Jew*, 62–65, 138; Noah, *Discourse*, 19, 27. For background on other attempts at settlement, see Bernard D. Weinryb, "Noah's Ararat Jewish State in Its Historical Setting," in *The Jewish Experience in America*, ed. Benjamin J. Karp, 2 vols. (New York: Ktav, 1969), vol. 2, 136–57.

22   Sarna, *Jacksonian Jew*, 64–66; Joseph L. Blau and Salo W. Baron, eds., *The Jews of the United States 1790–1840: A Documentary History*, 3 vols. (New York: Columbia University Press, 1963), vol. 3, 894–97.

23   Blau and Baron, *Jews of the United States*, 897–900.

Noah received encouragement. Eduard Gans and Leopold Zunz, leaders of the German Society for the Culture and Scientific Study of the Jews, made Noah an "Extraordinary Member," assuring him that "the better part" of European Jewry were looking to the United States with hope. However, he received more ridicule than praise. Newspapers charged that "the corner-stone" was a ruse to "fill the pockets of Mr. Noah." American Jews attacked his project as "contrary to scriptural authority." European Jews judged Noah a "crazy man." The project went nowhere.[24]

Ararat was an early forerunner of Zionism, but also the vision of a Jeffersonian New York Jew. America was a tolerant, enlightened society where Jewry could find fulfillment. For Noah, Jewish identity had grown from an insular synagogue community to a worldwide communal identity within a republican nation.[25]

Noah was also the focus of the most noteworthy outbreak of antisemitism in early republican New York when he ran for the office of Sherriff in 1821. The *Commercial Advertiser* expressed alarm that on the second day of the election "the Jews prevailed against the Gentiles." A leader of the American Society for Meliorating the Condition of the Jews warned that an outbreak of yellow fever was "God's judgement" brought on by prominent citizens "publically abetting the election of an infidel in preference to a Christian." Noah wrote that "Churchmen, Sextons, Bell-ringers [and] Deacons . . . of the Church Militant scoured the wards to oppose what they called the unbeliever." Lamenting that the campaign against him could threaten members of other religious sects as well, he lost, attracting forty-one percent of the vote in a strongly Democratic electorate. Republican New York was a welcoming society for Jews, but it had not eliminated antisemitism.[26]

---

24 Schappes, Documentary *History,* 157–160; "Mordecai M. Noah. A Letter to Him, Dated 1822, from Eduard Gans and Leopold Zunz, Relating to the Emigration of German Jews to America," *PAJHS* 20 (1911): 147–148; Sarna, *Jacksonian Jew*, 64, 72–74.

25 For a Zionist perspective, see Robert Gordis, "Mordecai M. Noah: A Centenary Evaluation," *PAJHS* 41, no.1 (1951): 1–27; Marcus, *United States Jewry*, vol. 1, 620–22.

26 Sarna, *Jacksonian Jew*, 45–46; Jaher, *Scapegoat in the Wilderness*, 137. In 1790, when the Federalists realized that New York's Jews were supporting the Jeffersonians, they unleashed "a wide and fetid stream of Antisemitism." David Hackett Fischer, *The Revolution of American Conservatism: The Federalist Party in the Era of Jeffersonian Democracy* (New York: Harper and Row, 1965), 164. See also Rock, *Haven of Liberty*, 109–11.

A Republican Synagogue Community

The republican spirit of the New Republic was apparent in the reorganization of Shearith Israel after the Revolution. In 1790 the congregation drafted a new Constitution. Its "Bill of Rights" opened with a ringing statement:

> Whereas in free states all power originates and is derived from the people, who always retain every right necessary for their well being individually. . . . Therefore we the profession [professors] of the Divine laws . . . conceive it our duty to make this declaration of our rights and privileges. . . .

The first right, entitling "every free person of the Jewish religion . . . who lives according to its holy precepts" to a seat in the synagogue "as a brother," hinted at a worldwide brotherhood of Jews, perhaps reflecting the French Revolution's idea of *fraternité*. The charter's preamble declared that the congregation had authority, "in the presence of the Almighty" and in "a state happily constituted upon the principles of equal liberty civil and religious," to formulate a "compact" containing "rules, and regulations" for the "general good." Fulfilling their duty "to themselves and posterity," the "congregation of *yehudim*" pledged to "perform all acts" required for the support of "our religious and holy divine service." Republicanism shaped the world of Jewish spirituality.[27]

The constitution offered membership to every Jewish male twenty-one years of age or over (except indentured or hired servants) not married "contrary to the rules of our religion" and "conforming hereunto." It enumerated duties of officers and officials, allowed all members to vote for the synagogue's leadership, and directed that internal controversies be settled through arbitration.[28]

Despite the optimistic words of the constitution, the future of Shearith Israel was in doubt. Ironically, the welcoming society of early republic New York posed a threat to the Jewish community. The colonial concept of the synagogue-community was incompatible with a republican society in which Jews no longer had to seclude themselves in a plainly constructed sanctuary. Jews needed to huddle together no longer. Could such a small minority maintain its identity? Could it survive integration and assimilation? The

---

27   Jacob Rader Marcus, *American Jewry, Eighteenth Century: Documents* (Cincinnati: Hebrew Union College Press, 1958), 149–155.

28   Ibid., 151–54, 157–58, 163–66.

numbers were not in its favor. When Washington took his oath in 1789, New York's population had reached 33,000, of whom around 350 were Jews, slightly more than 1%. By 1825 the city's population had grown to over 166,000 inhabitants, only 500 of whom were Jews, about 0.3%. With immigration limited by the wars in Europe and intermarriage more common, Jews were shrinking as a percentage of the population.[29]

Though Shearith Israel remained critical to the maintenance of Judaism in Gotham, its standing became precarious. For many Jews the synagogue assumed relevance for only part of their lives: primarily life cycle ceremonies and the High Holy Days. Its physical condition deteriorated. Services, lasting as long as four to five hours, were often conducted in a cacophonous manner that seemed less and less relevant to most of the community. Attendance dwindled; it was more and more difficult to gather a minyan of ten adult males. Ritual observance lessened, especially outside the home. Finances were "in a very deranged state"; the synagogue's trustees had difficulty raising the funds needed to pay the *hazan*, *shohet* (ritual slaughterer), *shamash* (caretaker), and clerk. At times they resorted to debt collectors against members in arrears for dues.[30]

But Shearith Israel persevered, sustained by a small but loyal membership. During a short period of national prosperity, it refurbished its sanctuary, doubling its size and making the synagogue a more visible presence in the metropolis. A closer look at the minutes of the synagogue also reveal that, as in the nation as a whole, the congregation was split between Hamiltonian and Jeffersonian outlooks.

The Hamiltonian approach, stressing deference and tradition, is apparent in the minutes of the congregation. Decorum and order were a constant theme. This included increasing the fine for disruptive behavior to a hefty $250 and forbidding members from chanting psalms in any key other than that of the *hazan*. The Board denied the request of a group of young congregants to form a choir for services on grounds that "innovations" must be approached "with great cautions and defference" so as not to create a greater "evil." In another case, though it could find no Talmudic source for requiring men to wear a tallit, it did so anyway, declaring that any "departure" from tradition would be

---

29 Grinstein, *Rise of the Jewish Community*, 469.
30 Marcus, *United States Jewry*, vol. 1, 240, 256, 598; Minutes of the Board of Trustees (MBOT), May 18,1806; November 1, 1807; October 27, 1812; February 15, March 13, and July 11, 1813; March 27, 1814; May 7 and 28, 1815, July 27, 1817, Microfilm, American Jewish Archives; Blau and Baron, *Jews of the United States*, vol. 1, 91.

an "innovation," which "could lead to further "deviations" and, finally, to the "subversion of all the venerable and established usages of this Congregation." The board expected obedient behavior from its employees, and reprimanded the *hazan* for behaving in an "unbecoming manner" and the *shamash* for failing to close a window when so ordered. Members summoned before the board for disruptive behavior generally struck a deferential attitude. Finally, its most conservative decision was to refurbish the existing sanctuary rather than move to a new synagogue uptown where most members were or would soon be living.[31]

The Jeffersonian outlook was also apparent. Most notable was a controversy from 1811 to 1814 that saw the removal or resignation of some of the congregation's most respected members. Isaac Moses, for example, noting that he had been a trustee for years, abandoned his post with "great pain and anxiety" because of a "combination tending to destroy the peace and happiness of the Congregation" by driving away men "who have unremittingly and honestly laboured to promote their prosperity," and selecting individuals who "have been steadily hostile to the present constitution," a charter "drafted and ratified by the congregation." There is no mention of the controversy that caused this disruption, though a dispute over the retention of the *shohet* appears to have been a cause.[32]

After hiring a new *shohet*, the new Board persuaded the Common Council to grant Shearith Israel the sole right to certify that meat was kosher, which in practice meant that only the congregation's *shohet* could be used. The former officers (who when on the Board expressed Hamiltonian ideals in their demands for deference and order) and their member supporters protested on grounds that monopolies were harmful to the common good. This Jeffersonian argument led the Council to repeal its ordinance and the new Board to deny that it intended a monopoly. Jeffersonianism was

---

31 *Bye Laws of the Congregation of Shearith Israel As Ratified on the 24 June 1805*, Lyons Collection, American Jewish Historical Association (AJHS). MBOT, July 21, 1805; January 11, 1807; February 23, 1809; May 8, 1814; July 27, 1817; August 25, October 18, November 23, and December 28, 1817; March 8 and April 5, 1818; September 6, 1820, January 16, 1824; October 26, 1825. Only in the 1820s did the synagogue regain fiscal health. For example, the expenses for salaries in 1814, a dark war year, were $1350. In 1824, a year of growth and prosperity, they were $8427. Sarna, *American Judaism,* 47; Lee M. Friedman, "An Early Reference to the Jews," *PAJHS* 24 (1917): 131. A proposal in 1815 to establish a branch of the synagogue in Greenwich Village was defeated.

32 MBOT, October 15 and November 19 and 20, 1811; August 30, 1812; July 11, 1813; October 3, 1824; Blau and Baron, *Jews of the United States,* vol. 2, 536, n.100.

also apparent in Shearith Israel's attempts to gain state funds for a Jewish public school in accord with Jefferson's ideas on common education. Too, when the son of Hazan Seixas was disciplined for contemptuous behavior in protesting an inadequate pension for his mother, seventeen members defended him, invoking egalitarian Jeffersonianism. Claiming that due process had been denied (he was not given a hearing), they declared that "laws . . . enacted for the rights and Liberties of individuals ought not to be thus precipitously disrespected." This was a violation of the congregation's constitution, a charter in conformity "with that universal law of our country which requires the accuser and accused to be confronted."[33]

Republican thought was central to the secession of members of Shearith Israel in 1825 to form the city's second congregation, Bnai Jeshurun. The split was triggered by the dissatisfaction of young Ashkenazi members with the congregation's Sephardic services. The group, Hevra Hinuch Nearim ("Society for the Education of Youth") organized itself along republican lines. Its governing board was a three-member committee that would hold office for three months at a time. All honors were to be distributed equally and new members would be admitted by a majority vote. The *hazan* would have no special standing in the community.[34]

Once organized, the Hevra asked Shearith Israel for permission to hold morning services when the sanctuary was not in use. Their request was denied on the grounds that that such a practice would have "a tendency to destroy the well-known and established rule and customs of our ancestors as have been practiced . . . for one hundred years past." With no alternative, the Hevra chose to withdraw from Shearith Israel and form its own congregation. Its public statement gave a number of reasons for its action, including the distance between residence and the sanctuary, the inadequate capacity of Shearith Israel to serve the city's Jewish community, and its desire to conduct services under the Ashkenazi *minhag*. Jefferson had written that when "a government no longer served the right of the people to seek life, liberty and the pursuit of happiness" it was their right to "abolish it and institute new Government" that would "seem more likely

---

33 Samuel Oppenheim, "A Question of Kosher Meat Supply in 1813 with a Sketch of Earlier Conditions," *PAJHS* 25 (1917): 31–60; MBOT, June 6, 1809, March 3 and December 12, 1812; January 10, 1813; July 15 and 20, 1814; December 28, 1817; February 4 and March 5, 1821; August 8, 1823; Grinstein, *Rise of the Jewish Community*, 228–38.

34 Blau and Baron, *Jews of the United States*, vol. 2, 540–45; Grinstein, *Rise of the Jewish Community*, 45–47.

to effect their . . . Happiness." When the Hevra argued that they, "acted out of necessity," and invoked the "religious and . . . equitable claim" that they possessed the right to separate, they likely had in mind the words of the American colonists fifty years earlier. The preamble to the new congregation's constitution praised the "wise and republican laws of this country . . . based upon universal toleration giving to every citizen and sojourner the right to worship according to the dictate of his conscience." [35]

The founding of Bnai Jeshurun heralded great changes in the New York Jewish community, especially in its overall growth and greater complexity. At the time of its founding, the local Jewish population was only about 500. By the time of the Civil War, the Jewish population had risen nearly 40,000 in a city of 813,000. Shearith Israel was the only synagogue in New York for nearly a century. Thirty-five years after Bnai Jeshurun became the city's second synagogue, there were twenty-seven congregations in Gotham.[36]

A final important question to consider is whether or not nineteenth-century republicanism was compatible with traditional Judaism. This issue is apparent in the sermons of Gershom Seixas, the beloved *hazan* of Shearith Israel. As we noted, he was a strong Jeffersonian. His talks include many republican themes. He viewed God as "prime mover," spoke of the works of "an almighty providence" that proved "the necessity of a first cause," described the "disinterested benevolence of our Creator" who endowed humanity with "the faculty and power of reasoning," a great gift as it is "by reason that we arrive to the knowledge of infinite Goodness." He was certain that Scripture would be "verified" by science. He despised inequality, remaining in New York at great peril during the yellow fever epidemics. He spoke of classical republican duty: responsibility for the common good. "Virtue" was not "of a passive nature." It must be "active, fulfilling the Law of God, exercising ourselves in good works, and by an exemplary Life, inducing others to pursue the path of righteousness." The task of each citizen was to "ameliorate" the condition of his brethren.[37]

35 Grinstein, *Rise of the Jewish Community*, 45–49; MBOT, June 27, July 10 and 31, September and October 6, 19, and 26, 1825; Israel Goldstein, *A Century of Judaism in New York: B'nai Jeshurun, 1825–1925* (New York: Congregation B'nai Jeshurun, 1930), 44–45, 54–62.
36 Grinstein, *Rise of the Jewish Community*, 469, 472–74; Kenneth Jackson, ed., *The Encyclopedia of New York City*, 2nd ed. (New Haven: Yale University Press, 2010), 1019.
37 Gershom Seixas, *A Religious Sermon Delivered . . . November 26, 1789* (New York, 1789), 6, 9, 21, 24; 1799 sermon, 4, 22; 1803 sermon, 3, 6–7, 9, 16, 22.

Seixas identified with the American cause, which he saw as God's work. The "conclusion of the last war" and the "establishment of public liberty" were "a wonderful display of divine providence," including the "adoption of the new constitution." Consequently, as Jews were fortunate to live "in a country where we possess every advantage that other citizens of these states enjoy," Seixas asked congregants to work toward the "public good," suppress "every species of licentiousness," promote "the welfare of the United States, and "return thanks to benign Goodness" for placing them "in a country where they are free to act, according the dictates of conscience."[38]

Seixas was also a deeply traditional Jew influenced by his years of friendship with local Calvinist divines. Salvation was a central theme of his sermons. In 1789 he reminded his congregants that "the Almighty" was "ever watchful over his people." Only those who both held a "firm belief in God" and followed His commandments could "truly hope for Salvation." Sin and reformation were entwined with Salvation. The ten lost tribes were dispersed because the Jews were "sinners in the eyes of the sight of their Creator," unwilling to "follow His commandments." A "late melancholy visitation" of the yellow fever epidemic (1799), was "a manifestation of his displeasures," a moment when "the finger of God" pointed out "the atrocities of our sins." These events of ancient and current history called for "strict reformation." Survivors must "rejoice that he has saved us alive, that we may have time to repent us our manifold Sins, and to become *regenerated*."[39]

Salvation implied a day of judgment. Seixas described the agony of a dissolute sinner facing the "presence of infinite justice": he has only "horror" for his prospects. In "paroxysms of Phrenzy," he beholds the "moment of his dissolution." The world to come was a presence in his sermons. Indeed, "were it not for the hopes and promises of an hereafter," what man would wish to be "a creature of this transitory existence," with its troubles and pains? Mankind alone possessed the "glorious prerogative" of "the power of free agency." Only the choice of a life of "virtue" prepared man for his "future state, when our immortal Soul shall be freed from this unstable tenement of flesh."[40]

---

38 Seixas, *A Religious Discourse*, 13–14; *Sermon Delivered*, 9, 23–24; Isidore E. Meyer, "The Hebrew Oration of Sampson Simson, 1800," *PAJHS* 46, no. 1 (1956): 41–48.

39 Jacob R. Marcus, *The Handsome Young Priest in the Black Gown: The Personal World of Gershom Seixas* (Cincinnati: Hebrew Union College, 1970), 42, 53; Seixas, *A Religious Discourse*, 9–12; *Sermon Delivered*, 11–12; 1799 sermon, 2–7, 12, 22–24; 1803 sermon, 6.

40 Seixas, *A Discourse Delivered*, 12; 1799 sermon, 13, 14, 18–19; 1803 sermon, 3–4.

Another traditional theme in Seixas's theology was restoration. The "sins of our progenitors" had transformed Jews into "wandering exiles through the habitable Globe." But the long banishment was nearing an end. The war convulsing the world in 1798 was a sign that "the glorious period of redemption is near at hand," a moment when God would keep "his divine promise" to collect "the scattered remnant of Israel." The scourge of yellow fever a signal of "that great and glorious day" when the "people of Israel . . . purged of our Sins," would be released from "their long and gloomy captivity" and be "reinstated in our land, there to dwell in Safety, in Peace, in Happiness."[41]

Seixas never sought to reconcile the gap between Jeffersonian republicanism and traditional Jewish belief. Rather he managed to live happily within both worlds. So too did the minority of New York's Jews, who took Jewish theology and commandments to heart. For New York Jewry early republican New York was a golden age. Antisemitism was not gone, but it was uncommon. Moreover, the republicanism of the new nation offered Jews the opportunity to enter freely into all aspects of society, commercial, fraternal, political, and religious, in the spirit that they were part of a great experiment to demonstrate to the world that men and women were capable of self-government. American Jewish history would reveal that while this acceptance was still incomplete, the ideals of this era were a significant factor in America's becoming a magnet, a new Jerusalem, for world Jewry, most of whom entered via the Port of New York.

---

41   Seixas, *A Religious Discourse*, 10; *A Discourse Delivered*, 10, 29; 1799 sermon, 25–26; 1803 sermon, 12, 13; "Items Relating to Gershom M. Seixas," *PAHS* 27 (1920): 131.

For Further Reading

Appleby, Joyce. *Capitalism and a New Social Order: The Republican Vision of the 1790s.* New York: NYU Press, 1984.

Blau, Joseph L. and Salo W. Baron, eds. *The Jews of the United States 1790-1840: A Documentary History*, 3 vols. New York: Columbia University Press, 1963.

Burrows, Edwin, and Mike Wallace. *Gotham: A History of New York City to 1898.* New York: Oxford University Press, 1999.

Cohen, Theodore. "Walter Jonas Judah and New York's 1798 Yellow Fever Epidemic." *American Jewish Archives Journal (AJA)* 48, no. 1 (1996): 23–34.

Elkins, Stanley, and Eric McKitrick. *The Age of Federalism: The Early American Republic, 1788–1800.* New York: Oxford University Press, 1995.

Faber, Eli. *Jews, Slaves and the Slave Trade: Setting the Record Straight.* New York: NYU Press, 1999.

Fischer, David Hackett. *The Revolution of American Conservatism: The Federalist Party in the Era of Jeffersonian Democracy.* New York: Harper and Row, 1965.

Fuchs, Lawrence H. *The Political Behavior of American Jews.* Glencoe, IL: Free Press, 1956).

Goldstein, Israel. *A Century of Judaism in New York: B'nai Jeshurun, 1825–1925.* New York: Congregation B'nai Jeshurun, 1930.

Gordis, Robert. "Mordecai M. Noah: A Centenary Evaluation." *PAJHS* 41, no.1 (1951): 1–27.

Gottesman, Rita Susswein. *The Arts and Crafts in New York, 1800–1804.* New York: New-York Historical Society, 1965.

Grinstein, Hyman B. *The Rise of the Jewish Community of New York, 1654–1860.* Philadelphia: Jewish Publication Society, 1947.

Jackson, Kenneth, ed. *The Encyclopedia of New York City*, 2nd ed. New Haven: Yale University Press, 2010.

Jaher, Frederic Cople. *A Scapegoat in the Wilderness: The Origin and Rise of Anti-Semitism in America.* Cambridge, MA: Harvard University Press, 1994.

Maier, Pauline, *American Scripture: Making the Declaration of Independence.* New York: Knopf, 1997.

Marcus, Jacob Rader. *Memoirs of American Jews 1775–1865.* Philadelphia: Jewish Publication Society, 1955.

———. *American Jewry, Eighteenth Century: Documents.* Cincinnati: Hebrew Union College Press, 1958.

———. *The Handsome Young Priest in the Black Gown: The Personal World of Gershom Seixas.* Cincinnati: Hebrew Union college, 1970.

———. *United States Jewry, 1776–1985,* 4 vols. Detroit: Wayne State University Press, 1989.

Pencak, William. *Jews and Gentiles in Early America, 1654–1800.* Ann Arbor: University of Michigan Press, 2005.

Pocock, J. G. A. *The Machiavellian Moment: Florentine Political Thought and the Atlantic Republican Tradition.* Princeton: Princeton University Press, 1975.

Rock, Howard B. *Haven of Liberty: New York Jews in the New World.* New York: NYU Press, 2012.

Sadowski, Edmund R. "A Jewish Masonic Prayer." *PAJHS* 48, no. 2 (1958–1959): 134–35.

Sarna, Jonathan. *Jacksonian Jew: The Two Worlds of Mordecai Noah.* New York: Holmes and Meier, 1981.

Schappes, Morris U. *A Documentary History of the Jews of the United States, 1654–1875.* New York: Citadel, 1950.

Schuldiner, Michael, and Daniel J. Kleinfeld, eds. *The Selected Writings of Mordecai Noah.* Westport, CT: Praeger, 1999.

Sokobin, Samuel. "The Simson-Hirsch Letter to the Chinese Jews, 1795." *PAJHS* 49, no. 1 (1959): 39–52.

Weinryb, Bernard D. "Noah's Ararat Jewish State in Its Historical Setting," in *The Jewish Experience in America*, 2 vols., edited by Benjamin J. Karp, vol. 2, 136–57. New York: Ktav, 1969.

Wilentz, Sean. *The Rise of American Democracy: The Crisis of the New Order, 1787–1815.* New York: W. W. Norton, 2007.

Wills, Gary. *Inventing America: Jefferson's Declaration of Independence.* New York: Doubleday, 1978.

Chapter 3

The Other Jews:
Jewish Immigrants
from Central Europe in
New York, 1820–1880

Tobias Brinkmann

A Curious Gap

With the end of the Napoleonic Wars in 1815 a growing number of
Europeans began moving to the New World, especially from Central
Europe and the British Isles. Among the millions of migrants who settled
in the United States between 1820 and 1880 were at least 100,000 Jews from
the German states and adjacent territories, especially the Austrian province
of Bohemia, the French territory of Alsace, but also from further east, especially from the Lithuanian provinces in the Russian Empire. Until recently,
pre-1880 Jewish immigrants were often described as "German Jews." The
following essay will show that this description is problematic. Key questions are where in New York Jewish immigrants lived, how they interacted
with other immigrants, especially from the German states, and why more
than a few Jewish immigrants considered German culture as an important
part of their Jewish identity.

During the nineteenth century, New York emerged as the largest center of Jewish life in the world. Admittedly, the decisive push only occurred after 1880 when the immigration from Eastern Europe began to increase sharply, but by that time the earlier Central European wave had already created a significant community. Even though New York was also the oldest Jewish community in North America, it is worthwhile to recall that around 1800 the city's Jewish population was declining. It is estimated that in 1810 not more than 450 Jews were living in a city of almost 100,000 inhabitants. Around 1820 the bustling port city Charleston in South Carolina had a larger Jewish population (ca. 700) than New York (ca. 550). But after 1820 New York attracted more Jewish immigrants than its rivals and soon reclaimed its spot as home of America's largest Jewish community. Thanks to strong Jewish immigration after 1820 New York's Jewish population had grown to about 80,000 in 1880. A mere twenty years later, in 1900, an estimated 600,000 Jews lived in New York (and Brooklyn), more than in any other city in the world. Ten years later, in 1910, the number had doubled to 1.2 million, thanks to the strong immigration from the Russian and Austro-Hungarian Empires. The Jewish share of the general population also increased strongly from 0.5% in 1800, to about 7% in 1880, over 15% in 1910, and ca. 30% in 1920 when New York City was home to more than 1.6 million Jews.[1]

It is thus not surprising that New York Jewish history is one of the best researched subfields of American Jewish history. Indeed, the Jewish history of New York is well-documented, not only for the period of mass Eastern European immigration, but even for the 1600s and 1700s.[2] A closer look reveals that one period remains understudied. Scholars seem uncertain how to assess the sixty years between 1820 and 1880. On the one hand, this is understandable: Since most of the tremendous growth of

---

1   Paul Ritterband, "Counting the Jews of New York, 1900–1991: An Essay in Substance and Method," *Jewish Population Studies* 29 (1997): *Papers in Jewish Demography*, 199–228; Eli Faber, *A Time for Planting: The First Migration, 1654–1820* (Baltimore, MD: Johns Hopkins University Press, 1992), 111; Howard B. Rock, *Haven of Liberty: New York Jews in the New World, 1654–1865* (New York: NYU Press, 2012), 93, 155; Moses Rischin, *The Promised City: New York's Jews 1870–1914* (Cambridge, MA: Harvard University Press, 1962), 116, 270.

2   See especially the three volumes of *City of Promises: A History of the Jews of New York*, ed. Deborah Dash Moore, with a visual essay by Diana L. Linden (New York: NYU Press, 2012): Rock, *Haven of Liberty*; Annie Polland and Daniel Soyer, *The Emerging Metropolis: New York Jews in the Age of Immigration, 1840–1920*; and Jeffrey S. Gurock, *Jews in Gotham: New York Jews in a Changing Metropolis, 1920–2010*.

the New York Jewish population came as a result of the post-1880 wave of mass immigration, the pre-1880 history can seem almost insignificant. On the other hand, though, this gap is curious, because the middle decades of the nineteenth century witnessed a remarkable shift in American urban and economic history. As the country's main Atlantic gateway, New York became the epicenter of America's dramatic transition from an agricultural settler society to a modern urban-industrial economy. As urban historian Janet Abu-Lughod puts it, between 1820 and 1870 New York emerged as America's "first global city." This transformation depended on access to technological innovation and on the availability of cheap immigrant labor and capital. Most of the millions of European immigrants who moved to the United States between 1820 and 1880 arrived in New York. These immigrants came overwhelmingly from Central Europe and the British Isles, especially Ireland. A significant number moved on after a few days or weeks, or returned to Europe, but many settled in New York and Brooklyn, boosting both the cities' populations. In 1825 only about ten percent of New York's inhabitants were foreign-born. By 1860 almost half of the much larger population was made up of immigrants, not counting their American-born children. Mass immigration and economic growth were mutually dependent processes, but the economic development was uneven. Throughout the nineteenth century, growth spurts were interrupted by periods of economic stagnation when thousands of workers were laid off and migration rates declined. Low wages and high unemployment during repeated recessions explains why many New Yorkers lived in great misery in notorious slum neighborhoods such as Five Points. Growing inequality and exploitation led to strikes and violent conflicts.[3]

Different Explanations

How did Jews contribute to New York's rise to America's metropolis *before* the onset of the strong Jewish migration from Eastern Europe in the 1880s? Jewish immigrants played a prominent role in New York's and America's

---

3   Janet Abu-Lughod, *New York, Chicago, Los Angeles: America's Global Cities* (Minneapolis: University of Minnesota, 1999), 35, 41; Sven Beckert, *The Monied Metropolis: New York City and the Consolidation of the American Bourgeoisie, 1850–1896* (Cambridge: Cambridge University Press, 2001); John Bodnar, *The Transplanted: A History of Immigrants in Urban America* (Bloomington: Indiana University Press, 1985), xviii; Mary P. Ryan, *Civic Wars: Democracy and Public Life in the American City during the Nineteenth Century* (Berkeley: University of California Press, 1997), 151–57.

economic transformation, primarily as entrepreneurs in crucial sectors such as wholesale and retail businesses, in the garment trade, and in finance. By the turn of the century some of the most successful and wealthiest American Jews lived in New York.

Some called themselves "Our Crowd." This was the title author Stephen Birmingham chose for his bestselling popular history of New York's Jewish establishment. The book was first published in 1967 and remains in print. Birmingham perpetuated the popular image of extremely wealthy "uptown" Jews who lived a world apart from hundreds of thousands of working-class Jews from Eastern Europe who toiled for low wages in sweatshops and lived in run-down tenements. In the popular imagination "Our Crowd" became synonymous with the Jews who arrived before 1880, primarily from "Germany." In his beautifully narrated book Birmingham concentrated on a few rags-to-riches careers, revealing hardly anything about almost all other Jews who moved to New York before 1880. Perhaps it would be unfair to criticize him for this omission, since his main interest as a writer seems to have been the colorful lives of very rich Americans, a subject on which his later works of fiction and non-fiction focus. But as a scholarly work, *Our Crowd* is lacking. It contains hardly any references and no bibliography, raising questions about its reliability. It is doubtful whether Birmingham used any German-language sources. Some passages of the book betray a crude and undifferentiated understanding of New York Jewish history. For instance, Birmingham asserted that the extensive support established Jews provided to Jewish immigrants from Eastern Europe after 1880 was not genuine and was driven by self-interest and intense embarrassment—an assessment that many historians now dispute.[4]

Most academic historians who wrote about the social history of Jews in New York after the 1950s concentrated on the post-1880 Jewish mass immigration from Eastern Europe. For understandable reasons authors who examined Jewish trade unions and *Yidishkayt* did not devote much attention to the wealthy Jewish establishment or the period before 1880, let alone to sources containing information about the "other" Jews. In his path-breaking and widely praised 1962 study about Eastern European Jews in New York, *The Promised City*, Moses Rischin provided a well-documented, in-depth analysis of how Jewish immigrants from Eastern Europe made

4 Stephen Birmingham, *Our Crowd: The Great Jewish Families of New York* (New York: Harper & Row, 1967), 289, 291, 294.

New York "their" city. The chapter on "Germans vs. Russians" reflects the perspective of the newly arriving immigrants and reveals little about the actual "Germans." In fact, a close reading reveals that Birmingham mined Rischin's chapter for his discussion of the German Jews' attitude towards the new immigrants, albeit without giving Rischin any credit.[5]

A few aspects of pre-1880 Jewish New York Jewish history received some attention, especially religious history. Yet the scholarship tended to concentrate on a few prominent rabbis and scholars who shaped the Reform movement and contributed to the rise of Conservative Judaism. Little was written about average Jewish immigrants who moved to New York between 1820 and 1880.[6] Most of the few publications about mid-century Jewish immigrants can be traced to scholars such as Rudolf Glanz and Eric E. Hirshler who grew up in Austria and Germany respectively and fled to America after the rise of the Nazi regime.[7]

Tellingly, it was the author of a 1990 study about German-speaking immigrants in New York who made the first serious attempt to look beyond the small wealthy and educated Jewish elite. During his research, historian Stanley Nadel noticed many immigrants belonging to German-American *Vereine* (associations) who openly identified as Jewish. German-language papers in New York regularly published articles about Jewish congregations and associations. German was widely spoken among Jewish immigrants during the 1840s and 1850s, not least in newly founded Reform congregations. Nadel decided to treat Jews as a subset of New York's bustling mid-century German immigrant community, devoting a few pages to Jews in the chapter about religion in his book on *Kleindeutschland*.[8] Nadel's social history was one of the first in the field of local German American studies to include Jews. Studies about German-speaking immigrants in other American cities hardly mentioned Jewish immigrants, in part because

---

5 Rischin, *The Promised City*, 95–111.
6 Michael Meyer, *Response to Modernity: A History of the Reform Movement in Judaism* (New York: Oxford University Press, 1988); Bruce L. Ruben, *Max Lilienthal: The Making of the American Rabbinate* (Detroit: Wayne State University Press, 2011).
7 Rudolf Glanz, *The German Jew in America: An Annotated Bibliography including Books, Pamphlets and Articles of Special Interest* (Cincinnati: Hebrew Union College Press, 1969); Rudolf Glanz, "The German-Jewish Mass Immigrations 1820–1880," *American Jewish Archives* 22, no. 1 (1970): 49–66; Eric E. Hirshler, ed., *Jews from Germany in the United States* (New York: Farrar, Straus and Cudahy, 1955). See also Lloyd Gartner, "Necrology: Rudolf Glanz (1892–1978)," *American Jewish History* 69, no. 2 (1979): 270–73.
8 Stanley Nadel, *Little Germany: Ethnicity, Religion and Class in New York City 1845–80* (Urbana: University of Illinois Press, 1990), 99–103.

scholars considered them part of a different ethnic group. Realizing that he had identified a striking gap, Nadel published an article in the journal *American Jewish History* criticizing the focus on the German Jewish elite and the "artificial division" of immigrant historians reinforcing the myth of supposedly separate ethnic groups. He argued that Jewish immigrants from the German states belonged to German-American immigrant communities. As he put it, "the German-American and German-Jewish communities were overlapping and inextricable entities."[9]

Shortly after Nadel, two other scholars presented hypotheses about mid-century Jewish immigrants that approached the history of the mid-century Jewish migration from entirely different angles. In a survey about the nineteenth century that was part of a five-volume series about American Jewish history and published under the auspices of the American Jewish Historical Society, Hasia Diner questioned the widely accepted position that three distinct "waves" of Jewish immigrants had shaped the American Jewish community—and by default the history of Jews in New York. According to this model, Sephardic immigrants arriving during the colonial period constituted the first wave. They were followed by "German Jews" who started immigrating after the end of the Napoleonic Wars in 1815. The German wave declined after the Civil War. The third Eastern European wave lasted from the early 1880s to the period after World War I, when the United States Congress passed restrictive immigration legislation. Diner rejected this model by arguing that the immigrations overlapped in several ways. Indeed, earlier studies had shown that most eighteenth-century Jewish immigrants were Ashkenazim rather than Sephardim. In a later study Diner made a convincing case for treating the period between 1820 and the 1920s in American Jewish history as the "age of migration."[10] Diner also described the term "German Jews" as misleading because in her view many Jewish immigrants came from borderland provinces with overwhelmingly non-German-speaking populations such as Bohemia, the Prussian province of Posen, and western Hungary, rather than "Germany." Moreover, the Jews who originated in German states, such as Bavaria, often were young men and women from small rural communities, who were

---

9   Stanley Nadel, "Jewish Race and German Soul in Nineteenth-Century America," *American Jewish History* 77, no. 1 (1987): 6–26, quote on 26.
10 Hasia R. Diner, *A Time for Gathering: The Second Migration 1820–1880* (Baltimore, MD: Johns Hopkins University Press, 1992); Diner, *The Jews of the United States, 1654 to 2000* (Berkeley: University of California Press, 2004).

Orthodox and spoke Yiddish. According to Diner, these migrants had only been superficially exposed to German culture and language when they left for America, more closely resembling their Eastern European coreligionists than their gentile German fellow emigrants. In her view only a "thin layer" of educated rabbis could reasonably be described as Germanized.[11] Diner did not consult German-language sources.

In 1994, Avraham Barkai, an Israeli scholar who had widely published on the history of German Jews in Germany, published a survey about the German Jewish immigration to the United States. Until then scholars working on German Jewish history had largely ignored the strong Jewish emigration, even though the number of Jews who left was not negligible. More research is necessary to ascertain accurate numbers, but current estimates range from 100,000 to over 200,000 Jews who moved from the German states to the United States between 1820 and 1880. The Jewish population in the states that would form Imperial Germany in 1871 increased from about 250,000 in 1816 to more than 500,000 in 1871, thanks in large part to natural growth. The departure of at least 100,000 mostly younger Jews during this period, therefore, was significant.[12] Barkai focused more on the migration process than Diner, and on ties between the immigrants and German Jews in Germany. Like Nadel he highlighted the immigrants' identification with German culture and their ties to other German-speaking immigrants. For Barkai "German Jews" in America represented a transplanted branch of German Jewry.[13] And indeed, even a superficial look at the German Jewish press, especially the main weekly, the *Allgemeine Zeitung des Judenthums*, betrays an intense interest in the state of Jewish life in America. The *Allgemeine Zeitung* regularly published reports about Jewish communities in the United States. During the lengthy emancipation process German Jews often looked to the United States as a model

11   Diner, *A Time for Gathering*, 232–33.
12   Tobias Brinkmann, *Sundays at Sinai: A Jewish Congregation in Chicago* (Chicago: University of Chicago Press, 2012), 11–30; Stefi Jersch-Wenzel, "Population Shifts and Occupational Structure," in *German-Jewish History in Modern Times: Emancipation and Acculturation, 1780-1871*, ed. Michael A. Meyer (New York: Columbia University Press, 1997), 52; Gabriel E. Alexander, "Die jüdische Bevölkerung Berlins in den ersten Jahrzehnten des 20. Jahrhunderts: Demographische und wirtschaftliche Entwicklungen," in *Jüdische Geschichte in Berlin: Essays und Studien*, ed. Reinhard Rürup (Berlin: Hentrich, 1995), 117–48.
13   Avraham Barkai, *Branching Out: German-Jewish Immigration to the United States 1820-1914* (New York: Holmes & Meier, 1994).

of freedom and the place where Jews (or rather, Jewish men) enjoyed full citizenship.[14]

Most scholars agree that the members of a few wealthy Jewish families whose members sat on the boards of Jewish congregations, associations, and institutions were not representative of the Jewish migrants who moved to New York between 1820 and 1880. Should Jewish immigrants who came to New York in this period be considered as part of German immigrant communities, as Nadel argued? Were German Jews perhaps even a transplanted branch of German Jewry? Or is the term "German Jews" completely misleading because most immigrants differed little from the Eastern European immigrants who arrived after 1880? It would be too simple to dismiss any of these hypotheses because each contains important insights. It has to be stressed that extensive research has not been conducted on the history of Jewish immigrants who settled in New York before 1880. Nevertheless, studies about other cities, and some original sources, do allow for some insights.

Making Sense of the "German" Nexus

At issue are the territories from which Jewish migrants actually originated, the language(s) they spoke after moving to the United States, their links with non-Jewish immigrants, and how they (re-)defined themselves in the setting of a rapidly changing metropolis that offered remarkable economic and social opportunities. It is important to look at each of these questions carefully. Moreover, in the entrepôt New York the in- and out-movement of Jewish and other immigrant populations was high. In his pioneering study *The Other Bostonians*, urban historian Stephan Thernstrom showed that the net growth of urban populations obscures high rates of movement to and from a city. While Boston's population grew only by 65,000 during the 1880s, between 180,000 and 800,000 people passed through the city.[15]

A key question concerns where Jewish immigrants who moved to New York before 1880 actually came from. Most authors do not distinguish between images of Germany, Poland, and Russia, and actual

---

14   Steven M. Lowenstein, "The View from the Old World: German Jewish Perspectives," in *The Americanization of the Jews*, ed. Norman J. Cohen and Robert M. Seltzer (New York: NYU Press, 1995), 19–40.

15   Stephan Thernstrom, *The Other Bostonians: Poverty and Progress in the American Metropolis, 1880–1970* (Cambridge, MA: Harvard University Press, 1973), 15–20.

political entities. A Polish state did not exist during the nineteenth century, a German nation-state was only founded in 1871, and the Russian Empire was home to a religiously and ethnically diverse population which included many Polish speakers, German speakers, and Jews, among others. Positive and negative images of "German" and "Polish" Jews require critical analysis, as the following example illustrates. In 1846 a correspondent of the German Jewish weekly *Allgemeine Zeitung des Judenthums* described the Jewish population in New York as an ethnic-social hierarchy. He lamented that Jewish immigrants from different parts of Europe seemed unable and unwilling to form a community:

> It is easy to understand that this mixture of many nations cannot come together. The Portuguese behaves like a nobleman among the Jews . . . and indeed, he is a gentleman. The Pole here is the dirtiest creature of all classes, and he is responsible for the derogatory use of the name "Jew". . . . The German represents the majority among the Jews; he is efficient and knows how to assimilate to the conditions here. . . . The German is proud towards the Pole and avoids him, for this the latter despises him.[16]

Obviously, the correspondent was not an impartial observer. But who made up the sub-communities that he described? The ethnic labels he gave them do not, in fact, identify precisely the actual places of origin of the different groups of Jews in New York. "Portuguese" refers to members of the small long-settled Jewish establishment whose members largely belonged to congregations founded by Sephardi settlers like New York's oldest congregation, Shearith Israel. Detailed research has shown that most Jews arriving during the seventeenth century, admittedly in small numbers, were actually Ashkenazi migrants from Central and Eastern Europe who joined the small Sephardi establishment, for instance through marriage.[17] The "Polish" and "German" Jewish migrants were more recent arrivals. By 1846 they outnumbered the longer settled Jewish population. But where did they actually come from?

In 1846, neither a German nor a Polish state existed. Prussia's eastern provinces, especially the Posen province, comprised both German and Polish speakers. Adjacent areas in East Central Europe also contained populations who belonged to different religious groups and spoke different

---

16   *Allgemeine Zeitung des Judenthums*, July 27, 1846.
17   Faber, *A Time for Planting*, 58–66.

languages. In Bohemia, which belonged to the Austrian Empire, German and Czech speakers lived in the same villages and towns. Many Jews who moved to New York before 1880 came from Bohemia and Posen. Like Christian migrants, they were often multilingual. Jewish migrants also originated in Alsace, a region that belonged to France before 1871 but that was largely settled by German-speakers. Another sizeable group of Jews moved to the United States from the southern German states of Baden, Württemberg, and Bavaria. Moreover, not all Jewish migrants moved straight from their home villages to New York or other American cities. Quite a few Lithuanian Jews stopped over in German cities, especially in the East Prussian capital and port city of Königsberg during the 1870s and 1880s. London was also an important point of passage for Jewish migrants heading to the United States before and after 1880.[18] It is also important to distinguish between ethnic labels applied by observers and the self-identification of migrants. Even a superficial look at contemporary newspapers in Central Europe and the United States indicates that migrants themselves frequently defined themselves as Jews from Bohemia, Posen, or Bavaria, rather than as Czech, Polish, or German. The same applied to non-Jewish migrants.[19]

These self-definitions had social significance. Studies of Jewish immigrants in Midwestern cities before 1880 demonstrate that Jews moved in close-knit networks, comprising relatives and acquaintances from adjacent villages. Members of the networks married each other, formed businesses together, and even established congregations and smaller associations which resembled the *landsmanshaftn* of later Polish, Lithuanian, and Galician Jewish immigrants.[20]

For members of an educated Jewish public in Central Europe and the United States in the 1840s and 1850s the broad terms "German Jewish" and "Polish Jewish" frequently did not refer to origin in specific places,

---

18   Ruth Leiserowitz, *Sabbatleuchter und Kriegerverein: Juden in der ostpreußisch-litauischen Grenzregion 1812-1942* (Osnabrück: Fibre, 2010), 226; Bernard Horwich, *My First Eighty Years* (Chicago: Argus Books, 1939), 79–121; Klaus Weber, "Transmigrants between Legal Restrictions and Private Charity: The Jews' Temporary Shelter in London, 1885–1939," in *Points of Passage: Jewish Transmigrants from Eastern Europe in Scandinavia, Germany, and Britain 1880-1914*, ed. Tobias Brinkmann (New York: Berghahn Books, 2013), 85–106.

19   Brinkmann, *Sundays at Sinai*, 11–30.

20   Ibid.; Marc Lee Raphael, *Jews and Judaism in a Midwestern Community: Columbus, Ohio, 1840–1975* (Columbus: Ohio Historical Society, 1979), 35–58.

let alone to political entities, but rather to different concepts of time. "German" was a synonym for the future. "German" Jews were seen as progressive and open to modernity. "Polish," on the other hand, stood for the Jewish past and for the refusal of traditional Jews to accommodate to a rapidly transforming society. The roots of these images can be traced to the eighteenth-century Enlightenment. Apart from promoting universal ideals such as education and individual rights, several German-speaking Enlightenment authors called for Jewish emancipation. In their view, Jewish difference was a consequence of the isolation of the Jewish population by governments and society. After years of enforced social and economic marginalization the Enlightenment represented a powerful vision of a new and inclusive society. A key question was whether there would be a place for Jews in this new society. Some Enlightenment thinkers expected Jews to give up their separate religion and identity and become part of mainstream society by converting to Christianity. Others felt that once Jews had been fully emancipated they would become a part of the society and consider Judaism exclusively a religious identity. A growing number of younger Jews embraced Enlightenment ideas and acquired an education at newly founded schools and universities. An initially relatively small minority of Jews called for a thorough theological "reform" of traditional Judaism. The Reform movement emerged in the 1820s and 1830s in the German states. Its proponents were academically trained rabbis who completely overhauled Jewish theology and ritual. Traditional Jews vehemently opposed Reform, and though the new movement made a growing impact in most Jewish communities after 1850, it nevertheless had to compromise with traditional Jewish leaders. The main German Jewish weekly paper, the *Allgemeine Zeitung des Judenthums*, which printed the description of Jewish life in New York in 1846, was edited by Reform Rabbi Ludwig Philippson. During the 1850s a growing number of Reform rabbis moved to the United States, several of them recruited by newly founded Reform congregations in cities such as Baltimore, Philadelphia and New York.[21]

Immigrant Reform rabbis like David Einhorn were aware that the founding fathers of the United States were inspired by the same Enlightenment ideals as most Reform Jews. And yet, Einhorn struggled to accommodate to his new home. When he moved to Adas Jeshurun congregation in New York in 1866, after serving Reform congregations in

---

21 Meyer, *Response to Modernity*, 10–142.

Baltimore and Philadelphia, he still had a hard time preaching in English. Einhorn often complained that America was a cultural wasteland. Still, it would be too simplistic to describe him as an elitist Germanizer. Einhorn explicitly embraced America as a land of freedom where the state did not interfere in religious affairs. He knew that his vision of radical Reform was not viable in the German setting.[22]

While Reform remained a relatively small force during the middle decades of the nineteenth century, most Jewish communities across Central Europe had begun to transform after 1800. In the German states, emancipation was granted in stages, partly because state governments expected Jews to modernize in order to qualify for full citizenship. As a result of government pressure, even small rural Jewish communities began reorganizing their religious education. More importantly, in many states Jewish children began attending newly established state elementary schools. In the province of Posen, 75% of Jewish children were educated under the umbrella of the Prussian school system by the early 1830s, compared to only a little more than 50% of the Christian (and overwhelmingly Polish-speaking) children. In Bohemia, Jewish children also attended German-language elementary schools. Historian Simone Lässig has argued that a thorough elementary school education equipped Jews in the German states with significant "cultural capital" that they invested effectively in a transforming economy and society. Jewish children not only learned how to read and write but were also exposed to key ideas of the Enlightenment. Thus, Jews developed a bourgeois mentality when they were still living on the margins of rural societies. A solid education partly explains why most Jews rose from the margins of rural societies into the urban bourgeoisie. As in the United States, some Jews in the German states were spectacularly successful entrepreneurs but their rise overshadows the broad and rapid embourgeoisement of German Jews as a group—in just one generation.[23]

---

22 Kaufmann Kohler, "David Einhorn: The Uncompromising Champion of Reform. A Biographical Essay," *Yearbook of the Central Conference of American Rabbis* 19 (1909): 215–70; Diner, *A Time for Gathering*, 221.

23 Simone Lässig, *Jüdische Wege ins Bürgertum: Kulturelles Kapital und sozialer Aufstieg im 19. Jahrhundert* (Göttingen: Vandenhoeck & Ruprecht, 2004); Hillel Kieval, *Languages of Community: The Jewish Experience in the Czech Lands* (Berkeley: University of California Press, 2000), 28; Sophia Kemlein, *Die Posener Juden 1815–1848* (Hamburg: Dölling und Gallitz, 1997), 78–89; Bernhard Breslauer, *Die Abwanderung der Juden aus der Provinz Posen* (Berlin: Levy, 1909).

Before 1871, for many educated Jewish men and women in the German states "Germany" was primarily a cultural concept rather than a state that, in any case, did not exist—a concept that they linked with the inclusive vision of a universal society and modern Judaism. The distorted negative image of "Polish" Jews or *Ostjuden* (eastern Jews) among Jews in Central Europe was a product of the emancipation and modernization process described above. Jews who became part of the urban bourgeoisie often projected the negative image of their own past on Jews in or from the "East" who were widely associated with Orthodoxy, poverty, and even dirt, as the 1846 passage quoted above demonstrates. This disassociation can be partly traced to lingering opposition to full Jewish emancipation and the rise of modern antisemitism in the 1870s, a movement that was in part a response to full Jewish emancipation in the German states.[24] Negative images of *Ostjuden* were widespread among Jews in the German states and in the United States. For example, in its 1864 report Chicago's main Jewish charity organization described the growing number of newly arriving *Ostjuden*—probably referring to a growing migration of Jews from Lithuania—as a burden for the Jewish community, using the German word in an otherwise English text.[25]

Jewish and German American Immigrants

Since the terms "German Jews" and *Ostjuden* carry such complex baggage, they should not be used as descriptive terms. Research for Chicago and Cincinnati corroborates Nadel's findings for New York—Jewish immigrants participated in the cultural life of other immigrants from Central Europe, often in leading positions. Michael Meyer has convincingly argued that German immigrant associations included newly arrived Jewish immigrants when they were still social outsiders in America. Many German American elected officials and newspaper editors were liberals who fled to the United States after the failed Revolution of 1848. "Forty-Eighters" like Carl Schurz, Friedrich Hecker, and Lorenz Brentano supported full Jewish emancipation before they emigrated. Once they settled in the United States

---

24 Steven Aschheim, *Brothers and Strangers: The East European Jew in German and German Jewish Consciousness, 1800–1923* (Madison: University of Wisconsin Press, 1982); Reinhard Rürup, *Emanzipation und Antisemitismus: Studien zur "Judenfrage" der bürgerlichen Gesellschaft* (Frankfurt am Main: Fischer, 1987), 93–119.

25 Rudolf Glanz, "The 'Bayer' and the 'Pollack' in America," *Jewish Social Studies* 17, no.1 (1955): 27–42; *5th Annual Report of the United Hebrew Relief Association* (Chicago, 1864).

they condemned the rise of modern antisemitism in Germany in the 1870s. German American newspapers echoed these views.[26]

Nevertheless, detailed research on Jewish and other German-speaking immigrants in Chicago and other cities throws doubt on Nadel's assertion that the German and Jewish immigrant communities were "inextricable entities." German-speaking immigrants differed from other groups such as Irish or Polish immigrants. They constituted a very large group and shared relatively little, apart from a common language. It was even doubtful that they spoke a common language, since immigrants spoke many different dialects. German-speaking immigrants were Protestant, Catholic, and, of course, in small numbers, Jewish. After 1870, working-class immigrants were often influenced by Socialism and rejected organized religion. Unlike many other groups, German-speaking immigrants had already begun moving to the United States in the late seventeenth century. Longer settled migrants shared little with later arrivals. It is, therefore, problematic to speak of German-American "communities," especially for large cities like New York. There was relatively little cohesion among hundreds of German-American associations and congregations, and overarching organizations often lacked grassroots support. German-speaking immigrants primarily came together for cultural events. In several American cities, not least New York, large festivities that included singing contests and other entertainments (and of course copious beer drinking) attracted tens of thousands of participants throughout the nineteenth century. These giant events impressed outside observers but overshadow the lack of strong organizations. The author of a recent German study about these festivities has emphasized that German-speaking immigrants in New York struggled even more than those in other cities to organize large-scale events because their backgrounds were diverse and population movement high. When New York hosted a large singing event, most participants were visitors from out of town, while only relatively few German-speaking New Yorkers participated.[27]

---

26 Michael A. Meyer, "German-Jewish Identity in Nineteenth-Century America," in *Toward Modernity: The European Jewish Model*, ed. Jacob Katz (New Brunswick, NJ: Transaction, 1987), 247–67. For background, see essays in *German Forty-Eighters in America*, ed. Charlotte Brancaforte (New York: Peter Lang, 1989).

27 Heike Bungert, *Festkultur und Gedächtnis. Die Konstruktion einer deutschamerikanischen Ethnizität 1848–1948* (Paderborn: Ferdinand Schöningh, 2016); Bruce Levine, "Community Divided: German Immigrants, Social Class, and Political Conflict in Antebellum Cincinnati," in *Ethnic Diversity and Civic Identity: Patterns of Conflict and*

In New York many Jewish immigrants did settle in the *Kleindeutschland* neighborhood on the Lower East Side of Manhattan in the 1840s and 1850s. The changing location of congregations founded by new immigrants after 1820, such as Anshe Chesed and Temple Emanu-El, indicates that many Jews lived in *Kleindeutschland* before the Civil War. But common language and sociability were not the only factors determining where immigrants chose to live. During the 1850s, as more recently arrived immigrants pushed into the southern part of *Kleindeutschland*, upwardly mobile residents began moving north.[28]

Moreover, the overlap of Jewish and German identities had its limits. As in New York, Jews in other American cities, such as Chicago, were also active as members and leaders of German immigrant associations. But even though individual rabbis and leading Jewish businessmen helped to organize events such as the big parade celebrating German unification in 1871, a Jewish community developed separately. In contrast to Christian congregations, Jewish congregations did not participate in German parades in Chicago. The Jews who marched in German parades did so as members and leaders of secular associations. In 1867 Jews held their own parade when the first Jewish hospital in Chicago was dedicated. For Jews, community building, especially the organization of an overarching institution that looked after poor and needy Jews, mattered greatly. Jews in Chicago managed to organize the overarching United Hebrew Relief Association that most Jewish congregations and associations joined as corporate members already in 1859. Jews in other cities, not least New York, struggled for decades to build similar umbrella institutions that were the forerunners of modern Federations. Among German-speaking immigrants, a much larger group than Jews, the divisions and different orientations in most major cities ran too deep to organize institutions that were backed by a majority of associations.[29]

Cohesion in Cincinnati since 1820, ed. Jonathan Sarna and Henry D. Shapiro (Urbana: University of Illinois Press, 1992), 46–93.

28   Polland and Soyer, *Emerging Metropolis*, 31; Ruben, *Max Lilienthal*, 103.

29   Tobias Brinkmann, "Charity on Parade—Chicago's Jews and the Construction of Ethnic and Civic 'Gemeinschaft' in the 1860s," in *Celebrating Ethnicity and Nation: American Festive Culture from the Revolution to the Early Twentieth Century*, ed. Jürgen Heideking, Geneviève Fabre (New York: Berghahn Books, 2001), 157–74; Arthur Goren, *New York Jews and the Quest for Community: The Kehillah Experiment 1908–1922* (New York: Columbia University Press, 1970), 1–24.

For Jewish immigrants the loss of the tight-knit Jewish communities they left behind in Europe was an ambiguous experience. In America, they were free to shape their lives and did not have to observe the Jewish tradition. Yet, even non-observant immigrants wanted to make sure they would be buried in a Jewish cemetery and felt an obligation to care for poor Jews. A growing number of immigrants felt the need to address the growing divisions between Jewish immigrants from different parts of Central Europe. They worried that younger immigrants, especially, would drift away from Jewish life, especially in the vibrant setting of a rapidly expanding metropolis like New York. In 1843 several recent immigrants founded the Independent Order of the B'nai B'rith (Sons of the Covenant) in New York "to overcome the geographical differences, to unite the German and the Pole, the Hungarian and the Dutchman, the Englishman and the Alsatian on one platform; it must extinguish narrow stereotypes and the misguided belief in divided sections and provinces." The B'nai B'rith founders intended to revive the spirit of Jewish unity—they used the term *das gemeinschaftliche Verständnis* ("the common identity")—which, they believed, had eroded over the centuries in the diaspora. On the local level B'nai B'rith brothers were at the forefront of building overarching Jewish institutions, such as Chicago's United Hebrew Relief Association.[30]

Jews were also an important part of the loose network of German immigrant associations and celebrations but these links were primarily a matter of individual involvement. Jewish associations and congregations usually had a more distant relationship to the loose German immigrant network. Curiously, the same applies to another much larger group, German-speaking Catholics. In many American towns and cities, they primarily socialized with other Catholics and did not have close affiliations with non-Catholic German speakers.[31] The claim that Jewish immigrants from the German states were a transplanted branch of German Jewry is also problematic. This is true even if limited to those who were active in a few radical Reform congregations like New York's Temple Emanu-El,

---

30   Quoted after Herman Eliassof, "The German-American Jews," *Deutsch-Amerikanische Geschichtsblätter* 14 (1914): 319–92. For background see Cornelia Wilhelm, *The Independent Orders of B'nai B'rith and True Sisters: Pioneers of a New Jewish Identity, 1843–1914* (Detroit: Wayne State Press, 2011), 13–56.

31   Kathleen Neils Conzen, "Immigrant Religion and the Public Sphere: The German Catholic Milieu in America," in *German-American Immigration and Ethnicity in Comparative Perspective*, ed. Wolfgang Helbich and Walter Kamphoefner (Madison: Max Kade Institute, 2004), 69–116.

where the German roots of the movement were a matter of much pride and German sermons were preached into the 1870s. Many sources indicate that Jewish immigrants identified as American Jews early on. They were often conscious of the fact that by moving to the United States they literally took their emancipation into their own hands, as the following example illustrates. The Bavarian government was particularly reluctant to grant emancipation to its Jewish subjects. Younger Jews were especially forced to leave, if they wanted to marry, because the government had fixed the number of Jewish households in villages and towns at artificially low levels. A Jewish emigrant, asked in 1845 in Mainz whether he might consider returning to his Bavarian home village, replied: "I will only come back when North America becomes Bavarian."[32] The first German state to fully emancipate its population was Baden in 1862. Jews in Bavaria were only fully emancipated in 1871 upon the unification of the German states, at a time when many Jews had already moved to the United States. The rise of antisemitism in Imperial Germany during the 1870s only increased the distance of many Jews.[33]

Conclusion

New York's Jewish history for the period between 1820 and 1880 requires more research. Thanks to the digitization of public records it is now much easier to track the movement of Jewish migrants. But researchers still face challenges, not least geographic mobility, which was particularly high in a port city such as New York, and makes it hard to trace individuals. Many immigrants spent only a few days or weeks in the city before moving on. Others returned to the city, sometimes for years, or relocated to other places after spending some time in New York. Jewish immigrants who arrived before 1880 were highly mobile after arriving in the United States. Most men worked as peddlers to accumulate capital for opening a store or small business, selling their wares in the wider vicinity of New York. A close analysis of the founders of congregations

---

32 *Der Orient* [Leipzig], May 28, 1845, 22. The original German reads: "Ich werde nicht eher zurückkehren, als bis Nordamerika baierisch wird!" On the Bavarian policy toward Jews, see Manfred Treml, "Von der Judenemanzipation: Zur bürgerlichen Verbesserung: Zur Vorgeschichte und Frühphase der Judenemanzipation in Bayern," in *Geschichte und Kultur der Juden in Bayern—Aufsätze*, ed. Manfred Treml and Josef Kirmaier (Munich: Haus der Bayerischen Geschichte, 1988), 247–65.

33 Rürup, *Emanzipation und Antisemitismus*, 36.

and B'nai B'rith chapters should make it possible to identify networks of relatives and acquaintances and migration routes.[34] Another important feature of the pre-1880 migration was its diversity. Jewish immigrants came from different regions in Central and East Central Europe. Many did identify with German culture and socialized with other German-speaking immigrants, but some did not. During the 1860s the Jewish migration from Lithuania increased. As Jews faced increasingly challenging economic conditions in the Lithuanian provinces of the Russian Empire the expansion of the Central European railroad network to Vilna and Kovno in 1862 opened the gates to a better future elsewhere. By the 1870s, *Litvaks* had settled in considerable numbers in London, New York and Chicago. Surprisingly, relatively little is known about the history of *Litvaks* in New York before 1880.[35] Pre-1880 Jewish migrants were highly socially mobile. Historian John Higham even described Jewish immigrants from Central Europe as the most successful immigrant group in American history.[36] The available evidence suggests that most Jewish immigrants from the German states managed to establish themselves in solid economic circumstances by the 1870s, even though most arrived with little capital and men frequently worked as peddlers. The parallels to the high social mobility of Jews in the German states are striking. To shine more light on this aspect of nineteenth-century American Jewish history, it is necessary to take a closer look at business and economic history, not least in the retail and garment sector where many Jewish immigrants launched businesses.[37] And finally, Nadel's demand that scholars working on American immigration history should move beyond the "artificial" ethnic boundaries has to be taken seriously. Hardly anything

---

34 Hasia Diner, *Roads Taken: The Great Jewish Migrations to the New World and the Peddlers Who Forged the Way* (New Haven: Yale University Press, 2015).

35 Gideon Shimoni, "From One Frontier to Another: Jewish Identity and Political Orientations in Lithuania and South Africa, 1890–1939," in *Jewries at the Frontier: Accommodation, Identity, Conflict*, ed. Sander L. Gilman and Milton Shain (Urbana: University of Illinois Press, 1999), 129–54; Anne Kershen, *Uniting the Tailors: Trade Unionism amongst the Tailors of London and Leeds 1870–1939* (London: Frank Cass, 1995), 128–29; Hyman Meites, *History of the Jews in Chicago* (Chicago: Chicago Jewish Historical Society, 1924), 489.

36 John Higham, *Send These to Me: Immigrants in Urban America* (Baltimore: Johns Hopkins University Press, 1975), 123.

37 For a pathbreaking study in this field with a focus on New York, see especially Adam Mendelsohn, *The Rag Race: How Jews Sewed Their Way to Success in America and the British Empire* (New York: NYU Press, 2015).

is known about links between Jewish and non-Jewish immigrants from Eastern Europe, for instance, even though local studies indicate that Jewish and Polish immigrants lived in close proximity and socialized with each other. In Chicago, the same applies to Jewish immigrants from Bohemia and Czech immigrants who lived in the same neighborhoods and cooperated, especially in the political sphere.[38]

---

38   Ewa Morawska, "Polish-Jewish Relations in America, 1880–1940: Old Elements, New Configurations," *Polin* 19 (2007): 71–86; Adolf Kraus, *Reminiscences and Comments, the Immigrant, the Citizen, a Public Office, the Jew* (Chicago: Toby Rubovits, 1925).

For Further Reading

Abu-Lughod, Janet. *New York, Chicago, Los Angeles: America's Global Cities.* Minneapolis: University of Minnesota, 1999.

Alexander, Gabriel E. "Die jüdische Bevölkerung Berlins in den ersten Jahrzehnten des 20. Jahrhunderts: Demographische und wirtschaftliche Entwicklungen." In *Jüdische Geschichte in Berlin: Essays und Studien*, edited by Reinhard Rürup, 117–48. Berlin: Hentrich, 1995.

Aschheim, Steven. *Brothers and Strangers: The East European Jew in German and German Jewish Consciousness, 1800–1923.* Madison: University of Wisconsin Press, 1982.

Barkai, Avraham. *Branching Out: German-Jewish Immigration to the United States, 1820–1914.* New York: Holmes & Meier, 1994.

Beckert, Sven. *The Monied Metropolis: New York City and the Consolidation of the American Bourgeoisie, 1850–1896.* Cambridge: Cambridge University Press, 2001.

Bodnar, John. *The Transplanted: A History of Immigrants in Urban America.* Bloomington: Indiana University Press, 1985.

Birmingham, Stephen. *Our Crowd: The Great Jewish Families of New York.* New York: Harper & Row, 1967.

Brancaforte, Charlotte, ed. *German Forty-Eighters in America.* New York: Peter Lang, 1989.

Brinkmann, Tobias. "Charity on Parade—Chicago's Jews and the Construction of Ethnic and Civic 'Gemeinschaft' in the 1860s," in *Celebrating Ethnicity and Nation: American Festive Culture from the Revolution to the Early Twentieth Century*, ed. Jürgen Heideking and Geneviève Fabre, 157–74. New York: Berghahn Books, 2001.

Brinkmann, Tobias. *Sundays at Sinai: A Jewish Congregation in Chicago.* Chicago: University of Chicago Press, 2012.

Bungert, Heike. *Festkultur und Gedächtnis. Die Konstruktion einer deutschamerikanischen Ethnizität 1848–1948.* Paderborn: Ferdinand Schöningh, 2016.

Conzen, Kathleen Neils. "Immigrant Religion and the Public Sphere: The German Catholic Milieu in America." In *German-American Immigration and Ethnicity in Comparative Perspective*, ed. Wolfgang Helbich and Walter Kamphoefner, 69–116. Madison: Max Kade Institute, 2004

Diner, Hasia R. *A Time for Gathering: The Second Migration, 1820–1880.* Baltimore, MD: Johns Hopkins University Press, 1992.

———. *The Jews of the United States, 1654 to 2000.* Berkeley: University of California Press, 2004.

———. *Roads Taken: The Great Jewish Migrations to the New World and the Peddlers Who Forged the Way.* New Haven: Yale University Press, 2015.

Faber, Eli. *A Time for Planting: The First Migration, 1654–1820.* Baltimore, MD: Johns Hopkins University Press, 1992.

Gartner, Lloyd. "Necrology: Rudolf Glanz (1892–1978)." *American Jewish History* 69, no. 2 (1979): 270-273.

Glanz, Rudolf. "The 'Bayer' and the 'Pollack' in America." *Jewish Social Studies* 17, no.1 (1955): 27–42.

———. *The German Jew in America: An Annotated Bibliography including Books, Pamphlets and Articles of Special Interest.* Cincinnati: Hebrew Union College Press, 1969.

Goren, Arthur. *New York Jews and the Quest for Community: The Kehillah Experiment 1908–1922.* New York: Columbia University Press, 1970.

Gurock, Jeffrey S. *Jews in Gotham: New York Jews in a Changing Metropolis, 1920–2010.* New York: NYU Press, 2012.

Higham, John. *Send These to Me: Immigrants in Urban America.* Baltimore: Johns Hopkins University Press, 1975.

Hirshler, Eric, ed. *Jews from Germany in the United States.* New York: Farrar, Straus and Cudahy, 1955.

Horwich, Bernard. *My First Eighty Years.* Chicago: Argus Books, 1939.

Jersch-Wenzel, Stefi. "Population Shifts and Occupational Structure." In *German-Jewish History in Modern Times: Emancipation and Acculturation, 1780–1871*, edited by Michael A. Meyer, 50–89. New York: Columbia University Press, 1997.

Kershen, Anne. *Uniting the Tailors: Trade Unionism amongst the Tailors of London and Leeds 1870-1939.* London: Frank Cass, 1995.

Lässig, Simone. *Jüdische Wege ins Bürgertum: Kulturelles Kapital und sozialer Aufstieg im 19. Jahrhundert.* Göttingen: Vandenhoeck & Ruprecht, 2004.

Leiserowitz, Ruth. *Sabbatleuchter und Kriegerverein: Juden in der ostpreußisch-litauischen Grenzregion 1812–1942.* Osnabrück: Fibre, 2010.

Levine, Bruce. "Community Divided: German Immigrants, Social Class, and Political Conflict in Antebellum Cincinnati." In *Ethnic Diversity and Civic Identity: Patterns of Conflict and Cohesion in Cincinnati since 1820*, edited by Jonathan Sarna and Henry D. Shapiro, 46–93. Urbana: University of Illinois Press, 1992.

Lowenstein, Steven M. "The View from the Old World: German Jewish Perspectives." In *The Americanization of the Jews*, ed. Norman J. Cohen and Robert M. Seltzer, 19–40. New York: NYU Press, 1995.

Kemlein, Sophia. *Die Posener Juden 1815–1848*. Hamburg: Dölling und Gallitz, 1997.

Kieval, Hillel. *Languages of Community: The Jewish Experience in the Czech Lands*. Berkeley: University of California Press, 2000.

Mendelsohn, Adam. *The Rag Race: How Jews Sewed Their Way to Success in America and the British Empire*. New York: NYU Press, 2015.

Meyer, Michael A. "German-Jewish Identity in Nineteenth-Century America." In *Toward Modernity: The European Jewish Model*, edited by Jacob Katz, 247–67. New Brunswick, NJ: Transaction, 1987.

———. *Response to Modernity: A History of the Reform Movement in Judaism*. New York: Oxford University Press, 1988.

Morawska, Ewa. "Polish-Jewish Relations in America, 1880–1940: Old Elements, New Configurations." *Polin* 19 (2007): 71–86.

Nadel, Stanley. "Jewish Race and German Soul in Nineteenth-Century America." *American Jewish History* 77, no. 1 (1987): 6–26.

———. *Little Germany: Ethnicity, Religion and Class in New York City, 1845–80*. Urbana: University of Illinois Press, 1990.

Polland, Annie, and Daniel Soyer. *The Emerging Metropolis: New York Jews in the Age of Immigration, 1840–1920*. New York: NYU Press, 2012.

Raphael, Marc Lee. *Jews and Judaism in a Midwestern Community: Columbus, Ohio, 1840–1975*. Columbus: Ohio Historical Society, 1979.

Rischin, Moses. *The Promised City: New York's Jews 1870–1914*. Cambridge, MA: Harvard University Press, 1962.

Ritterband, Paul. "*Counting the Jews of New York*, 1900–1991: An Essay in Substance and Method." *Jewish Population Studies* 29 (1997): *Papers in Jewish Demography*, 199–228.

Rock, Howard B. *Haven of Liberty: New York Jews in the New World, 1654–1865*. New York: NYU Press, 2012.

Ruben, Bruce L. *Max Lilienthal: The Making of the American Rabbinate*. Detroit: Wayne State University Press, 2011.

Rürup, Reinhard. *Emanzipation und Antisemitismus: Studien zur Judenfrage« der bürgerlichen Gesellschaft*. Frankfurt am Main: Fischer, 1987.

Ryan, Mary P. *Civic Wars: Democracy and Public Life in the American City during the Nineteenth Century.* Berkeley: University of California Press, 1997.

Shimoni, Gideon. "From One Frontier to Another: Jewish Identity and Political Orientations in Lithuania and South Africa, 1890–1939." In *Jewries at the Frontier: Accommodation, Identity, Conflict*, edited by Sander L. Gilman and Milton Shain, 129–154. Urbana: University of Illinois Press, 1999.

Thernstrom, Stephan. *The Other Bostonians: Poverty and Progress in the American Metropolis 1880–1970.* Cambridge, MA: Harvard University Press, 1973.

Treml, Manfred. "Von der Judenemanzipation: Zur bürgerlichen Verbesserung: Zur Vorgeschichte und Frühphase der Judenemanzipation in Bayern." In *Geschichte und Kultur der Juden in Bayern—Aufsätze*, edited by Manfred Treml and Josef Kirmaier, 247–265. Munich: Haus der Bayerischen Geschichte, 1988.

Wilhelm, Cornelia. *The Independent Orders of B'nai B'rith and True Sisters: Pioneers of a New Jewish Identity, 1843–1914.* Detroit: Wayne State Press, 2011.

Weber, Klaus. "Transmigrants between Legal Restrictions and Private Charity: The Jews' Temporary Shelter in London, 1885–1939." In *Points of Passage: Jewish Transmigrants from Eastern Europe in Scandinavia, Germany, and Britain 1880-1914*, edited by Tobias Brinkmann, 85–106. New York: Berghahn Books, 2013.

Chapter 4

From the Pale of Settlement to the Lower East Side: Early Hardships of Russian Immigrant Jews

Gur Alroey

Ten minutes' walk brought me to the heart of the Jewish East Side. The streets swarmed with Yiddish-speaking immigrants. The sign-boards were in English and Yiddish, some of them in Russian. The scurry and hustle of the people were not merely overwhelmingly greater, both in volume and intensity, than in my native town. It was of another sort.

—Abraham Cahan, *The Rise of David Levinsky*

Between 1875 and 1924, nearly 2.5 million Jews immigrated to the United States from Eastern Europe in search of a better life. It was the modern exodus of a people seeking to free themselves from economic servitude and political persecution, and to begin a new life across the sea. For many of the immigrants the initial period of adjustment in America was difficult, marked by crises major and minor, but most of them achieved their longed-for freedom relatively quickly and they or their children saw their economic situation and social status improve beyond recognition.

Although they are often regarded as such, however, the 1870s should not be considered a watershed in the history of Jewish migration to the United States. In some ways the mass migrations in the 1870s and subsequent decades simply continued an existing trend. Historian Hasia Diner has emphasized the continuity of the immigration process to the United States, denying that the 1870s constituted a true turning point. According to Diner, some of the immigrants who supposedly arrived from "Germany" were in fact from areas of Poland controlled by German states, or had earlier migrated from Poland to Germany. Moreover, by the1860s and 1870s, parts of the Jewish population had characteristics that are usually associated with the later arrivals. It was already possible, for example, to find Jews in the nascent American garment industry and there was even a Yiddish press.[1]

A number of factors motivated the mass migration of Jews from Eastern Europe to the United States: rapid Jewish demographic increase in Eastern Europe, onerous poverty, significant improvement in the means of transportation (railroads and steamships), and pogroms and persecution encouraged and practiced by the authorities. In fact, the last of these were not really the cause of emigration, but rather a catalyst for existing trends in European Eastern Jewish society.[2]

Of course, not all poverty necessarily leads to displacement and migration. But the economic reality in Imperial Russia gravely damaged the fragile economic fabric of Jewish society. While thousands of Russian, Ukrainian and Polish peasants, uprooted from their lands, were absorbed into the large industries and created a strong proletarian class, the Jews found themselves employed in dark and oppressive workshops of Minsk,

---

1   See Hasia Diner, *A Time for Gathering: The Second Migration 1820–1880* (Baltimore, MD: Johns Hopkins University Press, 1992). See also Diner, "Before the Promised City: Eastern European Jews in America before 1880," in *An Inventory of Promises: Essays on American Jewish History: In Honor of Moses Rischin*, ed. Jeffrey S. Gurock and Marc Lee Raphael (Brooklyn: Carlson, 1995), 43–62.

2   See Saul Stampfer, "The Geographic Background of East European Jewish Migration to the United States before World War I," in *Migration across Time and Nations: Population Mobility in Historical Contexts,* ed. Ira Glazier and Luigi De Rosa (New York: Holmes and Meier, 1985), 220–30; Joel Perlmann, *The Local Geographic Origins of Russian-Jewish Immigrants, Circa 1900*, Working Paper 465 (Annandale-on-Hudson, NY: The Levy Economics Institute of Bard College, 2006), 1–41. See also Leah Platt Boustan, "Were Jews Political Refugees or Economic Migrants? Assessing the Persecution Theory of Jewish Emigration, 1881–1914," in *The New Comparative Economic History: Essays in Honor of Jeffrey G. Williamson*, ed. Timothy J. Hatton, Kevin H. O'Rourke and Alan M. Taylor (Cambridge: MIT Press, 2007), 267–90.

Vilna, and other cities in the Pale of Settlement. The Jewish proletariat in Eastern Europe had been a proletariat of crafts since its inception. In its ranks there were almost no union workers with central positions in the process of economic production. The status of Jewish workers in the labor market was insecure and unstable. By the end of the nineteenth century, a Jewish labor movement had arisen, led by the Bund and other organizations. But the concentration of Jews in small workshops, and the unemployment that threatened them, limited their ability to improve their economic situation. The Jewish worker remained economically marginal to the emerging industrial order. The Jews' difficulty in integrating into the evolving economic reality aggravated their distress and led to intense competition and depressed prices and wages.

Another important stimulus for the Jewish migration was the abundant information that began flowing back from the United States to Eastern Europe about the economic possibilities available in the New World. Dudley Baines has asserted that "the key to emigration may have been availability of information. Information was important because it reduced uncertainty."[3] The economist and historian Arcadius Kahan observed that "another precondition for voluntary migrations is knowledge about imagined information that would provide a rational justification for migration. The information might be first- or second-hand based upon some recognizable authority, but it has a critical influence on the actual decision to migrate."[4] Chain migration and informal networks influenced the decision to pull up stakes and cross the ocean. The newcomers wrote back to their relatives about the job opportunities, wages, housing, and the cost of living, and even promised to help them get acclimated and adjust to the new country after they landed. The journey west became a much safer bet as time went on.

The availability and reliability of information explains the wave of immigration to the United States and its volume between 1875 and the 1920s. Despite Diner's caution, it has been conventional to take 1881 as the beginning of the mass East European Jewish immigration to America. But even that movement actually began in the previous decade, when there was severe famine in Lithuania. By the time of the pogroms in 1881–1882, more than 10,000 Jews had already immigrated to the United States from the

3 See Dudley Baines, *Emigration from Europe, 1815–1930* (Cambridge: Cambridge University Press, 1995), 8.
4 See Arcadius Kahan, *Essays in Jewish Social and Economic History* (Chicago: University of Chicago Press, 1986), 118.

Russian Empire. All told, during the last quarter of the nineteenth century, slightly more than half a million Jews made the journey. The immigrants in the first waves wrote letters to their families, and reports about the new Jewish communities on the other side of the Atlantic were published in Eastern European periodicals. A world-embracing link between the Jewish population centers of Eastern Europe and the new communities took shape.

A dramatic increase in migration took place from the turn of the century until the start of the First World War. In that brief span, 1.4 million Jews immigrated to the United States. In the five years at the crest of the wave (1904–1908), more than 600,000 Jews entered the country: 106,000 in 1904, 130,000 in 1905, 154,000 in 1906, 149,000 in 1907, and 103,000 in 1908. The Jewish migration had a family character. Generally, a male Jewish immigrant arrived with his wife and children; if he came alone, they followed soon after. On average, 44% of the immigrants were women, and 25% children below age fourteen. The age and gender breakdown of the immigrants indicates that their intention was to settle permanently in the new country.[5] Such a high percentage of women and children was nearly unique to Jewish migration. Among Italians, women made up only an estimated 23% and children 12% of immigrants; among Poles, 33% were women and 10% were children; and among Lithuanians, 32% women and 8% children.[6]

Although the Jews who landed in New York found themselves on a new continent and in a city whose ways were very different from what they had known in Eastern Europe, they arrived equipped with ample information that was essential for rapid and smooth integration. New York was one of the American cities about which information was available to Jews in Eastern Europe, and they understood its inherent economic potential before they took the fateful decision to leave home. The prevalent image of the greenhorn who arrives in the big city and is taken advantage of by those who preceded him is far from accurate. Reliable and precise information about New York was conveyed to Eastern Europe both by those who had already made the journey and shared their experiences with their families

---

5   See Liebman Hersch, "International Migration of the Jews," *International Migrations,* vol. 2: *Interpretations,* ed. Imre Ferenczi and Walter Wilcox (New York: National Bureau of Economic Research, 1931), 471–520; Simon Kuznets, "Immigration of Russian Jews to the United States: Background and Structure," *Perspectives in American History* 9 (1975): 35–126.

6   Hersch, "International Migration," 484, 486.

and by Jewish organizations that wanted to help potential immigrants and prepare them for their future before they landed in the New World.

As early as the mid-1870s, New York was a preferred city for Jewish immigrants who favored the big city over small cities and towns. In 1874, Aharon Yehudah Leib Horovitz published his book, *Romanyah ve-Amerikah:... Mas'otai be-Romanyah, tuv Artsot ha-Berit u-moreh derech lalechet la-Amerikah* (Romania and America: My Travels in Romania, the Goodness in the United States, and a Guide to Reach America).[7] Horovits was one of the first who tried to inform the East European Jewish public of the potential of the United States and to persuade them to immigrate there. Horowitz wrote:

> This book of mine will be like eyes to those of our brothers who look to America and desire to flee from whatever troubles and burdens them in their homeland, whether spiritual or material, and there [in America] escape from exile and poverty.[8]

Horowitz does not mention the number of immigrants who had immigrated to the United States before his book was written, but it is clear from his text that the number of those interested in this possibility was large:

> Experience has shown us these days that many Jews from all European countries come [to America] every year by the thousands, for the spirit of emigration lives amongst our brothers, and their eyes are turned to that good and happy country. When the word came to out in Romania two years ago that the Jews of America would help the Jews of Romania leave their country and come to America, some ten thousand households wrote and signed their names in the book to leave Romania. But most of them know nothing about the way of life in the United States; many more of them believe that much silver and gold covers the streets of America and anyone wishing to take it can come and take as much as he desires.[9]

The first few who did arrive started sending letters back to their relatives describing the potential of the country. Gradually the press also started dedicating space—initially only few lines and then whole articles—to America. For example, in *Hatzfira* in 1879, Yehuda David Eisenstein published a

---

7   Aharon Yehudah Leib Horovitz, *Romanyah ve-Amerikah: . . . Mas'otai be-Romanyah, tuv Artsot ha-Berit u-moreh derech lalechet la-Amerikah* (Berlin, 1874).
8   Horovitz, *Romanyah ve-Amerikah*, iii.
9   Horovitz, *Romanyah ve-Amerikah*, 51.

series of articles about New York, in general, and the life of Jews there, in particular.

Jewish migration to the United States had a distinct geographical pattern that could explain why the masses of immigrants streamed to New York. This geographical pattern shows that the highest rates of immigration came from the north-west regions of the Pale of Settlement—regions that were undergoing accelerated industrialization. The Minsk region was the region with the largest proportion of people leaving to the United States: 89% of the emigrants from Pinsk and Minsk went to the United States; from Bobruisk 84% did so. The majority of Jews from these areas reached New York, and this explains the high percentage of Jews there. Of those who arrived in the United States from Pinsk, about 62% settled in New York and the remainder dispersed in other cities. Out of all the regions and cities in the Pale of Settlement, those from Minsk settled in New York at the highest rate (75%). In contrast, only 36% of the immigrants from Grodno settled in New York and a relatively high proportion (15%) preferred Boston. Immigrants from Volyn settled in New York at the lowest rate of any from the Pale of Settlement, only 26%. 27% of Jewish immigrants from Volyn settled in Boston, and the rest were scattered in cities across the United States.[10]

The geographic location of New York on the other side of the Atlantic Ocean was also a major attraction for immigrants. The ship voyage from European ports to New York was relatively quick and easy, without any stops on the way. However, arrival at ports of origin was complex and sometimes even dangerous. The realization of the decision to emigrate was no small matter. The immigrant and his family had to cope with the many difficulties that accompanied them from the moment they set out on their journey to boarding the ship: obtaining the necessary documents to legally leave the country; purchasing train tickets; traveling thousands of kilometers by train from their hometown to the port; purchasing travel tickets; and selling their businesses and homes. For many of the immigrants, the bureaucratic procedures for immigration were complicated and unattainable, they sought the help of migration agents.

The agents were people who knew the inner secrets of migration, and for a price promised immigrants solutions to their problems. Various kinds

---

10   See Gur Alroey, "Patterns of Jewish Emigration from Russian Empire from the 1870s to 1914," *Jews in Russia and Eastern Europe* 57, no. 2 (Winter 2006): 41.

of crooks hid behind the title "travel agent" and exploited the innocent immigrants, at times risking their clients' lives and those of their families. These charlatan agents, or in the language of the period *agentn shvindler* or *geheyme agentn*, were the main source of the immigrants' troubles. "Agents of all sorts—secret officials and officials who own companies, and all kinds of helpers. They sprout up like fungi and cover every locality in the country." According to one contemporary newspaper, "each city has its own agents, as does every town. And cities and towns have not just one agent but entire groups who compete, fight, struggle, target, and inform on one another."[11]

Many Jews who understood the economic potential exploited those who wanted to get out of Eastern Europe. People who were unable to obtain all the necessary documents offered to pay them to get passports. These agents succeeded in obtaining the passports through the use of bribes, acquaintance with local clerks, and especially knowledge of bureaucratic process and its lacunas—but for a price:

> The deceit and fraud on the part of the agents has been especially great with respect to the preparation for papers needed to travel abroad. Ninety percent of the immigrants, if not more, do not know how to prepare such documents by themselves and are afraid to do so. The inhabitants of the big cities and small towns, and sometimes the poor city dwellers as well, imagine the process of preparing the travel documents to be a hard job, so they turn for help to the "almighty" agent. . . .[12]

The agents took advantage of the emigrants' helplessness to charge more and more for obtaining the documents: "The agents and shipping companies will use it, of course, to their own benefit and swindle the migrants."[13] Every bureaucratic complication caused delays and superfluous expenses, depleting the reserves intended for the initial absorption in the destination country. The largest sums were paid for accommodation and food in the port city; in order to save money, most emigrants stayed in the cheaper hotels under difficult conditions:

> And there are hundreds of migrants who have to stay here months on end, waiting for the travel documents, living in cramped, dark places like fish in

---

11   "Ha-emigratsya derech hof Libau," *Ha-zeman* 123, June 19, 1907, 3.
12   "Ha-emigratsya derech hof Libau," *Ha-zeman* 121, June 17, 1907, 3.
13   Ibid.

a barrel. Three or four in a bed, males and females in one room—there is no decency or proper hygienic conditions.[14]

Another kind of deceit and fraud occurred at the time of purchasing a ticket for the ship. Those who did not have prepaid tickets could purchase tickets directly from shipping companies in the big cities in the Pale of Settlement or through authorized agents. Quite a few people pretended to be such agents; they collected money and promised their customers that they would receive the tickets upon arrival at the port. After the emigrants had traveled hundreds of kilometers and had undergone medical exams in the border station, they approached the shipping company to get their tickets, only to discover that the agent had not transferred the money. They had to wait there, sometimes for many weeks, trying to get in touch the agent to demand that he settle the payment. Meanwhile, the emigrants ran out of money and had to go door to door begging, while being supported by Jewish philanthropic organizations.

Due to the bureaucratic difficulties, the frauds, and the tragic situations that ensued, there was need for organizations and institutions to come to the prospective emigrants' aid, support them, and save them from conmen. The Jewish Colonization Association (ICA) filled this need by founding the Information Bureau for Jewish Migration Affaires.[15] At the start of the twentieth century, ICA opened information bureaus throughout the Pale of Settlement, which provided potential Jewish immigrants with all the information they needed before leaving home. In 1904, in the wake of the Kishinev pogrom and the significant increase in the number of migrants, and especially because of the immigrants' travails, the ICA Central Committee in Russia decided to open an information bureau in St. Petersburg. From then on, ICA was the most important Jewish philanthropy that handled all matters of emigration from the Russian Empire. So that the Bureau could succeed in its mission and create a solid base of information for hundreds of thousands of Jewish migrants, it began opening regional offices all over the Russian Empire. Within a very few years it had authorized branches in all the major cities and important centers of

---

14   Ibid.
15   See Mark Wischnitzer, *To Dwell in Safety: The Story of Jewish Migration since 1800* (Philadelphia: Jewish Publication Society, 1948), 105–12.

emigration: 160 information bureaus throughout the Pale of Settlement in 1906, 296 in 1907, 449 in 1910, and 507 in 1913.[16]

The Bureau's publications, which appeared in both Yiddish and Russian, covered many fields. The pamphlet with the widest circulation, published in 1906 and sold at the nominal price of six kopeks, was *Algemeyne yedies far di vos vilen foren in fremde lender* (General Information for Those Wishing to Emigrate to Foreign Countries). It offered a brief survey in plain language of everything that a migrant needed to know before setting out, with many practical suggestions. After reading the pamphlet, a migrant knew how much money he needed to take with him, exchange rates and border crossings, and the dangers of unscrupulous agents; what seasickness was and how to cope with it; where to buy steamer tickets and the dangers of prepaid vouchers; how to obtain a passport and what he should include in his baggage; and, finally, concise information about the destination countries—the United States, Canada, South Africa, South America, Australia, and Palestine—and the basic conventions of behavior there.[17]

There was detailed and up-to-date information about destination countries in separate pamphlets about Argentina, Australia, Canada, South Africa, Chile, and the United States. Revised and updated as required, each pamphlet provided migrants with information about the country's geography (including a map), its climate and fauna, the local population, and the exchange rate and purchasing power of the local currency. There was also information about farming and other possible occupations, the cost of living, and the cost of passage from various ports to the destination. The most comprehensive booklet was that about the United States; it included information about each state and the job possibilities there.

Jews from Eastern Europe who wanted to get to New York could consult *Di fereynigte shtaten fun Amerika: Algemeyne yedies un onvayzungen far di vos vilen foren in dem land* (The United States of America: General Information and Instructions for Those Wishing to Emigrate to this Country). They would learn how many Jews lived in New York State (Albany, 3,500; Brooklyn, 250,000; Buffalo, 1,000; New York, 900,000; Troy, 1,800), the length of the workday in factories (10 to 12 hours; and longer in the sweatshops), the wages received by factory workers and craftsmen (1 to 3 dollars a day), working conditions for women and children, labor laws in

---

16 See Gur Alroey, *Bread to Eat and Clothes to Wear: Letters from Jewish Migrants in the Early Twentieth Century* (Detroit: Wayne State University Press, 2011), 15.

17 Ibid., 25.

the city, labor unions, and the cost of living (bread, three cents a loaf; meat, 15–20 cents a pound; a quart of milk, 8 cents; a dozen eggs, 20 cents; and a bushel of potatoes, 20 cents).

The importance of such information as a stimulus to migration did not escape the keen eye of the editor of the *Forverts*, Abraham Cahan. In his novel *The Rise of David Levinsky*, published in 1917, he emphasized his hero's image of America as an important element in the decision to immigrate. It was not his mother's murder in the marketplace of Antomir that made young David resolve to leave Russia, but the image that enchanted him:

> Letters full of wonders from emigrants already there went the rounds of eager readers and listeners until they were worn to shreds in the process.
>
> I succumbed to spreading fever. It was one of these letters from America, in fact, which put the notion of emigrating to the New World definitely in my mind. An illiterate woman brought it to the synagogue to have it read to her, and I happened to be the one whom she addressed her request. The concrete details of that letter gave New York tangible form in my imagination. It haunted me ever after.[18]

At the start of the twentieth century, New York was the largest and most densely populated city in the United States. Its population grew rapidly as immigrants streamed there from all over Europe. The area that became the united city of Greater New York in 1898 added roughly a million persons each decade: There were 1.9 million residents in 1880, 2.5 million in 1890, 3.4 million in 1900, 4.7 million in 1910, and more than 5.6 million in 1920. Jews became an inseparable part of its human and cultural scene. Between 70% and 90% of the Jews who migrated from Eastern Europe to the United States at the start of the twentieth century settled in the city. On the eve of the First World War the New York Jewish community was the largest in the world, having grown from an estimated 60,000 in 1880 to 672,000 in 1905, 1,330,000 in 1913, and 1,500,000 in 1917—an astounding twenty-fold increase in the short span of thirty-four years.[19]

---

18 See Abraham Cahan, *The Rise of David Levinsky* (Mineola, NY: Dover, 2002), 42.
19 See *The Jewish Communal Register of New York City, 1917–1918* (New York: Kehillah [Jewish Community of New York], 1918), 90.

The Socioeconomic Composition of the Jews on the Lower East Side

At the midpoint of the nineteenth century the area that later became known as the Lower East Side of Manhattan was inhabited mainly by Irish and German immigrants. The solution for their housing needs was the tenement house. Tenements came into being in response to a housing shortage in New York that arose during the 1830s, when landlords divided private houses into apartments for rent. Later, they developed whole blocks of four-, five- and six-story, multiple-unit apartment houses intended for working-class residents, including immigrants. These structures spread through lower Manhattan and became the homes of tens of thousands of recent immigrants. The legal definition of a tenement was "any house, building, or portion thereof, which is rented, leased, let, or hired out to be occupied or is occupied, as the home or residence of three families or more living independently of each other, and doing their cooking upon the premises, or by more than two families upon any floor, so living and cooking and having a common right in the halls, stairways, yards, water closets or privies, or some of them." But in common parlance, a "tenement" was different from a well-maintained middle- or upper-class apartment building, which were also becoming common in New York. In short order the tenements became neglected, filthy, and overcrowded.

The living conditions in these buildings were investigated by federal and municipal commissions that were interested in how the immigrants were living. Notable among them was the eleven-member Joint Congressional Commission on Immigration, chaired by Sen. William Paul Dillingham of Vermont, which operated from 1907 to 1910. In 1911 it published a forty-two-volume report that dealt with various issues related to immigration, including three volumes on the lives and socioeconomic integration of "Immigrants in Cities." The report is one of the most important sources of information on how immigrants lived in the United States, and especially the Jews on the Lower East Side.

We learn from the Dillingham Commission report that the proportion of New Yorkers living in tenements had increased since 1900. At the turn of the century, the city had 82,600 tenements, home to 2.3 million of its 3.4 million residents (67%). But the flood tide of immigrants during the subsequent decade accelerated their construction; by 1910 around 80% of New Yorkers lived in them.[20] As noted, Jewish immigrants were at first

---

20   *Reports of the Immigration Commission*, vol. 26: *Immigrants in Cities* (Washington, D.C.: Government Printing Office, 1911), 159.

concentrated on the Lower East Side of Manhattan. According to the *Jewish Communal Register*, in the area bounded by Allen, Houston, Essex, Canal, Eldridge and Grand Streets, and East Broadway, there were 134,000 Jews in the Eighth Ward, and 137,000 in the Ninth. Across the East River, in Brooklyn, the Williamsburg neighborhood was home to 107,000 Jews. [21]

Some interesting figures about New York Jews can be extracted from the Commission's report.

- Of 619 surveyed Jewish households on the Lower East Side, the members of 77% had immigrated from the Russian Pale of Settlement, 15.5% from the Austro-Hungarian Empire, and 5% from Romania.
- 21% had lived in the city for no more than 5 years; 31% for 10–19 years; and 18% for more than 20 years. This distribution of longer-settled and recent immigrants was favorable to the absorption of those who just arrived in New York since they came into contact with long-time residents.
- Some 39% of the Jewish residents were children under sixteen, a figure similar to that for other ethnic groups: 42% among the Italians and 38% among the Irish.
- The average wages of a Jewish man on the Lower East Side came to $509 a year, significantly lower than the income of other ethnic groups in the city. By contrast, the average annual income of Jewish women, $324, was the highest of all immigrant women. Moreover, Jewish households were more likely than others to include boarders and lodgers, meaning that women's labor was a significant source of household income. Including the income brought in by working children as well as women, Jewish household income compared favorably to that of other ethnic groups in the city, particularly with that of Italians.
- Jews had the second worst command of English—only 33% of male heads of Jewish households sampled spoke English, though the ability to do so increased significantly the longer the respondent had been in the country; only the Italians, at 22%, came in behind them. Some 82% of the Jewish men and 44% of the women could

---

21   *Jewish Communal Register of New York City, 1917–1918*, 85.

read and write. Compared to the other main "new immigrant" group in New York—the Italians—these figures were high.[22]

• Moreover, the next generation was the best educated of all immigrant groups. The percentage of Jewish children in the public schools was larger than the representation of any other ethnic group: more than a quarter of the 560,000 schoolchildren in New York were Jewish.[23]

The Slums of the Lower East Side

The two most common types of tenements in New York were the double-decker and the dumbbell. Property owners who perceived the potential return on rental apartments for immigrants turned the one-story buildings in the neighborhood into apartment houses and took advantage of every open space and square foot of ground. First, they added a residential building at the back of the lot; later, to increase their profits even more, they covered what remained of the lot with additional units. They erected apartment blocks with dozens of tenants on lots that were twenty-five feet wide and a hundred feet deep. The characteristics of the tenement, as defined by the New York State Tenement House Commission were:

> 1. Insufficiency of air, light, and ventilation due to narrow courts or airshafts; undue height, owing to the occupation by the building and adjacent buildings of too great a proportion of land area; 2. Overcrowding; 3. Danger in case of fire; 4. Lack of separate water-closets and washing facilities; 5. Foul cellars and courts.[24]

The commission found in 1905 that on an area of roughly 7,500 square meters 39 six-story apartment buildings had been built. Their 605 units had 2,700 tenants. But there were only 264 water-closets in all of them. Only 40 of the apartments had running water. Many rooms were interior, dark and unventilated; others received minimal light and air from narrow air shafts. The average size of the apartments was only 30 square meters,

---

22 *Immigrants in Cities*, 238–39.
23 *Reports of the Immigration Commission*, vol. 32: *The Children of Immigrants in Schools* (Washington, D.C.: Government Printing Office, 1911), 610.
24 Quoted from Maurice Fishberg, "Health and Sanitation: (A) New York," in *The Russian Jew in the United States*, ed. Charles S. Bernheimer (Philadelphia: John C. Winston, 1905), 284.

with two small rooms and the kitchen.[25] Until 1905 most of the toilets and water taps were in the courtyards; some residents had to go down as many as six flights to use them. The congestion and filth affected the immigrants' health. Diseases such as diphtheria, dysentery, and tuberculosis were rampant, spread by the inadequate sanitation, poor nutrition, overcrowding, and shortage of fresh air and natural light.[26]

The immigrants' living conditions attracted the attention of philanthropic organizations, welfare officials, and journalists. One 1905 study by Maurice Fishberg pointed out that "these wards [on the East Side, south of Fourteenth Street and east of the Bowery] enjoy the evil distinction of being the most densely populated spots in the United States, and probably on the earth."[27] It added that the tenements were unfit for human habitation. The apartments in these buildings were supposedly ventilated by air shafts. Some of those who testified to the Tenement House Commission called them "stinking air shafts." The narrow opening did not admit light and actually kept air out. Many residents used the air shaft to dispose of their garbage. It frequently sat at the bottom of the shaft for weeks, where it rotted and emitted a disgusting odor. Often laundry lines were hung in the shafts, and the clothes hanging there to dry blocked the air and light.[28]

The average Jewish family on the Lower East Side had six members and really needed a three-room apartment, but that was beyond its economic capacity. Because most of the Jews were desperately poor and hard-pressed to pay their rent, many took in lodgers.

> They therefore resort to lodgers to obtain part of their rent. In the four-room apartments, one bed-room is usually sublet to one or more, frequently to two men or women, and in many houses the front room is also sublet to two or more lodgers for sleeping purposes. The writer [Fishberg] on many occasions while calling professionally at night at some of these houses, beheld a condition of affairs like this: A family consisting of husband, wife, and six to eight children whose ages range from less than one to twenty-five years each. The parents occupy the small bed-room, together with two, three or even four of the younger children. In the kitchen, on cots and on the floor, are the older children; in the front room two or more (in rare cases as many

---

25 Deborah Dwork, "Health Conditions of Immigrant Jews on the Lower East Side of New York: 1880–1914," *Medical History* 25, no. 1 (1981): 8.

26 Ibid.

27 Fishberg, "Health and Sanitation," 283–84.

28 Ibid.

as five) lodgers sleep on the lounge, on the floor and on cots, and in the fourth bed-room two lodgers who do not care for the price charged, but who desire to have a "separate room" to themselves.[29]

The Sweatshops

Many of the immigrants to the United States from Eastern Europe in the later nineteenth and early twentieth centuries were skilled craftsmen. Roughly two-thirds (65%) of Jewish wage-earners worked in industry, and two-fifths of this group were employed in the garment trade. In the second half of the nineteenth century, this sector—which came to be closely identified with Jewish immigrants—began expanding for a number of reasons: the rapid growth of the urban population and the rise of a new urban middle class which had constant demand for clothing; the demand for uniforms during the Civil War that led to the creation of a standard sizing system in men's clothes; the availability of cheap labor and the advent of mechanization—the sewing machine, invented in 1850, and later the electric fabric-cutter, which could cut cloth rapidly and in bulk; and the railway network, which facilitated speedy and efficient marketing of the finished product. Taken together, these gave a strong push to the garment industry precisely in the years when the Jewish immigrants were arriving, first from Central and then from Eastern Europe. Their penetration of the garment industry was not necessarily due to skills they brought with them from home, but chiefly because they arrived in America when this industry was growing fast and begging for working hands. The immigrants of those years adapted themselves to the local labor market and soon found jobs.[30]

The most common employment model in the garment industry was through contractors: the manufacturer purchased the cloth, designed the garment, and employed skilled cutters to produce the pieces of garments. The parts were then sent to contractors, most of them Jews from Eastern Europe, who undertook to return the finished garments to the manufacturer. The contractor hired workers who toiled in what came to be known as "sweatshops," that were often located in converted tenement apartments, or even the contractor's own residence. In 1899, women's clothing shops

---

29 Fishberg, "Health and Sanitation," 286.
30 See Eli Lederhendler, *Jewish Immigrants and American Capitalism, 1880–1920: From Caste to Class* (New York: NYU Press, 2009), 46.

employed an average of 31 workers, but most had 20 or fewer workers. In 1919 the average dropped to 21 workers. In 1914, men's clothing shops employed 36 workers on average, but in three quarters of the workshops there were 5 employees or fewer.[31]

In these harsh conditions, the Jewish "operator" spent many hours bent over his, or more often her, sewing machine. This model increased the manufacturer's profits, because he did not have to pay to maintain the workshops or pay the workers wages in the off season.

The Danish American journalist Jacob Riis (1849–1914) was an influential social reformer who devoted his life to bettering the lives of the immigrants in New York. As the police reporter for the *New York Tribune* he came into contact with the residents of New York's backyard: the poor, the immigrants, the most wretched and miserable of all.[32] His reportage, accompanied by his pioneering photographs, forced newspaper readers to take a steely glance at the other half of New York's population. His book, *How the Other Half Lives* (1890), sold well and was praised by reviewers.[33] This is what he wrote about a sweatshop he visited on Ludlow Street:

> Up two flights of dark stairs, three, four, with new smells of cabbage, of onions, of frying fish, on every landing, whirring sewing machines behind closed doors betraying what goes on within, to the door that opens to admit the bundle and the man. A sweater, this, in a small way. Five men and a woman, two young girls, not fifteen, and a boy who says unasked that he is fifteen, and lies in saying it, are at the machines sewing knickerbockers, "knee-pants" in the Ludlow Street dialect. The floor is littered ankle-deep with half-sewn garments. In the alcove, on a couch of many dozens of "pants" ready for the finisher, a bare-legged baby with pinched face is asleep.[34]

Despite the exploitation and long hours, the contractor system had a number of advantages for immigrants in their first years in the United States. Operating a sewing machine did not require prior knowledge and basic competence was easy to acquire. This meant that immigrants could find

---

31 See Daniel Soyer, "Cockroach Capitalists: Jewish Contractors at the Turn of the Twentieth Century," in *A Coat of Many Colors: Immigration, Globalization, and Reform in New York City's Garment Industry*, ed. Daniel Soyer (New York: Fordham University Press, 2005), 94–95.

32 Bonnie Yochelson, *Jacob A. Riis: Revealing New York's Other Half: A Complete Catalogue of His Photographs* (New Haven: Yale University Press, 2015), 10-11.

33 Ibid., 13-14.

34 Jacob Riis, *How the Other Half Lives*, reprint ed. (New York: Dover, 1971), 100.

jobs very quickly. At times employers waited at the pier to scoop them up for their establishments; other times employers turned to the immigrants' hometown networks for workers.[35] The immigrants felt safer working among their co-ethnics and were spared manifestations of the antisemitism and xenophobia that pervaded American society. Finally, the low capital requirements for becoming a contractor held open the promise of moving up in the industrial hierarchy, even if such mobility was uncertain.

The immigrants' working conditions, like their housing, were bad. The inadequate lighting, poor ventilation, filthy surroundings, long hours, and low wages affected their physical and mental health. A number of studies conducted in the early twentieth century looked at the impact of working conditions on the immigrants' health; their conclusions were troubling. In 1911, a majority of those employed in the fur industry were unwell, because of the dust that collected on the fur and the noxious chemicals used to dye it. That same year, medical examinations of 800 bakers in New York, a third of them Jews, found that the extreme heat, high humidity, and poor ventilation in which they worked made them vulnerable to disease. A 1912 commission that investigated the health of 800 workers who made women's coats (half of them Jews) reached similar conclusions: more than 60% of them were suffering from at least one and sometimes multiple diseases.[36]

Despite their poor working and living conditions, however, the Jewish mortality rate and, notably, infant mortality, were strikingly low compared to those of other immigrants. There are a number of explanations for this. First of all, the largely non-Jewish immigrants who worked in mining, forestry, agriculture, and construction were much more vulnerable to natural disasters and work accidents than the tailors in the sweatshops.[37] Another cause for the lower mortality rate was that the Jewish immigrants were accustomed to the urban living conditions of New York, as the physician and physical anthropologist Maurice Fishberg explained:

> The immigrant Jew has not made a material change in his removal from Eastern Europe to London or New York. He lived there in a city and settled again in a city; he worked before at some indoor occupation, and does again the same in his new home; he lived there in an over-crowded home, and

---

35 See Annie Polland and Daniel Soyer, *Emerging Metropolis: New York Jews in the Age of Immigration, 1840–1920* (New York and London: NYU Press, 2012), 118.

36 See Dwork, "Health Conditions of Immigrant Jews," 20.

37 See, for example, June Granatir Alexander, *Daily Life in Immigrant America, 1870–1920* (Chicago: Ivan R. Dee, 2009), 114–15.

move again into American tenement or a London slum dwelling. He has paid the price for urbanization already for several hundred years.[38]

New York, the Pale of Settlement, and Jaffa: A Comparison

Want and poverty are relative. We can obtain a better understanding of Jewish life in New York by comparing the conditions there to the places the immigrants had left and other destinations they chose instead. There is no doubt that New York was far superior to Eastern Europe. The Jewish proletariat in Eastern Europe consisted exclusively of manual laborers. The Jewish laborer in the Russian Empire always had a weak and uncertain position in the job market. The high percentage of Jews who toiled in small workshops and the constant threat of unemployment deterred them from fighting to better their conditions. Jewish workers remained economically isolated; the demands advanced by the unionized workers in heavy industry had nothing to do with them. The Jews' difficulty in finding their place in the emerging economic landscape exacerbated their distress and pitted Jewish shopkeepers and craftsmen against one other, competing for every sale and job. The resulting price cuts forced many to sell their wares at a loss and made the life of Jewish craftsmen and merchants miserable. Their living conditions were intolerable: many families lived in cramped basements or dim rooms on a lower floor of apartment blocks in the big cities. Often their home was a single damp room, which served in turn as bedroom, workroom, dining room, and living room.[39] Many children had to work to supplement the family's income. The work hours were very long: in winter, from 8 AM to midnight, in summer from 6 AM to 9 PM, and sometimes longer. In Vitebsk, for example, Jewish craftsmen worked 13 to 18 hours a day; in Gomel, 16 to 17 hours; and in the textile center of Łódź, known as the "Manchester of Congress Poland," 13 to 15 hours.[40] The overcrowding, filth, and stench in their neighborhoods were even worse than in New York; both the local and imperial authorities were quite indifferent to the

---

38   Maurice Fishberg, *The Jews: A Study of Race and Environment* (New York: Charles Scribner's Sons, 1911), 294.

39   Isaac Rubinow, "Economic Condition of the Jews in Russia," *Bulletin of the Bureau of Labor* 72 (September 1907): 487–583 (repr. separately, New York, 1970), 526. See also Ezra Mendelsohn, *Class Struggle in the Pale: The Formative Years of the Jewish Workers' Movement in Tsarist Russia* (Cambridge: Cambridge University Press, 1970), 1–25.

40   Rubinow, "Economic Condition of the Jews of Russia," 527–28.

hardships of the people and did little or nothing to improve their quality of life.

By contrast, the comparison between New York and Jaffa in the early twentieth century suggests that immigrants to Palestine were better off. Instead of pieceworkers in sweatshops, they were hourly wage-earners in factories where the foreman felt responsibility for his workers. The relatively short workday was appropriate to the lifestyle of the Middle East, where "the natives, who like their ease, are not inclined to keep working after sunset."[41] The workshops closed at sunset and did not open before 7 AM:

> Except for a few factories and shops in the Jewish neighborhoods, which are open 11–13 hours a day, none of the other craftsmen or stores are open more than eight or nine hours a day. And if you deduct the lunch hour from this, it turns out that in practice all the assistants in the workshops and stores work for 7 to 8 hours a day. That is, the length of workday they are still fighting for in Europe has already been introduced in our land.[42]

As the immigrants became an integral part of the local population and Middle Eastern scene, they assimilated and adopted its lifestyle; after work they too would "go to the coffeehouses and sit at their ease, enjoying every sip of coffee and taking pleasure in the smoke of the nargila."[43] Businesses owned by non-Jews closed relatively early, so in the time until it got dark people could frequent cafes, bathe in the sea, or promenade along the beach. The Mediterranean attracted many people in Jaffa, both Jews and non-Jews, for an end-of-day swim; there is no doubt that this had a major impact on the immigrants' life and leisure-time culture:

> Bathing in the sea off Jaffa is done in the altogether, under the open sky. . . . In the evening the Arabs flock to the beach from every corner of the city to feast their eyes on the Jewish girls bathing half-naked in the sea. Year after year the rabbis protest this desecration of God's name, . . . but the world continues in its course. The Arab women bathe only at night, out of greater modesty.[44]

---

41   Z. Smilansky, "The Jewish Community in Jaffa, on the Basis of Statistical Records from 1904/5" [Hebrew], *Ha'omer* 1, no. 2 (1907): 108.
42   Smilansky, "Jewish Community in Jaffa," 107.
43   Ibid.
44   J. D. Freier, "The Season in Palestine" [Hebrew], *Hed hazman* 229, November 2, 1910, 1–2.

In Jaffa and subsequently in Tel Aviv the apartments were larger and more comfortable. There were no basement apartments in Jaffa and all the rooms were bright and airy. There was no need to heat them in the winter, which meant significant savings for immigrants. Palestine's major disadvantage in comparison with America was the more limited job opportunities and fewer prospects for immigrants who wanted to move up on the economic ladder.

Crime and Migration

The poverty, want, and harsh living conditions of the immigrants on the Lower East Side pushed some into crime. According to an article that Theodore Bingham, the New York police commissioner, published in the *North American Review* in September 1908, a majority of the criminals in the city were immigrants—and half of them were Jews. His article stunned the Jewish leaders in the city, who rejected his conclusions and sought to refute them. But they also feared that even if his statements were not totally on the mark there was nevertheless something to them. One response to the unfortunate situation of the Jews on the Lower East Side was the establishment of the Kehillah, at the initiative of Rabbi Judah L. Magnes.[45] Two of the new organization's goals were to better the Jewish immigrants' lives and to improve their image among other inhabitants of the city.

Crime statistics for the United States in general and for New York in particular in the early twentieth century indicate that Bingham's numbers were way off base.[46] According to a survey conducted in 1908, almost half of 12,853 convicts born outside the United States belonged to four groups: 2,336 from southern Italy (18.2%). 1,312 from Ireland (10.2%), 1,229 from Poland (9.6%), and 1,191 from Germany (9.3%). Nationwide, the Jews ranked only fifth in this dubious category.[47]

In New York, the proportion of Jewish criminals was much higher, but Bingham still overestimated the Jewish share of criminals. The Tombs, the municipal prison in Manhattan, housed 1,578 prisoners at the end of 1914,

---

45 See Arthur A. Goren, *New York Jews and the Quest for Community: The Kehillah Experiment, 1908–1922* (New York: Columbia University Press, 1970).

46 See Jenna Weissman Joselit, "An Answer to Commissioner Bingham: A Case Study of New York Jews and Crime, 1907," *YIVO Annual of Jewish Social Science* 18 (1983): 121–40.

47 *Reports of the Immigration Commission*, vol. 36: *Immigration and Crime* (Washington, D.C.: Government Printing Office, 1911), 29.

including 270 Jews (17.1%); Riker's Island had 288 inmates, including 58 Jews (20%); and the New York City Reformatory in New Hampton had 432 prisoners, including 85 Jews (19.6%).[48]

The war against Jewish crime was one of the Kehillah's main projects. Its researchers kept precise records of the criminal hotspots in the city, mapped by neighborhoods and addresses. They identified about six hundred brothels; drug dens; gambling houses; hangouts for gangsters, thieves, and pimps; shady billiard clubs; and other disreputable places, most of them on the Lower East Side, on East Fourteenth and Twenty-Third Streets, and in Harlem.

The congested streets of the Lower East Side became a magnet for crime and a source of concern for law-abiding immigrants. The neighbors of the building at 242 East Third Street sent Magnes the following letter (in flowery Hebrew) to complain about the nuisance:

> Honored rabbi, the distinguished and enlightened eminent scholar, the glory of the sages and crown of the prophets, the strong shield of all Jewry, Dr. J. L. Magnes, peace and blessings. Honored rabbi! Knowing that our people's honor is very dear to you, and so that the honor of Israel not be defiled among the poor, we have seen and become aware of his efforts concerning 242 East 3rd Street, having shut down a year and a half ago the tavern that brought shame and disgrace to the honor of Israel, and today the residents of this street from among our people and the residents of the whole area thank, praise, and honor him. Now, to our heart's distress, Number 242 has returned to its vomit, having been leased again as a tavern, before the air of this area had been cleansed of the impure sources of theft and adultery and murder. Now, with the opening of the tavern at Number 242, theft and adultery and murder will again proliferate seven- or seventy-fold, because a moving-picture theater has opened near Number 242, which more than 500 Jewish girls and boys, youngsters with nothing to do, will frequent every night. [...] For which reason we are addressing a question to his excellency, who has the capacity to protest and remove stumbling blocks.
>
> [Signed] The residents of East 3rd Street and the vicinity, near Number 242.[49]

---

48   See Judah Leib Magnes papers, P3, File 1774, Central Archives for the History of the Jewish People, Jerusalem (CAJP).

49   See undated letter to J. L. Magnes (1914?), File 1772, P3, CAJP.

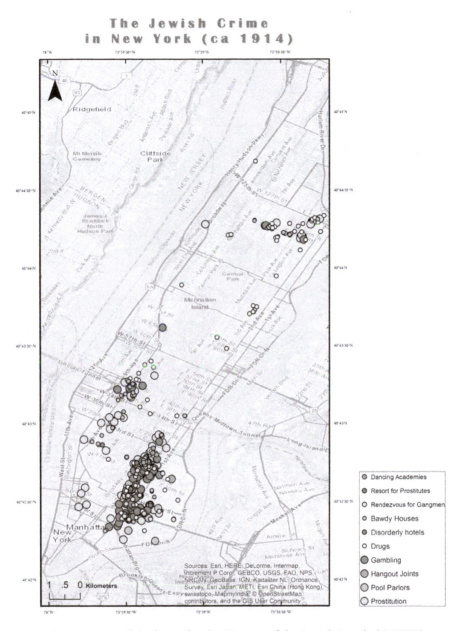

The Jewish Crime
in New York (ca 1914)

Legend:
- ◎ Dancing Academies
- ● Resort for Prostitutes
- ○ Rendezvous for Gangmen
- ○ Bawdy Houses
- ● Disorderly hotels
- ○ Drugs
- ◉ Gambling
- ◯ Hangout Joints
- ◯ Pool Parlors
- ◯ Prostitution

Fig. 1. Source: Central Archives for the History of the Jewish People (CAHJP), file P3/1774. The map was prepared by processing 588 addresses related to Jewish crime in New York, which were reported to the Kehila organization. Addresses were encoded into a database and processed by GIS software.

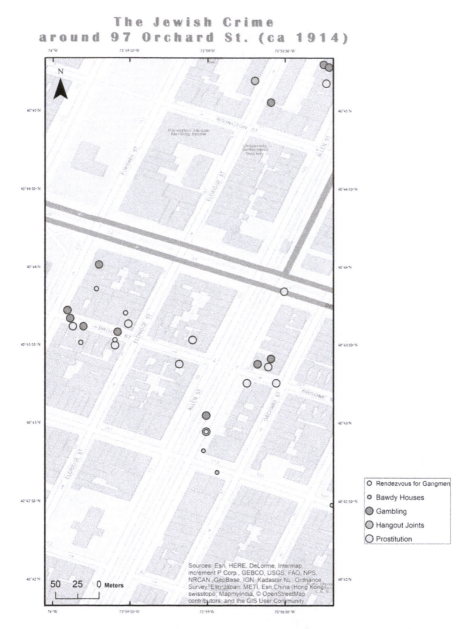

Fig. 2. Source: Central Archives for the History of the Jewish People (CAHJP), file P3/1774. The map was prepared by processing 588 addresses related to Jewish crime in New York, which were reported to the Kehila organization. Addresses were encoded into a database and processed by GIS software.

Prostitution and Drug Dens
in New York (ca 1914)

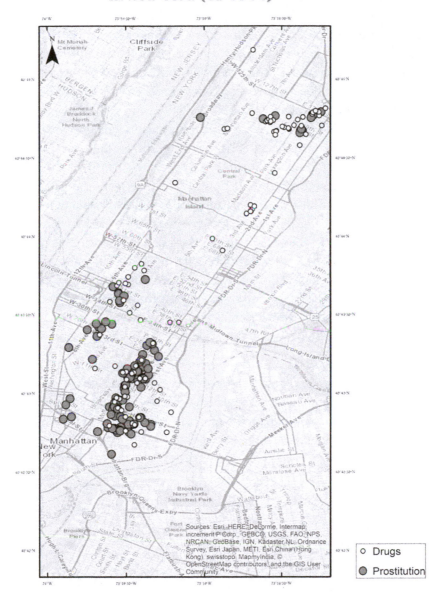

Fig. 3. Source: Central Archives for the History of the Jewish People (CAHJP), file P3/1774. The map was prepared by processing 588 addresses related to Jewish crime in New York, which were reported to the Kehila organization. Addresses were encoded into a database and processed by GIS software.

Many Jewish criminals were convicted of theft, dealing in stolen property, breaking and entering, and fraud. Only 2% were convicted of murder. The Jews were grossly overrepresented in the sex trade as compared to every other ethnic group. According to the Dillingham report, "the largest proportion of alien prisoners under sentence for offenses against chastity is that of the Hebrews. . . More than one-third of the Hebrew prisoners confined for such offenses were imprisoned for crimes of prostitution." Of 2,093 prostitutes arrested by the New York police in 1908, 581 were immigrants (28%) including 225 Jews.[50] This percentage seems proportional to the Jewish population at the time. And as Fig. 3 shows, there were brothels all up and down the Lower East Side.

In addition to the pimps and prostitutes, there were the gangs, both large and small, that disturbed the routine of New York Jews and non-Jews alike. Much has been written about the Jewish gangsters and the key role of Jewish immigrants in the rise of organized crime in America. Bugsy Siegel, Meyer Lansky, Mickey Cohen, Arnold Rothstein, Lepke Buchalter, and others became synonymous with merciless evil and cruelty, but were sometimes a source of pride as folk heroes who stood up against society and its conventions.[51] But most of the Jewish criminals, such as the members of the Yiddishe Camorra, were smalltime local thugs who never had an aura about them.

> The Yiddishe Camorra focused on extorting teamsters and demanding protection money from them. It operated on the Lower East Side, in Harlem, and in all the densely populated neighborhoods where Jews were involved in the garment trade, milk deliveries, transport, ice cream, and other businesses that relied on horse-drawn conveyances.[52]

Poisoning their horses was a lethal blow to teamsters and others who depended on carts and wagons. They had to find a way to maneuver between the gang's extortionate demands and their need to save their businesses and make a living.

***

50 *Reports of the Immigration Commission*, vol. 37: *Importation and Harboring of Women for Immoral Purposes* (Washington, D.C.: Government Printing Office, 1911), 62.
51 See Rich Cohen, *Tough Jews: Fathers, Sons, and Gangster Dreams* (New York: Simon and Schuster, 1998). See also Robert Rockaway, *But He Was Good to His Mother: The Lives and Crimes of Jewish Gangsters* (Jerusalem: Geffen, 2000).
52 File 1774 (undated; 1914?), P3, CAJP.

Sometimes, when I think of my past in a superficial, casual way, the metamorphosis I have gone through strikes me as nothing short of a miracle. I was born and reared in the lowest depths of poverty and I arrived in America—in 1885—with four cents in my pocket. I am now worth more than two million dollars and recognized as one of the two or three leading men in the cloak-and-suit trade in the United States.

—Abraham Cahan, *The Rise of David Levinsky*

The mass Jewish immigration from Eastern Europe to the United States effected a real change in the life of the Jewish people. Just as modernization in their countries of birth was a key factor behind their emigration, their migration was a key factor in the modernization of Jewish society. The Jewish migrants left the old religious and economic elite of Eastern Europe behind them. It was the shoemakers, the tailors, and the other craftsmen, who lived on the margins of Jewish society in Eastern Europe, who, thanks to the decision to emigrate and their improved economic situation in their new home, became a powerful and influential social force.

The lives of the Jews on the Lower East Side, both during the era of mass immigration and later, after the United States shut its gates, encapsulated the migratory experience of Eastern European Jews in America. The Lower East Side is the "sacred space of the American Jewish past."[53] Almost all Jewish immigrants, no matter whether they lived in New York or elsewhere in the country, were interested in what was taking place there, influenced by it, and saw it as an important and influential Jewish center.[54] It was a sort of microcosm of American Jewry in general and of the mass immigration era in particular.

Jewish immigrants started out in America with very few resources. Living hand to mouth in dark and crowded apartments, working long hours in sweatshops in inhuman conditions, they raised their children in an environment where criminals and prostitutes were a regular part of daily life. Nevertheless, they arrived with some advantages, including relatively high skill levels and a few more dollars than the other main new immigrant group in New York.[55] Thus, Jewish immigrants were able to take advantage

---

53 Hasia Diner, *Lower East Side Memories: A Jewish Place in America* (Princeton: Princeton University Press, 2000), x.

54 See ibid., 8–9.

55 See Thomas Kessner, *The Golden Door: Italian and Jewish Mobility in New York City, 1880–1915* (New York: Oxford University Press, 1977), 41–42; Stephen Steinberg, *The*

of the economic opportunities offered by the big city and to make steady progress up the socioeconomic ladder. The demanding urban life of the metropolis, American freedom, and the unlimited opportunities enabled the Jewish immigrants to find their place in American society and take part in building it. For many of them, the period of adjustment was difficult and traumatic, but most won their longed-for freedom in a relatively short time. The Jews' integration in New York and assimilation into the host society made the story of their immigration into a fascinating and dramatic success story in the history of the Jewish people in the modern age.

Ethnic Myth: Race, Ethnicity, and Class in America, 3rd ed. (Boston: Beacon Press, 2001), 94–99.

For Further Reading

Alexander, June Granatir. *Daily Life in Immigrant America, 1870–1920.* Chicago: Ivan R. Dee, 2009.

Alroey, Gur. "Patterns of Jewish Emigration from Russian Empire from the 1870s to 1914." *Jews in Russia and Eastern Europe* 57, no. 2 (Winter 2006): 24–51.

———. *Bread to Eat and Clothes to Wear: Letters from Jewish Migrants in the Early Twentieth Century.* Detroit: Wayne State University Press, 2011.

Baines, Dudley. *Emigration from Europe, 1815–1930.* Cambridge: Cambridge University Press, 1995.

Boustan, Leah Platt. "Were Jews Political Refugees or Economic Migrants? Assessing the Persecution Theory of Jewish Emigration, 1881–1914." In *The New Comparative Economic History: Essays in Honor of Jeffrey G. Williamson*, edited by Timothy J. Hatton, Kevin H. O'Rourke, and Alan M. Taylor, 267–90. Cambridge: MIT Press, 2007.

Cahan, Abraham. *The Rise of David Levinsky.* Mineola, NY: Dover, 2002.

Cohen, Rich. *Tough Jews: Fathers, Sons, and Gangster Dreams.* New York: Simon and Schuster, 1998.

Diner, Hasia. "Before the Promised City: Eastern European Jews in America before 1880." In *An Inventory of Promises: Essays on American Jewish History: In Honor of Moses Rischin*, edited by Jeffrey S. Gurock and Marc Lee Raphael, 43–62. Brooklyn: Carlson, 1995.

———. *A Time for Gathering: The Second Migration, 1820-1880.* Baltimore, MD: Johns Hopkins University Press, 1992.

———. *Lower East Side Memories: A Jewish Place in America.* Princeton: Princeton University Press, 2000.

Dwork, Deborah. "Health Conditions of Immigrant Jews on the Lower East Side of New York: 1880–1914." *Medical History* 25, no. 1 (1981): 1–40.

Goren, Arthur A. *New York Jews and the Quest for Community: The Kehillah Experiment, 1908-1922.* New York: Columbia University Press, 1970.

Hersch, Liebman. "International Migration of the Jews." In *International Migrations*, vol. 2: *Interpretations*, edited by Imre Ferenczi and Walter Wilcox, 471–520. New York: National Bureau of Economic Research, 1931.

Joselit, Jenna Weissman. "An Answer to Commissioner Bingham: A Case Study of New York Jews and Crime, 1907." *YIVO Annual of Jewish Social Science* 18 (1983): 121–140.

Kahan, Arcadius. *Essays in Jewish Social and Economic History.* Chicago: University of Chicago Press, 1986.

Kessner, Thomas. *The Golden Door: Italian and Jewish Mobility in New York City, 1880–1915.* New York: Oxford University Press, 1977.

Kuznets, Simon. "Immigration of Russian Jews to the United States: Background and Structure." *Perspectives in American History* 9 (1975): 35–126.

Lederhendler, Eli. *Jewish Immigrants and American Capitalism, 1880–1920: From Caste to Class.* New York: NYU Press, 2009.

Mendelsohn, Ezra. *Class Struggle in the Pale: The Formative Years of the Jewish Workers' Movement in Tsarist Russia.* Cambridge: Cambridge University Press, 1970.

Perlmann, Joel. *The Local Geographic Origins of Russian-Jewish Immigrants, Circa 1900*, Working Paper 465. Annandale-on-Hudson, NY: The Levy Economics Institute of Bard College, 2006.

Polland, Annie and Daniel Soyer. *Emerging Metropolis: New York Jews in the Age of Immigration, 1840-1920.* New York and London: NYU Press, 2012.

Riis, Jacob. *How the Other Half Lives*, reprint ed. New York: Dover, 1971.

Rockaway, Robert. *But He Was Good to His Mother: The Lives and Crimes of Jewish Gangsters.* Jerusalem: Geffen, 2000.

Soyer, Daniel, ed. *A Coat of Many Colors: Immigration, Globalization, and Reform in New York City's Garment Industry.* New York: Fordham University Press, 2005.

Stampfer, Saul. "The Geographic Background of East European Jewish Migration to the United States before World War I." In *Migration across Time and Nations: Population Mobility in Historical Contexts,* edited by Ira Glazier and Luigi De Rosa, 220–30. New York: Holmes and Meier, 1985.

Steinberg, Stephen. *The Ethnic Myth: Race, Ethnicity, and Class in America,* 3rd ed. Boston: Beacon Press, 2001.

Wischnitzer, Mark. *To Dwell in Safety: The Story of Jewish Migration since 1800.* Philadelphia: Jewish Publication Socety, 1948.

Yochelson, Bonnie. *Jacob A. Riis: Revealing New York's Other Half: A Complete Catalogue of His Photographs.* New Haven: Yale University Press, 2015.

Chapter 5

Yiddish New York

Ayelet Brinn, Eddy Portnoy, Daniel Soyer

According to statistics published by the US Department of Commerce, more people spoke Yiddish than English in 1920s New York City. On the face of it, this is an astounding statistic. Of course, New York City was at the time largely a city of immigrants speaking a variety of languages, but of the 52 languages documented as being spoken in the city, Yiddish had the most speakers. In fact, in 1920, only 20.9% of city residents declared English to be their mother tongue, whereas 22% declared Yiddish to be their mother tongue.[1] These remarkable statistics demonstrate the significance of New York's Yiddish-speaking population in relation to the city as a whole.

But even before the Department of Commerce published its statistics on language, it was already well known among Jews that New York had become the world's leading Yiddish city. "After New York, Warsaw is considered to be the biggest Yiddish center in the world" is the opening sentence of the first-column, front-page article in the first issue of *Der veg*, the first Yiddish daily permitted in Warsaw.[2] In 1905, it was thus already clear that New York had become the major center for Jewish cultural production, the great bulk of which took place in Yiddish.

But what a strange phenomenon it really was that New York should achieve that status. The peregrinations of Yiddish had, for centuries, taken place in Europe, moving eastward in a contiguous trajectory across the continent. That

---

1   "946,139 Jews Speak Yiddish in New York," *American Israelite*, August 17, 1922, 7.
2   *Der veg,* August 14, 1905.

the language was able to transplant itself across an ocean and establish itself as a major cultural center in an era dominated by print media is astounding, even more so when one considers that Yiddish newspapers were a phenomenon that began only during the second half of the nineteenth century.

The building of Yiddish culture in New York depended most of all on the development of a critical mass of Yiddish speakers. This critical mass was a result of the huge numbers of Yiddish-speaking Jewish immigrants who were drawn to New York by the city's economic dynamism. By 1920, New York's Jewish community numbered a million and a half, the largest Jewish population in the world. There they found their economic niche in garment manufacturing (most famously) and other growing industries. The upward mobility afforded the immigrants and their children enabled them to support a burgeoning Yiddish cultural scene—in the heart of America's cultural capital—even as it eventually threatened the language's viability as a spoken vernacular.

But Yiddish actually had a long history in New York. In the colonial period, a few Yiddish-speaking Jews from Germany and Poland began to trickle into North America. This small number of colonial-era Yiddish-speaking Jews were, of course, mainly preceded by Sephardim, who began to arrive in the 1650s. However, by 1750, the majority of North America's approximately 2,000 Jews were Ashkenazim and, very likely speakers of Western Yiddish. These Jews are nearly always categorized as "German" Jews, a designation that, while technically accurate, ignores the fact that German Jews prior to the Haskalah (Jewish Enlightenment) mainly spoke Yiddish.

In fact, Yiddish words and phrases can be found in eighteenth-century documents and even some created by Sephardim, an indication of the increasing influence of Yiddish. Notably, minutes of the city's one synagogue, Shearith Israel, include words like *shul*, *yortsayt*, and *rebbe*. Personal correspondence also shows the influence of Yiddish. Letters written by Sephardic businessman Abraham Halevy to Aaron Lopez in the 1770s contain many Yiddish words and phrases, an indicator that Yiddish was fairly prevalent among all Jews, not just Ashkenazim. If Yiddish was so influential in both the official documentation and in the correspondence of Sephardim, one can only wonder how prevalent it was as the spoken language among both Ashkenazim and Sephardim.[3]

---

3   Milton Doroshkin, *Yiddish in America: Social and Cultural Foundations* (Rutherford, NJ: Fairleigh Dickinson University Press, 1970), 51.

Ashkenazim in Colonial New York doubtlessly conducted business in Yiddish. The archives of the American Jewish Historical Society contain a notebook from 1759 which includes copies of business letters written by Uriah Hendricks, many of which are in Yiddish.[4] Perhaps the best known Jew of the Colonial period, alleged financier of George Washington's armies, Haym Solomon, corresponded with his parents in Poland in Yiddish. He is also known to have sprinkled Yiddish words and phrases into his English, writing to an uncle in London, for example, that, "in America, there is little *Yidishkayt*" (Jewishness).[5]

Hebrew and Yiddish books were also brought to America by early colonial-period immigrants. Popular Yiddish fare like the *Bove bukh* and the *Tsene rene* was common among European Jews and certainly made its way to America with these early immigrants. One such book, found in the collection of the Jewish Theological Seminary, is the seventeenth-century *Sefer ha-maggid*, a sequel to the *Tsene rene*, and bears a Yiddish inscription by a New York ritual slaughterer, dated 1720. In any case, there wasn't much cultural creation during this early period and colonial American Jews were consumers, not producers. That would eventually change.

Although some Jews in New York used Yiddish as a communal language in the early nineteenth century, the real growth of the language's presence as a private and public language came later as a result of mass immigration, first from Central, and later from Eastern Europe.[6] Only after the Civil War, for a prime example, did a viable Yiddish press gradually appear, as a mass market formed, Jewish publishers gained experience, and funds became available.[7] The first Yiddish newspaper in America appeared in 1870. Bankrolled by Tammany Hall in hopes of reaching a growing population of potential Jewish voters, *Di nyu-yorker yidishe tsaytung*, or, *The Hebrew Times*, was an intermittent weekly written by an educator named K. Bukhner. Primitive and unprofessional, it is not clear what the reaction to this first newspaper was. But its very existence attests to the close

---

4   See Hendricks Family Papers Archive, MS 295, Box 1, American Jewish Historical Society.

5   Arthur Hertzberg, *The Jews in America: Four Centuries of an Uneasy Encounter: A History* (New York: Columbia University Press, 1997), 51.

6   For an early document in Yiddish, see Morris Schappes, *A Documentary History of the Jews in the United States, 1654-1875* (New York: Schocken Books, 1950), 195–98, 615, n.1.

7   See Mordecai Soltes, *The Yiddish Press: An Americanizing Agency* (New York: Teachers College, Columbia University, 1925), 16–17.

relationship between the Yiddish press and American cultural and political institutions.[8]

At the time, Yiddish newspapers were still relatively rare. Even in Russia's Pale of Settlement, which held the world's largest Jewish population, there was only one weekly paper in the Jewish vernacular. Whereas Yiddish publishing in Russia suffered under government censorship, the nascent New York Yiddish press faced no external impediments. As a result, after the first Yiddish newspaper appeared in 1870, others quickly followed. Most of these early efforts were short-lived. Only one managed to survive for any length of time: *Di yidishe gazeten*, a weekly broadsheet founded by Kasriel Sarasohn in 1874. Eventually, this publication was so successful that Sarasohn was also able to launch the first long-running Yiddish daily, *Dos yidishes tageblat*. Not only had Sarasohn begun to cultivate a reading audience, but by 1885, when his daily first appeared, a massive influx of Yiddish-speaking immigrants—all potential customers—had arrived in New York City.[9]

"He who is without a newspaper," wrote P. T. Barnum in 1880, "is cut off from his species."[10] And, indeed, by the end of the nineteenth century, newspapers became the dominant medium among Jews, providing readers with local, national, and international news, information on local and national politics, advertisements offering employment and a plethora of goods, information, advice, and entertainment. It was the newspaper that guided immigrants through the complexities of the daunting new urban environment and introduced them to American life. Yiddish newspapers brought a sense of community and order for readers, and became authority figures that replaced or supplemented those of the old world.[11]

In addition to the influx of new potential readers, the nascent Yiddish press also benefited from innovations pioneered by a new style of American

---

8   Moshe Shtarkman, "Vikhtikste momentn in der geshikhte fun der yidisher prese in Amerike," in *Finf un zibetsik yor yidishe prese in Amerike, 1870-1945*, ed. Jacob Glatstein et al. (New York: I. L. Peretz shrayber fareyn, 1945), 11; Joseph Chaikin, *Yidishe bleter in Amerike: a tsushtayer tsu der 75 yoriker geshikhte fun der yidisher prese in di Fareynikte Shtatn un Kanade* (New York: M. S. Shklarshy[, 1946]), 53; A. R. Malakhi, "Der baginen fun der yidisher prese," in *Pinkes far der forshung fun der yidisher literatur un prese*, vol. 2 (New York: Alveltlekher yidisher kultur-kongres, 1972), 271.

9   Soltes, *The Yiddish Press*, 15; Shtarkman, "Vikhtikste momentn."

10 Gunther Barth, *City People: The Rise of Modern City Culture in Nineteenth-Century America* (New York: Oxford University Press, 1982), 61.

11 See Barth, *City People*, 58–59. Though he discusses this theme in connection to internal migration, it is very much applicable to any immigrant experience.

journalism emerging at this time. Whereas earlier American newspapers served small, elite audiences, and received funding from political parties, publishers like William Randolph Hearst and Joseph Pulitzer revolutionized the market by introducing sensationalism, human interest stories, and commercial advertisements. These transformations created a model for newspapers aimed at a mass audience, encompassing a mix of news, entertainment, advice, and advertising.[12] This fusion of ideological, commercial, and cultural aims would also come to characterize the American Yiddish press, including papers aligned with religious orthodoxy and political radicalism.

Sarasohn's tag-team of *Dos yidishes tageblat* and *Di yidishe gazeten* dominated the New York Yiddish publishing scene in the late nineteenth century. Multiple publications were launched, and Sarasohn became famous not for competing with these papers, but buying them out. This period also featured the first battles between newspapers espousing different ideologies. The first Yiddish socialist paper, *Di Nyu Yorker yidishe folkstsaytung* provided ideologically-minded fare for working-class readers. Socialist publishers became Sarasohn's bitter enemies and the two camps took frequent journalistic swipes at one another. While *Di Nyu Yorker yidishe folkstsaytung* folded in 1889, other radical papers followed, including *Dos abend-blat*, *Di arbeter tsaytung*, and *Di fraye arbeter shtime*.[13] In fact, New York's large, highly concentrated Yiddish-speaking proletariat made it a prime area for the development of radical Yiddish publishing. This led many pioneers of radical Yiddish journalism, who had never themselves regularly spoken Yiddish, or had rejected the language in their youths, to write and speak Yiddish to reach their desired audience.[14]

Over the ensuing decades, Yiddish newspaper circulation continued to grow—reaching the hundreds of thousands by World War I. By that time, New York's Yiddish press blossomed from a handful of short-lived papers into a broad, influential array of publications espousing various ideological perspectives. The mostly widely read was the socialist *Forverts*

---

12 Michael Schudson, *Discovering the News: A Social History of American Newspapers* (New York: Basic Books, 1978); Julia Guarneri, *Newsprint Metropolis: City Papers and the Making of Modern Americans* (Chicago: University of Chicago Press, 2017).

13 Y. Lifshits, "Di Nyu Yorker yidishe folkstsaytung," in *Pinkes far der forshung fun der yiddisher literatur un prese,* vol. 3 (New York: Alveltlekher yidisher kultur-kongres, 1975).

14 Tony Michels, *A Fire in their Hearts: Yiddish Socialists in New York* (Cambridge, MA: Harvard University Press, 2005).

(founded 1897 and commonly called the *Jewish Daily Forward* in English), which under its shrewd and domineering editor Abraham Cahan overtook Sarasohn's *Tageblat* by 1910. Drawing on his experience as an English-language journalist, Cahan fashioned his paper into a unique combination of earnest socialism and populist sensationalism. With this formula, the *Forverts*'s profits enabled it to build a ten-story building on East Broadway that became headquarters to the city's Jewish socialist and labor movements. The *Forverts*'s masthead bore the legend, "Workers of all countries, unite," but on its stationary ca. 1920 it proclaimed itself the "gateway to the Jewish market."

Other newspapers carved out other ideological and journalistic niches. The *Morgen zhurnal* (*Jewish Morning Journal*), founded in 1901, was the first Yiddish morning newspaper, and favored orthodoxy in religion and conservatism in politics. It absorbed the *Tageblat* in 1928. The *Tog* (*Day*) appeared in 1914, calling itself the "newspaper for the Jewish intelligentsia." Its editorial line was liberal and Zionist, but it prided itself in being politically independent and in its high-quality columns espousing a variety of views. Shorter lived was the *Varhayt* (*Truth*, 1905–1919), established by Louis Miller, Cahan's one-time friend turned rival. Finally, the *Frayhayt* (*Freedom*) was the Yiddish mouthpiece of the Communist Party from its appearance in 1922. In addition to these major dailies, many Yiddish weeklies, monthlies, annuals and occasional publications appeared in New York, catering to a wide spectrum of audiences from anarchists to small businesspeople.[15]

Newspaper writers, editors, and publishers became crucial cultural and political arbiters, sponsoring rallies, celebrations, and commemorations, and holding formal and informal debates about politics or the future of Yiddish culture in New York's cafes and lecture halls.[16] The fact that most Yiddish newspapers were produced on the Lower East Side, the first area of settlement for many Yiddish-speaking immigrants, afforded the newspapers particularly close relationships with their readers. But letters from

---

15   Moses Rischin, *The Promised City: New York's Jews, 1870–1914* (1962; Cambridge, MA: Harvard University Press, 1977), 117–27; Irving Howe, *World of Our Fathers* (New York: Harcourt Brace Jovanovich, 1976), 518–51.

16   Arthur A. Goren, "Pageants of Sorrow, Celebration and Protest," in *The Politics and Public Culture of American Jews* (Bloomington: Indiana University Press, 1999), 30–47; Shachar M. Pinsker, *A Rich Brew: How Cafes Created Modern Jewish Culture* (New York: New York University Press, 2018), chap. 5.

readers from around the country, and around the world, attested to the power and reach of these New York-based newspapers.

The turn of the twentieth century thus marked New York's emergence as the world's leading Yiddish cultural center. The influence of New York's Yiddish newspapers radiated back to Eastern Europe, where New York endeavors greatly influenced the development of Yiddish newspapers.[17] As a center of Yiddish cultural production, New York lacked the traditional and literary pedigrees of Eastern Europe. But what it lacked in pedigree it made up in numbers and economic power. The success of Yiddish culture in New York was often determined by pragmatism as much as by quality of product. This pragmatism, combined with the freedom offered by the New World and the ambition of immigrant entrepreneurs, were the driving forces behind New York's Yiddish cultural dominance.

The New York Yiddish press also served as an incubator for modern Yiddish literature. The earliest generation of Yiddish poets were the so-called Sweatshop Poets, most notably Morris Winchevsky, Morris Rosenfeld, David Edelstadt, and Joseph Bovshover, whose work both described and protested the poor conditions under which they and many of their fellow immigrants toiled. Set to music, some of their poems became the marching hymns of the Jewish labor movement not only in America, but in Europe as well. Around 1907–1908, however, a revolution took place in the world of Yiddish poetry. Led by Mani Leyb, Zishe Landau, and others, *Di yunge* (The Young Ones) rejected the propagandistic elements of the sweatshop bards (whom they derided as "the rhyme department of the Jewish labor movement") in favor of a lyrical aesthetic—art for art's sake. They in turn were followed in the aftermath of World War I by the modernist *In zikh* (Introspectivist) movement that included Jacob Glatstein and catered inevitably to an audience with more rarified taste. But this schematic chronology can be overdrawn. Some poets, such as Moyshe Leyb Halpern and H. Leivick, straddled movements, which in any case did not go away when "superseded" by the next. Neither did social themes disappear: Halpern wrote about the anarchist martyrs Sacco and Vanzetti, for

---

17 Eric L. Goldstein, "A Taste of Freedom: American Yiddish Publications in Imperial Russia," in *Transnational Traditions: New Perspectives on American Jewish History*, ed. Ava F. Kahn and Adam Mendelsohn (Detroit: Wayne State University Press, 2014), 105–39.

example, and the Communist-allied Proletpen movement that arose in the 1920s often commented on both class and racial injustice.[18]

New York formed not only the venue for these poets' creative activity, but a subject for their work. Halpern's poems, for example, featured the Jewish quarter's Seward Park, the subway, the surf off Coney Island, and Central Park, in ways that often expressed his profound alienation from his surroundings, but would still resonate with New Yorkers today. At the same time, the work of all these Yiddish poets reflected the influence of modern world culture. Readers might wonder how a poem like Anna Margolin's "The Girls of Crotona Park" was somehow "Jewish":

> Girls have woven themselves into autumn evenings
> as in a faded picture.
> Their eyes are cool, their smiles wild and thin,
> their dresses lavender, old rose, apple green.
> Dew flows through their veins.
> Their talk is bright and empty.
> Botticelli loved them in his dreams.

The answer is that not only was the poem written by a Jewish poet, in a Jewish language, and in a Jewish script, but the girls in the Bronx's Crotona Park were most likely Jewish as well, given that the Bronx was at the time the most Jewish of boroughs with a lively Yiddish cultural scene.[19]

In addition to poetry, New York also became a major center for the production of Yiddish prose. Several prominent Yiddish authors, including Sholem Rabinovich (aka Sholem Aleichem) and his bitter rival Nokhem Meyer Shaykevitch (aka Shomer), sent work to be published in New York while still living in Europe. Both eventually relocated to New York. New

---

18 Ruth Wisse, *A Little Love in Big Manhattan: Two Yiddish Poets* (Cambridge, MA: Harvard University Press, 1988); Irving Howe, Ruth Wisse, Khone Shmeruk, *The Penguin Book of Modern Yiddish Verse* (New York: Viking, 1987), 21–34, 84–85, 212–15; Benjamin Harshav and Barbara Harshav, *American Yiddish Poetry: A Bilingual Anthology* (Berkeley: University of California Press, 1986), 27–44; Alexandra Polyan, "Reflections of Revolutionary Movements in American Yiddish Poetry: The Case of Proletpen," in *Jewish Thought, Utopia and Revolution*, ed. Elena Namli, Jayne Svenungsson, and Alana Vincent (Amsterdam: Rodopi, 2014), 145–60; Dovid Katz, "Introduction: The Days of Proletpen in American Yiddish Poetry," in Amelia Glaser, *Proletpen: America's Rebel Yiddish Poets* (Madison: University of Wisconsin Press, 2005), 3–24.

19 Howe, Wisse, Shmeruk, *Penguin Book of Modern Yiddish Verse*, 174–75, 206–209, 222; Harshav, *American Yiddish Poetry*, 394–97, 400–405.

York also fostered the careers of local Yiddish literary talents, many of whom drew inspiration from life in New York's Jewish immigrant enclaves.[20]

The development of Yiddish prose was deeply intertwined with the development of the Yiddish press. Yiddish dailies, weeklies, and monthlies included short stories as well as longer, serialized fiction to entertain readers and to elevate their cultural literacy. There were also smaller literary journals, such as *Literatur un lebn* (Literature and Life), founded in 1913. Furthermore, many of the most successful newspapers also owned presses that were responsible for the majority of Yiddish book publishing in America.[21] At first, most Yiddish newspapers mainly published translations of world fiction into Yiddish. For example, in its first year publication, the *Forverts* serialized Victor Hugo's *Les Miserables*. Over time, Yiddish newspapers shifted to publishing primarily original Yiddish fiction.[22]

Many writers of Yiddish prose had fraught, complex relationships with the Yiddish press. Not only were newspapers and magazines the major venues in which Yiddish prose was published, but many Yiddish authors also supplemented their belletristic work by writing newspaper features. However, many of these authors resented having to rely on newspapers for patronage, as they felt that this often required them to sacrifice artistic merit in favor of mass appeal.[23]

In reality, Yiddish prose comprised a broad spectrum, from melodramatic, formulaic romance novels to what was often referred to as more "serious" fiction by writers such as Sholem Asch, Joseph Opatoshu, and Israel Joshua Singer.[24] And even the fiction that critics characterized as *shund* (trashy or lowbrow) often explored the tensions inherent in the immigrant experience. In addition, serialized fiction and short stories were

---

20 Ellen Kellman, "The Newspaper Novel in the Jewish Daily Forward, 1900–1940: Fiction as Entertainment and Serious Literature" (PhD diss., Columbia University, 2000); Justin Cammy, "Judging *The Judgment of Shomer*: Jewish Literature versus Jewish Reading," in *Arguing the Modern Jewish Canon*, ed. Justin Cammy et al. (Cambridge, MA: Harvard University Press, 2008), 85–127.

21 Hagit Cohen, *Nifla'ot ba-'olam he-hadash: sefarim ve-kor'im be-yidish be-Artsot ha-Berit, 1890–1940* (Ra'ananah: Open University Press, 2016).

22 Kellman, "The Newspaper Novel."

23 Wisse, *A Little Love in Big Manhattan*, 9–10; Reuben Iceland, *From Our Springtime: Literary Memoirs and Portraits of Yiddish New York*, trans. Gerald Marcus (Syracuse: Syracuse University Press, 2013); original: Reuben Iceland, *Fun unzer friling: literarishe zikhroynes un portretn* (New York: Inzl, 1954).

24 Kellman, "The Newspaper Novel"; Anita Norich, *The Homeless Imagination in the Fiction of Israel Joshua Singer* (Bloomington: Indiana University Press, 1991).

two of the only arenas, along with poetry and women's columns, where women writers were regularly featured within the Yiddish press. Writers such as Kadya Molodowsky and Miriam Karpilove wrote fiction for various publications, much of which focused on the particular challenges faced by immigrant Jewish women.[25]

The same mix of high and low culture, and commercial and ideological agendas, which was central to New York's Yiddish literary culture also characterized New York's Yiddish theater scene. Like newspapers, Yiddish theater was a relatively new art form when it took hold in the United States. Though there were several antecedents, including amateur skits on Jewish holidays and didactic plays by adherents of the Haskalah, scholars generally date the beginning of modern Yiddish theater to mid-1870s Romania, when Avrom Goldfadn organized the first professional Yiddish theater troupe. This troupe traveled throughout Europe, and eventually the United States, quickly achieving mass popularity. While some critics dismissed Goldfadn's work as overly melodramatic, his plays encompassed characteristics that would come to define New York's Yiddish theater as well: plots that reflected contemporary Jewish concerns as well as European and American cultural influences; fusions between drama, ideology, music, and comedy; and a broad audience encompassing sweatshop workers and intellectuals.[26]

The first Yiddish play performed in New York—an operetta by Goldfadn—premiered in 1882. Quickly, theater became one of the most important American Jewish cultural institutions. By 1918, there were twenty Yiddish theaters on New York's Lower East Side, staging approximately a thousand performances each year, with audiences exceeding two million spectators.[27] Most major areas of Jewish settlement in the United

---

25 Irena Klepfisz, "Queens of Contradiction: A Feminist Introduction to Yiddish Women Writers," in *Found Treasures: Stories by Yiddish Women Writers*, ed. Frieda Forman et al. (Toronto: Second Story Press, 1994), 21–62; Kathryn Hellerstein, "Introduction," in *Arguing with the Storm: Stories by Yiddish Women Writers*, ed. Rhea Tregebov (New York: City University of New York Press, 2007), xiv–xxvi; Anita Norich, "Translating and Teaching Yiddish Prose by Women," *In geveb* (April 2020), https://ingeveb.org/blog/translating-and-teaching-yiddish-prose-by-women, accessed May 29, 2020.

26 Alyssa Quint, *The Rise of Modern Yiddish Theater* (Bloomington: Indiana University Press, 2019); Edna Nahshon, ed., *New York's Yiddish Theater: From the Bowery to Broadway* (New York: Columbia University Press, 2016); Nahma Sandrow, *Vagabond Stars: A World History of Yiddish Theater* (Syracuse: Syracuse University Press, 1996).

27 Nahshon, *New York's Yiddish Theater*, 12; Gerald Sorin, *A Time for Building: The Third Migration, 1880–1920* (Baltimore: Johns Hopkins University Press, 1992), 99.

States had local Yiddish theater scenes—comprising a mix of professional and amateur productions, and traveling productions originating in New York. But New York served as the art form's major hub. The first Yiddish productions rented out spaces on the Bowery that had once housed German and Irish theater troupes—reflecting the polyglot, multiethnic nature of the neighborhood.[28] By the 1910s, the center of Yiddish theater shifted to Second Avenue, which became known as the Yiddish Rialto or Yiddish Broadway.

Yiddish-speaking immigrants looked to theater as an escape and as a way to process their transition to America. But Yiddish theater audiences also included a significant number of non-Yiddish speakers, including members of other immigrant groups and native-born Americans, drawn in by the interactive relationship between the actors and their audience. Journalists Hutchins and Norman Hapgood wrote glowing reviews of Yiddish productions for Anglophone newspapers. And their colleague, Lincoln Steffens, praised Yiddish theater as "about the best in New York at the time both in stuff and in acting."[29]

The diversity of Yiddish theater reflected the heterogeneous nature of its audience. While many early plays were melodramas, Yiddish theater grew to encompass dramas, operettas, vaudeville, comedies, and avant garde political art theater. Works by Ibsen, Chekhov, and Shakespeare were performed in translation, or adapted to conform to the perceived tastes of audiences. Other playwrights used current events to inspire their plots. One of the most successful Yiddish playwrights, Jacob Gordin, garnered particular acclaim for his ability to realistically dramatize the immigrant experience. This variety on the Yiddish stage led to a vibrant field of Yiddish theater criticism. And the fact that much of this criticism was published in Yiddish and English newspapers highlights the intertwined nature of these institutions. Critics debated the comparative merits and drawbacks

---

28 Nahshon, *New York's Yiddish Theater*, 18; Sabine Haenni, *The Immigrant Scene: Ethnic Amusements in New York: 1880–1920* (Minneapolis: University of Minnesota Press, 2008), chap. 3.

29 Lincoln Steffens, *The Autobiography of Lincoln Steffens* (New York: Harcourt, Brace and Co. 1931), 318; See also Hutchins Hapgood, *The Spirit of the Ghetto* (New York: Funk & Wagnall, 1902), chap. 5; Stefanie Halpern, "Yiddish Drama on the Broadway Stage," *Digital Yiddish Theater Project*, https://web.uwm.edu/yiddish-stage/yiddish-drama-on-the-broadway-stage, accessed June 27, 2020.

of *shund* (lowbrow theatrical productions) and realism. But for audiences, this diversity meant that they had a wide array of options to choose from.[30]

The Yiddish theater scene was dominated by powerful impresarios, such as Boris Tomashefsky and Jacob Adler, who produced, directed, and starred in their own productions. Their troupes were often family affairs, with Boris's wife, Bessie, and Adler's wives and children, including Dina, Sara, Luther, Celia, and Stella, becoming stars in their own rights. Several actresses achieved renown on the Yiddish stage, including Bertha Kalisch, Molly Picon, and, on tour, Esther Rokhl Kaminska. And there were a handful of female actor-managers who ran companies. However, like the press, the Yiddish stage remained a primarily male-dominated space, with male actor-managers exerting most of the control and benefitting the most financially.[31]

The heyday of Yiddish theater lasted from the 1880s through the end of the 1920s. But the reverberations of Yiddish theater continued long after its peak. Several stars became cross-over successes in other venues, including Stella Adler, who achieved great renown as an acting teacher and a central force in New York's Group Theatre. And Yiddish theater was a major source of talent for the Borscht Belt and variety shows of the mid-twentieth century. In addition, works by Yiddish playwrights have been performed in translation ever since the early twentieth century.[32] Sholem Asch's *God of Vengeance* served as the inspiration for Paula Vogel's 2017 Broadway play *Indecent*, and was simultaneously revived in Yiddish by New Yiddish Rep— one of two troupes, along with the National Yiddish Theater Folksbiene, still regularly performing Yiddish theater in New York in the twenty-first century.

While the heydays of the Yiddish press and theater were over by the end of the 1920s, that same decade saw the proliferation of a new Yiddish-language medium: radio. By the 1930s, New York had twenty-three stations broadcasting some form of Yiddish programming, all running on frequencies that also carried programs in other languages. The fact that Yiddish radio thrived in the 1930s and 1940s, at a time when immigration

---

30   Nina Warnke, "Immigrant Popular Culture as Contested Sphere: Yiddish Music Halls, the Yiddish Press, and the Processes of Americanization, 1900–1910," *Theatre Journal* 48 (1996): 321–35; Nahshon, *New York's Yiddish Theater*, 70.

31   Nahshon, *New York's Yiddish Theater;* Nahma Sandrow, "Yiddish Theater in the United States," in *Jewish Women: A Comprehensive Historical Encyclopedia,* Jewish Women's Archive, https://jwa.org/encyclopedia/article/yiddish-theater-in-united-states, accessed June 27, 2020.

32   Nahshon, *New York's Yiddish Theater.*

from Eastern Europe had been suspended, suggests that many American Jews continued to engage with Yiddish-language media even after they had transitioned to living their lives mainly in English.[33] In devising their programming, Yiddish radio stations drew on pre-existing Yiddish media. The most successful Yiddish radio station—WEVD—was closely connected to the Socialist Party, and was taken over by the socialist Yiddish daily *Forverts* in 1932. But other newspapers like *Der tog* expanded into radio as well.[34] Many figures involved with Yiddish theater also worked in radio as a way to supplement their income. Playwright and actor Nukhem Stutchkoff, for example, wrote radio melodramas, and actress Molly Picon performed in radio broadcasts throughout the interwar period. Like newspapers and theater, these programs offered a mix of formats and content, including melodramas, comedies, advice programs, variety hours, and advertisements for local and national businesses. While the audience for Yiddish radio began to decline after World War II, some programs continued for decades, with a small, but devoted, audience still listening to Yiddish programs into the twenty-first century.[35]

As New York emerged as one of the premier centers of Yiddish culture, the city's linguistic environment altered the language itself. Not surprisingly, the Yiddish speech of East European Jewish immigrants, and especially their children, absorbed not only many English words and expressions, but also English syntax. In his massive study, *The American Language*, H. L. Mencken listed dozens of loanwords, many of them denoting such mundane concepts as *boy, chair, window, floor, trouble, bother, school, grocery, shop, wages,* and *boss.* Mencken (whose chief Yiddish informant was Abraham Cahan) also reported that such expressions as *Di boyz mit di meydlekh hobn a good time* ("The boys and girls have a good time"), or *Rosie hot shoyn a fella* ("Rosie already has a fella") were already "excellent American Yiddish." Yiddishist purists like philosopher Chaim Zhitlowsky might bemoan "the wild-growing Yiddish-English jargon, the potato-chicken-kitchen language," but there

---

33 Ari Y. Kelman, *Station Identification: A Cultural History of Yiddish Radio in the United States* (Berkeley: University of California Press, 2009).

34 Kelman, *Station Identification*; Brian Dolber, *Media and Culture in the U.S. Jewish Labor Movement: Sweating For Democracy in the Interwar Era* (New York: Palgrave Macmillan, 2017). For *Der tog*'s forays into Yiddish radio, see its archival collection at YIVO Institute for Jewish Research, "Day-Morning Journal ('Der Tog')," RG 639, box 1, folders 8–9.

35 "Yiddish Radio Project," https://www.yiddishradioproject.org/, accessed June 27, 2020.

was little they could do about it.[36] By 1941, even the distinguished literary critic Shmuel Niger argued for pronouncing many English loanwords kosher and, mixing his metaphors, giving them their "citizenship papers" in proper Yiddish speech and writing.[37]

But other local languages besides English also influenced New York Yiddish. German, especially, left a strong impression on the immigrants' journalistic, organizational, and political lingo. New York was, when Yiddish-speakers started arriving in great numbers, the third-largest German-speaking city in the world, and the newcomers moved into the neighborhoods already inhabited by German immigrants. Members of the two groups also often interacted in business. In their early years in America, Jewish radicals looked up to the powerful German labor and socialist movement in city, reading German Socialist periodicals and attending German labor meetings. As Abraham Cahan later self-consciously pointed out, it was no wonder that German permeated Yiddish Socialist discourse, including that of the *Forward*. Likewise, the thousands of East European Jewish mutual aid societies adopted much of their organizational culture from the similar, and very widespread, German groups that preceded them. In both cases, borrowing from German was encouraged by German's much higher social prestige, a sense shared even by many Yiddish speakers.[38]

Moreover, influence was exerted in the other direction as well. If English influenced Yiddish, so Yiddish left its mark on New York English. Mencken, once again, reported dozens of Yiddish words that had entered the American language. But he argued that the presence of Yiddishisms was especially notable in New York, and not only among Jews. "In New York City," he wrote, "the high density of Eastern Jews in the population has

---

36 H. L. Mencken, *The American Language: An Inquiry into the Development of English in the United States*, 4th ed. (1936; reprint ed., New York: Knopf, 1962), 633–36. In the quotes, we have corrected Mencken's transcriptions of the original Yiddish words.

37 Sh. Niger, "Lomir zey kashern (a briv in redaktsie)," *Yidishe shprakh* 1, no. 1 (1941): 21–24.

38 Stanley Nadel, *Little Germany: Ethnicity, Religion, and Class in New York City, 1845–1880* (Urbana: University of Illinois Press, 1990), 1, 41; Y. A. Benequit, *Durkhgelebt un durkhgetrakht*, vol. 2 (New York: Kultur federatsie, 1934), 53–54, 81–82; Abraham Cahan, *Bleter fun mayn leben*, vol. 2: *Mayne ershte akht yor in Amerike* (New York: Forward Association, 1926), 314–15; Michels, *A Fire in their Hearts*, 4–5, 41–49, 110–13; Daniel Soyer, *Jewish Immigrant Associations and American Identity in New York, 1880–1939* (Cambridge, MA: Harvard University Press, 1997), 72–73.

made almost every New Yorker familiar with a long list of Yiddish words," idioms, and grammatical structures.[39]

And yet, despite all of this cultural creativity, in 1925, Mordecai Soltes, an educator and historian of the Yiddish press, predicted the imminent decline of New York's role as a major center of Yiddish culture. As potential consumers of Yiddish culture grew increasingly comfortable with English, he argued, "the present tendencies, if maintained, point to the gradual decline" of Yiddish institutions in the United States.[40] Indeed, even producers of Yiddish culture had made similar predictions since the advent of American Yiddish theater and newspapers in the late nineteenth century, assuming their institutions would be short-lived, transitional phenomena.[41] But the imposition of immigration quotas in 1924 that severely restricted new immigration from Eastern Europe—squelching the influx of potential consumers and producers of Yiddish culture—created an even more dire situation for Yiddish culture in New York.

By 1950, however, Soltes felt compelled to revise his predictions about the future of American Yiddish culture. In some ways, his predictions had been borne out. Beginning in the 1930s, and increasingly in the next decades, many Yiddish cultural institutions saw drastic declines in consumption and advertising revenue. Many once-prominent newspapers, for example, folded or combined with former rivals in the face of the combined stressors of immigration restriction and the Great Depression. But in other ways, the story of New York Yiddish culture in the preceding decades had been one of remarkable resilience. Many consumers continued to subscribe to Yiddish newspapers, attend Yiddish theatrical productions, or listen to Yiddish radio, even after transitioning to living their lives primarily in English. And these institutions continued to exert a strong influence in Jewish communal life.[42]

Soltes's description of Yiddish culture after 1925—fusing decline, resilience, and creative adaptation—is an apt window into New York's Yiddish culture after its heyday, and foreshadowed the history of Yiddish culture after World War II as well. In many ways, this period saw a decline in the centrality of Yiddish in New York culture. But in others, New York took

---

39 Mencken, *American Language*, 216–18.
40 Soltes, *The Yiddish Press*, 174.
41 Michels, *A Fire in their Hearts*, 22–23; Mordecai Soltes, *The Yiddish Press*, preface to reprint ed. (New York: Teachers College, Columbia University, 1950), xii.
42 Soltes, *The Yiddish Press*, preface to reprint ed., xii–xiv.

on new importance in the preservation and continuance of Yiddish, as the Holocaust, Soviet repression, and Hebraization in Israel decimated other centers of Yiddish culture.

In 1940, for example, New York became the new home of YIVO (the Yidisher visnshaflekher institut, or Yiddish Scientific Institute). Originally founded in Vilna in 1925, YIVO was the leading center of scholarship on Eastern European Jewish history and culture. Among YIVO's priorities were documenting folklore practices throughout Jewish Eastern Europe and its diaspora, as well as cultivating the academic study of the Yiddish language. In pursuit of these aims, YIVO set up satellite offices through-out the world, including New York. With the outbreak of World War II, the New York branch was transformed into the center of YIVO's activity. YIVO-affiliated scholars found ways to smuggle documents out of Europe to the United States to preserve for posterity. And several key figures associ-ated with YIVO, including Max Weinreich and Jacob Leshtschinsky, man-aged to escape Europe and resettle in New York.[43]

In its New York headquarters, YIVO continued to promote the study of Jewish history and Yiddish culture. In a time before Jewish Studies was a common discipline on college campuses, YIVO-affiliated scholars pio-neered the academic study of the Holocaust; sponsored the publication of reference works, journals, and books; and organized a 1942 autobiography contest cataloging the experiences of immigrants to America.[44] YIVO also became a major center of Yiddish-language instruction and Jewish public programming, and housed unparalleled archival and library collections on Jewish history and culture. In this way, New York became the major center of the academic study of Yiddish in the postwar period.

Moreover, while New York's Yiddish newspapers, and Yiddish writing in general, saw a decline in its audience in the postwar period, some writers continued to produce new, innovative Yiddish poetry and prose. As was true of the heyday of New York's Yiddish cultural institutions, many authors still looked to Yiddish newspapers, magazines, and journals as major areas of publication for their work. But the particular challenges faced by Jewish

43   Cecile E. Kuznitz, *YIVO and the Making of Modern Jewish Culture: Scholarship for the Yiddish Nation* (New York: Cambridge University Press, 2014); Kalman Weiser, "Coming to America: Max Weinreich and the Emergence of YIVO's American Center," in *Choosing Yiddish: New Frontiers of Language and Culture,* ed. Hannah S. Pressman et al. (Detroit: Wayne State University Press, 2013), 233–52.

44   Jocelyn Cohen and Daniel Soyer, eds., *My Future Is in America: Autobiographies of Eastern European Jewish Immigrants* (New York: New York University Press, 2005).

communities worldwide, and the Yiddish language, in the postwar period, also led these authors to shift their previous artistic priorities. Some, like playwright and novelist Sholem Asch, poet and essayist Jacob Glatstein, and future Nobel laureate novelist Isaac Bashevis Singer, drew on the particular challenges of the Holocaust and its aftermath as inspiration for their work, or ruminated in their work on the challenges of writing in a language with a dwindling audience. Increasingly, several of these authors also relied on translation into other languages, especially English, in order to reach a broader audience. This often meant producing two simultaneous, yet divergent, versions of the same work in Yiddish and English—meant to speak to audiences with different relationships to Yiddish and Jewish culture.[45]

The postwar period also saw the creation of various projects and institutions aimed at preserving historical Yiddish culture as well as ensuring Yiddish's future in America. While the National Yiddish Book Center was purposely founded in 1980 outside of New York, other Yiddishist groups, including YIVO, the Workmen's Circle, Yugntruf, and others, were based in New York, creating Yiddish immersion programs, teachers' seminars, summer camps, youth movements, klezmer festivals, and summer retreats—all aimed at creating environments for Yiddish speakers to interact with each other in Yiddish, or at nurturing future generations of Yiddish speakers in the United States and abroad.[46] This period also saw the rise of Yiddish courses on college campuses throughout the country. Unlike prewar efforts, which aimed to foster literature, culture, and a more serious, scholarly engagement with a vernacular language spoken by millions, these programs often meant to introduce new speakers to the language.[47]

---

45 Saul Zaritt, "'The World Awaits Your Yiddish Word': Jacob Glatstein and the Problem of World Literature," *Studies in American Jewish Literature* 34, no. 2 (2015): 175–203; Monika Adamczyk-Garbowska, "Isaac Bashevis Singer's Works in English and Yiddish: The Language and the Addressee," *Prooftexts* 17, no. 3 (1997): 267–77; Leah Garrett, "Cynthia Ozick's 'Envy': A Reconsideration," *Studies in American Jewish Literature* 24 (2005): 60–81; Kathryn Hellerstein, "The Envy of Yiddish: Cynthia Ozick as Translator," *Studies in American Jewish Literature* 31, no. 11 (2012): 24–47.

46 Aaron Lansky, *Outwitting History: The Amazing Adventures of a Man Who Rescued a Million Yiddish Books* (Chapel Hill: Algonquin Books, 2004).

47 Jennifer Young, "Down with the 'Revival': Yiddish is a Living Language," *YIVO Institute for Jewish Research*, September 12, 2014, https://yivo.org/down-with-the-revival-yiddish-is-a-living-language, accessed June 28, 2020; Sandra F. Fox, "'Laboratories of Yiddishkayt': Postwar American Jewish Summer Camps and the Transformation of Yiddishism," *American Jewish History* 103, no. 3 (2019): 279–301.

In addition to postwar efforts to maintain Yiddish as a literary and spoken language, the second half of the twentieth century saw the proliferation of a form of engagement with Yiddish language and culture that scholar Jeffrey Shandler has designated "postvernacularism."[48] Postvernacularism refers to the cultural roles that Yiddish has continued to play even for those who no longer speak the language in their everyday life. For some, postvernacular engagement with Yiddish represents a way to connect to a history of radical Jewish activism.[49] For others, it represents a nostalgia for the Jewish past, real or imagined. By engaging with Yiddish literature in translation, by continuing to translate world literature into Yiddish, or by performing klezmer music or Yiddish plays for audiences who do not necessarily speak the language, the producers and consumers of postvernacular Yiddish culture continue to infuse the language with symbolic value and meaning. Yiddish words and phrases continue to appear in English-language popular culture, including television shows, writing, and material culture such as board games and T-shirts. These projects and practices represent a very different form of engagement with Yiddish than many New York Jews practiced before World War II, when Yiddish was the language in which they listened to radio, spoke to their families, read their newspapers, and bought their groceries. But they also suggest that the history of New York Yiddish culture in the postwar period was not only one of decline, but one of creative adaptation as well.[50]

Moreover, there were still pockets of New York in which Yiddish *was* an every-day language. Some 86,356 city residents spoke Yiddish at home in the second decade of the twenty-first century, according to the US census bureau, almost all of them in Brooklyn. Indeed, a majority of American Yiddish speakers lived in that borough. In largely Hasidic neighborhoods such as Williamsburg, Borough Park, and Crown Heights, it was not unusual to hear Yiddish spoken on the street and in businesses, by adults and children alike. Store signs, communal notices, and product labels all featured Yiddish. The number of weekly Yiddish newspapers and glossy magazines actually grew at the turn of the century, packed with advertisements and rich reading material, even as the older secular Yiddish press all but disappeared. A new Yiddish children's and adult literature arose,

---

48   Jeffrey Shandler, *Adventures in Yiddishland: Postvernacular Language and Culture* (Berkeley: University of California Press, 2006).

49   Fox, "'Laboratories of Yiddishkayt,'" 300.

50   Shandler, *Adventures in Yiddishland.*

alongside a vibrant popular music scene. This is not to say, however, that use of the language was completely unselfconscious or "natural." Rather, Hasidic communities—especially the Satmar sect—made a conscious commitment to the perpetuation of Yiddish as a spoken language and language of instruction in their schools. Yiddish was valorized as a link to the European Jewish communities of the past, where life was presumed to be more pious, even as it served to differentiate Hasidim not only from gentiles, but also from less-observant Jews. Not simply entertainment, all genres of Yiddish cultural production aimed to reinforce the community's religious values.[51]

At the same time, language use differed among Hasidic communities and, most interestingly, by gender. Both boys and girls spoke Yiddish at home, and both received schooling in Yiddish. But beginning at around age five, girls and women began to speak English among themselves, while boys and men continued to speak Yiddish. Partly, this reflected a degree of ambivalence about Yiddish among girls and women: English was seen as more modern and "with it." Moreover, while traditional study, in which Hebrew and Aramaic texts were parsed in Yiddish, reinforced boys' and men's Yiddish fluency, women's task of mediating between their families and the outside world mandated greater familiarity with English.[52]

Yiddish also continued to influence New York English, especially among Jews. Indeed, though few non-"ultra-Orthodox" Jews could speak Yiddish, many integrated Yiddish words, and sometimes syntax, into their English in order to emphasize either a sense of strong religiosity or, paradoxically, of a strong secular ethnic identity. In fact, younger people in the early twenty-first century may have used Yiddish in these ways more than did their parents. But the strongest influence of Yiddish on New York English was felt among the English-speaking ultra-Orthodox—both

---

51 On the numbers, see "Language Spoken at Home by Ability to Speak English for the Population 5 Years and Over," 2007–2011 American Community Survey 5-Year Estimates, https://factfinder.census.gov/faces/tableservices/jsf/pages/productview.xhtml?src=bkmk; "Top Languages Spoken at Home by Ability, NYC and Boros 2015 5yr," https://www1.nyc.gov/assets/planning/download/pdf/data-maps/nyc-population/acs/top_lang_2015pums5yr_nyc.pdf. See also Ayala Fader, *Mitzvah Girls: Bringing Up the Next Generation of Hasidic Jews in Brooklyn* (Princeton: Princeton University Press, 2007), especially chaps. 4 and 5; Rose Waldman, "Seizing the Means of Cultural Production: Hasidic Representation in Contemporary Yiddish Media," In geveb (April 2018), https://ingeveb.org/blog/seizing-the-means-of-cultural-production-hasidic-representation-in-contemporary-yiddish-media, accessed March 15, 2020.

52 Fader, *Mitzvah Girls*, chaps. 4 and 5.

Hasidic and "yeshivish." Both groups spoke variants of English that drew much vocabulary from Hebrew and Aramaic, as well as Yiddish, and were heavily influenced by Yiddish grammar and syntax, as well as intonation.[53]

In the twenty-first century, Yiddish was thus no longer the most widely spoken "foreign" language in New York, but it is far from gone—its presence still felt on the streets, in print, on the stage, and in institutions old and new.

---

53 Sarah Bunem Benor, "Echoes of Yiddish in the speech of Twenty-First-Century American Jews," in Pressman et al., *Choosing Yiddish*, 319–37; Benor, *Becoming* Frum: *How Newcomers Learn the Language and Culture of Orthodox Judaism* (New Brunswick: Rutgers University Press, 2012), especially 84–104.

For Further Reading

Adamczyk-Garbowska, Monika. "Isaac Bashevis Singer's Works in English and Yiddish: The Language and the Addressee." *Prooftexts* 17, no. 3 (1997): 267–77.

Barth, Gunther. *City People: The Rise of Modern City Culture in Nineteenth-Century America.* New York: Oxford University Press, 1982.

Benor, Sarah Bunin. *Becoming Frum: How Newcomers Learn the Language and Culture of Orthodox Judaism.* New Brunswick: Rutgers University Press, 2012.

——— (as Bunem Benor, Sarah). "Echoes of Yiddish in the speech of Twenty-First-Century American Jews." In *Choosing Yiddish: New Frontiers of Language and Culture,* edited by Hannah S. Pressman et al., 319–37. Detroit: Wayne State University Press, 2013.

Cammy, Justin. "Judging *The Judgment of Shomer*: Jewish Literature versus Jewish Reading." In *Arguing the Modern Jewish Canon,* edited by Justin Cammy et al., 85–127. Cambridge, MA: Harvard University Press, 2008.

Chaikin, Joseph. *Yidishe bleter in Amerike: a tsushtayer tsu der 75 yoriker geshikhte fun der yidisher prese in di Fareynikte Shtatn un Kanade.* New York: M. S. Shklarshy[, 1946].

Cohen, Hagit. *Nifla'ot ba-'olam he-hadash: sefarim ve-kor'im be-yidish be-Artsot ha-Berit, 1890–1940.* Ra'ananah: Open University Press, 2016.

Cohen, Jocelyn, and Daniel Soyer, eds. *My Future Is in America: Autobiographies of Eastern European Jewish Immigrants.* New York: New York University Press, 2005.

Dolber, Brian. *Media and Culture in the U.S. Jewish Labor Movement: Sweating For Democracy in the Interwar Era.* New York: Palgrave Macmillan, 2017.

Doroshkin, Milton. *Yiddish in America: Social and Cultural Foundations.* Rutherford, NJ: Fairleigh Dickinson University Press, 1970.

Fader, Ayala. *Mitzvah Girls: Bringing Up the Next Generation of Hasidic Jews in Brooklyn.* Princeton: Princeton University Press, 2007.

Fox, Sandra F. "'Laboratories of Yiddishkayt': Postwar American Jewish Summer Camps and the Transformation of Yiddishism." *American Jewish History* 103, no. 3 (2019): 279–301.

Garrett, Leah. "Cynthia Ozick's 'Envy': A Reconsideration." *Studies in American Jewish Literature* 24 (2005): 60–81.

Goldstein, Eric L. "A Taste of Freedom: American Yiddish Publications in Imperial Russia." In *Transnational Traditions: New Perspectives on American Jewish History*, edited by Ava F. Kahn and Adam Mendelsohn, 105–39. Detroit: Wayne State University Press, 2014.

Goren, Arthur A. *The Politics and Public Culture of American Jews.* Bloomington: Indiana University Press, 1999.

Guarneri, Julia. *Newsprint Metropolis: City Papers and the Making of Modern Americans.* Chicago: University of Chicago Press, 2017.

Haenni, Sabine. *The Immigrant Scene: Ethnic Amusements in New York: 1880–1920.* Minneapolis: University of Minnesota Press, 2008.

Halpern, Stefanie. "Yiddish Drama on the Broadway Stage." *Digital Yiddish Theater Project,* https://web.uwm.edu/yiddish-stage/yiddish-drama-on-the-broadway-stage. Accessed June 27, 2020.

Harshav, Benjamin, and Barbara Harshav. *American Yiddish Poetry: A Bilingual Anthology.* Berkeley: University of California Press, 1986.

Hellerstein, Kathryn. "Introduction." In *Arguing with the Storm: Stories by Yiddish Women Writers*, edited by Rhea Tregebov, xiv–xxvi. New York: City University of New York Press, 2007.

Hellerstein, Kathryn. "The Envy of Yiddish: Cynthia Ozick as Translator." *Studies in American Jewish Literature* 31, no. 11 (2012): 24–47.

Hertzberg, Arthur. *The Jews in America: Four Centuries of an Uneasy Encounter: A History.* New York: Columbia University Press, 1997.

Howe, Irving. *World of Our Fathers.* New York: Harcourt Brace Jovanovich, 1976.

Howe, Irving, Ruth Wisse, and Khone Shmeruk. *The Penguin Book of Modern Yiddish Verse.* New York: Viking, 1987.

Katz, Dovid. "Introduction: The Days of Proletpen in American Yiddish Poetry." In *Proletpen: America's Rebel Yiddish Poets*, edited by Amelia Glaser, 3–24. Madison: University of Wisconsin Press, 2005.

Kellman, Ellen. "The Newspaper Novel in the Jewish Daily Forward, 1900-1940: Fiction as Entertainment and Serious Literature." PhD diss., Columbia University, 2000.

Kelman, Ari Y. *Station Identification: A Cultural History of Yiddish Radio in the United States.* Berkeley: University of California Press, 2009.

Klepfisz, Irena. "Queens of Contradiction: A Feminist Introduction to Yiddish Women Writers." In *Found Treasures: Stories by Yiddish Women Writers*, edited by Frieda Forman et al., 21–62. Toronto: Second Story Press, 1994.

Kuznitz, Cecile. *YIVO and the Making of Modern Jewish Culture: Scholarship for the Yiddish Nation.* New York: Cambridge University Press, 2014.

Lansky, Aaron. *Outwitting History: The Amazing Adventures of a Man Who Rescued a Million Yiddish Books.* Chapel Hill: Algonquin Books, 2004.

Lifshits, Y. "Di Nyu Yorker yidishe folkstsaytung." In *Pinkes far der forshung fun der yiddisher literatur un prese,* vol. 3. New York: Alveltlekher yidisher kultur-kongres, 1975.

Malakhi, A. R. "Der baginen fun der yidisher prese." In *Pinkes far der forshung fun der yidisher literatur un prese,* vol. 2. New York: Alveltlekher yidisher kultur-kongres, 1972.

Michels, Tony. *A Fire in their Hearts: Yiddish Socialists in New York.* Cambridge, MA: Harvard University Press, 2005.

Nadel, Stanley. *Little Germany: Ethnicity, Religion, and Class in New York City, 1845–1880.* Urbana: University of Illinois Press, 1990.

Nahshon, Edna, ed. *New York's Yiddish Theater: From the Bowery to Broadway.* New York: Columbia University Press, 2016.

Norich, Anita. *The Homeless Imagination in the Fiction of Israel Joshua Singer.* Bloomington: Indiana University Press, 1991.

———. "Translating and Teaching Yiddish Prose by Women." *In geveb* (April 2020). https://ingeveb.org/blog/translating-and-teaching-yiddish-prose-by-women.

Pinsker, Shachar M. *A Rich Brew: How Cafes Created Modern Jewish Culture.* New York: New York University Press, 2018.

Polyan, Alexandra. "Reflections of Revolutionary Movements in American Yiddish Poetry: The Case of Proletpen." In *Jewish Thought, Utopia and Revolution,* edited by Elena Namli, Jayne Svenungsson, and Alana Vincent, 145–160. Amsterdam: Rodopi, 2014.

Quint, Alyssa. *The Rise of Modern Yiddish Theater.* Bloomington: Indiana University Press, 2019.

Rischin, Moses. *The Promised City: New York's Jews, 1870–1914.* Cambridge, MA: Harvard University Press, 1977. Original edition, 1962.

Sandrow, Nahma. *Vagabond Stars: A World History of Yiddish Theater.* Syracuse: Syracuse University Press, 1996.

———. "Yiddish Theater in the United States." In *Jewish Women: A Comprehensive Historical Encyclopedia,* Jewish Women's Archive. https://jwa.org/encyclopedia/article/yiddish-theater-in-united-states.

Schappes, Morris. *A Documentary History of the Jews in the United States, 1654–1875.* New York: Schocken Books, 1950.

Schudson, Michael. *Discovering the News: A Social History of American Newspapers.* New York: Basic Books, 1978.

Shandler, Jeffrey. *Adventures in Yiddishland: Postvernacular Language and Culture.* Berkeley: University of California Press, 2006.

Shtarkman, Moshe. "Vikhtikste momentn in der geshikhte fun der yidisher prese in Amerike." In *Finf un zibetsik yor yidishe prese in Amerike, 1870–1945,* edited by Jacob Glatstein et al. New York: I. L. Peretz shrayber fareyn, 1945.

Soltes, Mordecai. *The Yiddish Press: An Americanizing Agency.* New York: Teachers College, Columbia University, 1925.

Sorin, Gerald. *A Time for Building: The Third Migration, 1880–1920.* Baltimore: Johns Hopkins University Press, 1992.

Soyer, Daniel. *Jewish Immigrant Associations and American Identity in New York, 1880–1939.* Cambridge, MA: Harvard University Press, 1997.

Waldman, Rose. "Seizing the Means of Cultural Production: Hasidic Representation in Contemporary Yiddish Media." In geveb (April 2018). https://ingeveb.org/blog/seizing-the-means-of-cultural-production-hasidic-representation-in-contemporary-yiddish-media.

Warnke, Nina. "Immigrant Popular Culture as Contested Sphere: Yiddish Music Halls, the Yiddish Press, and the Processes of Americanization, 1900–1910." *Theatre Journal* 48 (1996): 321–35.

Weiser, Kalman. "Coming to America: Max Weinreich and the Emergence of YIVO's American Center." In *Choosing Yiddish: New Frontiers of Language and Culture,* edited by Hannah S. Pressman et al., 233–52. Detroit: Wayne State University Press, 2013.

Wisse, Ruth. *A Little Love in Big Manhattan: Two Yiddish Poets.* Cambridge, MA: Harvard University Press, 1988.

Young, Jennifer. "Down with the 'Revival': Yiddish is a Living Language." *YIVO Institute for Jewish Research*, September 12, 2014. https://yivo.org/down-with-the-revival-yiddish-is-a-living-language.

Zaritt, Saul. "'The World Awaits Your Yiddish Word': Jacob Glatstein and the Problem of World Literature." *Studies in American Jewish Literature* 34, no. 2 (2015): 175–203.

Chapter 6

"Impostors": Levantine Jews and the Limits of Jewish New York*

Devin E. Naar

Caricaturing the ways in which Jews who came from the Ottoman Empire did not fit the typical mold of twentieth-century American Jews, one satirist recalled: "How could you be a Jew when you looked like an Italian, spoke Spanish, and never saw a matzoh ball in your life?"[1] As reflected in this quip, Jews from the Ottoman Empire were stereotyped as darker-complected and speaking languages and eating cuisines not readily identifiable as "Jewish" in the American context.[2] Perhaps fifty or sixty

*   Research for this chapter was undertaken with generous support from the University of Washington's Royalty Research Fund and the Isaac Alhadeff Professorship in Sephardic Studies.
1   Quoted in Aviva Ben-Ur, *Sephardic Jews in America: A Diasporic History* (New York: New York University Press, 2009), 108.
2   Ironically, as Susan Glenn notes, Jews in general and Italians were often confused with each other: "'Funny, You Don't Look Jewish': Visual Stereotypes and the Making of Modern Jewish Identity," in *Boundaries of Jewish Identity*, ed. Susan Glenn and Naomi Sokoloff (Seattle: University of Washington Press, 2010), 64–90.

thousand Jews from the Ottoman Empire and successor states arrived in the United States between the end of the nineteenth century and 1924, when the Immigration Restriction Act came into effect.[3] Also designated as "Oriental" or "Levantine" Jews due to their ostensible origin beyond Europe in the Middle East (historically referred to as the "Orient") and the eastern Mediterranean region (known as the Levant), as the descendants of those Sephardic Jews expelled from Spain in 1492, they principally spoke Ladino (also known as Judeo-Spanish, Judezmo, and Djudyo).[4] While in the Ottoman context, their language, surnames, customs, and cuisine had been recognized as unambiguously Jewish, upon their arrival in the United States, it became clear that the categories of "Jew" and "Jewish" were already taken.[5] Levantine Jews constituted a demographic minority, less than five percent of the more than two million principally Yiddish-speaking Jews from Eastern Europe, who arrived between the 1880s and 1924, and whose language, names, culture, cuisine, religious practices, experiences, and memories have stood in for all American Jews.[6]

It may be tempting to explain the invisibility of Levantine Jews within broader historical narratives of American and New York Jews as a logical consequence of macrolevel demographics. But to do so would be to misunderstand the extent to which specific neighborhoods remembered today as quintessentially "Jewish" a century ago—most famously the Lower East

---

3   Ben-Ur, *Sephardic Jews in America*, 193–96.
4   A smaller segment of so-called Oriental or Levantine Jews, from Syria, spoke Arabic as their principal language, whereas another group from Janina, in central Greece, spoke Greek. The term "Levantine Jews" will be used throughout because it roots the population under consideration in the geography of the eastern Mediterranean and distinguishes them from the other Sephardic Jews in the United States, those Spanish and Portuguese Jews established in the Americas since colonial times who are not the focus of the present study. Often pejorative like the term "Oriental," "Levantine" referred to the purportedly half-Europeanized, half-Oriental Mediterranean world that became an object of scorn during an era of ascendant nationalism in the twentieth century. Esther Benbassa and Aron Rodrigue, *Sephardi Jewry: A History of the Judeo-Spanish Community, 14th–20th Centuries* (Berkeley: University of California Press, 2000), xvii.
5   Judezmo and Djudyo refer to the "Jewish" character of Ladino just as Yiddish means "Jewish" in Yiddish. David Bunis, "Native Designations of Judezmo as a 'Jewish Language,'" in *Studies in Language, Literature and History Presented to Joseph Chetrit*, ed. Yosef Tobi and Dennis Kurzon (Jerusalem: Carmel, 2011), 41–81.
6   In his classic study, Irving Howe set the template for the demographic argument: "Among the Jews settling in America, the East Europeans were by far the largest component and the most influential. To tell their story is, to a considerable extant, to tell the story of twentieth-century American Jews. . . . The Sephardic Jews as a group hardly figure at all." See his *World of Our Fathers* (New York: Harcourt Brace Jovanovich, 1976), xix.

Side—were at the time considered "Jewish" due to the imprint not only of Yiddish—but also of Ladino-speaking Jews.[7] Such was the assessment of the Lower East Side superintendent of the New York Public Libraries at the end of World War I. In a pamphlet with a revealing title, *Exploring a Neighborhood: Our Jewish People from Eastern Europe and the Orient*, the libraries' superintendent highlighted the principal constituents in her jurisdiction, the forty square blocks around Rivington Street: "66,000 people, chiefly new-come Russian and Oriental Jews."[8] She then described both communities in considerable detail and their imprints on the neighborhood while acknowledging the vast divides that separated them despite living side by side: "But for the saving consciousness of the bond of blood and faith, you will discover differences as broad and deep as any to be found in our common humanity."[9]

The contemporary elision of Levantine (or "Oriental") Jews from the dominant narratives of Jewish New York and the Jewish Lower East Side therefore has less to do with demographics than with the conceptual, methodological, and political challenges that the inclusion of Levantine Jews would pose to those dominant narratives, which until now have rendered the Eastern European Yiddish-speaking Jewish experience *the* American Jewish experience par excellence. That alleged "bond of blood and faith" that outsiders like the libraries' superintendent saw as linking Yiddish- and Ladino-speaking Jews a century ago on the Lower East Side has been powerless in the face of the persistence of the narrative of American Jewish exceptionalism, which claims that, unlike elsewhere, Jews have been uniquely welcomed in the United States where they prosper, contribute to society, and synthesize their Jewishness and their Americanness. No place is held up as evidence of such an exceptional dynamic than New York City and no neighborhood more than the Lower East Side.

While indeed a "city of promise" for hundreds of thousands of Jews and a place where they found security, indeed prosperity, New York did not become a city where, as one prominent scholar recently phrased it, "all Jews could flourish and express themselves." The notions that "New York Jews understood that there were many ways to be Jewish" and that "the city

---

7   See Hasia Diner, *Lower East Side Memories: A Jewish Place in America* (Princeton: Princeton University Press, 2000), 41.

8   Mary Frank, *Exploring a Neighborhood: Our Jewish People from Eastern Europe and the Orient* (New York: Immigrant Publication Society, 1919), 1.

9   Frank, *Exploring a Neighborhood*, 10.

welcomed Jews in all their variety" need to be reconsidered.[10] As evidenced by the experiences of Levantine Jews in New York during the early twentieth century and their general invisibility in historical narratives about Jewish New York still today, there was and remains a limit to the variety of ways in which Jews could express their identity and be unquestionably accepted by other Jews in New York. While many Jews from the Ottoman Empire came to identify strongly with New York as a place to which they felt a deep connection and sense of belonging, they did not necessarily feel that same embrace on the part of New York's Jews. Rather, central to the experience of Levantine Jews in twentieth-century New York was often painful alienation, marginalization, and exclusion—from mainstream Ashkenazi Jews and their institutions. Acknowledging the Levantine Jewish experience compels us to grapple with the inconvenient truth of intra-Jewish prejudice often expressed in racist terms in New York, the limits of the whiteness among American Jews, and the mythology of American Jewish triumphalism.

Already in 1921, the dynamic of intra-Jewish prejudice was apparent to two prominent sociologists, who reported that Levantine Jews in New York were denigrated by European Jews as "dagoes" (a racially coded derogatory term generally reserved for Italians) and "feel more discrimination from the other wings of the Jews than they do from the non-Jews."[11] In response to this sense of rejection, Jews from the Ottoman Empire—especially men, who were the first to arrive in the United States—went to great lengths in order to "prove" that they were indeed Jews to their new Eastern European Jewish neighbors in New York City—people who, as fellow Jews, they anticipated would be most likely to extend a welcoming hand. They did so by displaying their *taletóth* (prayer shawls) and *tefilín* (phylacteries), reading aloud from Hebrew prayer books (albeit in a "different" or "strange" accent), showing the Hebrew fonts of their Ladino newspapers, or even revealing their circumcisions.[12] These often humiliating efforts were not always successful: an Ottoman Jewish lawyer recalled that a prospective Yiddish-speaking landlord on the Lower East Side assumed that someone with his surname, Amateau, who could not speak Yiddish, could not be Jewish, and forced him to disrobe. Even after seeing that Amateau was

---

10 Deborah Dash Moore, "Forward," in *City of Promises: A History of the Jews of New York*, ed. Deborah Dash Moore (New York: New York University Press, 2012), xi.

11 Robert E. Park and Herbert A. Miller, *Old World Traits Transplanted* (New York: Harper & Brothers, 1921), 200.

12 Ben-Ur, *Sephardic Jews in America*, 108-149.

circumcised, the landlord concluded that he must be Muslim and refused to rent him an apartment.[13] These kinds of interactions not only reveal a latent Islamophobia among Yiddish-speaking Jews but also contributed to a deep sense of alienation on the part of Levantine Jews in the United States—a sense that they were not welcome in mainstream American Jewish life. These kinds of interactions should not be interpreted as mere personal slights but rather as manifestations of structural dynamics inherent in the formation of Jewish communal life under the pressures imposed by the dominance of whiteness and Eurocentrism in the United States.

In oral histories, memoirs, and communal publications, Ottoman-born Jews and their descendants became preoccupied with the deep sense of rejection they experienced from other Jews. New York-born writer Miriam Israel Moses recalled the traumatizing effects of the denial of her Ottoman-born grandparents' Jewish identity by other Jews in New York, where "all Jews were the same Jews":

> And some of the Ashkenazi Jews did not believe that the Sephardic Jews were real Jews because they did not speak Yiddish and all real Jews that they believed were real Jews spoke Yiddish. So some of the Ashkenazi Jews accused the Sephardic Jews of being impostor Jews, for it may certainly be assumed that many people aspire to successfully impersonate Jews.[14]

Moses emphasized the pain experienced by her grandparents when accused of being "impostor Jews." In response to the denial of their Jewish identity, Moses's grandparents returned to their native Salonica along with their American daughter, born in 1920 on the Lower East Side on the corner of Broome and Allen Streets. According to Moses, her grandparents reasoned that in Greece, at least they would be "treated like real Jews." Indeed, they were—in the most devastating way. In 1943, during the German occupation of Greece, they were deported to Auschwitz and murdered, with the exception of the daughter, who later returned to New York and became Moses's mother. Not only does Moses's family story counter the lingering myth that Jewish migrants never returned (anecdotal evidence further suggests

---

13 "One Century in the Life of Albert J. Amateau, 1889–: The Americanization of a Sephardic Turk," interview by Rachel Amado Bortnick (Berkeley, CA, 1989), 54–55; Ben-Ur, *Sephardic Jews in America*, 115.

14 Miriam Israel Moses, "Survivors and Pieces of Glass," in *Jewish American Literature: A Norton Anthology*, ed. Hilene Flanzbaum et al. (New York: W. W. Norton, 2011), 1111–20.

that Levantine Jews returned at much higher rates than Eastern European Jews); it also reveals that Moses conceptualized her grandparents' decision to return not due to economic woes, antisemitism, homesickness, or other factors, but rather the lack of recognition of their status as Jews by fellow Jews—a dynamic that spurred a decision with horrifying consequences.

Grappling with the initial and powerful sense of rejection, Levantine Jews did not succumb to a sense of victimhood but rather actively developed their own institutions and sense of community that occasionally intersected with but generally remained separate from mainstream American Jewish life until World War II. The recovery of the Levantine Jewish experience reveals the ways in which Jews of all varieties are implicated, indeed complicit, in the racial hierarchies that serve as a foundation of American society and, by extension, of the American Jewish experience.[15] The qualitative distinctiveness of the story of Levantine Jews therefore compels us to think critically about the assumptions that underpin the accepted narrative of Jewish New York and invite us to rewrite that narrative, to expand its boundaries, and to embrace its margins.

Becoming "Jewry's Stepchildren"

There was nothing unusual about representatives of an already established group of immigrants looking down on new arrivals in the United States. Expressing xenophobia, especially in racist terms, became a mechanism for longer-established immigrants to prove their patriotic bona fides. Maligned in the nineteenth century, Irish became some of the most ardent advocates for Asian exclusion. Peninsular Italians invoked racialized language and epithets to denigrate Sicilians as "black dagoes."[16] Within the Jewish context, tensions between various groups also developed. The small contingent of Spanish and Portuguese Jews established since colonial times looked down on German Jews who arrived in the mid-nineteenth century, and together they looked down on the Eastern European Jewish masses arriving toward the end of the nineteenth century into the twentieth.[17] But in

15 See Eric Goldstein, *The Price of Whiteness: Jews, Race, and American Identity* (Princeton: Princeton University Press, 2008).
16 Stefano Luconi, "Black Dagoes? Italian Immigrants' Racial Status in the United States: an Ecological View," *Journal of Transatlantic Studies* 14, no. 2 (2016): 188–99; Donna Gabaccia, *Italy's Many Diasporas* (Seattle: University of Washington Press, 2000).
17 Jack Wertheimer, "The German-Jewish Experience: Toward a Useable Past," in *German-Jewish Legacy in America, 1938–1988*, ed. Abraham Peck (Detroit: Wayne

these interactions, the basic Jewishness of either group was never called into question. Such denial only impacted Jews from the Ottoman Empire.[18]

Structurally embedded racial hierarchies set the dynamics that characterized the encounter between migrant groups, including Jews. In the United States, race functioned as much more than a description of skin color, but also a cipher for social class, economic status, moral standing, and suitability for absorption into white American society that were shaped by perceptions about geographic origin, language, and religion.[19] Those positioned as more European, more Western, closer to Protestant Christianity, and thus more "civilized" and more "white," could more benefit from the fantasy of the American Dream. Access to American citizenship was only available to immigrants legally recognized by the state as racially white or "of African descent" (from 1870 to 1952). Due to the persistent social stigma, legal discrimination, and violence experienced by Blacks, those who did not readily fit into either racial category—people of mixed-race descent, Native Americans, Chinese, Japanese, Asian Indians, Armenians, Syrians and others—exerted considerable effort to prove their whiteness in order to gain the right to become naturalized; most did not succeed as evidenced by a series of landmark court decisions.[20]

Although characterized as a "racial conundrum,"[21] European Jews were not barred from citizenship during this period, but rather sought to protect the right to naturalize. When the case of a (Christian) Syrian from the Ottoman Empire came before the court in 1909, Jewish leaders panicked: if Syrians were ruled not-white and thus ineligible for naturalization, would Jews—also perceived at the time to be racially "Semitic"—lose the right to

---

State University, 1988), 233–38, esp. 236; Steven Aschheim, *Brothers and Strangers: The East European Jew in German and German Jewish Consciousness, 1800–1923* (Madison: University of Wisconsin Press, 1982); Paula Hyman, *From Dreyfus to Vichy: The Remaking of French Jewry, 1906–1939* (New York: Columbia University Press, 1979).

18 Aviva Ben-Ur, "Funny, You Don't Look Jewish!: 'Passing' and the Elasticity of Ethnic Identity among Levantine Sephardic Immigrants in Early Twentieth-Century America," *Kolor: Journal on Moving Communities* 2 (2002): 9–18, esp. 11.

19 Cf. Matthew Frye Jacobson's observation: "Race is not just a conception; it is also a perception," in his *Whiteness of a Different Color: European Immigrants and the Alchemy of Race* (Cambridge, MA: Harvard University Press, 1998), 9. For an overview of race and migration, see Mae Ngai, *Impossible Subjects: Illegal Aliens and the Making of Modern America* (Princeton: Princeton University Press, 2014).

20 Ian Haney López, *White By Law: The Legal Construction of Race* (New York: New York University Press, 2006); John Tehranian, *Whitewashed: America's Invisible Middle Eastern Minority* (New York: New York University Press, 2009).

21 Goldstein, *The Price of Whiteness*, 1.

become citizens? Levantine or "Asiatic" Jews seemed to offer a detrimental link between the European Jew and the Syrian in this racial imagination: the lower court judge who ruled Syrian Christians ineligible to naturalize also explicitly stated that he would similarly deny naturalization petitions from Syrian Jews.[22] Indeed, some Ottoman Jews' petitions in other cities, such as Seattle, seem to have been denied on the grounds that they were not "white." In response to such a threat in New York, those who could position themselves higher in the racial hierarchy sought to protect their position and looked down upon those perceived to be lower in the order, especially those who, by association, might negatively impact their own position.

The desire of longer-established Jews to protect their status shaped their reactions to the new arrivals from the eastern Mediterranean. The rabbi of Shearith Israel, the historic Spanish and Portuguese congregation founded in New York during the colonial period, initially argued that the newcomers ought to be identified as "Oriental" or, more precisely, "Levantine" rather than "Sephardic" even if they were descendants of those expelled from Spain in 1492. He sought to preserve the designation "Sephardic" for his own Spanish and Portuguese Jewish community of "grandees," the true, Western, upper-class descendants of the Iberian Jews who had always dwelt in the lands of Christendom and had evaded the taint of Islam and the broader Orient.[23] Shared condescension toward the new arrivals even united Spanish and Portuguese Jews as well as Central and Eastern European Jews. As *Harper's Magazine* noted in 1933, the three constituencies "all get together to snoot the Levantine Jews."[24]

As these examples indicate, various groups of Jews internalized and redirected Orientalist and antisemitic attitudes in order to secure a favorable position in the oppressive racial hierarchy—a practice with a deep history stretching back into Europe. In the nineteenth century, European politicians and intellectuals especially in Germany perceived of Jews to be racially "Semitic," "Orientals" with roots in the Middle East—in

---

22   Sarah M. A. Gualtieri, *Between Arab and White: Race and Ethnicity in the Early Syrian American Diaspora* (Berkeley: University of California Press, 2009), 64–68.

23   Devin E. Naar, "'Sephardim Since Birth': Reconfiguring Jewish Identity in America," in *The Sephardi and Mizrahi Jews in America*, ed. Saba Soomekh (West Lafayette, IN.: Purdue University Press, 2016), 75–104, esp. 82–83; Ben-Ur, *Sephardic Jews in America*, 81–107; Joseph M. Papo, *Sephardim in Twentieth-Century America: In Search of Unity* (San Jose: Pelé Yoetz Books, 1987), 51–64.

24   Elmer Davis, "On the Gentility of Gentiles," *Harper's Magazine*, July 1933, 147–55; here 150.

Palestine—and thus foreign to European Christian society in terms of language, culture, geography, religion, and race. Those who sought to exclude Jews from European society, culture, and politics began to call themselves "antisemites," a term coined in 1879 invoked by its proponents as a declaration of their opposition to Jews. Seeking to prove that they belonged in European society, German-Jewish leaders tried to demonstrate that they were really European, capable of assimilation, and thus fit for citizenship as Germans.[25]

In the context of the United States, where whiteness served as a key prerequisite for access to the privileges of citizenship, German and Eastern European Jews, due to their appearance, geographic origin, and cultural orientation, could more readily stake a claim on European and thus white status in part by contrasting themselves with a group that was deemed the real "Orientals" among them—Jews from the Ottoman Empire and the broader Muslim world.[26] A designation of disrepute solidified with the Chinese Exclusion Act in 1882, which barred Asian immigration to the United States, the term "Oriental" literally means "eastern." Used interchangeably to refer to the "despotic," non-Western worlds of the "Near East" and the "Far East," the term "Oriental" was also deployed to describe Jews from the eastern Mediterranean. Designations like "Oriental" emphasized the purportedly non-European, non-Western, non-white, and thereby uncivilized status of those to whom the term referred.[27]

The Balkan Wars (1912–1913), followed by the Great War (1914–1918) and then a war between Greece and Turkey (1919–1922), resulted in the violent dissolution of the Ottoman Empire and the emergence of successor

---

25 James Pasto, "Islam's 'Strange Secret Sharer': Orientalism, Judaism, and the Jewish Question," *Comparative Studies in Society and History* 40 (1998): 437–74; Michael Brenner, *Prophets of the Past: Interpreters of Jewish History* (Princeton: Princeton University Press, 2010), 55–56; John Efron, "Orientalism and the Jewish Historical Gaze," in *Orientalism and the Jews,* ed. Ivan Davidson Kalmar and Derek J. Penslar (Waltham/Hannover: Brandeis University Press/University Press of New England, 2005), 80–93.

26 Daniel Schroeter, "From Sephardi to Oriental: The 'Decline' Theory of Jewish Civilization in the Middle East and North Africa," in *The Jewish Contribution to Civilization: Reassessing an Idea,* ed. Jeremy Cohen and Richard I. Cohen (Oxford: Littman Library of Jewish Civilization, 2008), 125–50; Devin E. Naar, "Fashioning the 'Mother of Israel': The Ottoman Jewish Historical Narrative and the Image of Jewish Salonica," *Jewish History* 28, no. 3-4 (2014): 337–72.

27 Henry Yu, *Thinking Oriental: Migration, Contact, and Exoticism in Modern America* (New York: Oxford University Press, 2001).

nation-states in the Balkans and European colonial regimes in the Middle East that compelled Jews—and others—to flee. Perhaps as many as one third of the Jews in the region departed during this period.[28] Those who fled from the newly solidified nation-states of Greece, Bulgaria, and Serbia did so to escape what they characterized as the crusader mentality of the new Christian leaders who directed their animosity against both Muslims and Jews.[29] Others saw in the rising tide of nationalism echoes of the fifteenth-century Spanish inquisition and viewed the exodus of Jews from former Ottoman lands as the result of a "new expulsion."[30]

Those heading to the United States faced numerous challenges upon their arrival at Ellis Island, which the Ladino press characterized as a "prison" where one prayed for "liberation" as opposed to "deportation."[31] US immigration officials could not readily identify the newcomers' "race" or "nationality," often perceiving them to be Greeks, Turks, Italians, or Syrians rather than Jews, but soon coined the designation: "Turks of the Hebrew Race." In the context of World War I, during which the Ottoman Empire and the United States fought on opposing sides, immigration officials questioned whether the newcomers ought to be excluded as "enemy aliens" or, after 1917, due to their origins in or near the "Asiatic barred zone." Once they could be identified as Jews, various Jewish institutions— motivated by an ambivalent sense of solidarity combined with paternalism and embarrassment—began to discuss how to handle their own "problem" of "Oriental immigration."[32]

At a meeting in 1913 organized by the National Conference of Jewish Charities, for example, Jewish communal leaders emphasized the radical differences between the new arrivals and already-established Jews and referred to the sense of shame felt by the latter when forced to recognize the former as "coreligionists." Maurice Hexter, who later became

28 Devi Mays, "'I Killed Her Because I Loved her Too Much': Gender and Violence in the 20th Century Sephardi Diaspora," *Mashriq & Mahjar* 3 (2014): 4–28, esp. 5.

29 Maír José Benardete, *Hispanic Culture and Character of the Sephardic Jews* (New York: Hispanic Institute in the United States, 1952), 160.

30 Shemuel Saadi Alevi, "La ora del sefardizmo es menester krear un komite de inisiativa," *El luzero sefaradi*, March 1927, 8–11.

31 Devin Naar, "From the 'Jerusalem of the Balkans' to the 'Goldene Medina': Jewish Immigration from Salonika to the United States," *American Jewish History* 93, no. 4 (December 2007): 461; Ben-Ur, *Sephardic Jews in America*, 25.

32 David de Sola Pool, "The Immigration of Levantine Jews into the United States," *Jewish Charities* 4, no. 11 (June 1914): 12–27 and "Discussion," ibid., 27–31.

the executive vice president of the Federation of Jewish Philanthropies in New York, argued that Levantine Jews ought to be treated in a manner completely differently from "our" Jews—already-established "European" Jews. He emphasized "the psychic and psychological difference between the Levantine Jew and our Russian, Austrian and Roumanian coreligionists. So great is the difference that there seems to be little in common. The points of similarity are few."[33] Another participant in the meeting, Joseph Gedalecia, an Ashkenazi-identified Jew whose family had spent time in Istanbul and therefore claimed to speak with authority on the subject, disparagingly insisted: "The Levantine Jew is as human, or almost as human, as any other."[34]

Influenced by ascendant fields of "race science" and eugenics that shaped the development of the social sciences, urban planning, health care, public policy, immigration laws, and other areas in the 1920s, Jewish researchers and philanthropists invoked racialized language to characterize differences between Oriental and European Jews, the former deemed "inferior," "uncivilized," and likely to become a burden on American society and an embarrassment; and the latter "superior," "civilized," and prepared for success. In these comparative discussions, European—predominantly Ashkenazi— Jews presented themselves as well-suited to assimilate into white American society, whereas the capacity—or even desirability—of Levantine Jews to become recognized as white and thus as American remained unresolved. In conjunction with its effort to determine the social welfare needs of Jews in New York, the Bureau of Jewish Social Research commissioned a well-known economic historian and future Columbia University dean, Louis Hacker, to study the conditions impacting the city's Oriental Jews in 1926. He began his report by observing that Ottoman-born Jews are "nearly as alien to their [Ashkenazi] kinsmen as are the negroes to the average white Southerner."[35]

---

33   "Discussion," 27.

34   "Discussion," 30. Gedalecia was a controversial figure who served as a leader of the Federation of Oriental Jews in New York, but was also criticized by peers for not being an authentic voice of the group he purported to represent, especially as he spoke Yiddish and not Ladino. While born in Istanbul of mixed Sephardi-Ashkenazi ancestry, Gedalecia attended a German school, married a Russian-Jewish woman in New York, joined her family's mutual aid society, and generally presented himself and was perceived as Ashkenazi. See Papo, *Sephardim in Twentieth-Century America*, 363–64.

35   Louis M. Hacker, "The Communal Life of the Sephardic Jews in New York City," *The Jewish Social Service Quarterly* 3 (December 1926): 32–40.

Hacker then proceeded to attribute the challenges faced by New York's Levantine Jews to their racial inferiority that he viewed as stemming from the "backward" Oriental and "Mohammedan" atmosphere of their birth that, he feared, they would not be able to "slough off."[36]

In a society shaped by systemic racial oppression, the legal segregation of Blacks and whites in the South, the absence of civil rights for the former, anti-miscegenation laws, and widespread lynching, the comparison of Ashkenazi Jews to whites and Levantine Jews to Blacks sought to emphasize the "alien" nature and immutable racial characteristics of Levantine Jews that rendered them unfit for assimilation into the general Jewish community or white American society.[37] The invocation of such racialized rhetoric by a representative of a mainstream and ostensibly upstanding Jewish communal institution also helps explain why Ottoman-born Jews experienced such a lasting sense of alienation and rejection on the part of other Jews. By likening them to two principal "others" with respect to white American society—the "Negro" within and the "Mohammedan" from afar—representatives of mainstream American Jewish institutions, while seeking to overcome their own status as "other" and to combat antisemitism, relegated Levantine Jews to the margins of American Jewish life.

Although not always framed in such provocative racialized language, tenuous dynamics shaped the relationships between established, Ashkenazi-dominated Jewish institutions and Ottoman-born Jews. The Kehillah, New York's main Jewish communal organization (1908–1922), rebuffed the request of two Ottoman Jewish leaders for support to establish a Ladino newspaper and a communal organization in 1910.[38] Although aiding some Levantine Jews upon their arrival at Ellis Island, the Hebrew Immigrant Aid Society (HIAS) encouraged them to relocate to Cuba not only because their Ladino would be more useful there, but also because their Mediterranean origins imbued them with a "lack of energy" that would impede their success in the "Northern Hemisphere." The Industrial

---

36 See Hacker's full, unpublished report in the Henry Besso Papers, Box 27, File 41, American Sephardi Federation, New York.

37 On Hacker's comparison, see Caroline E. Light, *That Pride of Race and Character: The Roots of Jewish Benevolence in the Jim Crow South* (New York: New York University Press, 2014), 183–86. On the image of Blacks in the Ashkenazi Jewish imagination, see Gil Ribak, *Gentile New York: The Images of Non-Jews among Jewish Immigrants* (New Brunswick: Rutgers University Press, 2012), 127–33.

38 Albert Amateau, "The Sephardic Immigrant from Bulgaria: A Personal Profile of Moise Gadol," *American Jewish Archives* 42, no. 1 (Fall/Winter 1990): 57–70.

Removal Office, an organization established in New York by German Jews to secure lodging and employment for Jewish immigrants, further refused to print its guide in Ladino translation despite requests from the Federation of Oriental Jews to do so (and despite the publication of versions in English, Yiddish, Italian, and Polish).[39] To fill the void, Moise Gadol, the editor of the Ladino weekly, *La Amerika*, independently published a guidebook in Ladino (with an exposé on the American lifestyle, preparatory material for the US citizen exam, and "useful" vocabulary in English and even [highly German-inflected] Yiddish) for "all the Spanish [sic] Jews immigrating or considering immigration here in America."[40]

In terms of social, business, and interpersonal relations, dynamics remained strained but more fluid. As Yiddish- and Ladino-speaking Jews dwelt in the same neighborhoods, they frequented each other's businesses as evidenced by myriad advertisements that appeared in Ladino newspapers for Ashkenazi-owned establishments: dentist office, furniture store, photo studio, merchant of ritual items. Gadol, the editor of *La Amerika*, employed Yiddish-speaking Jews as his first typesetters, adapted cartoons and other content from the Yiddish press, and even encouraged readers to learn Yiddish.[41] Business enterprises also developed across communal lines, such as Yohai and Goldemberg, fish and vegetable merchants.[42] A particular relationship developed between Ottoman and Romanian Jews, not only due to a sense of proximity to the Balkans and the existence of an important Ladino-speaking community in Bucharest, but also due to cuisine: Romanian Jews were the only Ashkenazim for whom eggplant was also a culinary staple, and it was from them that Ottoman Jews purchased their kosher meat.[43]

Setting the limits of rapprochement between Yiddish- and Ladino-speaking Jews, "intermarriage" between them remained uncommon prior to World War II. The Ladino press, for example, reported on an affair

---

39   On the Hebrew Immigrant Aid Society and the Industrial Removal Office, see Ben-Ur, *Sephardic Jews in America*, 117–25.

40   Julie Scolnik, "'Libro de embeźar las linguas ingléśa y yudiš': *La América*'s Guidebook to Learning English and Yiddish and Becoming an American Citizen," *Miscelánea de Estudios Árabes y Hebraicos* 63 (2014): 1–13.

41   Amateau, "The Sephardic Immigrant from Bulgaria."

42   "Yohai i Goldemberg, 160 Allen Street," *La vara*, October 20, 1922, 4.

43   Amateau, "The Sephardic Immigrant from Bulgaria," 59; Isaac Jerusalmi, "The Constitution of the Burial Society of the Bucharest Sephardic Community, April 30, 1850," *Hebrew Union College Annual* 76 (2006): 235–58.

between a Ladino-speaking woman and *un Yiddish* (an Ashkenazi man) in 1922, and advised the woman—and all readers—to refrain from pursuing relationships with *ajenos* ("foreigners," a term applied to Ashkenazim as well as Italians, Irish, Puerto Ricans, and so forth). The newspaper threatened to out the woman and publish her name if she were caught again.[44] This incident reveals both the role that the Ladino press played in social policing and that romance across communal lines was frowned upon at the time. Even once they began to develop, as recalled by Joy Zacharia, the New York-born granddaughter of the chief rabbi of Kastoria (a town in present-day Greece), they were the subject of tension and mockery:

> The *Yiddishim* or *Ziggizooks*[45], as the Ashkenazic Jews are called . . . were commonly referred to as *fediendo* ("rotten"), especially their women. If your son married a *Yiddisha*, he would rue the day! These overbearing women, who not only handled the household accounts, often participated in the family business. They were pushy and domineering. Besides, your grandchildren would never be named for you, since the Ashkenazim only name after the dead. If, on the other hand, your daughter married an Ashkenazic man, this was good. Ashkenazic men were so brow-beaten by their mothers and sisters, that they could feel very compatible with a more docile, homebound Sephardic woman.[46]

Reciprocating the denigration experienced by Jews of Ottoman background, Zacharia drew upon gendered anti-Jewish images ("overbearing" woman and "brow-beaten" man) to illustrate her point.

But underlying the jocular tone is an element of serious critique that reinforced the perceived different natures of the two groups. The son of an "intermarriage" conducted at Shearith Israel, the Spanish and Portuguese synagogue, between an Ashkenazi father and a Sephardi mother from Izmir, art critic Richard Kostelanetz recounted the rumor that, when he was born in 1940, his parents considered sending out a birth announcement that drew upon racialized language—indeed slurs: "Now we present

---

44   "Postadas diversas," *La vara*, December 29, 1922, 8.
45   A term derived from the common Yiddish greeting, *zay gezunt*, meaning "be healthy; be will; farewell." See Sarah Bunin Benor, "Lexical Othering in Judezmo: How Ottoman Sephardim Refer to Non-Jews," in *Languages and Literatures of Sephardic and Oriental Jews*, ed. David M. Bunis (Jerusalem: Misgav Yerushalayim, 2009), 65–85, esp. 82.
46   Joy Zacharia Appelbaum, "Growing up in a Polyglot Sephardic Household," in *From Iberia to Diaspora: Studies in Sephardic History and Culture*, ed. Yedida Kalfon Stillman and Norman Stillman (Leiden: Brill, 1999), 451–57, here 453.

our son Dick, one part kike, some other parts spic."[47] The sentiment behind this rumor intriguingly, indeed derogatorily, fixed the difference between Sephardim and Ashkenazim. His Jewishness ("kike") does not overlap with his Sephardiness, which is racialized as Hispanic: he is "some *other* parts spic." The persistent sense of Levantine Jews as not fully or legitimately Jewish explains why Joseph Papo, a native of Ottoman Palestine who served as president of the Sephardic Jewish Community of New York, continued to lament the second-class status of his community as "Jewry's stepchildren" even after World War II.[48]

From *Turkino* Colony to Sephardic Community and Beyond

The family metaphor that envisioned Ashkenazim and Sephardim as kin—at least partly so, as parent and stepchild—was not always apparent to observers. Whether "Levantine Jews" should be classed among Jews, in general, or as their own discrete group, perplexed analysts of American immigration. During World War I, a commentator cataloging the racial and religious diversity of the United States characterized the arrival of "Levantine Jews" as the "most surprising feature of Jewish immigration."[49] In contrast, describing the "mosaics of little language colonies" and "cultural enclaves" established by immigrants in the United States, an urban sociologist in 1922 identified "Jews" and "Levantine Jews" as two discrete groups, as distinct from each other as either were from Chinese, Italians, or Swabians precisely because language served as the key criterion of differentiation. "Each one of these little communities," the sociologist explained, "is certain to have some sort of co-operative or mutual aid society, very likely a church, a school, possibly a theater, but almost invariably a press."[50] Largely left to their own devices and not integrated into the broader Jewish institutional life in New York, Levantine Jews followed the broader pattern establishing their own institutions that fomented a sense of community, such as mutual aid societies, cafes, and periodicals.

---

47 Richard Kostelanetz, "Sephardic Culture and Me," *European Judaism* 33, no. 1 (Spring 2000): 20–23.

48 Joseph Papo, "The Sephardim: Jewry's Stepchildren," *Chicago Jewish Forum* (Fall 1949): 1–8.

49 Archibald McClure, *Leadership of the New America: Racial and Religious* (New York: George H. Doran Co., 1916), 170.

50 Robert E. Park, *The Immigrant Press and its Control* (New York: Harper & Bros, 1922), 6–7.

While Ottoman-born Jews who arrived in the United States congregated primarily in New York City, they soon established other communities in New Brunswick (NJ), Rochester (NY), Peabody (MA), Atlanta, Montgomery, Cincinnati, Indianapolis, Chicago, Los Angeles, Portland, and Seattle. Despite their distance from the Ottoman Empire, Levantine Jews across the country formed what they referred to as "*Turkino* colonies," settlements linked not only to each other but also to their empire of origin ("Turkey" was a common designation for the entirety of the Ottoman Empire; *Turkinos* refer to "those from Turkey").[51] In New York, where eighty to ninety percent of the Levantine Jews in the United States initially settled, the Lower East Side from Christie to Essex Streets and East Houston to Canal Streets became the "*Turkino* center," the location of the Ladino printing presses and a range of Ottoman Jewish-owned shops and cafes that catered to *Turkino* clientele, who dwelt in the surrounding tenements.[52] From 110th to 125th Streets and from First to Fifth Avenues, Harlem served as the other principal area of Levantine Jewish settlement. By the start of World War I, about two-thirds resided on the Lower East Side and one-third in Harlem, whereas a decade later the numbers began to even out between the two neighborhoods.[53] In the 1930s and 1940s, families began to move from Manhattan to Brooklyn and the Bronx. As Brooklyn was the cite of several early burial plots for Levantine Jewish associations, the Ladino expression, *se fue a Brooklee* ("he went to Brooklyn"), referred euphemistically to someone who passed away, but also captured the sense of distance between the boroughs.[54] The Grand Concourse in the Bronx became a major center of Levantine Jewish life in the immediate post-World War II era—the neighborhood where several well-known American-born personalities imbibed the Ladino of their elders, such as the famed classical pianist Murray Perahia (who received his first lessons from an Auschwitz survivor from his parents' hometown of Salonica); the Emmy-award winning actor Hank Azaria (whose family came from Salonica and Izmir); and

---

51 See Devin E. Naar, "*Turkinos* beyond the Empire: Ottoman Jews in America, 1893–1924," *Jewish Quarterly Review* 105, no. 2 (Spring 2015): 174–205.

52 "Eldridge Street sentro Turkino," *La bos del pueblo*, August 4, 1916, 2.

53 Albert Matarasso to the Sephardic Brotherhood of America, New York, February 23, 1924, Records of the Sephardic Jewish Brotherhood of America, Box 27, File 33, American Sephardi Federation.

54 Hank Halio, *Ladino Reveries: Tales of the Sephardic Experience* (New York: Foundation for the Study of Sephardic Studies and Culture, 1996), 96.

Shelley Morrison (née Rachel Mitrani, with family roots in Edirne), the television actress known for playing Latina and other "ethnic" characters.

The move from neighborhood to neighborhood accompanied the gradual economic advancement of Levantine Jews, especially men, who—even the well-educated among them—initially worked as pushcart peddlers; postcard or flower sellers; janitors; check-room attendants in hotels and restaurants; candy and ice cream vendors in movie theaters; workers in garment factories, tailoring shops, and electrical and phonographic plants; or as bootblacks. Women also worked in textile factories.[55] Very few gained wealth as quickly as Moris Schinasi, who had arrived for the Chicago World's Fair in 1893 and subsequently established a cigarette factory in Harlem that imported tobacco and rolling papers from Greece, Turkey, and Egypt; by 1919, he served as the chairman of New York's Tobacco Trading and Finance Corporation.[56] By the 1920s, a professional class of lawyers, doctors, dentists, and teachers emerged and the most ambitious attended Columbia University or New York University.[57] Education served as one of the main conduits for class mobility and geographic decentralization. By World War II, Manhattan was home to several prominent Levantine Jews, such as two from Salonica: Maurice Abravanel, the conductor of the New York Metropolitan Opera; and Daniel Carasso, the founder of Danon Yogurt, which popularized the Ottoman delicacy for the American market.

Following the broader pattern, Ottoman Jews initially established their own mutual aid organizations based on specific town of origin, referred to in Judeo-Spanish (and in Ottoman Turkish) as *hemşerilik* (in Yiddish, the *landsmanshaft* principle).[58] Notably, while a general practice among immigrants, commentators often drew on Orientalist tropes to present the "separation" or "breakdown" of the Levantine Jews according to place of origin as a sign of their "clannishness." In contrast, Levantine Jews initially viewed their hometown organizational principle both as a product of practicality and a representation of legitimate differences that distinguished each group, although some leaders soon internalized the critique and

---

55 Papo, *Sephardim in Twentieth-Century America*, 30; "Find Ample Space for Pushcart Men," *New York Times*, July 12, 1912, 18.

56 "Prominent Men in New Tobacco Concern," *United States Tobacco Journal*, September 27, 1919, 6.

57 Papo, *Sephardim in Twentieth-Century America*, 328.

58 "'Korespondensia de Amerika," *El mundo sefaradi* 1, no. 2 (1923): 92–95; Lisa DiCarlo, *Migrating to America: Transnational Social Networks and Regional Identity among Turkish Migrants* (London: I. B. Tauris, 2008), 55.

demanded institutional unification in order to prove the civilized status of their community.[59]

By the conclusion of World War I, nearly forty hometown institutions operated in New York and twenty more throughout the country, each comprised of members from specific locales: Salonica, Istanbul, Kastoria, Monastir, Rhodes, Edirne, Izmir, Ankara, Gallipoli, Çanakkale, Marmara, Chios, Silivria, Çorlou, Tekirdag, Janina, Damascus, and Aleppo. The Salonican Brotherhood of America (established 1915) became the largest of the organizations, and, when reorganized as the Sephardic Brotherhood of America in 1922, became the first of the associations to admit members from any city of origin. In 1924, several of the smaller organizations merged to create the Sephardic Jewish Community of New York, which served as the Brotherhood's chief competitor. These organizations established their own synagogues, schools (Talmude Tora), mutual aid, sick and death benefits, and raised funds to support their poorer members and—often by putting on theater productions in Judeo-Spanish—to support institutions in their native cities or aid Jews back home during wartime and other crises.

In addition to the mutual aid societies, cafes or coffee houses played a key role in the development of the social, cultural, political, and institutional life in the *Turkino* colony. To the outsider, however, the "Oriental cafe," perhaps more than any other institution, represented the "alien" status of Levantine Jews in the New York.[60] It was precisely via reference to the cafe that Istanbul-born Ashkenazi Jewish journalist, Samuel Auerbach, who wrote for prominent newspapers like the *New York Times*, emphasized the alien nature of Levantine Jews from the mainstream American Jewish gaze:

> Who are these strangers who can be seen in the ghetto of the [Lower] East Side, sitting outside of coffee-houses smoking strange-looking waterpipes, sipping a dark liquid from tiny cups and playing a game of checkers and dice, a game that we are not familiar with? See the signs on these institutions. They read: "Cafe Constantinople," "Cafe Oriental," "Cafe Smyrna," and there are other signs in Hebrew characters that you perhaps cannot read. Are they Jews? No it cannot be; they do not look like Jews; they do not speak Yiddish. Listen; what is that strange tongue they are using? It sounds like Spanish

---

59   Benardete, *Hispanic Culture and Character of the Sephardic Jews*, 164ff.
60   A recent book celebrates the cafe as the site of the genesis of modern culture for European Jews while acknowledging its roots in the Ottoman Empire: Shachar Pinsker, *A Rich Brew: How Cafes Created Modern Jewish Culture* (New York: NYU Press, 2018).

or Mexican. Are they Spaniards or Mexicans? If so, where did they get the coffee-houses, an importation from Greece and Turkey? [61]

Depictions like this in the English-language American press described the "Turkish-Jewish coffee houses" not only as markers of the strangeness of Levantine Jews, but also as places that developed "not altogether desirable influences" by allegedly promoting laziness, idle chatter, and vices like gambling, alcoholism, and illicit substance abuse.[62] That cafes were often full during the day appeared to support the accusations of Levantine Jewish men's lack of initiative, absence of gainful employment, and liability as potential public charges. New York police indeed raided several of the cafes, but sometimes on faulty pretenses, as in one infamous case in which nineteen Levantine Jews were handcuffed and hauled away on suspicion of gambling and only released after a night in jail once it was determined that they had merely been playing an Ottoman board game, *tavle* (*sheshbesh*).[63]

The reality, of course, was more complex. The cafes served as the initial communal organizing entities for Jews from across the former Ottoman Empire. Jews from Salonica, Istanbul, Izmir and elsewhere each established their own cafe, which served as a place to meet friends and relatives, to consume kosher cuisine prepared in the accustomed styles, to receive mail, and to read American newspapers and those imported from Greece and Turkey. The cafes appeared to be full during the day because Levantine Jewish men often worked night shifts at factories and sought out the cafes for solace and camaraderie during the day. Many of the most important mutual aid societies—including the Salonican (subsequently Sephardic) Brotherhood of America—were founded at meetings at these cafes, which served as key venues for communal debate, political discussion, reading circles, charitable fundraising, and labor organizing. Some Levantine Jews thus preferred to characterize their cafes more along the lines of the salons of the European Enlightenment.[64]

In addition to the mutual aid societies and the cafes, the press served a primary role in cultivating a collective consciousness among Levantine Jews

61 Samuel M. Auerbach, "The Levantine Jew," *The Immigrants in America Review* 2 (July 1916): 47–53, republished in *Jewish Immigration Bulletin* 7 (August/September 1916): 10–13.

62 David de Sola Pool, "The Levantine Jews in the United States," *American Jewish Year Book* 15 (1913/1914): 207–20, here 218.

63 "Sefaradim arestados en bloko aptaun," *La luz*, July 9, 1922, 4.

64 Henry Besso to editor of *The Jewish Daily Forward*, August 11, 1926, in Besso Papers, Box 27, File 41.

in New York and in linking them to other colonies across the country and to their native communities. Despite the *Jewish Daily Forward*'s characterization of "Turkish Jews" as "a backward people from a backward country" who had "no cultural life of their own worth speaking of,"[65] Levantine Jews published twenty-one newspapers and magazines in New York between 1910 and 1948. Bulgarian-born Moise Gadol published the first Ladino weekly, *La Amerika* (1910–1925), but most of the editors of the other periodicals hailed from Salonica. Edited by Albert Levy, Albert Torres, and Moise Soulam, *La vara* (1922–1948) emerged as the longest-lived Ladino publication in the United States and became the last Ladino newspaper anywhere in the world to be printed in Hebrew letters. Most of the newspapers had modest subscription numbers of just a few thousand, whereas *La vara* claimed 16,500 subscribers in 1928 not only in New York, but also in cities across the United States as well as in Mexico City, Havana, Rio de Janiero, Vienna, London, Belgrade, Jerusalem, and beyond.[66] Publishers, however, generally supplemented the modest income derived from their newspapers with printing and paper supplies businesses and by selling the latest records in Ladino, Greek, Turkish, and Arabic as well as novels and religious books in Ladino.

Intended to provide information, education, and entertainment, the newspapers published the latest news from New York, across the country and abroad, with specific attention to happenings in the Ottoman Empire and its successor states. Many articles focused on events in the New York "colony," including meetings, fundraisers, and theater productions organized by mutual aid societies. Whereas *La Amerika* pushed both Americanizing and Zionist agendas, *La vara* drew on the well-establish Salonican tradition of political satire and also promoted Socialism. Editorials and letters to the editor in the Ladino newspapers debated every conceivable issue—whether the mutual aid societies should remain independent, federate, or merge; whether Levantine Jews should seek rapprochement with Ashkenazi Jews and Spanish and Portuguese Jews or retain their own independence; whether the colony ought to throw its lot in with Americanization or retain hope for a possible return to the Old Country; whether the Ladino language was sustainable in the United States or ought to be reformed to

---

65 Nathaniel Zalowitz, "The Thirty Thousand Turkish Jews in New York—Who They Are, What They Do, and How They Live," *Jewish Daily Forward*, July 25, 1926, 1–2.

66 Aviva Ben-Ur, "In Search of the American Ladino Press: A Bibliographic Survey, 1910–1948," *Studies Bibliography and Booklore* 21 (Fall 2001): 11–51.

make it closer to standard Castilian or abandoned altogether in favor of English; which candidates to vote for in elections; and many other themes.[67] Drawing on the Ottoman Jewish practice of recording and commenting upon contemporary events in poetic form that dated back to the seventeenth century, New York Ladino newspapers published myriad articles on all of the above-mentioned themes in rhymed verse, known as *koplas*.[68]

The mutual aid societies, the cafes, and the press served as three pillars of the *Turkino* colony in New York. But already during World War I, some Levantine Jewish leaders sought to recast the "*Turkino* colony" and their sense of community and identity in a way that would resonate more positively with the mainstream Jewish community and with white American society. The rhetoric of the "Terrible Turk" during the Great War compelled them to minimize their expressions of allegiance to their empire of birth. Seeking to navigate the complex political, cultural and racial dynamics in America, Ottoman-born Jewish leaders in America began to recast themselves not as Oriental Jews, Turks, or Levantines, but rather as the heirs of the famous Jewish golden age of medieval Spain. Emphasizing their ancestral, cultural, and intellectual linkages to Spain—and hence to Europe, to Western civilization, and to whiteness—Ottoman-born Jews began to insist on calling themselves "Sephardic Jews" or "Spanish Jews." The embrace of their distant Spanish and thus European origins sought to overturn their association with the purportedly backward Orient and to raise their prestige in the eyes of mainstream American Jews.[69]

Initiated in 1915 by the New York Ladino newspaper, *La America*, the so-called "Sephardic campaign" demanded that institutions catering to Ottoman-born Jews refer to themselves as "Sephardic" or "Spanish" and to their "colony" as the "Sephardic community." Such a move involved the internalization of Orientalist rhetoric. Rather than defend the validity of Ottoman society and culture, proponents of the Sephardic campaign accepted the claim that their land of birth was a land of stagnation, and insisted that their true cultural and intellectual roots should be recognized as stemming from Spain and its famed Jewish theologians, philosophers, scientists, and diplomats. The rhetoric of the Sephardic campaign gained

---

67 Marc Angel, *La America: The Sephardic Experience in the United States* (Philadelphia: Jewish Publication Society, 1982).

68 Elena Romero, *Entre dos (o más) fuegos: Fuentes poéticas para la historia de los sefardíes de los balcanes* (Madrid: Consejo superior de investigaciones científicas, 2008).

69 I describe this process in more depth in Naar, "'Sephardim since Birth.'"

momentum through the Depression, as encapsulated in this defense published in 1930 by Leon Saady, a founder of New York's Sephardic Brotherhood of America:

> We are Jews like the others, and if we are still called the People of the Book, we will prove it: we are not the gypsies of our people, we have the same Jewish character, we have a glorious past, and we still possess the intelligent Jew capable of drawing upon all that they [our ancestors] have bequeathed to us. We will show to our brothers [the Ashkenazim] that the descendants of Maimonides, [Ibn] Gabriol, Rashi [sic], and Abravanel still count [among them] individuals who can become leaders of their people and if we still have our dignity, we will show that we are the true Spanish Jews who made Spain rich in money, the Jew rich in knowledge, and if we still cannot shake ourselves, our status in America will have constituted a period of stagnation continued since our expulsion from Spain.[70]

Saady's apologia stemmed from his desire to prove the worth of his community to mainstream American Jews by internalizing the Orientalist image of the "stagnant" Ottoman Empire and promoting the glory of medieval Jewish Spain as an antidote.

A sign of the limit of Sephardic-Ashkenazi rapprochement in the 1930s, the first major initiative to legitimize the Sephardic Jewish experience for the New York public transpired beyond the realm of the Jewish institutions. A Çanakkale-born professor of Spanish at Brooklyn College, Mair J. Benardete, and a few other Levantine Jewish intellectuals, established the country's first Sephardic Studies program—at Benardete's alma mater, Columbia University. While the distinguished Columbia scholar Salo Baron, the first professor of Jewish history at an American university, occasionally lectured on topics such as "The Hebraic Civilization in Spain," Benardete succeeded in establishing the Sephardic Studies program under the aegis of Columbia's Hispanic Institute.[71] The prominent Spanish scholars who supported the initiative saw in the Levantine Jews' Ladino language a vestige of the Spanish literary golden age of Cervantes, whereas figures like Benardete capitalized on the Spanish embrace to secure an entrée for his community into European civilization, and thus, in the American context, whiteness. The convergence of interests positioned this short-lived

---

70   Yeuda Saady, "20 anyos despues. Progreso i estagnasion," *El ermanado* (1930): 23–24.
71   Ben-Ur, *Sephardic Jews in America*, 161–73.

Sephardic Studies initiative of the 1930s firmly within the framework of the Spanish world—Benardete even began to refer to himself as "Mercedes José"—and decidedly beyond the orbit of Jewish institutions. It would take six more decades before the first stirrings of Sephardic Studies within the framework of Jewish Studies would emerge.

If Levantine Jews tended to be excluded from mainstream Ashkenazi-dominated Jewish institutions or were viewed as "impostor Jews" on the streets of New York, they could play the role of Spaniard, Latino, Greek, Turk, Italian, or French person to their benefit in various scenarios. Such cultural flexibility and even the capacity to "pass" as non-Jews enabled them to take advantage of opportunities not readily available to those identified as Jews—controversially posing as Italian or French to secure jobs from employers known to not hire Jews.[72] Drawing upon their multiple cultural affinities not only served instrumental ends, but also enabled alienated Levantine Jews to cultivate a sense belonging among various non-Jews with whom they developed cultural, economic, and political ties: whether Spaniards through the Sephardic Studies initiative at Columbia, Puerto Ricans through labor organizing and radical politics in Harlem, Greeks via a *rembetika* (underground Greek blues) music revival in cafes and nightclubs across Manhattan, or Turks through fundraising campaigns in support of the Ottoman Red Crescent and Turkish war orphans. Yet they often encountered a limit to such interactions, a sense of pushback that they were *really* Jews and operating as impostor Italians, French people, Greeks, Turks, Spaniards, or Latinos. Just as their language, culture, and geographic origins rendered them unrecognizable as Jews in an Ashkenazi-dominated Jewish environment in New York, their Jewishness impinged upon their claims as legitimate members of the various other groups. Such encounters not only revealed the instability of national, cultural, and racial categories, but also the ways in which the marginalization of Levantine Jews by mainstream Jewish institutions opened new, perhaps unexpected, opportunities for them beyond the framework of organized Jewish life.

New York as a "Jewish City"

Arriving in the United States during the Great Depression, a Jewish traveler from Greece marveled over the extent to which New York represented a

---

72   Ben-Ur, "Funny, You Don't Look Jewish."

"Jewish city." As he reported to a Ladino newspaper back in his native city, Salonica:

> New York, the city of hundreds of nationalities, the home of Black African Jews, of Yemenite Jews coming from the deserts of Arabia, of Syrian Jews, of Jews descended from those expelled from Spain, of Russian, German, and Polish Jews, and, ultimately, of Jews speaking innumerable languages—New York, the home of three rabbinical seminaries, of the largest Jewish library in the world, of the only Jewish museum, of the only Jewish college. New York, the city with the largest Jewish community in the world.[73]

Describing his stroll from lower Manhattan all the way up to Harlem, the journalist pinpointed locations along the way that he viewed as key Jewish "monuments": the Chatham Square cemetery of the Spanish and Portuguese congregation, Shearith Israel, the building of the *Jewish Daily Forward*, the Hebrew Immigrant Aid Society, the Amalgamated Bank, the Fifth-Avenue headquarters of the Zionist Organization of America, Hadassah, and the Jewish Federation, Temple Emanu-El, Mount Sinai Hospital (New York's "most sacred Jewish monument"), the Jewish Theological Seminary, and even the Beth B'nai Abraham Synagogue of Black Jews on West 131st Street.

Despite his reference to the multiplicity of Jews who called New York home, the visitor presented a vision of Jewish New York bereft of "monuments" marking the imprint of his own community—Ladino-speaking Jews from the former Ottoman Empire. He could have noted the offices of the main Ladino newspaper, *La vara*, on Rivington Street; the headquarters of the Sephardic Brotherhood of America, the Sephardic Jewish Community of New York, or several dozen mutual aid societies and synagogues; the Sephardic Talmud Torah schools on the Lower East Side and in Harlem; or the Sephardic Studies Program at Columbia University. In rendering invisible the mark of Levantine Jews on the Jewish landscape of New York, the visitor, perhaps unwittingly, internalized the dominant, popular image of Jewish New York that centers the narrative and physical imprint of European, principally Ashkenazi, Jews who have come to stand in for all New York—and by extension, all American—Jewry.

But the writer's description also hinted at another dynamic at play in the representation of Jewish New York through the exoticization of other

---

73   D. K., "Letra de Nu York. Nu York, Sivdad Djudia," *El tiempo*, ca. 1933, clipping in Archive of the Jewish Community of Salonica, Gr/Sa 379, Central Archives for the History of the Jewish People, Jerusalem.

Jewish populations ("Yemenite Jews coming from the deserts of Arabia"). As a result of both internalizing and seeking to overcome Orientalist imagery targeting their own community, Ladino-speaking Jews replicated the process of creating their own "other"—Arabic-speaking Jews. Similar to how non-Jews scorned Jews, Spanish and Portuguese Jews initially looked down on German Jews, who in turn denigrated Russian Jews, and who all together alienated Ladino-speaking Jews, the latter group also established distance from Jews from places like Syria. Joy Zacharia captures the attitude:

> The *Yiddishim* [Ashkenazi Jews], however, are not as bad as the Syrians. They are the worst of all! The Syrians and other groups of Mizrachi Jews are simply *gorsus* ["evil"]. If your family members get mixed up with them, you will never see them again! These people have their own tight community and demand total conformity. Of course, they are all rich and your relative will live well, as long as a child is produced almost every year. How they earn their money is another story! They are all horse thieves in their hearts![74]

Drawing on a wide variety of disparaging stereotypes, this kind of rhetoric permitted Ladino-speaking Jews to elevate themselves in the Jewish and broader American racial hierarchies, and to soothe themselves by emphasizing that others rank lower than they. But the emphasis on difference also stemmed from a practical reality: just as Yiddish- and Ladino-speaking Jews could not communicate with each other, neither could either with Arabic-speaking Jews. Such differentiation also led Ladino-speaking leaders to insist on dissolving categories like "Oriental Jews," which created a false sense of unity by lumping together Ladino- and Arabic-speaking Jews. They did not go as far as some Yiddish-speaking Jews, who sometimes referred to Ladino-speaking and later Yemenite Jews in New York—as in Israel—as *schvartze khayes* ("nigger beasts").[75]

---

74 Zacharia, "Growing Up in a Polyglot Sephardic Household," 453.
75 Jodi Varon, *Drawing to an Inside Straight: The Legacy of an Absent Father* (Columbia, MO: University of Missouri Press, 2006), 52; Aviva Ben-Ur, "Diaspora Reunions: Sephardi/Ashkenazi Tensions in Historical Perspective," *Conversations: The Journal of the Institute for Jewish Ideas and Ideals* 13 (Spring 2012): 107-127; Ben-Ur, *Sephardic Jews in America*, 112, citing Dina Dahbany Miraglia, "An Analysis of Ethnic Identity among Yemenite Jews in the Greater New York Area" (PhD diss., Columbia University, 1983), 179, who notes that Yemenite Jewish men internalized the slur and used it to refer to each other. Ashkenazim regularly denigrated Mizrahim as *schvartze hayes* in Israel. The Mizrahi power movement took its name, Black Panthers, as an allusion to its American counterpart and as a way to reclaim the epithet *schvartze haye*; the panther

The irony is that the coming-of-age of the first American-born generations of Levantine Jews, the entrance of the men into the US Armed Forces during World War II, the devastation of the Holocaust which resulted in the annihilation of some of the largest Ladino-speaking communities (like Salonica, Monastir, Rhodes), the creation of the state of Israel in 1948, the folding of the last Ladino newspaper that same year, the dissolution of the old neighborhoods and the suburbanization of New York's Levantine Jews (the wealthier of whom moved to Long Island where they established the Sephardic Temple in 1961), and the greater acceptance of Ashkenazi and Sephardic Jews as whites (rather than a distinct race of "Hebrews") in broader American society both contributed to the unraveling of organized Levantine Jewish life in New York and partially facilitated the rapprochement between Levantine and Ashkenazi Jews.[76] While mixed marriages between the two groups became commonplace after World War II, the city's Jewish institutions, leaders, and cultural figures remained almost exclusively Ashkenazi. The victory of the Sephardic campaign initiated in 1915 resulted in the category of "Sephardic Jews" gaining predominance, but it became a term still defined in relationship to the dominant group: Sephardic Jews came to refer to all "non-Ashkenazi Jews," a framework internalized and adopted by the New York's American Sephardi Federation (established 1972), which seeks to represent all "Greater Sephardi communities": "the traditional Sephardim (Jews who traced their lineage to Spain and Portugal), as well as Jews stemming from the Mediterranean basin, the Balkans, the Middle East, Africa, and Asia)."[77] Even as representatives of the various "non-Ashkenazi" communities may still view themselves as distinct from each other, the entrenched Ashkenazi and Eurocentric visions of Jewish New York—and of world Jewry—combined with demographics and other factors, continues to group all of the "other" Jews together at the margins of the story or renders them invisible.

But perhaps the greatest irony may be found in one of New York's most emblematic contemporary (Jewish) monuments: the Tenement Museum

---

became their "black beast." See Ella Shohat, "Sephardim in Israel: Zionism from the Standpoint of its Jewish Victims," *Social Text* 19–20 (Fall 1988): 1–35, esp. 6.

76 A caveat should be introduced that not all Ashkenazi Jews are white: Lewis R. Gordon, "Rarely Kosher: Studying Jews of Color in North America," *American Jewish History* 100, no. 1 (January 2016): 105–16.

77 Caryn Aviv and David Shneer, *New Jews and the End of the Jewish Diaspora* (New York: New York University Press, 2005), 148–49.

on the Lower East Side. With reconstructed apartments that seek to provide visitors access to "living history" at 97 Orchard Street, the Museum offers stories of Irish, Italian, German, Russian-Jewish, German-Jewish, Chinese, and Puerto Rican families.[78] Its longest-running and most popular tour features the reimagined apartment of fourteen-year-old Ottoman-born Victoria Confino and her Ladino-speaking family, natives of Kastoria, a town near Salonica. From a historical perspective, the Tenement Museum's elevation of the Confino family story makes sense: it channels the view of the New York Public Libraries' superintendent who saw the Lower East Side a century ago as a Jewish neighborhood due to both the "Russian" and "Oriental" Jews who resided there. From today's vantage point, however, there is a certain irony in highlighting a Levantine Jewish family as an iconic representation of early twentieth-century Jewish life on the Lower East Side precisely because the Confino family's very status as Jews may have been questioned by fellow Jews and because their community has generally been rendered invisible in Jewish accounts of the neighborhood and city they once called home.[79] The emphasis on the Confino family does not represent heightened visibility for Levantine Jews writ large in American Jewish consciousness today—precisely the opposite. By making the story about an individual family—whose origin, culture, and identity are mentioned in passing—and by not acknowledging the broader structures at play that otherwise continue to render the collective experience of Levantine Jews marginal, the Tenement Museum, perhaps unwittingly, confirms the liminal status of Levantine Jews.

What would narratives of Jewish New York look like not only if individual Levantine Jews, like Victoria Confino, were added to the story not merely as tokens, but on a structural level, if space were made to recover, highlight, and contextualize the qualitative difference not only of her individual and family experience but also of the community of which she was a part? The narrative contours would be transformed by taking into account the historically charged, racialized, and tenuous relationships among various Jewish groups—not only those of "European" origin—and the attendant power dynamics; and the narrative frame and geographic scope would be expanded

---

78 Jack Kugelmass, "Turfing the Slum: New York City's Tenement Museum and the Politics of Heritage," *Remembering the Lower East Side: American Jewish Reflections*, ed. Hasia Diner, Jeffrey Shandler, Beth Wenger (Bloomington: Indiana University Press, 2000), 179–211.

79 I thank Aron Rodrigue for sharing this observation with me.

to account for Levantine Jews—and other non-European, non-Ashkenazi, or non-white Jews—and their ambivalent interactions with, and ability to pass as and build community with, other national, ethnic, or racial groups. In this way, the narrative of American Jewish exceptionalism may begin to be unraveled, the historically entrenched nature of intra-Jewish prejudice may begin to be confronted, and a new paradigm may emerge that could imbue "imposter Jews" with status as legitimate Jews and finally transform the narrative of white Ashkenazi New York into more capacious, inclusive, and representative stories of the multiplicities of *Jewish* New York.

For Further Reading

Amateau, Albert. "The Sephardic Immigrant from Bulgaria: A Personal Profile of Moise Gadol." *American Jewish Archives* 42, no. 1(Fall/Winter 1990): 57–70.

Angel, Marc. *La America: The Sephardic Experience in the United States.* Philadelphia: Jewish Publication Society, 1982.

Appelbaum, Joy Zacharia. "Growing up in a Polyglot Sephardic Household." In *From Iberia to Diaspora: Studies in Sephardic History and Culture*, edited by Yedida Kalfon Stillman and Norman Stillman, 451–57. Leiden: Brill, 1999.

Aschheim, Steven. *Brothers and Strangers: The East European Jew in German and German Jewish Consciousness, 1800–1923.* Madison: University of Wisconsin Press, 1982.

Aviv, Caryn, and David Shneer. *New Jews and the End of the Jewish Diaspora.* New York: New York University Press, 2005.

Benbassa, Esther, and Aron Rodrigue. *Sephardi Jewry: A History of the Judeo-Spanish Community, 14th–20th Centuries.* Berkeley: University of California Press, 2000.

Benardete, Mair José. *Hispanic Culture and Character of the Sephardic Jews.* New York: Hispanic Institute in the United States, 1952.

Benor, Sarah Bunin, "Lexical Othering in Judezmo: How Ottoman Sephardim Refer to Non-Jews." In *Languages and Literatures of Sephardic and Oriental Jews*, edited by David M. Bunis, 65–85. Jerusalem: Misgav Yerushalayim, 2009

Ben-Ur, Aviva, "In Search of the American Ladino Press: A Bibliographic Survey, 1910–1948." *Studies Bibliography and Booklore* 21 (Fall 2001): 11–51.

———. "Funny, You Don't Look Jewish!: 'Passing' and the Elasticity of Ethnic Identity among Levantine Sephardic Immigrants in Early Twentieth-Century America." *Kolor: Journal on Moving Communities* 2 (2002): 9–18.

———. *Sephardic Jews in America: A Diasporic History.* New York: New York University Press, 2009.

Brenner, Michael. *Prophets of the Past: Interpreters of Jewish History.* Princeton: Princeton University Press, 2010.

Bunis, David. "Native Designations of Judezmo as a 'Jewish Language.'" In *Studies in Language, Literature and History Presented to Joseph Chetrit,* edited by Yosef Tobi and Dennis Kurzon, 41–81. Jerusalem: Carmel, 2011.

Dahbany-Miraglia, Dina. "An Analysis of Ethnic Identity among Yemenite Jews in the Greater New York Area." PhD diss., Columbia University, 1983.

DiCarlo, Lisa. *Migrating to America: Transnational Social Networks and Regional Identity among Turkish Migrants.* London: I. B. Tauris, 2008.

Diner, Hasia. *Lower East Side Memories: A Jewish Place in America.* Princeton: Princeton University Press, 2000.

Efron, John. "Orientalism and the Jewish Historical Gaze." In *Orientalism and the Jews,* edited by Ivan Davidson Kalmar and Derek J. Penslar, 80–93. Waltham/Hannover: Brandeis University Press / University Press of New England, 2005.

Frank, Mary. *Exploring a Neighborhood: Our Jewish People from Eastern Europe and the Orient.* New York: Immigrant Publication Society, 1919.

Gabaccia, Donna. *Italy's Many Diasporas.* Seattle: University of Washington Press, 2000.

Geldfand Alexander. "Eastward Expansion: Bringing Sephardic Music into the Fold." *Tablet Magazine,* December 26, 2008.

Glenn, Susan. "'Funny, You Don't Look Jewish': Visual Stereotypes and the Making of Modern Jewish Identity." In *Boundaries of Jewish Identity,* edited by Susan Glenn and Naomi Sokoloff, 64–90. Seattle: University of Washington Press, 2010.

Gordon, Lewis R. "Rarely Kosher: Studying Jews of Color in North America." *American Jewish History* 100, no. 1 (January 2016): 105–16.

Goldstein, Eric. *The Price of Whiteness: Jews, Race, and American Identity.* Princeton: Princeton University Press, 2008.

Gualtieri, Sarah M. A. *Between Arab and White: Race and Ethnicity in the Early Syrian American Diaspora.* Berkeley: University of California Press, 2009.

Halio, Hank. *Ladino Reveries: Tales of the Sephardic Experience.* New York: Foundation for the Study of Sephardic Studies and Culture, 1996.

Haney-López, Ian. *White By Law: The Legal Construction of Race* (New York: New York University Press, 2006).

Howe, Irving. *World of Our Fathers.* New York: Harcourt Brace Jovanovich, 1976.

Hyman, Paula. *From Dreyfus to Vichy: The Remaking of French Jewry, 1906–1939.* New York: Columbia University Press, 1979.

Jacobson, Matthew Frye. *Whiteness of a Different Color: European Immigrants and the Alchemy of Race.* Cambridge, MA: Harvard University Press, 1998.

Jerusalmi, Isaac. "The Constitution of the Burial Society of the Bucharest Sephardic Community, April 30, 1850." *Hebrew Union College Annual* 76 (2006): 235–58.

Kostelanetz, Richard. "Sephardic Culture and Me." *European Judaism* 33, no. 1 (Spring 2000): 20–23.

Kugelmass, Jack. "Turfing the Slum: New York City's Tenement Museum and the Politics of Heritage." *Remembering the Lower East Side: American Jewish Reflections*, edited by Hasia Diner, Jeffrey Shandler, and Beth Wenger, 179–211. Bloomington: Indiana University Press, 2000.

Light, Caroline E. *That Pride of Race and Character: The Roots of Jewish Benevolence in the Jim Crow South.* New York: New York University Press, 2014.

Luconi, Stefano. "Black Dagoes? Italian Immigrants' Racial Status in the United States: an Ecological View." *Journal of Transatlantic Studies* 14, no. 2 (2016): 188–99.

Mays, Devi. "'I Killed Her because I Loved Her Too Much': Gender and Violence in the 20th Century Sephardi Diaspora." *Mashriq & Mahjar* 3 (2014): 4–28.

Moore, Deborah Dash. "Forward." In *City of Promises: A History of the Jews of New York*, edited by Deborah Dash Moore, 11–23. New York: New York University Press, 2012.

Moses, Miriam Israel. "Survivors and Pieces of Glass." In *Jewish American Literature: A Norton Anthology,* edited by Hilene Flanzbaum et al., 1111–20. New York: W. W. Norton, 2011.

Naar, Devin. "From the 'Jerusalem of the Balkans' to the 'Goldene Medina': Jewish Immigration from Salonika to the United States." *American Jewish History* 93, no. 4 (December 2007): 435–73.

———. "Fashioning the 'Mother of Israel': The Ottoman Jewish Historical Narrative and the Image of Jewish Salonica." *Jewish History* 28, no. 3-4 (2014): 337–72.

———. "*Turkinos* beyond the Empire: Ottoman Jews in America, 1893–1924." *Jewish Quarterly Review* 105, no. 2 (Spring 2015): 174–205.

———. "'Sephardim since Birth': Reconfiguring Jewish Identity in America." In *The Sephardi and Mizrahi Jews in America,* edited by Saba Soomekh, 75–104. West Lafayette, Ind.: Purdue University Press, 2016.

Ngai, Mae. *Impossible Subjects: Illegal Aliens and the Making of Modern America.* Princeton: Princeton University Press, 2014.

Papo, Joseph M. *Sephardim in Twentieth-Century America: In Search of Unity.* San Jose: Pelé Yoetz Books, 1987.

Park, Robert E. and Herbert A. Miller. *Old World Traits Transplanted.* New York: Harper & Brothers, 1921.

Park, Robert E. *The Immigrant Press and Its Control.* New York: Harper & Bros, 1922.

Pasto, James. "Islam's 'Strange Secret Sharer': Orientalism, Judaism, and the Jewish Question." *Comparative Studies in Society and History* 40 (1998): 437–74.

Pinsker, Shachar. *A Rich Brew: How Cafes Created Modern Jewish Culture.* New York: NYU Press, 2018.

Ribak, Gil. *Gentile New York: The Images of Non-Jews among Jewish Immigrants.* New Brunswick: Rutgers University Press, 2012.

Romero, Elena. *Entre dos (o más) fuegos: Fuentes poéticas para la historia de los sefardíes de los balcanes.* Madrid: Consejo superior de investigaciones científicas, 2008.

Scolnik, Julie. "*Libro de embeźar las linguas ingleśa y yudiš: La América*'s Guidebook to Learning English and Yiddish and Becoming an American Citizen." *Miscelánea de Estudios Árabes y Hebraicos* 63 (2014): 1–13.

Schroeter, Daniel. "From Sephardi to Oriental: The 'Decline' Theory of Jewish Civilization in the Middle East and North Africa." In *The Jewish Contribution to Civilization: Reassessing an Idea,* edited by Jeremy Cohen and Richard I. Cohen, 125–50. Oxford: Littman Library of Jewish Civilization, 2008.

Shohat, Ella. "Sephardim in Israel: Zionism from the Standpoint of its Jewish Victims." *Social Text* 19-20 (Fall 1988): 1–35.

Tehranian, John. *Whitewashed: America's Invisible Middle Eastern Minority.* New York: New York University Press, 2009.

Wertheimer, Jack, "The German-Jewish Experience: Toward a Useable Past." In *German-Jewish Legacy in America, 1938-198,* edited by Abraham Peck, 233–38. Detroit: Wayne State University, 1988.

Yu, Henry. *Thinking Oriental: Migration, Contact, and Exoticism in Modern America.* New York: Oxford University Press, 2001.

Chapter 7

Jewish Builders in New York City, 1880–1980

Deborah Dash Moore

New York's identity as a twentieth-century city owes much to its Jewish builders. This chapter examines the impact of New York Jewish builders on the cityscape over the course of a century. It first looks at the nineteenth-century origins of Jewish participation in construction of tenements and single- and two-family houses. These experiences prepared the ground for the 1920s, years of explosive growth when Jewish builders helped to define the physical dimensions of the modern city. The chapter then examines the postwar decades when glass, steel, and aluminum replaced brick and mortar. Not only in new neighborhoods emerging in Brooklyn, the Bronx, and Queens, but also in the heart of Manhattan, Jewish builders left their stamp upon the city. Building for where Jews would live and work, they helped to transform substantial sections of New York's residential, industrial, and commercial areas.

During the twentieth century, a relatively small percentage of New York's roughly two million Jews found employment in construction, development, and real estate.[1] Family firms typified some of the most

---

1   Jewish population figures in New York ranged from 750,000 in 1900 to 950,000 in 2000, but during the middle decades of the century, roughly two million Jews lived in New York.

successful Jewish builders, endowing this industry with a measure of intimacy. Many Jewish builders knew each other, joined the same congregations, sent their children to a handful of private schools, supported Jewish philanthropies, and sat on the boards of cultural and social welfare institutions. Although it is difficult not to celebrate the types of rags-to-riches story promoted by these men and the public relations firms they employed, often only the buildings themselves survived the bankruptcies and deaths of their builders. Despite individuals' financial failures, skyscrapers, apartment complexes, industrial lofts, shopping centers, and cooperative houses often endured. Their presence shaped the patterns of daily life of millions of New Yorkers who lived and worked in these buildings, usually unaware of who built them.

A nexus of work and living formed a crucial element of Jewish construction in the city. The creation of the Brownsville neighborhood of Brooklyn at the end of the nineteenth century epitomized this process. In 1887 Elias Kaplan moved his clothing factory to Watkins Avenue, a largely rural, swampy section of eastern Brooklyn, far from the East River and downtown. He was seeking cheap land where he could build housing for the workers in his factories.[2] Kaplan rented rooms to his garment workers and to other Jews as well. Soon speculative builders joined him in constructing multi-family wooden houses and brick tenements, along with new factories for food production and jewelry making, plus stores, with residences above them. This development produced buildings whose "conditions fluctuated between bad and barely satisfactory."[3] Tenants liked the apartments because they were new and close to jobs. Basic infrastructure—paved streets, sewers, street lamps—didn't arrive until the early twentieth century. Then approximately 25,000 people, the vast majority Jewish immigrants, lived in the growing neighborhood, accessible from Manhattan via an elevated railway. Brownsville's combination of high population density and inferior infrastructure prompted Jews with some socioeconomic resources to move out as poorer Jews poured in. Population turnover accompanied a churning real estate market. In the space of two years of peak immigration,

---

2   This was not quite the "company town" model of Pullman, but it initially shared some aspects of it. On Pullman, see Stanley Buder, *Pullman: An Experiment in Industrial Order and Community Planning, 1880–1930* (New York: Oxford University Press, 1967).
3   Wendell Pritchett, *Brownsville, Brooklyn: Blacks, Jews, and the Changing Face of the Ghetto* (Chicago: University of Chicago Press, 2002), 2.

lots soared from $50 in 1907 to $3000.[4] Brownsville's population rose rapidly, reaching over 200,000 by 1930, with a median income of $2,490. It was a working-class neighborhood somewhat more prosperous than the immigrant Lower East Side and Williamsburg.[5]

Speculative construction produced ever denser concentrations of multistory tenements. By 1930 Brownsville's density reached 92,000 people per square mile—high, but far less than another relatively new Jewish neighborhood of the East Bronx.[6] In general, Brownsville's tenements were of a better quality than those on the Lower East Side, due to the 1901 Tenement House law that mandated new multifamily housing include windows in all rooms, indoor plumbing, and electric lighting. Ethnic tensions on Brownsville's borders restricted expansion of the neighborhood and stimulated construction of ever taller tenement houses. "Most of these developers were small, operated on tight profit margins, and relied on locally acquired capital that often dried up. Sixty-four percent of the builders in the area produced fewer than five houses," notes Wendell Pritchett, a historian of Brownsville. "A few developers like Ira and Jacob Goell created stable, large-scale operations, but most builders did not achieve lasting success. Financially insecure and opportunistic developers built for quick profit, not for long-term occupancy, which contributed to the low quality of housing in Brownsville."[7] Nevertheless, these low-capital construction projects that fashioned ethnic neighborhoods allowed Jews who stayed in construction to learn the business.

The 1925 publication, *Building Up Greater Brooklyn*, paid tribute to many of the borough's more successful builders, a majority of them Jews. Some of them got their start in Brownsville while others began in neighborhoods, like Williamsburg and Borough Park, that became heavily Jewish after the construction of the Williamsburg and Manhattan bridges in 1903 and 1909 respectively. Almost all of these Jews immigrated to New York City from Eastern Europe. Some came with building experience; others possessed such craft skills as carpentry or house painting. Many began by remodeling older buildings; newcomers also apprenticed to learn modern construction techniques, such as plumbing. A number of Jewish builders

4   Pritchett, *Brownsville*, 14–15.
5   Deborah Dash Moore, *At Home in America: Second Generation New York Jews* (New York: Columbia University Press, 1981), 66.
6   The East Bronx had a density of 130,000 per square mile. Moore, *At Home*, 66.
7   Pritchett, *Brownsville*, 15.

and their brothers entered the construction business together. This family pattern of work characterized a significant segment of Jewish builders, especially those who managed to remain in the business.[8]

An absence of discriminatory barriers to enter the field of speculative building partially accounted for the outsized presence of Jews as builders in the city. There were many routes to becoming a builder, but in the years before World War II all of them usually involved some form of apprenticeship rather than formal training. Aspiring builders worked on construction projects of friends or relatives. Newcomers learned on the job, watching how various trades were coordinated and supervised. Once they thought they understood the process and could get financing, they set off on their own. These networks drew expanding circles of Jews into construction. Even men with college educations entered the field. Some joined family firms, often working with their fathers, brothers, uncles, and cousins.[9]

John Tishman, who benefited from the prosperity produced by his grandfather's eponymous firm, acknowledged the significance of such family businesses. In an era of discrimination against Jews "by the predominantly Protestant mainstream society in the U.S.," establishing a family construction and real estate firm allowed Jews "to control their destinies, to fend for themselves and to make their way up the economic ladder. These firms," observed this third-generation member of Tishman Realty and Construction, "called themselves 'owner-builders.' It was an apt and comprehensive description, since the families' stock in trade was to acquire land, erect a structure on that property, and after the building was completed to continue to own and manage it and make income from it."[10]

The widespread puffery promoting Jewish builders, who imagined houses where swamps and farms existed and crowed about their rags-to-riches capitalist accomplishments, provoked angry responses from Communist and Socialist Jewish writers. The Communist novelist Michael Gold in his 1930 semi-autobiographical novel, *Jews without Money,* mocked their pretensions through the sensitive response of his mother to a possible purchase of a new house in Borough Park. "My mother would not go

---

8   Leon Wexelstein, *Building Up Greater Brooklyn with Sketches of Men Instrumental in Brooklyn's Amazing Development* (New York: Brooklyn Biographical Society, 1925), passim.

9   Moore, *At Home,* 39–53.

10   John Tishman with Tom Schactman, *Building Tall: My Life and the Creation of Construction Management* (Ann Arbor, MI: University of Michigan Press, 2011), 9–10.

in," to view the suburban house. "She remained on the porch like a beggar," he wrote. "With troubled eyes she stared around at the suburb, at the lots covered with slush and weeds, at the eight banal houses."[11] Abraham Cahan, the perceptive editor of the Yiddish Socialist daily *Forverts*, similarly depicted the ambition of Jewish builders in his 1917 novel, *The Rise of David Levinsky*. "Vast areas of meadowland and rock were turned by them, as by a magic wand, into densely populated avenues and streets of brick and mortar," he wrote. "Under the spell of their activity cities larger than Odessa sprang up within the confines of Greater New York in the course of three or four years."[12] The gradual erasure of vacant plots of land thrilled builders, who delighted in the changes they wrought. Many chose to honor family members, especially wives and daughters, by naming buildings after them.

Jewish builders left a lasting impress on Brooklyn and the Bronx during the interwar period, turning farms into streets lined with tenements and erecting multistory elevator-equipped apartment buildings along broad, tree-lined avenues. Their vision of a modern urban neighborhood departed from the mixed-use pattern of Brownsville and other immigrant areas. Instead they segregated commerce onto larger streets, leaving many blocks with exclusively residential buildings. Jewish builders would similarly remake Queens in the postwar decades, accommodating shifting styles of what was considered modern and desirable. Ten-year tax incentives in the 1920s spurred construction, as did expansion of the subway system. Jewish "builders anticipated population movement, constructing speculative buildings that would become the basis for Jewish neighborhoods. In the process, Jews introduced standards that would define both middle-class living and upper-class urban luxury as well as aesthetics that conveyed what it meant to be modern and up-to-date. Of course, in all cases, zoning laws restricted height and mass of commercial office buildings and factories, and tenement laws governed residential construction, not only height and mass but also plumbing, ventilation—especially light and air—heating, and fireproofing."[13] What these Jews built reflected their ambitions and dreams within standard urban constraints. As one chronicler of New York

---

11   Michael Gold, *Jews without Money* (1930; reprint ed., New York: Avon Books, 1965), 155.

12   Abraham Cahan, *The Rise of David Levinsky* (1917; reprint ed., New York: Harper, 1960), 512. He exaggerated only slightly. Odessa boasted a population of roughly 125,000 Jews in 1897, around 30% of the total population.

13   Deborah Dash Moore, "Who Built New York?: Jewish Builders in the Interwar Decades," *American Jewish History* 101, no 3 (July 2017): 316.

residential builders observed, "The builder determines the size, appearance and manner of the structure; this is obvious. But it is *not* so obvious that he determines the class of people who would seek to live on his property."[14]

Although Jewish builders put up single- and two-family homes, especially in Brooklyn, and modern walk-up tenements, especially in the Bronx, the greater residential density of apartment houses came to characterize distinctive Jewish urban neighborhoods. The sociologist Marshall Sklare labeled the apartment house "the emblem of the Jews' love affair with the city." As he observed, "the elevator building was designed for people who had moved up from the working class and walk-up building, and who, though financially able to buy a one-family home in the suburbs, chose to remain in the city."[15] Jewish builders embraced apartment houses as a way of synthesizing American modern with Jewish ethnic values. "The public space of lobbies, hallways, rooftops, stairwells, and elevators allowed for controlled social action among tenants and mediated the encounter with what some Jews perceived as the American world of the streets."[16] Builders advertised the latest conveniences—self-operating elevators, switched outlets, tiled bathrooms, and refrigerators—along with such luxurious elements as parquet floors and entrance foyers. These accompanied the new basic requisites of light and air from windows in every room, including bathrooms and kitchens.[17]

During the 1920s, New York City, with a population of approximately six million, accounted for 20% of new residential construction in the United States. Apartment buildings, 39% of such residential construction in 1919, soared to 77% by the peak year 1926. These numbers indicated many opportunities for Jews to enter the speculative housing market.[18] In Brooklyn alone, the decade produced 118,000 new houses along with "a whole array of streets."[19] Jews built all types of apartment buildings, from

14 Emphasis in the original. Franklin J. Sherman, *Building Up Greater Queens Borough* (New York: Brooklyn Biographical Society, 1929), 62.

15 Marshall Sklare, "Jews, Ethnics, and the American City," *Commentary*, April 1972, 72.

16 Deborah Dash Moore, "On the Fringes of the City: Jewish Neighborhoods in Three Boroughs," in *The Landscape of Modernity: Essays on New York City, 1900–1940*, ed. David Ward and Olivier Zunz (New York: Russell Sage Foundation, 1992), 253.

17 Moore, "Who Built New York?," 328.

18 Steven Ruttenbaum, *Mansions in the Clouds: The Skyscraper Palazzi of Emery Roth* (New York: Balsam Press, 1986), 66–67.

19 Quote from Wexelstein, *Building Up Greater Brooklyn*, xv–xvii. Eleanora Schoenbaum, "Emerging Neighborhoods: The Development of Brooklyn's Fringe Areas, 1850–1930" (PhD diss., Columbia University, 1977), 292, notes the correlation of the ethnicity

monuments to luxury on Manhattan's Upper East and West sides to middle-class versions in the Bronx, Brooklyn, and Washington Heights, to utilitarian cooperatives for workers in the Bronx. These apartment houses shared common elements that set them apart from tenements: they all featured light and air, modern fixtures, the latest in plumbing. Many were fire-proof and all followed the revised tenement housing codes.

Among the hundreds of Jewish builders, several stand out. Irwin Chanin introduced art deco style to apartment construction just as the Depression hit. He had started with two single-family houses in Bensonhurst, Brooklyn, after World War I and made his reputation initially as a builder of theaters in Times Square and then with the monumental eponymous Chanin office building on Forty-Second Street. In 1929 he decided to take advantage of new rules allowing construction of taller apartment buildings with setbacks, similar to office buildings. Despite the stock market crash, he continued to build during the early thirties, putting up two elegant apartment houses on Central Park West that occupied an entire block front: the Century between Sixtieth and Sixty-First Streets and the Majestic between Seventy-First and Seventy-Second Streets. Having acquired an architect license, Chanin designed both with signature art deco features, a style previously reserved for theaters, restaurants and office buildings. Such items as corner windows, sunken living rooms, and free-standing showers set his twin-towered buildings apart, along with solaria and exuberant detailing in the main entry and lobby.[20]

The style caught on, particularly along the Grand Concourse in the Bronx. During the Depression, Jewish builders constructed block after block of yellow brick apartment houses along the boulevard, buoyed by the building of the Independent subway line underneath the street. This neighborhood attracted middle-class Jews who relished the modern elegance of their mostly six-story apartment houses. These residents delighted in the recessed entrances with molded, precast concrete panels that looked like curtains, ceilings with mosaic ornamentation, curving apartments

---

of builders with the subsequent ethnic group dominant in the neighborhood by comparing Italian and Jewish builders in Canarsie and Flatlands respectively.

20 On Chanin, see Moore, "Who Built New York?" For details see Landmarks Preservation Commission, Century Apartments, July 9, 1985, Designation List 181, LP-1517, 1–5. Report prepared by Andrew Dolkart; and Landmarks Preservation Commission, Majestic Apartments, March 8, 1988, Designation List 201, LP-1518, 1–5. Report prepared by Andrew Dolkart.

with geometric motifs, elevator doors incised with arching designs, corner windows, and accessible roof tops with stylish metal railings.[21]

Henry Mandel's career exemplifies the ongoing presence of Jewish builders in New York even after bankruptcy and death. Although often touted like Chanin for his skyscrapers, Mandel's two innovative residential projects constructed in Manhattan and completed during the Great Depression—London Terrace and Chelsea Corners—were perhaps more important. Mandel anticipated that the attraction of a short walk or subway ride to work would offset living in a less prestigious, largely industrial neighborhood. He bet that an economical apartment, combined with access to shared amenities, would prove attractive even to white-collar workers.[22] Like many builders, he appealed to women, based on convenience and style. To that end, he set up an "Apartment Shop" on Fifth Avenue and Thirty-Sixth Street with five different apartment layouts. A brochure promoted the galley-style kitchens, designed to save "precious steps."[23]

Mandel built London Terrace on a full square block between Twenty-Third and Twenty-Fourth Streets and Ninth and Tenth Avenues, within easy walking distance of the new garment center to the north as well as to shopping on Thirty-Fourth Street. The "colossally scaled complex of fourteen continuous buildings" contained 1,670 apartments, most of them studios or one-bedrooms for white collar workers, not families, and cost more than $25 million to build. At the time, it was the largest apartment building in the world and produced an astonishing density of population. Although a courtyard existed in the interior, the nineteen-story buildings addressed the street with shops and three restaurants along the avenues. Garage space was nearby. Mandel envisioned London Terrace as a city within a city, offering its five thousand residents a host of modern amenities rarely available even in upper-class Park Avenue apartment houses—such as an Olympic-sized swimming pool and a rooftop clubhouse that resembled the deck of an ocean liner. (From the roof deck, actual ocean liners could be seen docked at the nearby Hudson River piers.) Internal tunnels

21   Donald G. Sullivan and Brian J. Danforth, *Bronx Art Deco Architecture: An Exposition* (New York: Hunter College, 1976), 49, 56.

22   "Henry Mandel, 58, Realty Man, Dies: Builder of London Terrace, Park Vendome Apartments, a Native of Russia; Erected Brittany Hotel: Responsible for the Pershing Square, Hearst and Postal Life Office Structures," *New York Times*, October 11, 1942, 57.

23   Ed Lewis, "201 West 16th Street: A History," http://201west16.org/history/; accessed September 9, 2017.

connected the buildings and allowed residents to access many amenities without going outside.[24]

While Mandel completed London Terrace by May of 1930 and rented most of its apartments, he failed to fulfill his even more ambitious ideal for Chelsea Corners. Looking at a rather mundane stretch of Seventh Avenue south of Twenty-Third Street filled with small buildings, random shops, and a few industrial lofts, Mandel saw an opportunity to secure corner lots along the avenue for apartment houses that would allow white-collar workers to live near their employment in Manhattan. Billed as "one of the greatest residential developments in New York, creating a new skyline on the avenue, replacing the existing buildings with lofty apartment buildings, uniform in their general architectural conception and ranging from seventeen to twenty stories in height," Chelsea Corners encompassed a staggering seventeen buildings to be located on the corners of Seventh Avenue and Fifteenth, Sixteenth, Eighteenth, Nineteenth, Twentieth and Twenty-Second Streets.[25] Both the printing and garment districts as well as the flower district were located within a mile of Mandel's corners and the subway ran beneath the avenue.[26] In fact, a number of printing plants occupied Seventh Avenue, including a large bindery on the southeast corner of Sixteenth Street. Ignoring the onset of the Depression, in 1931 Mandel quickly erected four nineteen-story corner buildings, three facing each other across Seventh Avenue at Sixteenth Street and one at Fifteenth Street.[27] But his ambitious

---

24 Robert A. M. Stern, Gregory Gilmartin, and Thomas Mellins, *New York 1930: Architecture and Urbanism between the Two World Wars* (New York: Rizzoli International Publications, 1987), 417; Andrew Alpern, *Luxury Apartment Houses of Manhattan: An Illustrated History* (New York: Dover, 1993), 149–150. London Terrace rented apartments for $30 per room to secretaries, accountants, engineers, and attorneys.

25 "Big Apartment Row on Seventh Avenue: Henry Mandel Plans Seventeen Tall Structures to Be Known as Chelsea Corners," *New York Times,* March 29, 1931.

26 "Mandel Companies Plan Seven Flats in Chelsea Area to Cost $15,000,000," *New York Times,* May 16, 1930. The article totals the number of apartments in both Chelsea Corners and London Terrace as 2,269, with 5,534 rooms and 2,392 baths.

27 He also completed the Parc Vendome east of Ninth Avenue running from Fifty-Sixth to Fifty-Seventh Street with 600 apartments, the Lombardy apartment hotel on East Fifty-Sixth Street where he lived, and the Pershing Square building at Forty-Second Street and Park Avenue (later the Continental Can building). Christopher Gray, "Streetscapes/Seventh Avenue Between 15th and 16th Streets; 4 30s Apartment Buildings on 4 Chelsea Corners," *New York Times,* May 23, 2004, http://www.nytimes.com/2004/05/23/realestate/streetscapes-seventh-avenue-between-15th-16th-streets-four-30-s-apartment.html, accessed August 30, 2017.

plans stumbled. Unable to weather the Depression, in 1932 he plunged into bankruptcy and his buildings went into foreclosure.[28] Rumors circulated that he had committed suicide.

While Mandel died in 1942, his vision endured. Other owners acquired his properties, and the appeal of living in a neighborhood with a mix of industry, commerce, and white-collar employment survived. Indeed, the buildings remained attractive residential choices for generations of white-collar workers who liked the idea of living near their offices. In some ways, Mandel's concept updated aspects of Jewish immigrant areas that he had known growing up. These neighborhoods routinely mixed residences with commerce and industry. Having started out with his father, Samuel, in building tenements, Henry Mandel reimagined an older way of thinking about urban space. His high-density apartment buildings accepted Manhattan's streets as promiscuous rather than segregated spaces, although his developments retained biases and exclusion based on class and race.[29]

In contrast to bourgeois apartment houses, Jewish workers developed cooperative housing in the Bronx as a blue-collar alternative. Through cooperation, workers aimed to acquire the benefits of middle-class living at reduced rates, thus effectively improving their socio-economic status. By eliminating landlords and gaining tax abatements for limited dividends, cooperative housing substantially lowered monthly fees, reducing the cost of living and enhancing wage-earners' purchasing power. While many politically engaged Jews experimented with cooperatives, the Amalgamated Clothing Workers of America produced the most successful iteration in 1927. Located in the northern Bronx overlooking Van Cortlandt Park, the initial six buildings incorporated a courtyard design that featured separate entrances for the different wings. Although the five-story buildings were walk-ups, all of the apartments had windows in every room, cross ventilation, bathtubs, kitchens with iceboxes and gas ranges, hot and cold running water, and electricity. The Depression forced most of the Jewish cooperatives into the hands of mortgagees and landlords, but the Amalgamated survived

---

28   See obituary, "Henry Mandel, 58, Realty Man, Dies," *New York Times*, October 11, 1942, 57.

29   Alpern, *Luxury Apartment Houses,* 150, quotes the rental agent, William A. White & Sons, "Restrictions are especially important in London Terrace," promising a "careful check of business, social and financial references before a lease is signed."

with the help of its union and the Forward Association, the organization that published the Yiddish daily *Forverts*.[30]

Despite foreclosures, the cooperatives' political culture endured. Common rooms, nursery schools, libraries, and clubs that sponsored theatrical performances and lectures complemented shared purchasing of milk, ice, and groceries. Cooperation meant more than having a single electrical meter for the entire complex; it expressed collective communal values.[31] After World War II, Abraham Kazan, who championed cooperatives, took this vision of urban living to other parts of the city with the support of the union's Amalgamated Dwellings Corporation. Eventually, a partnership of state and federal monies would stimulate Jews to build cooperatives designed for the middle as well as the working class.

Jewish builders did not focus only on residential construction. During the interwar decades, they rebuilt extensive sections of midtown with loft buildings designed specifically for the garment industry. As clothing manufacturing evolved, "interwar jobbers directly supervised cutting and perhaps finishing, but subcontracted out the sewing. Their small cutting shops and showrooms became increasingly concentrated in the midtown garment district."[32] Women's clothing manufacturers could not afford to be separated from the jobbers. So, they moved north to the streets between Seventh and Eighth Avenues in the twenties and thirties where Jewish builders constructed loft buildings to accommodate them. The needle trades concentrated in a new garment district that became known as Seventh Avenue. These buildings all featured fireproof construction, a heritage of the disastrous Triangle Shirtwaist Factory fire. That 1911 fire on the upper floors of the fireproof Asch building took the lives of 146 workers, mostly Jewish women, although the building itself survived without serious damage. The new fireproof loft buildings possessed features to save the lives of workers in case of fire and not just keep the building safe. These modern loft buildings had fireproof stairs, complete sprinkler systems, elevators with safety devices, and fire towers for speed in putting out fires. Mostly utilitarian in design, garment factory lofts in midtown guaranteed

30 Moore, *At Home*, 53–55.
31 Katherine Rosenblatt, "Cooperative Battlegrounds" (PhD diss., University of Michigan, 2016), chap. 2, 106–11.
32 Nancy L. Green, "From Downtown Tenements to Midtown Lofts: The Shifting Geography of an Urban Industry," in *A Coat of Many Colors: Immigration, Globalism and Reform in New York City's Garment Industry*, ed. Daniel Soyer (New York: Fordham University Press, 2005), 34.

that industrial production remained a visible part of New York City. Similar trends led to the relocation of the printing industry from the east to the west side of lower Manhattan. Jewish builders constructed lofts with structural steel and reinforced concrete that would support heavy printing presses. They also installed special acid-proof soil lines to carry off liquid wastes from the presses.[33]

Many of these Jewish builders flourished when New York City was expanding and increasing in population. Builders of speculative office buildings and industrial lofts especially benefited from the enormous growth of New York City after consolidation with Brooklyn in 1898. New York's population doubled from 3.4 million in 1900 to 6.9 million by 1930.[34]

As Jews entered the field of speculative building, they followed in the footsteps of immigrants, like the Irish and Germans, who had arrived in the nineteenth century. Ethnicity shaped the city's extensive construction industry, from the various trades to the foremen and builders. The building trades attracted diverse immigrants, but relatively few immigrant builders became active in the formal real estate and construction market, which relied on commercial banks and mortgage companies for loans. Rather, immigrant builders drew upon fellow ethnics for resources when they decided to go into construction. Jews, too, started by entering the informal market directed at their fellow working-class immigrants. They received financing from other Jews, turning to friends, family, Jewish businessmen with money to loan, and eventually, as they succeeded, to Jewish mortgage companies and banks.[35] Often a builder borrowed money in stages so that he received additional funds as he completed different parts of the building, from laying the foundation and erecting the scaffolding, to enclosing the building and topping it off. With some luck in choice of location and timing, a builder easily found tenants.[36]

New York's construction industry was largely ethnically segregated, which meant that Jews entered a segment of the industry even as Italians or Irish or Germans entered other parts of construction. Entering an

33   Moore, "Who Built New York?," 322–25.
34   Ira Rosenwaike, *Population History of New York City* (Syracuse, NY: Syracuse University Press, 1972), 90–92.
35   On Jewish banks see Rebecca Kobrin, "Destructive Creators: Sender Jarmulowsky and Financial Failure in the Annals of American Jewish History," *American Jewish History* 97, no. 2 (2013): 105–37.
36   Moore, *At Home*, 35–36, 39–49.

ethnically segregated construction industry, Jewish builders regularly built specifically for Jewish tenants: residential, commercial, and industrial. Jews concentrated in certain niches of the city's economy, foremost among them the garment, printing, jewelry, baking, and entertainment industries.[37] Jewish business owners often turned to Jewish builders when they sought better facilities for their firms and Jewish builders often courted Jewish businessmen. On occasion, Jewish garment manufacturers like Abraham Lefcourt decided to try their hand in building. Lefcourt invested profits from his garment firm and entered the construction industry. Dubbed "the Miracle Man of Realty," Lefcourt became the garment center district's largest builder and "a major force behind the creation of this new industrial center."[38] In short, moving from buttons to building was not unheard of.

Depression and war reduced new construction in the city, but after the war a building boom occurred. In 1958, in the midst of that boom, the *New York Times* published an article comparing the "skyscraper builders of yesteryear" with current leading figures.[39] Although the *Times* did not mention it, their list of old and new builders contained almost exclusively Jewish names. Fred French, Walter J. Salmon, Abraham Lefcourt, Henry Mandel, and Irwin Chanin headlined the interwar list that also included Julius Tishman, Harris Uris, Abe Adelson, and the four partners of the Bricken Construction and Improvement Corporation: Abraham Bricken, Leo Schloss, Irving J. Friedman, and Samuel Lipman. This was an odd list: none of these men had constructed the Chrysler Building or the Empire State building, the iconic New York skyscrapers of those years. In focusing on mostly Jewish figures in construction, the *Times* article was instead pointing to the emergence of an ethnic segment of the industry that was

---

37 Jews also were extensively involved in food industries as well as commerce on large and small scales. However, while factories required loft buildings as did wholesale firms, retail shops, restaurants and lunchrooms did not necessarily lead to construction of buildings. Similarly, white-collar occupations as professionals—teachers, social workers, lawyers, dentists, and doctors—rarely led to construction work. The enormous physical expansion of the public-school system in the interwar years did not involve Jewish builders.

38 Andrew S. Dolkart, "From the Rag Trade to Riches: Abraham E. Lefcourt and the Development of New York's Garment District," in *Chosen Capital: The Jewish Encounter with American Capitalism,* ed. Rebecca Kobrin (New Brunswick: Rutgers University Press, 2012), 64.

39 Thomas W. Ennis, "Skyscraper Builders of Yesteryear Give Way to the New: Depression and Deaths Help Thin the Ranks of Speculators Who Helped Change Manhattan in Twenties," *New York Times,* April 13, 1958, R1, 10.

achieving greater visibility in the decades after World War II. Jewish firms were now headlining speculative office construction in Manhattan, rather than garment lofts, or even Broadway theaters.

Jewish builders Percy and Harold Uris, Joseph Blist, Norman Tishman, Erwin Wolfson, and Joseph Durst occupied the top of the postwar list. The *Times* added Sam Minskoff, Sam Rudin, William Kaufman, and Jack D. Weiler as "big names." Jewish builders' visibility as leading men in an important New York industry signaled the growing prominence of construction as an important economic niche for Jews.[40]

Although the *Times* avoided mentioning the Jewish identity of many of the men, it did point out that several were the sons of an earlier generation of builders, notably Norman Tishman, the youngest son of Julius Tishman, and Percy and Harold Uris, sons of Harris Uris. The article also reported that "a surprising diversity of pursuits" characterized builders of the 1920s. "Only one or two builders had started in the construction trades. The others were milliners, clothiers, house painters," or, more aptly, engaged in the less prestigious, low-capital alteration building trades remodeling tenements, and the proverbial "newsboys."[41] Garment manufacturing had served as a well-known ethnic niche, dominated by Jews as workers, jobbers, and manufacturers prior to World War II. By referencing a form of "common knowledge" among its readers, the *Times* implicitly acknowledged the Jewishness of these men who built skyscrapers. The article highlighted the significant visibility of Jewish builders together with its implications for the growth of New York. As one historian subsequently observed, these men were "unusual only in the scope of their real estate enterprises. Other Jewish developers, working on a smaller scale," had constructed thousands of buildings in the interwar years, "ranging from modest apartment houses to great commercial skyscrapers."[42]

The article's author looked back to the 1920s for precedents. Before 1920 only 34 office buildings over five stories were erected during the twenty-three-year period between 1897–1920. By contrast, between 1920 and 1933, 138 office buildings set a thirteen-year record for new skyscraper construction. The *Times* cited a number of distinctive prewar Manhattan skyscrapers, including the fifty-six-story Chanin building at 122 East Forty-Second Street, completed in 1929, the first building with

---

40   Ennis, "Skyscraper Builders," R1, 10.
41   Ibid.
42   Dolkart, "From the Rag Trade to Riches," 87.

its tower illuminated by floodlights at night. It also mentioned the Bricken Corporation's forty-five-story Transportation Building downtown at 225 Broadway, and Abraham Lefcourt's eponymous forty-story building at 521 Fifth Avenue (corner of Forty-Third Street), completed in 1929.[43]

However, postwar construction was challenging the interwar record. By 1958 over 100 new skyscrapers had been built in the space of thirteen years, dramatically modifying many of the city's streets. The postwar boom did not erase memories of what had been lost, of bankruptcies and foreclosures. The Great Depression had wiped out the fortunes of many builders, something the *Times* acknowledged. Still, looking at the differences between the 1920s and the 1950s, the *Times* optimistically pointed to aspects of the current postwar situation that made widespread foreclosures less likely. No longer was easy credit available; standard long-term leases now included escalator clauses to pass on increases in taxes and other costs to tenants; greater investments in equity were required to help construct or purchase an office building.[44] Revised zoning also spurred construction, as did dismantling the elevated trains that brought noise and dirt to residents.[45] The last one, the Third-Avenue elevated, came down in 1955. New buildings marched up wide avenues no longer shadowed by tracks overhead, especially Sixth Avenue (renamed Avenue of the Americas) and Third Avenue.[46]

The postwar years registered additional changes. While many Jewish builders continued in the speculative informal mode, others moved into a formal housing market that relied on government financing. This enmeshed Jews in politics and networks outside of their ethnic circles. In one of the most innovative postwar moves, John Tishman convinced his uncle to let him bid on construction work that would not be owned and operated by Tishman, reversing the firm's previous policy. An engineer by training, John Tishman called his innovation "construction management." Unlike Irwin Chanin who had secured an architect's license to gain control over construction, Tishman sought to professionalize his building operations substantively and promotionally. He aimed to transform his form of business entrepreneurship rooted in skilled trades into a new field that placed him on the same level as an architect. In fact, as a construction manager,

---

43   Ennis, "Skyscraper Builders," R1, 10.
44   Ibid.
45   Kim Moody, *From Welfare State to Real Estate: Regime Change in New York City, 1874 to the Present* (New York: The New Press, 2007), 3.
46   The other avenues with elevated trains were Second Avenue and Ninth Avenue.

Tishman challenged architectural designs and demanded modifications to accommodate construction requisites.[47]

The desire to move up in status touched most successful Jewish builders. "Every real estate family that made its money in Brooklyn, Queens or the Bronx eventually has children and grandchildren who want to make their mark in Manhattan or some other glamour location," remarked Mitchell Moss, a professor of urban planning at New York University.[48] Gradually, a gulf developed between prominent Jewish firms, like the ones mentioned in the *Times*' article, and other relatively small-scale builders.

But trends of the interwar years also continued after the war. Jewish builders adopted new designs, often surrounding tall apartment buildings with grass and trees instead of facing them toward tree-lined streets. Modern middle-class apartment houses now promoted affordable elegance only a brief subway ride from offices rather than factories. One example promoted "three luxurious 21-story skyscrapers" as "an entire suburb within a suburb."[49] Such apartment houses attempted to compete with the burgeoning suburbs by devoting a substantial portion of the site to landscaped grounds. The buildings offered both covered balconies and air conditioning (when it was too hot to sit on the balcony). As more city dwellers bought automobiles, new apartment houses incorporated garages, a feature distinguishing them from their prewar predecessors.[50]

If prewar Manhattan had been a city of brick and mortar, its postwar skyscrapers were increasingly sheathed in glass and aluminum. John Tishman embraced the use of exterior aluminum panels to skin a building's skeleton. It took weeks to finish an office building with bricks and mortar. Aluminum cut this to days. So pleased was he with his innovative engineering partnership with Alcoa that he decided to promote the system by covering two sides of a building in a single day. In early October 1960, Tishman invited *Life* photographers to shoot the process at 460

---

47   Tishman, *Building Tall*, 153–71.
48   Quoted in Charles V. Bagli, "Blue-Collar Builders Expand Empire to Glitzier Shores," *New York Times* [N.Y. Region], October 9, 2007. A version of the article appeared in print, *New York Times* [New York edition], under the title, "The Family Empire That Built Lefrak City Is Developing a Global Vision," B1.
49   Quoted in Deborah Dash Moore, Jeffrey S. Gurock, Annie Polland, Howard B. Rock, and Daniel Soyer, *Jewish New York: The Remarkable Story of a City and a People* (New York: New York University Press, 2017), 204–205.
50   "New Apartments Offer Terraces," *New York Times*, April 26, 1942.

Park Avenue, corner of Fifty-Seventh Street in midtown.[51] Manhattan increasingly became the home of corporate headquarters. The trend started in the 1950s and extended through the 1960s, signaled by the construction of the distinctive and expensive Seagram building on Park Avenue in what had been a residential area.[52] Jewish builders participated in this boom and sold more contemporary office buildings with flexible open floor plans to accommodate major national and international firms. A glorious building like the 1929 Chanin building, for example, had small, subdivided interior spaces. By contrast, engineering designs that cantilevered the floor supports between an external frame and an internal core that housed elevators made possible the open floor plan of the Fifth Avenue Tishman building.

Other successful builders, men like Samuel J. LeFrak, focused not on Manhattan skyscrapers but on expansive middle-class housing developments, mostly in the outer boroughs. These "blue-collar builders" aimed, as LeFrak quipped, to "serve the mass, not the class." For half a century after World War II, Sam LeFrak concentrated on construction projects in and around New York City, amassing in the process "a multibillion-dollar empire that comprises more residential and commercial property than can be found in most medium-sized cities. . . ."[53] Like many Jewish family firms, the LeFrak Organization housed its headquarters in its signature property. For Tishman, it was the distinctive aluminum-clad Tishman building at 666 Fifth Avenue. By contrast, LeFrak located its offices in its sprawling Queens residential development, Lefrak City. This huge complex, completed in 1959, boasted five thousand apartments—three times the number in Mandel's London Terrace—in twenty eighteen-story buildings and housed fifteen thousand people, including many families. During the years it took to complete, the project also served as summer school for Sam's son, Richard LeFrak. Richard was smitten. "The capacity to make something from nothing—that's the sex," he admitted. "The other stuff is kissing."[54]

Both of Richard's sons also entered the business, just as Sam had joined his father, Harry Lefrak, an immigrant glazier. Harry's initiatives had been

---

51 Tishman, *Building Tall*, 43.

52 The Seagram Building for the Canadian distillery was completed in 1958. Seagram Building, New York City, https://skyscraperpage.com/cities/?buildingID=2386, accessed May 25, 2018.

53 Bagli, "Blue-Collar Builders." Bagli notes: "There is little or no debt on the family's holdings. When the LeFraks build, as they are doing at their 600–acre Newport complex on the waterfront in Jersey City, they do so without any loans."

54 Quoted in ibid.

relatively modest; he started out building small houses in Williamsburg and then constructed tenements. Like John Tishman, Sam LeFrak entered the business in 1948 after studying engineering. Together, Sam and Harry built apartment houses in Queens, naming them after the different states. By 1950 they had already built the Oklahoma and Oregon in Forest Hills, with the Washington soon to follow.[55] With his decision to build and own, and to finance privately, LeFrak adopted a popular pattern of Jewish builders in the city, including such family firms as those of Rose and Rudin, Muss and Milstein.[56] LeFrak also innovated, for example, by setting aside twenty percent of almost 10,000 apartments under construction in Brooklyn and Queens for elderly tenants, with special features designed to make their lives easier.[57]

Perhaps the most iconic among later twentieth-century office buildings, the World Trade Towers, was built by Tishman Construction. But this was not a speculative office building. Tishman managed construction for the Port Authority of New York. His ability to work with a public client, the Port Authority, indicated a level of respectability that this Jewish builder had achieved, especially since Tishman was chosen over two giant general non-Jewish contractors, Fuller and Turner.[58] Similarly, after the LeFrak organization finished its eponymous complex in Queens, it built Gateway Battery Park City on landfill in lower Manhattan (some of it coming from the enormous "bathtub" that had to be dug to secure the trade towers from the Hudson River).[59] LeFrak's 1,700-apartment project, like the World Trade Center towers, was partially paid for with public funds.

Both of these huge projects reflected the integration of successful Jewish builders into the upper echelons of New York City construction. John Tishman was keenly aware of the significance of his firm's new status when he was subsequently chosen by Texaco to manage the construction of their new national headquarters in a suburb outside the city. Looking back at

---

55 "Queens Site Sold For Apartments: Builders Buy Blockfront in Forest Hills Area for a New Project," *New York Times*, May 14, 1950.

56 On Muss see Alison Gregor, "Away from the Limelight, A Builder Makes his Mark," *New York Times*, December 31, 2006.

57 "Apartment Builder is Designing 20% of Projects for the Elderly," *New York Times*, August 18, 1957. The innovations included an absence of thresholds in doorways, non-skid floors, amplified doorbells, and handrails on walls and in bathrooms.

58 Both of these firms were family firms, not Jewish; Fuller dated back to the mid-nineteenth century and Turner to 1902.

59 Tishman, *Building Tall*, 81–94, on building the World Trade Towers.

that moment in the early 1970s, he wrote, "I was particularly appreciative of the opportunity to build for Texaco, as it broke a barrier—a religious-based one. Prior to this time, most major industrial and financial corporations had been reluctant to award professional work to firms with Jewish owners."[60] In fact, his father and uncle had taken the firm public in 1928 in part as a means to raise funds for construction. The firm remained publicly owned until it was sold during the city's financial crisis and subsequently reconstituted in 1980 as privately owned.[61]

Beyond even Battery Park City and the World Trade Center, the impact of Jewish builders on New York City can perhaps be best assessed by standing at the corner of Twenty-Third Street and Ninth Avenue. North and west loom the massive towers of London Terrace. But north and east stretch fifteen relatively modest brick apartment houses, with 2,820 apartments, that make up Penn South, as the International Ladies' Garment Workers' Union cooperative is called (its official name is Mutual Redevelopment Houses). Funded in part by city tax abatements and completed in 1962, Penn South exemplifies the enduring impact of the residential cooperative ideal on New York City.[62] Both London Terrace and Penn South replaced tenements and industrial buildings. Both represent visions that celebrate living not far from one's place of work. One caters to middle- and upper-class tenants and the other to middle- and working-class residents. And both reflect Jewish builders' efforts to shape a livable urban environment.

---

60 Ibid., 164.

61 Ibid., 11–12, 104–109. Part of the financing for the stock float came through his mother's family and friends who were in the banking business in Chicago.

62 Raanan Geberer, "Affordable Living in Chelsea: A Look at Manhattan's Penn South Co-op," November 2004, https://cooperator.com/article/affordable-living-in-chelsea/full, accessed September 5, 2017.

For Further Reading

Alpern, Andrew. *Luxury Apartment Houses of Manhattan: An Illustrated History.* New York: Dover, 1993.

Buder, Stanley. *Pullman: An Experiment in Industrial Order and Community Planning, 1880–1930.* New York: Oxford University Press, 1967.

Cahan, Abraham. *The Rise of David Levinsky,* reprint ed. New York: Harper, 1960. Original edition, 1917.

Dolkart, Andrew S. "From the Rag Trade to Riches: Abraham E. Lefcourt and the Development of New York's Garment District." In *Chosen Capital: The Jewish Encounter with American Capitalism,* edited by Rebecca Kobrin, 62–90. New Brunswick: Rutgers University Press, 2012.

Gold, Michael. *Jews without Money,* reprint ed. New York: Avon Books, 1965. Original edition, 1930.

Green, Nancy L. "From Downtown Tenements to Midtown Lofts: The Shifting Geography of an Urban Industry." In *A Coat of Many Colors: Immigration, Globalism and Reform in New York City's Garment Industry,* edited by Daniel Soyer, 27–44. New York: Fordham University Press, 2004.

Kobrin, Rebecca. "Destructive Creators: Sender Jarmulowsky and Financial Failure in the Annals of American Jewish History." *American Jewish History* 97, no. 2 (2013): 105–37.

Moody, Kim. *From Welfare State to Real Estate: Regime Change in New York City, 1874 to the Present.* New York: The New Press, 2007.

Moore, Deborah Dash. *At Home in America: Second Generation New York Jews.* New York: Columbia University Press, 1981.

———. "On the Fringes of the City: Jewish Neighborhoods in Three Boroughs." In *The Landscape of Modernity: Essays on New York City, 1900–1940,* edited by David Ward and Olivier Zunz, 252–72. New York: Russell Sage Foundation, 1992.

———. "Who Built New York?: Jewish Builders in the Interwar Decades." *American Jewish History* 101, no 3 (July 2017): 311–36.

Moore, Deborah Dash, Jeffrey S. Gurock, Annie Polland, Howard B. Rock, and Daniel Soyer. *Jewish New York: The Remarkable Story of a City and a People.* New York: New York University Press, 2017.

Pritchett, Wendell. *Brownsville, Brooklyn: Blacks, Jews, and the Changing Face of the Ghetto.* Chicago: University of Chicago Press, 2002.

Rosenblatt, Katherine. "Cooperative Battlegrounds." PhD diss., University of Michigan, 2016.

Rosenwaike, Ira. *Population History of New York City.* Syracuse, NY: Syracuse University Press, 1972.

Ruttenbaum, Steven. *Mansions in the Clouds: The Skyscraper Palazzi of Emery Roth.* New York: Balsam Press, 1986.

Schoenbaum, Eleanora. "Emerging Neighborhoods: The Development of Brooklyn's Fringe Areas, 1850–1930." PhD diss., Columbia University, 1977.

Sklare, Marshall. "Jews, Ethnics, and the American City." *Commentary,* April 1972, 70–77.

Stern, Robert A. M., Gregory Gilmartin, and Thomas Mellins. *New York 1930: Architecture and Urbanism between the Two World Wars.* New York: Rizzoli International Publications, 1987.

Sullivan, Donald G., and Brian J. Danforth. *Bronx Art Deco Architecture: An Exposition.* New York: Hunter College, 1976.

Tishman, John, with Tom Schactman. *Building Tall: My Life and the Creation of Construction Management.* Ann Arbor, MI: University of Michigan Press, 2011.

Zunz, Olivier. *The Changing Face of Inequality: Urbanization, Industrial Development, and Immigrants in Detroit, 1880–1920.* Chicago: University of Chicago Press, 1982.

Chapter 8

New York Jews
and American Literature

David Mikics

"What could Emerson mean to a boy or girl on Rivington Street in 1929, hungry for books, reading voraciously, hearing Yiddish at home, yet learning to read, write, and think in English?" Irving Howe asked this question in 1977, in his essay "Strangers."[1] Howe, born Irving Horenstein in the Bronx in 1920, remembers being suspicious of Emerson's individualism and rhapsodic relation to nature, imbued as Howe was with what he called "our own tradition, long rutted in shtetl mud and urban smoke." New York Jewish writers did have a tradition of their own, for a while at least. But by the late seventies, when Howe wrote his essay, that tradition, based on the experience of immigrant life, was rapidly fading.

In his essay Howe complained about "those younger Jewish writers who are, so to say, exhausting the credit of their grandfathers' imaginations, making of the Lower East Side a sort of black-humored cartoon, half-Chagall, half-Disney. By now," Howe continued, "it is clear that the world

---

1   Irving Howe, "Strangers," reprinted in his *Selected Writings, 1950-1990* (New York: Harvest / Harcourt, Brace, Jovanovich, 1990), 325.
      One possible characteristic of Jewish American literature, Howe writes, is its interest in excitable, passionate talk, "a rapid, nervous, breathless tempo, like the hurry of a garment salesman trying to con a buyer or a highbrow lecturer trying to dazzle an audience" (338). Howe is thinking of Saul Bellow; but most of the writers I discuss sound rather different from him.

of our fathers, in its brief flare of secular passion, gave the American Jewish writers just enough material to see them through a handful of novels and stories. The advantages of remembered place soon gave way to the trouble of having lost their place." Howe's devastating assessment is probably correct: New York Jews had only a few generations' worth of time to carry their world into literature before the amnesia that America bestows on all its immigrants began to set in. There is still a genuine literature of Jewish New York centered on two well defined groups, Russian emigré Jews (like fiction writers Gary Shteyngart and Lara Vapnyar) and "off-the-*derech*" ex-Hasidim (like memoir writers Shulem Deen, Deborah Feldman, and Leah Vincent). These authors describe their departure from environments strange to outsiders, whether the former Soviet Union or strictly observant Hasidic enclaves, and their disoriented, questioning arrival in the American mainstream. They retain a sense of displacement not shared by most Jewish New Yorkers, who are more similar to than different from the gentiles around them.

From the very beginning, Jewish writers portrayed the trouble that came with having lost their place, a loss that started to occur with their arrival in the golden land of America, or perhaps even earlier, with their decision to emigrate or with a revolt against tradition in their old world homes. But they also turned this trouble into an imaginative source. New York Jewish writers were especially prone to take the chaos of urban life, and the Jew's hardscrabble effort to adapt to it, as their subject.

My focus in this essay is twofold: the effort of New York Jews to enter American literature, with the rich urban maelstrom that was and is New York as their calling card; and (secondarily) the project of the New York Intellectuals, especially Alfred Kazin and Lionel Trilling, to redefine the American canon. Both these enterprises owed something to the writer's or critic's consciousness of being a Jewish outsider, even as he or she laid claim to American tradition.

This is not an all-embracing survey. I have focused on New York Jewish writers who wrote about Jews and who relied on the city for their mise-en-scène. I discuss only one playwright, Tony Kushner, aware that Broadway and Yiddish theater are worlds in themselves, too large to be encompassed here. I omit poets writing in English in order to focus on the Yiddish poets who were bound together by a Jewish language and a close concern with Jewish immigrant life. My criteria are easy to quarrel with, but not adhering to them, or to something similar, would have turned this essay into a mere laundry list of writers who happen to be Jewish and happen to be from New York.[2]

For at least forty years, from the 1880s on, New York Jewish life meant the immigrant experience, which reached its peak in 1907, the year when close to a hundred and fifty thousand Jews came to America. The novel by a New York Jew that more than any other sums up an immigrant's life and prospects is Abraham Cahan's *The Rise of David Levinsky*. Cahan, as the editor of the *Forverts*, probably the most prominent of New York's Yiddish newspapers, had his finger on the pulse of Jewish life in the city.

Levinsky, Cahan's narrator, begins his story as a young greenhorn newly arrived at Castle Garden, the precursor to Ellis Island. (Cahan, born in 1860 in Lithuania, himself came to America in 1882.) Paying matter of fact attention to his various setbacks, Levinsky describes how he ascended from a pushcart peddler to a clothes cutter and then to the owner of a clothing business. By the end of the novel, he is worth millions. But he remains in the end a man at a loss, though measured in dollars a lucky one. The richer he becomes, the more adrift he seems.

Much to the reader's fascination, Levinsky describes the shrewd tactics he uses to build a business. Even more interesting are his odd responses when he courts women. During one successful seduction, of a married friend whom he has desperately desired, he listens to the woman's profession of love for him: "She spoke with profound, even-voiced earnestness,

---

2   The list of English-language Jewish poets from New York City is a long and distinguished one, including Emma Lazarus, Howard Nemerov, Delmore Schwartz, Alvin Feinman, John Hollander, Anthony Hecht, Irving Feldman, Samuel Menashe, Alicia Ostriker, Charles Reznikoff, Louis Zukofsky. My choice to discuss Yiddish poets instead is not a value judgment, but rather a decision about whether the lens of Jewishness is useful in dealing with a particular author. Feinman's verbal art is absolute, but thinking of him as a Jewish writer adds little to one's perspective on his work.

Among dramatists I have passed over Arthur Miller, George S. Kaufman, Moss Hart, Ben Hecht, Paddy Chayefsky, Harvey Fierstein, Wendy Wasserstein, and others. Though Miller is without doubt the preeminent Jewish American playwright, he usually avoided explicitly Jewish contexts on stage. Among fiction writers I have left out Daniel Fuchs, Wallace Markfield, Bruce Jay Friedman, E. L. Doctorow, and many others. I have also left out graphic novels and stories like Ben Katchor's *Julius Knipl, Real Estate Photographer* (1996) and Anya Ulinich's *Lena Finkle's Magic Barrel* (2014).

Philip Roth, born and raised in Newark, New Jersey, insisted on his local roots so thoroughly that he claimed to be not an American Jewish writer but a Newark Jewish writer. I take Roth at his word and exclude him, towering figure though he is. I have also left out Norman Mailer, indisputably Jewish and indisputably from Brooklyn, because he avoids depicting any Jewish milieu in his fiction; for the same reason, I have not discussed Nathanael West.

with peculiar solemnity, as though chanting a prayer. I was somewhat bored," Levinsky concludes.[3] Cahan has clearly read Stendhal, who expertly diagnosed the way that love affairs combine the rhapsodic and the banal, but his protagonist has none of the fire of Stendhal's Julien Sorel.

Cahan's Levinsky is in some ways a hard-hearted, though rarely mean-spirited, hero, apt to shut himself off from human complications when he senses trouble. Success excites him, but only up to a point—he is never in danger of losing control. The matter-of-factness of Cahan's narration makes his conclusion all the more mournful: "I cannot escape from my old self," Levinsky remarks in the book's last paragraph. "My past and my present do not comport well."[4] Once, he remembers, he was David the *yeshiva-bokher* [youth; student] swaying over a volume of Talmud: the thrill of Talmudic puzzle-solving represents an innocent passion more gripping than anything he encounters later in life, but also something strictly useless, even meaningless, in this world or any other. He ends a stranded man, nearly a broken one.

Levinsky's problem, Cahan hints, is connected to a lack in the Jewish culture of his day. A life like Levinsky's, reduced to the satisfactions of money-making, looks dry; it cannot nourish the soul. This conclusion Cahan voices in low-key accents, making it all the more persuasive. *The Rise of David Levinsky* points to what it suggests is an absence at the heart of New York Jewish life: a new sustaining culture, now that the old religious certainties have been lost.

For many New York Jewish writers, Cahan's subject, the successful businessman, failed to appeal. Instead, aided by the large circulation of Yiddish daily newspapers willing to publish their work, they produced proletarian literature (the so-called sweatshop poetry of the end of the nineteenth century) or writing influenced by the literary avant-garde of France, Germany and Russia. At the cutting edge of such bohemianism were *Di yunge* (The Young Ones), a group of Yiddish poets who published their first journal in New York in 1907. *Di yunge* revolted against what they called "*cholent* Jewishness," the deadening reliance on tradition that, they charged, weighs you down like a *shabbos* stew. *Di yunge*, with their long hair, canes, and wide-brimmed hats, sauntered down the jammed streets of the Lower East Side, easing their way past pushcarts, baby-carriages, herring sellers, men

3   Abraham Cahan, *The Rise of David Levinsky*, ed. Jules Chametzky (New York: Penguin, 1993), 280.
4   Cahan, *Rise of David Levinsky*, 530.

in yarmulkes and *tzitzes*.[5] They were ragtag rebels whose sense of urban life had more to do with Whitman and Baudelaire than with anything in Jewish lore.

Among the poets associated with *Di yunge* were Mani Leyb, a shoemaker; H. Leyvik, a paperhanger who had escaped from Tsarist prison in Siberia; and Moyshe Leyb Halpern, who lived hand to mouth, working at various trades. The women poets Anna Margolin and Celia Dropkin, both writing for *Di yunge's* journals, introduced a startling sexual frankness into Yiddish poetry.

A later group of poets, who called themselves the Introspectivists or the *In zikh* movement, hoisted their flag in 1919. The Introspectivists, like T. S. Eliot, borrowed from French Symbolism, and tended to be matter of fact rather than rhapsodic or ravishingly abstruse like their French sources. Among the major Introspectivist Yiddish poets were A. Leyeles and Jacob Glatstein. Leyeles displayed a sober formal dexterity in his kaleidoscopic wordplay, while Glatstein, at times equally groundbreaking in his technique, adeptly portrayed characters in his verse. The Introspectivists did not reject social and political themes, but they insisted that such themes had to be refracted through the intensely personal sensibility of the poet. The *In zikh* manifesto proclaims, "For us, everything is 'personal.' Wars and Revolutions, Jewish pogroms and the workers' movement, Protestantism and Buddha, the Yiddish school and the Cross. . . ."[6]

Glatstein's poem "Good Night, World," written in April 1938 when European Jewry was in enormous peril, is a culmination of the *In zikh* movement. Here Glatstein voices a rejection of gentile culture, along with the "Jesusmarxes" that tempt secular Jewry, and a defiant return to parochial, and collective, Jewish concerns. He embraces the "hunchbacked Jewish life" (*tsehoykert yidish lebn*) of the shtetl, an embrace colored by strange joy: "I kiss you, tangled Jewish life" [*Kh'kush dikh, farkoltent yidish lebn*], Glatstein croaks at the poem's end: "It cries in me, the joy of coming" [*S'veynt in mir, di freyd fun kumen*]. Glatstein's picture of the embattled old-world Jew is untainted by nostalgia, but it does suggest a harsh irony along with its doomed, defiant joy: Glatstein (born in 1896 in Lublin, and arriving

---

5 This description, by the writer Isaac Raboy, is cited in Ruth Wisse, *A Little Love in Big Manhattan: Two Yiddish Poets* (Cambridge, MA: Harvard University Press, 1988), 60.

6 Cited in Benjamin and Barbara Harshav, eds., *American Yiddish Poetry* (Stanford: Stanford University Press, 2007), 38.

in America in 1914) remained in New York, on the other side of the world from the Jewish masses living on the edge of destruction.

Often preoccupied with the old world, New York Yiddish poets were still more involved in New York City itself. Anna Margolin, born in Brest-Litovsk in 1887, a journalist as well as a poet, led a hectic romantic life, a fact reflected in her sometimes self-lacerating verse. By turns chilly, predatory, and wounded, Margolin's persona speaks with a bright bitterness. Margolin set her poem "Girls in Crotona Park" in a park in the Bronx well known as a meeting place for kibitzing Yiddish literati. Here the Jewish writers are absent, but Margolin's poem is still about New York as Jewish territory. She depicts a group of ethereal young women whom, she says, Botticelli would have loved. Their beauty, glazed and slightly deathly, is a rebuke to the usually agitated soul of the Yiddish poet; but they also resemble Margolin herself with their cool eyes and "wild, thin smiles" [*der shmeykhl vild un din*].

No New York Yiddish writer was more agitated than Moyshe Leyb Halpern. Halpern was born in 1886 in Galicia and arrived in New York in 1908, where he drifted from job to job, making a living by fits and starts. The critic Ruth Wisse describes Halpern's stance in his first book of poems, *In New York* (1919): "There is a motley cast of characters—drunks, derelicts, loose women, and other lonely souls—but the liveliest parts of the book are the personal lyrics in which a character named 'Moishe Leib' laughs, mocks, challenges, stabs the air for emphasis, and shrugs off what he does not want to confront. When he occasionally drops the bravado, his musings are uncommonly soft."[7] Halpern's "Watch your Step!"—the title in English rather than Yiddish—applies the spell-like lilt of a Heine ballad to that quintessential New York phenomenon, the subway. His uncanny and disconcerting "Memento Mori" shows the poet wooing death while surrounded by a crowd of summer bathers at (the reader assumes) Coney Island.

Like Margolin, two other women writers, the poet Kadya Molodovsky and the prose writer Anzia Yezierska, provided essential portraits of the lives of women, sometimes neglected in traditional Judaism. Anzia Yezierska in

---

7   Wisse, *A Little Love*, 101. Wisse, Howe, and Khone Shmeruk, in their introduction to *The Penguin Book of Modern Yiddish Verse*, characterize Halpern as "a master of grotesque playfulness," whose persona "Moyshe-Leyb the rascal" is "a lost urban creature, full of nostalgia for the old country, full of contempt for his nostalgia." Ruth Wisse, Irving Howe, and Khone Shmeruk, *The Penguin Book of Modern Yiddish Verse* (New York: Penguin, 1987), 32.

her novel *The Bread Givers* (1925) voiced a fierce condemnation of Jewish religion, seen as the province of brutal-minded men, who pored over the Talmud while their neglected wives and daughters struggled to survive without their help. While Molodovsky masterfully intimated a near-mystical depth of experience in her women, in Yezierska their lives remained too starkly impoverished to be reclaimed for the liberating imagination. Yezierska's realism seemed to reduce instead of enliven the people it described, and this dilemma was passed on into the New York Jewish fiction of the 1930s.

By the 1930s Cahan's anxiety about the meaning of Jewishness in materialistic America had been swept away by the tide of socialist realism. Writers like Mike Gold in *Jews without Money* (1930) fervently charged capitalism itself with responsibility for the poverty of Jewish existence in the slums of Brownsville and the Bronx. That poverty was literal, but also metaphorical: Gold's characters had little inward life to keep a reader's interest. Clifford Odets's plays *Waiting for Lefty* and *Awake and Sing!* (both 1935) now read like period pieces; their invocations of struggling workers and hard-pressed Jewish families ring with a heartiness that is hard to take seriously.

In the 1930s and 1940s the tenets of socialist realism largely held sway among fellow-travelling New York Jewish intellectuals, but the books produced according to Communist principles were instantly forgotten, or went unread. Yet the columnists at the *New Masses*, the *Nation*, and the *New Republic* frequently demanded that writers proclaim a proletarian consciousness, that they stress the battle between labor and capital and keep a tight rein on their characters' inwardness. The most memorable novel by a New York Jew during this period conformed to none of these criteria, and so was neglected for thirty years, until it was rediscovered in the 1960s. The author was Henry Roth, who was born in Galicia and who arrived in New York as a toddler, probably in 1908. The book was *Call It Sleep*, published in 1934.

Roth was a Communist, but in its review of *Call It Sleep* the Communist *New Masses* savaged the book by trumpeting the party line: the reviewer said, "It is a pity that so many young writers drawn from the proletariat can make no better use of their working class experience than as material for introspective and febrile novels."[8] Communism, Roth wrote years

---

8   Morris Dickstein, "Call It an Awakening," *New York Times*, November 29, 1987, http://www.nytimes.com/1987/11/29/books/call-it-an-awakening.html?pagewanted=all&mcubz=0.

later, "fell like a giant shunt across [my] career"—though Roth remained loyal to Communist principles until the Six Day War, when the Soviet bloc championed the Arab effort to destroy Israel. Roth finally published the multivolume sequel to *Call It Sleep* sixty years later. In it he divulges the crippling psychosexual experience that was an enormous factor behind his writer's block: childhood incest with his sister and his cousin.

Call It Sleep is an endlessly rewarding book, probably the greatest portrayal of the Jewish immigrant experience in America. Roth's language rivals the incandescent poetry of Hart Crane, and like Crane he makes the sublime this-worldly, not otherworldly. The novel is a long ecstatic hymn to mother love, and to the isolated prophet-like child who repeats the exaltation of Isaiah, his lips touched with a hot coal, in the grimy streets of New York. The squabbling and the squalor of the working-class block, with its kids who butcher English and tease and torment each other, proves perfectly suited to such illumination. *Call It Sleep* traces the collision courses between Jews and Christians, between rabbinical strictness and sexual experiment, between male and female. At the book's end, David, its nine-year-old protagonist, becomes a survivor, an inspired, whole figure who has passed through a crucible.

The New York Intellectuals did not discover Roth's novel until the sixties, when Howe celebrated it as a neglected classic. But all along they shared Roth's trouble with Communist strictures about acceptable art. The New York Intellectuals, most of whom were Jewish, revolted against socialist realism. They announced the essential role of thoughtfulness in literature and the other arts, in place of a brute allegiance to the "reality" of class warfare. I put reality in quotation marks because these critics, foremost among them Lionel Trilling and Alfred Kazin, insisted that thought and private emotion are just as real as the data of social and political life, and that any worthwhile conception of politics must take such inwardness into account. Kazin's *On Native Grounds*, published in 1942 when he was only twenty-seven, was a full-scale account of American literature from the end of the nineteenth century through World War II. Trilling wrote essays on Twain, Henry James, and other crucial American voices. Kazin and Trilling worked from an idea of what the American writer's task ought to be. Both grasped the roots of our twentieth-century literature in relation to the progressive movement and its inheritor, American liberalism. And both prized the flexibility and nuance of liberalism even as they wanted the liberal to be less fearful of literary imagination, which is by its nature often extreme.

The first astonishing thing about *On Native Grounds* is its title: this was an era when Jews were often barred from being professors of American literature because they were said to lack the "native" Protestant background needed to understand America. Kazin, born in Brownsville to poor Yiddish-speaking parents, spoke throughout the book of "our" culture and "our" literature, in a manner that left no doubt of his sense of belonging. Strikingly, Kazin wrote (in his 1955 postscript to a reissue of the book) that

> our perpetuation of the romantic tradition carries to both Americans and Europeans—in books like *Walden, Moby Dick, Leaves of Grass, Huckleberry Finn*—a kind of racial memory of the wilderness we have all lost. The truly unexpected, the explosive, the dynamic quality of the undefined, man's awareness of himself moving through an utterly new situation—this is the great fact of life in our time and was prophesied by the Ishmaels, the Walt Whitmans, and other world-wanderers of nineteenth-century American literature.[9]

Whereas Howe's "Strangers" was to insist decades later that the solitary wandering through the wilderness so favored by American romanticism was more or less foreign to Jewish writers, Kazin claimed such romantic solitude as his due. Yet Kazin hinted that he esteemed before all other American writers one who had nothing to do with wilderness, and everything to do with urban social life: Henry James. James, who had died in 1916, brought out by contrast the deficiencies of Kazin's own contemporaries. The two with the strongest affinity to wilderness were Ernest Hemingway and William Faulkner. Hemingway, Kazin charged in *On Native Grounds*, "brought a major art to a minor vision of life,"[10] in which Jamesian powers of thought seemed to have no place.

Kazin expertly diagnosed what he saw as Faulkner's "lack of a center": "that curious abstract magnificence . . . which holds his books together, yet seems to arise from debasement or perplexity or a calculating terror."[11] The antitype to Faulkner's passivity and confusion in Kazin's book—so he implies—is Henry James: he quotes James's ideal of the writer who will "feel and feel until he understands" and so will "have perception at the pitch of passion" (36). James was the discerning, the discriminating author, the fiction writer who incarnates the critical spirit. In *The American Scene*

---

9   Alfred Kazin, *On Native Grounds* (Garden City, NY: Doubleday Anchor, 1956), 408–409.
10 Ibid., 257.
11 Ibid., 353.

(1907) James had shown his distaste for the Jewish masses of the Lower East Side, but as the American author who embodied the marriage of critical and creative faculties, he became the darling of New York Jewish intellectuals.

Another Jewish critic, Leon Edel, wrote a magisterial biography of James, firmly enshrining him in the postwar American canon. But Lionel Trilling made the best case for the novelist in his essay on James's *The Princess Casamassima*. Trilling wrote that James's Princess, an aristocrat who falls for a simplistic radical cause, was a victim of "the chronic American belief that there exists an opposition between reality and mind and that one must enlist oneself in the party of reality." She becomes "a perfect drunkard of reality . . . ever drawn to look for stronger and stronger drams."[12]

It made perfect sense, given Stalinism and Hitlerism, that Trilling would warn against "the party of reality," whether Left or Right, with its adherence to crude versions of the world and its demand for propagandistic uniformity. Jewish history itself suggested the danger lurking in simplistic pictures of reality that would appeal to the masses. By taking a stand on behalf of ambivalence and complexity, Trilling and Kazin marked themselves as intellectuals wary of any party line. In an era when what to think about Russia was a burning issue for many American Jews, they argued against Stalinist fellow travelers, but were wary of McCarthyism, too.

The "Family," as the New York Intellectuals sometimes called themselves, thrived on squabbling and dissent. For the Family, one's opinions about art or politics remained profoundly personal, however commandingly voiced; such opinions stood in contrast to both Marxist doctrine and all-American conformity. Though Communists espoused the fiction of Theodore Dreiser, they did so, Kazin wrote, for the wrong reasons: Dreiser's true value was in the way he imagined human personality, not his occasional boilerplate claims about class struggle.

Another major figure in New York Jewish writing took after Dreiser in his deliberate plainness, but was focused, like Henry Roth, on the purgatorial and its result, secular illumination: Bernard Malamud. Malamud was born in 1914 in Brownsville, Brooklyn. Malamud's urban settings, like Henry Roth's, tend to be narrow—in his books life seems to take place within a few blocks—and this constriction serves his purpose. Malamud substitutes the spare economy of his style for Roth's condensed rhapsodic flights.

---

12 Adam Kirsch in his book *Why Trilling Matters* (New Haven: Yale University Press, 2011), notes that the Princess suffers, according to Trilling, from what Tom Wolfe would later call "radical chic" (66).

Malamud was, in some sense, a Jewish Puritan: he devoted himself to interesting sufferers who blossomed from self-punishment. Their careful decency turns extreme, even fanatical, in classic Puritan fashion. Among Malamud's truest achievements in the novel form are *The Assistant* and *The Fixer*, the latter based on the notorious 1913 blood libel trial of Mendel Beilis.[13] Both *The Assistant*'s Morris Bober, a shopkeeper, and *The Fixer*'s Yakov Bok are men of excruciating virtue, and Malamud puts them to the test.

Malamud's short stories, often marked by a vein of fantasy, are probably his most remarkable work. Here, too, he stresses how we are each locked in the prison of self. The two main characters at the end of his story "The Mourners" sit shiva together, each thinking of his own drastic moral inadequacy, and they remain isolated from each other. "The Jewbird," "The Magic Barrel," and "Angel Levine" follow from the Yiddish tales of Peretz and Sholem Aleichem, with schlemiel-like characters who are both blessed and cursed by their innocence.

Malamud's biographer, Philip Davis, reports that Malamud told his son Paul "that people in Brooklyn, when he was a child, were in every sense from a different world—not cultured, not articulately interesting, men talking mainly about cars and baseball and money."[14] But there was an advantage to this deprivation, Malamud explained: "They spoke then without voices, with their hands, eyes, even with inert bodies. If you were alive, could you hide it? They couldn't."[15] Malamud's picture of Jewish life does not feature fast talkers, schemers and *luftmentshn*, but instead obstinate, close-mouthed characters. (Though he does loosen up in his delightful yet somehow morose comic novel, *A New Life* [1961].)

Somewhere between the Puritans and Kafka resides Malamud's idea that whatever we do we are unworthy. If the life is a gift, then "the gift is pure," Malamud commented, and our "punishment renews the extraordinary value of the gift." Malamud credited to the Jews "the primal knowledge . . . that life is tragic, no matter how sweet or apparently full."[16] The world was a fallen one, and even its pleasures derived from this original fact.

---

13 For an account of the differences between Beilis's autobiography and Malamud's novel, see David Mikics, "The Beilis Conspiracy," *Tablet*, April 26, 2013, http://www.tabletmag.com/jewish-arts-and-culture/books/130606/the-beilis-conspiracy.

14 Philip Davis, *Bernard Malamud* (New York: Oxford University Press, 2010), 127.

15 Bernard Malamud, *Talking Horse* (New York: Columbia University Press, 1996), 189.

16 Davis, *Bernard Malamud*, 119.

Malamud was a sure hand at building prisons for his characters. For Isaac Bashevis Singer, who became a major force in American literature in the 1960s and 1970s, fate itself was the power that ruled the world, and fate he defined by turns as either God's work, the mischief done by the demons of Jewish mysticism, or the devastation wrought by Hitler and Stalin. Singer, born in 1902 in Poland, escaped the Shoah by coming to New York in 1935. (His brother I. J. Singer, also a talented fiction writer, came a year earlier.) The depth of Singer's Talmudic education as well as his knowledge of kabbalah suggested that the old Eastern European Jewish tradition lived within him. Singer wrote a fluent, pure Yiddish, and enlisted a series of talented translators to adapt his work for an American market that had little knowledge of the *shtetlekh* where he usually set his stories.

In the years when Singer was the favorite Jewish author of New Yorker readers (so much so that, as Kazin noted, one sometimes got the impression that Jewish tradition lived on only in his writing), he set a number of stories on the Upper West Side. Here he was a familiar figure, eating rice pudding in the cafeterias and feeding the pigeons on Broadway. One of his small masterpieces is "The Cafeteria," in which a writer very much like Singer meets an intriguing woman in an Upper West Side cafeteria where Jews, having barely escaped Hitler or Stalin, spend hours kibitzing or reading the Yiddish papers. The woman disappears, the cafeteria burns down. Then she reemerges and tells the narrator of her recent nightmare: she has seen Hitler and his Nazis conferring together in the cafeteria. Her vision's authority holds more sway than the narrator's skepticism: after all, ghosts do walk, and they sense more than we do. The Shoah and the Soviet labor camps still possess the cafeteria's chattering denizens, the *shtam-gest* ("regulars") who exist in a haunted afterlife. In Singer's Yiddish phrase the Hitler and Stalin years *hobn zikh opgerufn*: they recur like a symptom, or like a passing rumor that from time to time picks out one of the cafeteria's customers for death. *Der ruekh veyst im*, one character in "The Cafeteria" remarks about another: literally, "the (evil) spirit knows him." The dark forces from Singer's Europe, implacable and grimly knowing, eclipse the lives of his New York Jews.

Grace Paley, born in 1922 in New York, seems distant from the European disasters that haunt Singer. Her work as a short story writer took place in the intermissions of her life as a mother and a left-wing political activist. Her stories seem spoken as much as written: Paley instilled a voracity and a madcap on-the-ball quality into her characters' words that stem originally from *Huck Finn*, that ever-surprising dynamo of American speech. Her style is both bizarre and apt, a constantly piquant high-wire act. Along with Twain, Isaac Babel and Sholem Aleichem were major influences.

Paley was a definitively urban voice. The writer George Saunders remarks about her work, "All these agitated manic New York voices explaining themselves! . . . The city is the energy coming off a million hustling souls who have both forgotten they will die soon and are very actively feeling that, ah God, they most definitely will."[17]

In Paley's stories, life and love seem like they could be just as transitory as her ten-page monologues themselves, with their self-amused and nervous jabbering. Maybe there's a trick for making love a permanent truth, her characters ask. Paley's answer: Not so fast, buster. In the first story Paley ever wrote, "Goodbye and Good Luck," the heroine, now an old woman, resumes after many years her love affair with a flamboyant Yiddish actor. Here the illusion works: we can live for passion without being its dupes, and bring back as well, in a small way, the golden age of Yiddish theater. But such optimism becomes less and less usual in Paley's later work.

Paley dedicates herself to the transitory, appropriately so for the fading Jewish milieu she chronicles. Her story "Dreamer in a Dead Language" is set in that unavoidable Jewish environment, a rest home for the aged. At the story's end the narrator, having fled from the institution where her parents now live, gets her children to bury her playfully in the beach at Coney Island. With sand up to her shoulders, she can still wave her arms, like a Jewish Winnie (in Samuel Beckett's *Happy Days*).

Cynthia Ozick, six years older than Paley, is an important voice among Jewish writers, less for her rather studied novels than for her essays and her stories, foremost among them "The Shawl," a searing Holocaust fable, and "Envy, or Yiddish in America," a comic tale about the rivalry between Isaac Bashevis Singer and another writer usually identified as Glatshteyn. Ozick's celebrated essay "A Drugstore in Winter" recalls her childhood with a vivid nostalgic pang.

Some recent Jewish novelists, perhaps inspired in part by an Ozick novel like *The Messiah of Stockholm* (1987), think of their work as a scholarly project, fed by careful research into the history of Jewish writing and thought. Dara Horn and Joshua Cohen, among others, belong to this

---

17   George Saunders, "Grace Paley, the Saint of Seeing," *New Yorker*, March 3, 2017, http://www.New Yorker.com/books/page-turner/grace-paley-the-saint-of-seeing.

school. (Cohen is also a visionary postmodernist who follows in the train of Pynchon and Gaddis.) They are balanced by the memoir writers and personal essayists who look more immediately to their own Jewish families for their source. Two of these "life writers," Philip Lopate and Vivian Gornick, both from Brooklyn, and both born shortly after World War II, have been particularly influential. Kazin's superb *A Walker in the City* (1951) was an early prototype of the form, a lyrical memoir featuring the at times self-punishing and doomed characters of Kazin's native Brownsville.

Lopate in his personal essays appears a gentle, slightly sheepish figure, yet stubborn as well: he expertly charts the changes between his past and his present self. In her memoir *Fierce Attachments* (1987) Gornick recounts her Bronx childhood: she is poised between two unruly, outspoken women, her mother and a Ukrainian neighbor she calls Nettie, who becomes a rival maternal figure for her. The two quarrel bitterly, and Gornick decades later continues to reflect on how a parent's authority can be violently self-consuming. Gornick's *Fierce Attachments*, like a later memoir, *The Odd Woman and the City* (2015), sways between harsh telling-it-like-it-is and nostalgia.

Gornick paints the Jewish Communists of yore with a perhaps too-naive nostalgic brush; Lopate is more or less indifferent to them: too much stridency—the too-overt enjoyment of one's opinion—turns him off. Both Gornick and Lopate are masters of autobiographical ambivalence, and as such, they refuse to participate in the ferocious opinion making that was the specialty of the New York Intellectuals. Both were teenagers during the 1960s, but they bristle at the campaigns for easy emotional liberation characteristic of that era. Both reflect on the heated squabbles and occasional brutality, whether verbal or physical, that they experienced as children. For both Gornick and Lopate, home is a place certainly Jewish, and one that leads the grown-up child, now a writer, to an intense wish to figure out who one's parents were and what they wanted, and to give them not reverence but a dose of loving contention. And Gornick especially values New York as a place where, having left home, she can get lost in the pleasures of the streetwise observer, shared with the friends who have taken the place of family. Much of Gornick's work, like her recent *The Odd Woman and the City*, is a paean to the ever-shifting human cityscape of New York. She writes, "Most people are in New York because they need evidence—in large quantities—of human expressiveness; and they need it not now and then, but every day. That is what they need."[18] Gornick embodies such expressiveness in her stance and style.

It is fitting to close this essay with a New York Jewish writer who moves beyond purely Jewish contexts: the playwright Tony Kushner, author of *Angels in America* (1991–1992). Howe famously suggested that, when Yiddish stopped being the lingua franca of Ashkenazi Jews, Jewishness now meant either religion or Israel.[19] Howe's verdict may have been hyperbolic, but there was a basis for it. By the close of the twentieth century, the secular New York Jew was vanishing: New York had become too intermixed to convey the world of the grandparents into the present.

Kushner seems typical of the waning New York secular Jew: largely uninterested in Judaism and connected to Israel only as a subject of protest. Significantly, Mormons rather than Jews are the chosen people in *Angels*, and the play's charismatic villain is the infamous Roy Cohn, Kushner's Jewish Richard III. Cohn, the power-addicted macher, offers a contrast to Cahan's David Levinsky, who was a strikebreaking businessman but no figure of evil. As the sole figure of Jewish entrepreneurial talent in Kushner, he signals that such talent cannot be employed innocently.

Angels' antidote to Cohn's restless Satanic majesty is a rather lukewarm prophetic gesture, the meeting at Central Park's Bethesda Fountain of all colors, creeds, genders, and sexual orientations. Yet Cohn remains the white-hot core of *Angels in America*; he cannot be banished by liberal clichés. New York's wild gangsterish energies are at their highest pitch in this hustler and egomaniac, who easily defeats Kushner's collective affirmations of humanity. By the time of Kushner's play the collective has become largely featureless, and the Jewish writer an average American who is distinctive only in the tone of proud ownership she exhibits when she expresses liberal values. New York Jewish writers now feel perfectly at home, and for this reason are far less significant as a critical category than they once were. The past glories of Jewish writing in New York belong to them no more than to the rest of us, Jew or gentile.

---

18 Vivian Gornick, *The Odd Woman and the City* (New York: Farrar, Straus and Giroux, 2015), 173.

19 See Irving Howe, *A Margin of Hope* (New York: Harcourt, Brace, Jovanovich, 1982), 277–82.

For Further Reading

Cahan, Abraham. *The Rise of David Levinsky*, edited by Jules Chametzky. New York: Penguin, 1993.

Davis, Philip. *Bernard Malamud*. New York: Oxford University Press, 2010.

Dickstein, Morris. "Call It an Awakening." *New York Times*, November 29, 1987. http://www.nytimes.com/1987/11/29/books/call-it-an-awakening.html?pagewanted=all&mcubz=0.

Gornick, Vivian. *The Odd Woman and the City*. New York: Farrar, Straus and Giroux, 2015.

Harshav, Benjamin, and Barbara Harshav, eds., *American Yiddish Poetry*. Stanford: Stanford University Press, 2007.

Howe, Irving. *A Margin of Hope*. New York: Harcourt, Brace, Jovanovich, 1982.

———. *Selected Writings, 1950–1990*. New York: Harvest / Harcourt, Brace, Jovanovich, 1990.

Kazin, Alfred. *On Native Grounds*. Garden City, NY: Doubleday Anchor, 1956.

Kirsch, Adam. *Why Trilling Matters*. New Haven: Yale University Press, 2011.

Malamud, Bernard. *Talking Horse*. New York: Columbia University Press, 1996.

Mikics, David. "The Beilis Conspiracy." *Tablet*, April 26, 2013. http://www.tabletmag.com/jewish-arts-and-culture/books/130606/the-beilis-conspiracy.

Saunders, George. "Grace Paley, the Saint of Seeing." *New Yorker*, March 3, 2017. http://www.New Yorker.com/books/page-turner/grace-paley-the-saint-of-seeing.

Wisse, Ruth. *A Little Love in Big Manhattan: Two Yiddish Poets*. Cambridge, MA: Harvard University Press, 1988.

Wisse, Ruth, Irving Howe, and Khone Shmeruk. *The Penguin Book of Modern Yiddish Verse*. New York: Penguin, 1987.

Chapter 9

"I Never Think About Being Jewish—Until I Leave New York": Jewish Art in New York City, 1900 to the Present[1]

Diana L. Linden

In order to grow and thrive, an arts community demands avenues of training, wealthy patrons, an interested public, informed art critics, freedom from traditional constraints, and also museums where artists can study vast collections. Since the turn of the twentieth century, New York City has offered all of these, making it the premier American city for the visual arts. Concurrently, the massive Eastern European Jewish migration (nearly 2.5 million Jews) from 1870 to 1924 rapidly transformed New York into the global capital of the Jewish world. In the early decades of the twentieth century, the visual arts and immigrant Jews met up in New York City, and Jews have remained central to the New York art scene ever since. The flourishing of American-Jewish art could never have happened in any other location.

---

1   I titled this essay after a piece by contemporary artist Elaine Reichek discussed on page 200.

This chapter introduces artists, styles, and subject matter representative of New York City's Jewish artwork beginning in the early 1900s up to the present day. Its focus is on those artists who have self-identified as Jews, and whose work pointedly engages with the City. It concentrates on the ways in which artists interact with the city, either as their subject, or as the context within which the artist's work emerged. Due to the constraints of space, the essay limits itself to sculptors, painters, and a few photographers.

New York, circa 1900

Many Eastern European Jews arrived in New York already secularized, even radicalized, and were well prepared for the new world that beckoned to them.[2] The prior arrival of Central European Jews, some of whom had become wealthy and well established, served a vital function, providing both ideological and financial support. Alfred Stieglitz (1864–1946), photographer, essayist, and gallerist was one of the first to both promote both modern art and photography as an art form at 291, his innovative gallery named for its Fifth-Avenue address. In the words of photo-historian Max Kozloff, "The patriarch of early New York photography was Alfred Stieglitz, a Jew among gentiles."[3] Walter and Louise Arensberg's Manhattan apartment functioned as a salon for avant-garde artists and intellectuals, in particular Marcel Duchamp and New York Dada, up until 1921 at which point the couple decamped to Los Angeles for health reasons.[4]

The year 1902 stands as the symbolic start date for the manifestation of Jewish American art, with the publication of journalist Hutchins Hapgood's *The Spirit of the Ghetto: Studies in the Jewish Quarter in New York*. Believing that a Jewish artist would enliven his text, Hapgood commissioned Lower East Side-born Jacob Epstein (1880–1959) to create fifty-two vibrant black-chalk drawings. He praised Epstein's graphics as "typically Jewish" and

---

2   Milton W. Brown, "An Explosion of Creativity: Jews and American Art in the Twentieth Century," in *Painting a Place in America: Jewish Artists in New York, 1900–1945: A Tribute to the Educational Alliance*, ed. Norman L. Kleeblatt and Susan Chevlowe (New York / Bloomington: Jewish Museum / Indiana University Press, 1991), 22–27.

3   Max Kozloff, *New York: Capital of Photography* (New York / London and New Haven: The Jewish Museum / Yale University Press, 2002), 70.

4   Francis M. Naumann, *New York DADA, 1915–1923* (New York: Harry N. Abrams, Inc., 1994).

fine examples of "ghetto art."[5] Epstein drew Jewish street vendors peddling goods from pushcarts, Orthodox Jews at prayer and study, and clean-shaven intellectuals engaged in lively debate at downtown cafes. While Hapgood's book was a serious attempt to capture both the normalcy and the variety of Jewish life, it also evidences a fascination with the "other," in this case, poor Ashkenazi Jews who dwelled in the tenements.

It was around this time that several Jewish artists traveled to Paris, then the global center of artistic modernism. Between 1901 and 1911, such immigrants and children of immigrants, New Yorkers all—Samuel Halpert, Bernard Karfoil, Abraham Walkowitz, Max Weber, and William Zorach— went abroad to train. In 1905, Weber helped Matisse establish his first art classes in Paris. The whole of what these eager young modernists learned from Matisse, Picasso, and the School of Paris in terms of color, composition, and form, they brought back with them to New York City, making these painters among the most advanced artists in the city.

At the turn of the twentieth century several venues for serious artistic training existed in Manhattan, including the Cooper Union, the Art Students League, and the National Academy of Design with its conservative, traditional academic curriculum based on the classical nude. Jews also studied individually under the guidance of prominent, established American gentile artists; for example, realist painter and printmaker Theresa Bernstein (1890–2002) trained under painter William Merritt Chase.[6]

Many immigrant Jews took their first art classes at the Educational Alliance; possibly due to middle-class aspirations, Jewish parents wanted their children to study art.[7] Founded in 1889 on the Lower East Side by several Jewish charitable organizations, the Educational Alliance assisted foreign-born Jews' cultural, social, and economic acclimation to the United States. Simultaneously, the Alliance was a "major force in the cultural life of the community."[8] The Alliance ran art classes from 1895 to 1905, at which point funds were diverted to meet the more rudimentary needs of immigrants. In 1917, the Alliance resumed its art classes under the directorship

---

5   Diana L. Linden, *Ben Shahn's New Deal Murals: Jewish Identity in the American Scene* (Detroit: Wayne State University Press, 2015), 8–10.

6   Gail Levin, *Theresa Bernstein: A Century in Art* (Lincoln and London: University of Nebraska Press, 2013).

7   Matthew Baigell, *Jewish Art in America* (Lanham, MD: Rowman & Littlefield Publishers, Inc., 2007), 13.

8   Ibid., 14.

of Abbo Ostrowsky (1889–1975). The Educational Alliance constitutes the first organized effort to provide training specifically for Jews in the visual arts and produced a long list of illustrious graduates.

During the 1910s, New York artists formed important organizations and mounted significant art exhibitions. Art and leftist politics became closely entwined. Artists hotly debated the merits of socialism versus anarchism with a vigor comparable to their debates on abstraction versus realism. Jewish artists were intensely involved with all these events, organizations, and trends. In 1912 the reform-driven, uptown Ethical Culture Society with its German-Jewish origins, hosted an open-call exhibition at the Madison House Settlement. According to records, numerous "Russian Jewish immigrants" contributed works to the Madison House Settlement exhibition, as did such non-Jewish realists associated with the Ashcan School as painter George Luks who often depicted immigrant and working-class life on the Lower East Side.[9]

From January 1915 to 1918, Dr. John Weichsel—an educator, art critic, and anarchist—oversaw the People's Art Guild, both as an alternative to the exclusionary system of fine-arts galleries, and in opposition to the conservative ideals of beauty promoted by elite art academies.[10] As with the Educational Alliance, the membership was primarily Jewish, but not exclusively so. The initial call for a meeting of artists states, "In view of the now prevailing art conditions in our ghetto a number of Jewish painters and sculptors have decided to meet . . . for the purpose of organizing themselves into an association."[11] Artists gathered and drafted a constitution in both Yiddish and English. Toward its zenith, with dues set on a sliding scale, membership in the Guild reached close to three hundred. Weichsel curated exhibitions in such non-traditional spaces as the tenements and settlement houses on the Lower East Side, and reached out to labor unions for potential audiences and practitioners.[12] Through the Guild, Weichsel promoted "a class base for modernism in which artists would not only thrive but also find solidarity with the revolutionary struggle."[13] In May 1917, The

---

9   Rebecca Zurier, *Picturing the City: Urban Vision and the Ashcan School* (Berkeley, Los Angeles, and London: University of California Press, 2006).

10   See Sarah Archino, "The People's Art Guild and the Forward Exhibition of 1917," *Smithsonian Studies in American Art* 27, no. 3 (Fall 2013): 14–19.

11   John Weichsel Papers, Archives of American Art, Smithsonian Institution.

12   Archino, "People's Art Guild," 14.

13   Allan Antliff, *Anarchist Modernism Art, Politics, and the First American Avante-Garde* (Chicago: University of Chicago Press, 2007), 55.

People's Art Guild staged an exhibition at the Forward Building, home to the Yiddish daily socialist newspaper *Forverts*, an event popularly known as the Forward Exhibition, which offered works for sale at prices ranging from $5.00 to $2,500. Weichsel's dismissal of hierarchical notions of art making, training, and exhibition, became manifest by the Ferrer Center and Modern School, named in honor of Francisco Ferrer, the Spanish educator and anarchist. Anarchism held a special attraction to artists who positioned themselves as part of the avant-garde and in opposition to the status quo.[14] The Ferrer Center was a lively base for political radicalism, social comradery, and artistic experimentation.[15] Among those active at the Ferrer Center were Ben Benn, Samuel Halpert, Moses Soyer, Abrahahm Walkowitz, Max Weber, William Zorach, and the revolutionary Dadaist Man Ray.[16]

During the first decades of the twentieth century, the wealthy Stettheimer Family relished the exclusionary social life of New York City's prominent Jews who dwelled uptown. Painter Florine (1871–1944) along with her sister Carrie (1869–1944) hosted legendary salons studded with Jewish intellectuals and artists. Among salon regulars were Marcel Duchamp, Georgia O'Keeffe and Alfred Stieglitz (husband and wife), and Polish-Jewish sculptor Elie Nadelman.[17] Carrie's high-style dollhouse, which she crafted and outfitted between 1916 and 1935, now resides at the Museum of the City of New York.[18] Through her dollhouse, Carrie preserved the rarified social bubble in which she, her mother, and sisters lived at the fashionable Alwyn Court Building on Seventh Avenue and Fifty-Eighth Street, miles away from the firetraps and immigrants on the Lower East Side. The most extraordinary aspect of the dollhouse are the miniature works of art it contains, which were created by leading modernists whom Carrie

---

14 Paul Avrich and Francis M. Naumann, "Adolf Wolff: 'Poet, Sculptor, and Revolutionist, but Mostly Revolutionist,'" *Art Bulletin* 67, no. 3 (September 1985): 486.

15 Ibid., 487.

16 See Milly Heyd, "Man Ray/Emmanuel Radnitsy: Who is behind the Enigma of Isidore Ducasse?," in *Complex Identities: Jewish Consciousness and Modern Art*, ed. Matthew Baigell and Milly Heyd (New Brunswick, NJ, and London: Rutgers University Press, 2001), 115–41.

17 Teresa A. Carbone, *Youth and Beauty: Art of the American Twenties* (New York: Brooklyn Museum, 2011), 34–35.

18 Sheila W. Clark, ed., *The Stettheimer Doll House* (New York: The Museum of the City of New York, 2009); Emily D. Bilski and Emily Braun, *Jewish Women and their Salons: The Power of Conversation* (New York: The Jewish Museum, 2005), 126–37; Stephen Brown and Georgianna Uhlyarik, *Florine Stettheimer: Painting Poetry* (New York: The Jewish Museum, 2017).

called her friends. Alexander Archipenko, Duchamp, Gaston Lachaise, Marguerite and William Zorach, and others who frequented the salons, each gifted Carrie with a miniature canvas or sculpture in their signature style. Duchamp presented Carrie with a tiny copy of his scandalous *Nude Descending a Staircase, No. 2* (1912), a painting that when exhibited at the revolutionary Armory Show of 1913 created a tremendous uproar the likes of which the American art world had never known.

In 1915, excited by the modern times and modern city that was New York, Max Weber (1881–1961) wrote: "This is a wonderful age we are living in. Surely there will be new numbers, new weights, new colors, new forms." Influenced by the cubism of Picasso and Braque that he had previously seen in Paris, coupled with Matisse's vibrant palette, in New York Weber became affiliated with Stieglitz's roster of artists. Weber, like Stieglitz, was committed to the art of abstraction and of the new. His canvases from 1913 to 1915 were the most advanced abstract paintings created by any American artist up to that point.

In the late 1930s and 1940s, Weber would change his style and subject matter, remaking himself as the foremost American artist to render religious Jewish subject matter. Doing so meant that he had to step back from his modern experimentations. With an air of nostalgia, Weber began to paint genre scenes of religious Jews praying and studying sacred texts.[19] Such paintings as *Students of the Torah*, 1939, *Hassidic Dance*, 1940, and *Sabbath Reading*, 1943, evidence Weber's more subdued and monochromatic palette, his reembrace of figuration, and also, of legible narration.

The Ten: Avant-Garde Painters in the 1930s

In December 1935, a group of nine artists who called themselves The Ten debuted at New York's Montross Gallery.[20] The original group consisted of Ben-Zion, Adolph Gottlieb, Louis Harris, Yankel Kufeld, Marcus Rothkowitz (later, Mark Rothko), Louis Schanker, Joseph Solman, and Nahum Tschacbasov; they assumed that a tenth artist would eventually

---

19 On Weber's religious paintings, see Jacqueline Francis, *Making Race: Modernism and Racial Art in America* (Seattle and London: University of Washington Press, 2012), 57–63.

20 See Isabelle Dervaux, "The Ten: An Avant-garde Group in the 1930s," *Archives of American Art Journal* 31, no. 2 (1991): 14–20; Dervaux, *The Ten: Birth of the American Avant-Garde* (Boston: Mercury Gallery, 1998).

join them. Although their ranks remained steady at nine, the membership changed over the four years of the group's existence, 1935 to 1939; consistently, the majority of members were Jews. The creation of groups such as the Artists' Union and the American Artists' Congress based on political and collective activities was common during the Depression era. The Ten were all members of both the Union and the Congress and were politically active on the left.

As a whole, however, The Ten emphasized artistic concerns over political ones. Art historian Isabelle Dervaux points out, "the various forms of expressionism displayed by the Ten signaled a resurgence of modernism and experimentalism in New York that would grow during the second half of the 1930s."[21] The Ten represent an important group of expressionist painters and can be seen, in part, as a prelude to the abstract painting that would emerge in the 1940s and go on to dominate the art world.

Jews, Modernism, and Sculpture: 1920s–1940s

Abstraction remained a "negligible factor" among American sculptors through the 1930s, and figuration reigned supreme until the post-World War II period.[22] During the 1920s such sculptors as Saul Baizerman (1889–1957) and Adolf Wolff (1883–1994) produced thematically and stylistically innovative, even radical, sculptures. Born in Russia, Baizerman was imprisoned for participating in the 1905 Odessa Uprising. He managed to escape from a remote Russian prison, and made his way to New York. Having already begun artistic training in Russia, Baizerman enrolled in the National Academy of Design, Beaux-Arts Institute, and the Educational Alliance. Baizerman's subject matter were unskilled workers, most of whom were immigrants, African-Americans new to the North, and women.[23] One of the artist's finest pieces is *The Digger* (1923), which he rendered in a planar, simplified, modernist vocabulary that left the figure of the worker, the Digger, recognizable.

Emma Goldman introduced Adolf Wolff to the Ferrer Center, where he became one of its most passionate participants as a teacher of sculpture.

---

21   Dervaux, "The Ten," 14.
22   Ilene Susan Fort, ed., *The Figure in American Sculpture: A Question of Modernity* (Los Angeles: Los Angeles County Museum of Art, 1995), 8.
23   Melissa Dabakis, *Visualizing Labor in American Sculpture: Monuments, Manliness, and the Work Ethic, 1880–1935* (New York: Cambridge University Press, 1999), 176.

Born in Belgium, Wolff was influenced by the social themes of sculptor Constantin Meunier (1831–1905), who sympathetically represented workers in his small-scale statues. In the United States, Wolff was taken by the sleek, streamlined modernism of Romanian artist Constantin Brancusi (1876–1957) who exhibited at Stieglitz's 291. Arrested for participating in a meeting of the radical Industrial Workers of the World, Wolff served jail time on Blackwell's Island in 1914. In 1927, Wolff created the urn that holds the ashes of Italian anarchist martyrs Nicola Sacco and Bartolomeo Vanzetti, who were executed after their problematic conviction for a murder committed in the course of a robbery in Massachusetts.

The radical political views espoused by Wolff and Baizerman went on to resonate with sculptors during the 1930s, especially those involved with the Communist Party and its allied cultural organizations, the John Reed Clubs (1929–1935) and the American Artists Congress. Berta Margoulies, born in 1907 in Lovitz, Poland, brought together modernist formalism with the traditional subject matter of the human body. Her most famous work is *Mine Disaster* (1942), a cast bronze which presents an arrangement of anguished women, grouped tightly together behind a restraining fence, as they await word of their husbands' fate in the aftermath of an accident. Confronting America's racism, Seymour Lipton (1903–1986) carved *Lynched* (1933), a pedestal-sized wood statue of a murdered African-American man curled tightly in a fetal position, the noose that killed him still tight around his neck. Lipton's immediate inspiration was the infamous Scottsboro Case.[24] In contrast to Lipton's coiled up horizontal figure, Aaron J. Goodelman's Yiddish-titled *Kultur* (ca. 1940) is a taut, tall, elongated wood figure standing with his shackled hands high above his head. When the majority of artists, in all mediums, approached the theme of lynching they interpreted the lynched victim as dead. Goodelman's statue stands alive and upright its arms thrust upwards in resistance.[25] By referencing slavery and lynching, Goodelman was one of many socially conscious Jewish artists who drew parallels between their own community's history of oppression and that of African-Americans.

---

24 Diana L. Linden, "Visual Essay," in Jeffrey S. Gurock, *Jews in Gotham: New York Jews in a Changing City, 1920–2010* (New York: New York University Press, 2012), 229.
25 Ibid., 237.

Printmakers, Easel Painters, and Muralists during the 1930s-1940s

Art historian Helen Langa convincingly argues for a return to the 1930s term "social viewpoint" over the more popular term "social realism" which was coined much later in the twentieth century to describe realist art of the Left which agitated for progressive social change.[26] Jewish social-viewpoint or social realist printmakers included Selma Freeman, Boris Gorelick, William Gropper, Riva Helford, and Nan Lurie. During the Great Depression and the New Deal, "egalitarian ideals and economic constraints" led artists to produce prints to reach out to a broader audience beyond those few from the upper-class who frequented galleries and museums.[27] The New Deal's Works Progress Administration/Federal Arts Project funded the Graphic Arts Division, which employed numerous Jews, other minorities, and women who otherwise would not have been able to survive the Depression as working artists. New York City's WPA/FAP branch was the nation's largest. Many printmakers created works that were more overtly leftist in their private work, or in their illustrations for the Artist Union's magazine *Art Front,* than in their paid government work, most likely knowing such provocative work might be censored.[28]

"Surprisingly," writes Langa, "very few New York social viewpoint artists raised the problem of antisemitism either in Germany or in America in their political drawings or fine arts prints."[29] Florence Kent (1917–1998), however, did confront Nazism in her *Jewish Refugees,* ca. 1939, with strong symbols representative of both Kristallnacht and pogroms.[30] Langa notes the paucity of images that directly confronted the rise of German antisemitism, even at the 1938 exhibition organized by the World Alliance for Yiddish Culture, or *Yidisher kultur farband* (YKUF), this, in contrast to the outpouring of images responsive to the Spanish Civil War.[31] The Communist Party had organized YKUF the previous year in Paris to combat fascism, to protest antisemitism, and to bring attention to Jewish contributions to

---

26 Helen Langa, *Radical Art: Printmaking and the Left in 1930s New York* (Berkeley, Los Angeles, and London: University of California Press, 2004).

27 Ibid., 1.

28 See Francine Tyler, "Artists Respond to the Great Depression and the Threat of Fascism: The New York Artists Union and Its Magazine, *Art Front* (1934–1937)" (PhD diss., New York University, 1991).

29 Langa, *Radical Art,* 201.

30 Ibid., 11–16.

31 Ibid., 197, 199.

European culture and society. Approximately one hundred artists exhibited in the 1938 New York display, including non-Jewish artists who submitted work in order to show support for the Jews of Europe.

With the impact of the Great Depression and further radicalization of artists, the Soyer brothers—Isaac (1902–1981) and twins Moses (1899–1975) and Raphael (1899–1987)—drew praise for their compassionate easel paintings of New York City's urban poor, portraying such proletarian themes as homeless men in city parks, dejected women in unemployment offices, and the down and out gathered in transient centers, such as Isaac's *Unemployment Office*, 1937. In 1935, with great conviction and an eye toward the worsening situation in Germany, Moses Soyer critiqued the role of the artist in society in *Art Front*. He asserted: "Great art is national, but not nationalistic. Artists should not be misled by the chauvinism of the 'Paint America' slogan. Yes, paint America, but with your eyes open. Do not glorify Main Street. Paint it as it is—mean, dirty, avaricious. Self-glorification is artistic suicide. Witness Nazi Germany."[32] The Soyers, along with such other painters as Minna Citron (1896–1991), represented social hardships in their private easel paintings, in contrast to the federal works with the federal government's patronage that displayed a wholesome, nativist Main Street, and Midwest Regionalism.

The most famous New Deal arts program was its mural initiative. One of America's finest muralists, and one of the few to conquer the difficult art of true fresco, which he learned under the tutelage of Mexican master muralist Diego Rivera (1886–1957), was Lithuanian-born Ben Shahn (1898–1969). Shahn bravely countered government censors to address fascism, the rise of Nazism, the significance of labor unions, and the important history of refugees and immigrants to America for his mural at the Jersey Homesteads, New Jersey.[33] The Jersey Homesteads was a planned community funded in large measure by the Federal Government's Farm Security Administration to house and employ Jewish garment workers, most of them Leftists, who had relocated from New York to the farmlands of New Jersey. The community had a cooperative dual economy, maintaining both fields and garment factories, thus permitting the workers to be economically self-sufficient. Through his large-scale fresco, Shahn recounts the exodus from Eastern Europe to the United States on the heels of pogroms,

---

32 Moses Soyer, "The Second Whitney Biennial," *Art Front* (February 1935): 7.
33 Linden, *Ben Shahn*, chap. 2.

the oppressive conditions Jews found in the sweatshops and tenements of the Lower East Side, and their liberation through the garment unions based in New York. Shahn commences his mural's narrative in 1930s Germany, where a Nazi solider warns his fellow Germans not to buy from Jews; this threatening image with its accompanying German signage was the *only* reference to Nazi Germany and the rise of Hitler in *any* New Deal mural. Shahn's ultimate message is one of hope for working-class American Jews.

Radicals with a View Finder

New York's Photo League, 1936–1951, focused their cameras on the streets of the City to comment on issues of class, poverty, opportunity, and racial equality. Jews made up a large percentage of the League's membership, perhaps the majority, and, unusually for the time, one-third of the members were women. Indeed, women held important positions in the League, its school, and journal.[34] As the budding capital of modernity, New York City was home to a diverse spectrum of residents who served as subject matter for the photographers. [35] The photographers strongly felt that they held much in common with their subjects. The members of the League were urban types, more accustomed to the urban scene, than to the American tradition of nature photography. For Walter Rosenblum setting his lens on the Lower East Side was extremely personal, since he believed that "the kids are our images when we were young."[36]

The Holocaust: Responses in Sculpture

Throughout his lengthy career, Chaim Gross (1904–1991) repeatedly sculpted joyful mothers with their children in playful, nurturing poses. However, in one statue he completely shifted his style and intention— Gross's tribute to his murdered sister and his niece titled *In Memoriam: My Sister Sarah, Victim of Nazi Atrocities* (1947).[37] Gross, who had begun to collect African art in the early 1930s, looked to the attenuated statuary of

---

34   Mason Klein and Catherine Evans, *The Radical Camera: New York's Photo League, 1936 –1951* (New York: Jewish Museum, 2002).

35   Ibid., 12.

36   Ibid., 12.

37   Diana L. Linden, "Sculpting Joy: Experiencing the Artist and his Art at the Renee and Chaim Gross Foundation," *The Magazine Antiques,* September/October 2016, 104.

the Dogon people of West Africa for stylistic direction. The statue presents a seated woman, her elegantly elongated body curving inwards in a slight concave bend as she leans forward, her head solemnly dipped downwards. She tenderly and protectively presses the child, who sits in her lap, close to her own body. Sarah slightly envelopes the child, her pose and posture expressing the sense of mournfulness. The Holocaust would become a more prominent theme in Gross's later work.

By the late 1940s, sculptor Seymour Lipton dramatically changed his work stylistically, and abandoned realism and wood carving for welding abstract lead, steel, and metal sculptures, such as *Exodus No. 1* (1947). Like many others at the time, Lipton felt that figuration was too limited a vocabulary to confront the Holocaust. Lipton envisioned this piece as a model for a large, horizontal outdoor sculpture, which he described as "a kind of wailing wall monument to human suffering." Many other artists also experimented and struggled to develop a new visual rhetoric applicable to World War II, the Holocaust, the Nuclear Age, and the Cold War. While realists and such political artists as Hugo Gellert, William Gropper, Ben Shahn, and the Soyers continued to actively paint and to exhibit realist works, the art world became consumed by the great energy of Abstract Expressionism.

The Triumph of American Painting: The Rise of Abstract Expressionism

During the late 1940s and throughout the 1950s, artistic abstraction and non-objective painting were championed by the two most important, and competing art critics of the twentieth century: Clement Greenberg (1909–1994) and Harold Rosenberg (1906–1978), leading New York Jewish intellectuals.[38] Greenberg and Rosenberg dismissed realist, narrative, and political art as retrograde, in opposition to abstraction, which they considered the most advanced and appropriate means of visual expression for the era. Since the early 1970s, various art historians have tried to locate Jewishness within the canvases of the Abstract Expressionists, and within the artists' biographies and related artistic motivations.[39] While New York City gave rise to the movement, which is at times referred to as the New

---

38   Norman Kleeblatt, ed. *Action/Abstraction: Pollock, de Kooning, and American Art, 1940–1976* (New York / London and New Haven: The Jewish Museum / Yale University Press, 2008).

39   Thomas Hess, *Barnett Newman* (New York: Museum of Modern Art, 1971), 56.

York School, the development of Abstract Expressionism held global ramifications. Abstract Expressionism remains the most popular subject of study within twentieth-century American art, and the literature on it is therefore vast and ongoing.

Overwhelmingly, Abstract Expressionism was promoted as a white, male, heterosexual artform with Jackson Pollock, Willem de Kooning, Robert Motherwell, and Mark Rothko heading up the roster. As this list of names just cited indicates, and using Rothko as an example, Jewishness was melded into whiteness. In fact, there was a noteworthy racial, gender, and ethnic variety of practitioners, this according to revisionist scholar Ann Eden Gibson.[40] Recently, art historians Samantha Baskind and Larry Silver have pointed out that although Jews made up approximately three percent of the United States population at mid-century, a large number of first- and second- generation Abstractionists were Jews.[41] One repeated, yet facile, explanation for this prominence of Jewish among Abstract Expressionists is that the Jewish prohibition against graven images led to the traditional Jewish mastery of pure abstraction, which enabled artists to overcome a cultural resistance to depict the human figure. Yet as this essay has shown, Jews in America had long been engaged with figurative and narrative art-making. The erasure of overt Jewish symbolism—keeping in mind that pure abstraction and non-objective painting should not be read in order to glean legible symbols—has been claimed as the erasure of Jewish identity during the vulnerable post-World War II and Cold War era. But Jews were not the only ones who denounced figuration, realism, and narrative during this time, as many gentiles worked abstractly as well.

In 1971, curator Thomas Hess attempted to attribute the Judaic aspect of Barnett Newman's Zip or Stripe paintings, such as Newman's vertical oil on canvas *Onement I* (1948) on Kabbalah. Newman was familiar with Gershom G. Scholem's *Major Trends in Jewish Mysticism* (1946). The painter's vertical strips of pulsating colors seemingly emerge from a void as if symbolizing or replicating the very act of creation. For decades, Hess's interpretation, which celebrated art historian Matthew Baigell calls "a startling piece of information," had not be questioned, that is, until Baigell

---

40   Ann Eden Gibson, *Abstract Expressionism: Other Politics* (New Haven and London: Yale University Press, 1997).
41   Samantha Baskind and Larry Silver, *Jewish Art: A Modern History* (London: Reaktion Books, 2011).

himself took up the subject matter in his writings on Newman.[42] Newman, among Jewish abstractionists, was the one artist who most openly identified with Judaism.[43] Baigell takes apart Hess's conclusion by questioning his knowledge of Jewish texts and also how they applied to Newman. Newman painted additional canvases which reference major figures or themes within Judaism such as *Covenant* (1949) and *Eve* (1950).[44] Through his own close reading of Newman's ouvere and his knowledge of Jewish texts and traditions, which surpasses Hess's, Baigell proposes that in the late 1940s as Newman painted, "Jews throughout the world were deeply affected by the Holocaust and the creation of the state of Israel."[45] In this context, Baigell writes that Newman's Stripe paintings "might be understood as an act of resistance as well as a celebration of life and renewal and rebirth, an affirmation of life during a time of Jewish trauma and national revival."[46]

One of the pioneering figures of the movement was Brooklyn-born painter Lee Krasner (1908–1984), who has been pushed out of the male-dominated mythology of Abstract Expressionism. The fact that the figure whose celebrity loomed largest during this period, and ever since, was Krasner's husband Jackson Pollock, negatively impacted on the critical and popular awareness of the artist, and later on her legacy. Krasner described her situation as that of the "wife of famous artist," bluntly saying, "I happened to be Mrs. Jackson Pollock and that's a mouthful . . . I was a woman, Jewish, a widow, a damn good painter, thank you, and a little too independent." Krasner played a pioneering role in the formation of abstraction, and was one of the most schooled painters in terms of art theory and art history. She studied at New York's important art academies despite the obstacles she had to overcome because of her gender. Krasner, in fact, pioneered the all-over painting technique later made famous by Pollock, Cy Twombly, and others. Since the 1970s, art historians have brought greater attention to Krasner, beginning with the writings of feminist art historians. While gender was the first element assessed in her work and career, how

---

42 Matthew Baigell, "Barnett Newman's Stripe Paintings and Kabbalah: A Jewish Take," in his *Artist and Identity in Twentieth-Century America* (New York: Cambridge University Press, 2001), 232–42.

43 Matthew Baigell, *Jewish-American Artists and the Holocaust* (New Brunswick, NJ, and London: Rutgers University Press, 1997), 29.

44 Baskind and Silver, *Jewish Art,* 149.

45 Baigell, "Barnett Newman," 241.

46 Ibid. For Rothko, see Andrea Pappas, "Haunted Abstraction: Mark Rothko, Witnessing, and the Holocaust in 1942," *Journal of Modern Jewish Studies* 6, no. 2 (2007): 167–83.

Jewishness impacted on her identity and image making has also been of scholarly interest. Marcia Tucker's catalog and exhibition of the early 1970s helped bring Krasner back to greater public attention. Tucker posited that Krasner's first Little Image paintings of the mid- to late 1940s drew upon the artist's youthful lessons in Hebrew writing, and in fact these small paintings were worked on right to left the same direction as one writes Hebrew.[47] Art historian Barbara Rose builds upon this supposition suggesting that Krasner's calligraphic elements and style were based on ancient systems of writing, including Hebrew.[48]

New York's Jewish Museum

As stated early on, one reason that New York is so enticing to artists are its numerous museums, including the Jewish Museum. This heralded institution began with a gift of twenty-six ceremonial objects in 1904 to the library of the Manhattan's Jewish Theological Seminary. The Jewish Museum was the first of its kind to exist in the United States, and remains the largest of its kind in the Western Hemisphere.[49] For the first fifty years of its history, the Museum focused just on the acquisition and exhibition of ceremonial objects. The Museum in the 1960s became a force in the contemporary art work during the 1960s when, writes Maurice Berger, the curators showed a greater interest in cutting edge art of the avant-garde, the promoting geometric abstraction, pop art, and socially removed conceptual art, with little or no interest in the personal Jewish identity of the artist/creator.[50] This emphasis, or rather de-emphasis, on the artist's Jewishness has shifted over the years as curator Norman L. Kleeblatt has organized a great number of innovative exhibitions including *Too Jewish? Challenging Traditional Identities* (1996), which highlighted works by contemporary artists.

---

47 Marcia Tucker, *Lee Krasner: Large Paintings* (New York: Whitney Museum of American Art, 1973–1974).

48 Barbara Rose, *Lee Krasner: A Retrospective* (New York: Museum of Modern Art, 1983), 59.

49 Joan Rosenbaum, "The Jewish Museum and its History," in *Masterworks of the Jewish Museum*, ed. Joan Rosenbaum and Maurice Berger (New Haven and London: Yale University Press, 2004), 11–12.

50 Berger, *Masterworks of the Jewish Museum*, 22-23.

Contemporary Art

Artmaking has moved beyond paint and brush, steel and blowtorch, giving birth to such movements as installation art, graphic novels (such as the works of Art Spiegelman), process art, and performance art, to state just a few media. Jewish artists based in New York have been active in all these arenas. Contemporaneously, until the 1990s, open discussion of Jewishness within the New York art world was practically nonexistent, demonstrating the act of erasure and self-erasure, as well as striving to pass into "whiteness," writes Lisa E. Bloom.[51]

In 1979, pioneering feminist religiously-Jewish artist Mierle Laderman Ukeles debuted her performance piece "Touch Sanitation" (1979–1980), which drew upon her concern with women's role as providers of domestic and social cleanliness and maintenance. Ukeles is the New York Department of Sanitation's artist-in-residence, an honorary position she has held for many decades. Through connecting with the ten thousand New York City Sanitation workers personally, engaging with them, and shaking their hands, Ukeles's performance addresses issues of sanitation and the maintenance of daily life which she views as central issues in her life as a Jewish woman. Another prominent performance by Ukeles is her "Mikva Dreams," which likewise addressed feminism, Judaism, and ritual cleansing.[52] In this work, writes Lisa E. Bloom, Ukeles has successfully reclaimed the ritual from any negative connotations.

Installation, eco-feminist, and process artist Helene Aylon (1931-2020) was born and raised Orthodox in Brooklyn; she was the widow of a young rabbi while still in her twenties. Extremely knowledgeable in Torah and midrash, starting in the 1980s, Aylon started to read Torah through a feminist lens. Making art, she has said, "is a little like praying."[53] In the 1990s, Aylon, in her own words, sought to rescue "G-d from patriarchal projections." Her multi-media installation, "The Liberation of G-d" (1990–1996), addressed masculinist assertions in the Torah, along with other texts utilized

---

51   Lisa E. Bloom, *Jewish Identities in American Feminist Art: Ghosts of Ethnicity* (New York: Routledge, 2006), 105.

52   Mierle Laderman Ukeles, "Mikva Dreams—A Performance," *Heresies: A Feminist Publication on Art and Politics* 5 (Spring 1978), 52–54. See also Andrea K. Scott, "Mierle Laderman Ukeles and the Art of Work," *New Yorker*, November 7, 2016, newyorker.com/magazine/2016/11/07/mierle-laderman-ukeles-and-the-art-of-work (accessed August 12, 2017). See also, Bloom, *Jewish Identities* for more on Ukeles.

53   Baigell, *American Artists, Jewish Images*, 176.

for generations by religious scholars.[54] Her installation, which premiered at New York's Jewish Museum exhibition *Too Jewish?* consisted of an arrangement of sacred texts on glass shelves and placed on plexiglass stands to represent the five books of Moses. Respectful to the original text, Aylon layered the open books and unfurled scrolls with protective parchment on which she used a pink highlighter to call attention to those passage where the female presence had been obliterated or misaligned

Bloom writes about Elaine Reichek (b. 1945), an American born daughter of Jewish immigrants, that she deploys irony as well as parody to reveal how pervasive the practice of "passing" into white, gentile middle-class culture has been for American Jews such as her own family.[55] Reichek has used thread and needlework as central elements of her work beginning in the early 1970s. In a recreation of her childhood bedroom in Brooklyn titled *A Postcolonial Kinderhood* (1994, mixed media), she interprets how her parents sought to claim American authenticity through their acquisition of mid-1970s mass-produced Ethan Allan furnishings.[56] By focusing on the domestic sphere, Reichek focuses on the female sphere. Such furnishings, reworked, were displayed as part of the exhibition, *Too Jewish?* Alongside the furniture, the artist created and installed needlepoint samplers meant to evoke the WASP culture of the seventeenth–nineteenth centuries. Yet upon close looking and reading of what she has embroidered, one sees her biting commentary about Jewishness and dominant culture, such has her brother-in-law Paul Tannenbaum's quip: "I never think about being Jewish—until I leave New York."

When is Brooklyn not Brooklyn? Scholar Maya Balakirsky Katz tells us that "770" is a location, a symbol, and a brand representing the world headquarters of Chabad-Lubavitch Hasidism at 770 Eastern Parkway in the Crown Heights section of Brooklyn."[57] A brick apartment building built in the 1930s in the then popular Gothic Revival style, the building once housed the office of a physician who performed illegal abortions; with remaking of the building to become the Lubavitch headquarters, a "new vital life

---

54 Baigell, *Jewish American Art*, 214–15. See also Helene Aylon, *Whatever is Contained Must Be Released: My Jewish Orthodox Girlhood, My Life as a Feminist Artist* (New York: The Feminist Press at the City University of New York, 2012), 223–31.
55 Bloom, *Jewish Identities*, 114.
56 Leslie Friedman, *Masterworks of the Jewish Museum*, 140-41.
57 Maya Balakirsky Katz, *Visual Culture of Chabad* (New York: Cambridge University Press, 2010), 144.

force" was brought forth. The building was acquired to accommodate the Lubavitcher Rebbe, Rabbi Menachem Mendel Schneerson, on his arrival in Brooklyn. As of 2010, throughout the Jewish diaspora, there stand replicas of 770 in Israel, Italy, Australia, Chile, Argentina, Brazil, Canada, and Los Angeles. While the original building was designed to blend in with the tree-lined boulevard designed in the late nineteenth century by Frederick Law Olmsted, these assertive, masonry interpretations never aspired to blend with their new habitats, and in fact, are often pointedly at odds with their surroundings. In 2005, New York-based photographers Andrea Robbins and Max Becher shot their "Brooklyn Abroad" series throughout the diaspora, examining this iconic structure and its new iterations and meanings in varied locations, asking in part what the meaning is of this Brooklyn institution when transported and utilized elsewhere. Further, these replicas of 770 can be seen as symbolic of this traditional community's resistance to assimilation, and its simultaneous reassertion of its own identity.

"OY"—the blazing yellow aluminum sculpture in front of the Brooklyn Museum of Art assertively broadcasts its Jewishness. "YO"—bellows its reverse side making its New York attitude brashly known. Mimicking the planting of a flag to stake out territory, Deborah Kass's 2015 "OY/YO" (eight feet long and seventen feet wide) boldly claims its identity as both an urban and Jewish public sculpture. Kass's piece presents a twinned, inseparable identity. Her work is equal parts Jewish and New York, visual and vocal. Kass (b. 1952) a significant force within the contemporary art world, is best known for her works of appropriation and minimalism. The Jewishness of Kass's OY/YO placed solidly within the public sphere is undeniable.

Contemporary Jewish art in New York is the art of the now and of the moment. In the time that it has taken to write this essay and now, for you to have read it, an untold number of Jewish artists have decamped to New York City (skyrocketing rents and gentrification permitting) to pursue a career in what remains the nation's art capital. There is no one dominant media, theme, or style which describes the art of the new in these first two decades of the twenty-first century. Additionally, there are multiple means by which Jewish artists, including Jews who have migrated internationally to the City from throughout the United States or the global community, communicate their Jewishness, their relationship to the city, and their identity in plastic means. There is no neat conclusion to this chapter due to the continuation of artistic exploration. The story of Jewish art in New York City continues without seeming cessation.

For Further Reading

Antliff, Allan. *Anarchist Modernism: Art, Politics, and the First American Avante-Garde.* Chicago: University of Chicago Press, 2007.

Archino, Sarah. "The People's Art Guild and the Forward Exhibition of 1917." *Smithsonian Studies in American Art* 27, no. 3 (Fall 2013): 14–19.

Avrich, Paul, and Francis M. Naumann. "Adolf Wolff: 'Poet, Sculptor, and Revolutionist, but Mostly Revolutionist.'" *Art Bulletin* 67 no. 3 (September 1985): 486–500.

Aylon, Helene. *Whatever is Contained Must Be Released: My Jewish Orthodox Girlhood, My Life as a Feminist Artist.* New York: The Feminist Press at the City University of New York, 2012.

Baigell, Matthew. *Jewish-American Artists and the Holocaust.* New Brunswick, NJ, and London: Rutgers University Press, 1997.

———. *Artist and Identity in Twentieth-Century America.* New York: Cambridge University Press, 2001.

———. *Jewish Art in America.* Lanham, MD: Rowman & Littlefield Publishers, Inc., 2007.

Baskind, Samantha, and Larry Silver. *Jewish Art: A Modern History.* London: Reaktion Books, 2011.

Bilski, Emily D., and Emily Braun. *Jewish Women and their Salons: The Power of Conversation.* New York: The Jewish Museum, 2005.

Bloom, Lisa E. *Jewish Identities in American Feminist Art: Ghosts of Ethnicity.* New York: Routledge, 2006.

Brown, Milton W. "An Explosion of Creativity: Jews and American Art in the Twentieth Century." In *Painting a Place in America: Jewish Artists in New York, 1900–1945: A Tribute to the Educational Alliance,* edited by Norman L. Kleeblatt and Susan Chevlowe, 22–27. New York / Bloomington: Jewish Museum / Indiana University Press, 1991.

Brown, Stephen, and Georgianna Uhlyarik. *Florine Stettheimer: Painting Poetry.* New York: The Jewish Museum, 2017.

Carbone, Teresa A. *Youth and Beauty: Art of the American Twenties.* New York: Brooklyn Museum, 2011.

Clark, Sheila W., ed. *The Stettheimer Doll House.* New York: The Museum of the City of New York, 2009.

Dabakis, Melissa. *Visualizing Labor in American Sculpture: Monuments, Manliness, and the Work Ethic, 1880 –1935.* New York: Cambridge University Press, 1999.

Dervaux, Isabelle. "The Ten: An Avant-Garde Group in the 1930s."*Archives of American Art Journal* 31, no. 2 (1991): 14–20.

Fort, Ilene Susan, ed., *The Figure in American Sculpture: A Question of Modernity.* Los Angeles: Los Angeles County Museum of Art, 1995.

Francis, Jacqueline. *Making Race: Modernism and Racial Art in America.* Seattle and London: University of Washington Press, 2012.

Gibson, Ann Eden. *Abstract Expressionism: Other Politics.* New Haven and London: Yale University Press, 1997.

Hess, Thomas. *Barnett Newman.* New York: Museum of Modern Art, 1971.

Heyd, Milly. "Man Ray/Emmanuel Radnitsy: Who Is behind the Enigma of Isidore Ducasse?" In *Complex Identities: Jewish Consciousness and Modern Art,* edited by Matthew Baigell and Milly Heyd, 115–41. New Brunswick, NJ, and London: Rutgers University Press, 2001.

Katz, Maya Balakirsky. *Visual Culture of Chabad.* New York: Cambridge University Press, 2010.

Kleeblatt, Norman, ed. *Action/Abstraction: Pollock, de Kooning, and American Art, 1940–1976.* New York / New Haven and London: The Jewish Museum / Yale University Press, 2008.

Klein, Mason, and Catherine Evans. *The Radical Camera: New York's Photo League, 1936–1951.* New York: Jewish Museum, 2002.

Kozloff, Max. *New York: Capital of Photography.* New York / New Haven and London: The Jewish Museum / Yale University Press, 2002.

Laderman Ukeles, Mierle. "Mikva Dreams—A Performance." *Heresies: A Feminist Publication on Art and Politics* 5 (Spring 1978): 52–54.

Langa, Helen. *Radical Art: Printmaking and the Left in 1930s New York.* (Berkeley, Los Angeles, and London: University of California Press, 2004).

Levin, Gail. *Theresa Bernstein: A Century in Art.* Lincoln and London: University of Nebraska Press, 2013.

Linden, Diana L. "Visual Essay." In Jeffrey S. Gurock, *Jews in Gotham: New York Jews in a Changing City, 1920–2010,* 223–54. New York: New York University Press, 2012.

———. *Ben Shahn's New Deal Murals: Jewish Identity in the American Scene.* Detroit: Wayne State University Press, 2015.

———. "Sculpting Joy: Experiencing the Artist and his Art at the Renee and Chaim Gross Foundation." *The Magazine Antiques* (September/October 2016). https://www.themagazineantiques.com/article/

sculpting-joy-experiencing-the-artist-and-his-art-at-the-renee-and-chaim-gross-foundation/.

Naumann, Francis M. *New York DADA, 1915 –1923.* New York: Harry N. Abrams, Inc. 1994.

Pappas, Andrea. "Haunted Abstraction: Mark Rothko, Witnessing, and the Holocaust in 1942." *Journal of Modern Jewish Studies* 6, no. 2 (2007): 167–83.

Rose, Barbara. *Lee Krasner: A Retrospective.* New York: Museum of Modern Art, 1983.

Rosenbaum, Joan. "The Jewish Museum and its History." In *Masterworks of the Jewish Museum,* edited by Joan Rosenbaum and Maurice Berger, 10–17. New Haven and London: Yale University Press, 2004.

Scott, Andrea K. "Mierle Laderman Ukeles and the Art of Work." *New Yorker,* November 7, 2016. https://www.New Yorker.com/magazine/2016/11/07/mierle-laderman-ukeles-and-the-art-of-work.

Tyler, Francine. "Artists Respond to the Great Depression and the Threat of Fascism: The New York Artists Union and Its Magazine, *Art Front* (1934–1937)." PhD diss., New York University, 1991.

Zurier, Rebecca. *Picturing the City: Urban Vision and the Ashcan School.* Berkeley, Los Angeles, and London: University of California Press, 2006.

Chapter 10

Jewish Geography in New York Neighborhoods, 1945–2000

Jeffrey S. Gurock

I.

In 1960, a feature writer for *Fortune* magazine declared that for Jews "as no other city is, New York is their home: here a Jew can be what he wants to be." Living "out of the shadow of his historic crisis"—a decade and a half after the Holocaust decimated European Jewry—"in New York at least he does not live in the crisis of alienation." Sam Welles observed a "Jewish elan [was] contribut[ing] mightily to the city's dramatic character—its excitement, its originality, its stridency, its unexpectedness." On a day-by-day basis, New York Jews, whether "cab drivers . . . Wall Street bankers . . . hole-in-the-wall delicatessen owners . . . Nobel laureates in physics . . . Beatnik author[s]" or "some 15 percent of the city's civil servants who quietly do their work and will in due course retire on small pensions," all "exercise[d] . . . wide influence" upon life in Gotham. New York Jews were not totally of one brand, "as they constituted a widely diverse society in themselves." But rich or poor, the word on their streets was that the metropolis was home even as the city welcomed new groups of Jewish immigrants, many of whom were survivors of the Holocaust.[1]

Just a decade later, the way New York's Jews looked at their place in the city had changed. While many remained ensconced in stable middle-class neighborhoods and others in wealthy ones, still others lost that loving feeling as they became embroiled in racial controversies both where they resided and elsewhere. They began to question their future in their hometown. In the quarter-century that followed, as the municipality rode through the depths and crests of financial crises and revivals—amid continued racial strife—many of the disaffected exited the city. They looked towards suburbia for more favorable settings. Meanwhile, more than 100,000 of the Jewish community's poorest—often the elderly—were trapped in declining, crime-ridden neighborhoods. At the same time, while alienation was rife in so many quarters, groups of incipient gentrifiers began to carve out new Jewish spaces for themselves and their friends. At the turn of the new millennium, the patterns of diverse Jewish economic and social lives in Gotham continued apace. Then, as always, there was no one New York Jewish story. There were those who glorified in their own achievements and in the panache of the metropolis while others feared what the future held for them.

II.

Writer Vivian Gornick has rhapsodized about her early postwar West Bronx neighborhood as a symphony of Jewish sounds and sights. She has recalled that everywhere she turned there "was Jewishness in all its rich variety. Down the street were Orthodox Jews, up the street were Zionists, in the middle of the street were shtetl, get-rich-quick Jews, European humanist Jews." Notwithstanding differences of opinion that were debated loudly on park benches, often late into hot summer nights "Jewishness was the leveler." During Jewish holidays "the whole world shut down, everyone was dressed immaculately, and a sense of awe thickened the very air we breathed; the organic quality of the atmosphere told us who we were, gave us boundary and idiomatic reference, shaped the face of the culture in which each one of us assumed a vital albeit, primitive sense of identity."[2]

---

1   Sam Welles, "The Jewish Elan," *Fortune*, February 1960, 135–36.
2   Vivian Gornick, "There is No Community," *Interchange*, April 1977, 21–25.

What was true culturally and demographically in this "old" Bronx neighborhood applied to other enduring Jewish enclaves. If, in 1940, "55.6% of all Jews in New York City were still concentrated in fifteen neighborhoods that were at least 40% Jewish, in 1960, the total number of such neighborhoods—primarily in the Bronx and Brooklyn—held steady and comprised 57.6% of the city's Jews." Fifteen years after World War II "more than one of every four New York Jews lived in a neighborhood that was over half Jewish in composition." In other words, these predominantly American-born New Yorkers still lived largely among their own kind, continuing the way of life that they inherited from their mostly immigrant parents.[3]

Comfortable where they were and among whom they lived—tensions between them and other ethnic groups that had roiled neighborhood life died down after the war—in the early mornings, Jewish workers and tradespeople, took the cheap, if crowded, subways to work much as their parents did before them. As late as 1948, a single ride cost five cents, the fare only rising beyond twenty cents after 1966. Bronx subway commuters—perhaps a garment cutter, presser, or finisher—could leave home at 7:30 AM and be certain to punch the clock by 8. They returned home to shop and socialize on their Jewish streets. On occasion, they might go back into the inner city to take advantage of all that the metropolis's cultural venues had to offer.[4]

Still, suburbia beckoned. Although Jews were neither the first nor the largest group of New Yorkers to look for new homes outside the city's limits, very substantial numbers of their younger generation were on the move. Perhaps some did not want to live forever next door to their parents in buildings that were starting to become run-down. But for even more migrants, it was their search for "a more wholesome environment" for their baby-boomer children that drove them to new surroundings. Nassau County, Long Island, absorbed, as of 1959, some 329,000 Jews; more than a quarter of the county's overall population. North of the city, in Westchester, 15% of the population was Jewish. Over the George Washington Bridge

---

3   Joshua M. Zeitz, *White Ethnic New York: Jews, Catholics and the Shaping of Postwar Politics* (Chapel Hill: University of North Carolina Press, 2007), 16.

4   Welles, "Jewish Elan," 134–39; Robert A. Caro, *The Power Broker and the Fall of New York* (New York: Knopf, 1974), 851–52; Zeitz, *White Ethnic New York*, 23, 32–35, 236–37; Joshua Freeman, *Working Class New York: Life and Labor since World War II* (New York: Free Press, 2000), 37.

in Bergen County, by 1960, some 14,000 Jews had found new homes in townships like Englewood, Fair Lawn, Teaneck and Fort Lee.[5]

And then there was Queens; a borough which, ironically, during the interwar period had harbored neighborhoods off-limits to Jews. Unique among American metropolises, Gotham proffered what was essentially a "suburb" within the city's legal limits; only a subway ride to work in Manhattan. For Jews who previously lived in Brooklyn and the Bronx and, who still "look[ed] for urban virtues," Queens offered the kind of street life they were used to, especially if they opted for life in high-rise apartment buildings. Contrasting what day-by-day life could be like in Jewish neighborhoods like Forest Hills, Flushing, Bayside and Jackson Heights, as opposed to Long Island, a social scientist suggested that even if in "the mass-produced Levittown-type suburbs . . . their neighbors were still close by . . . on the other hand, there were no hallways, or lobbies, as in apartment houses, for chance meetings, no elevators for quick exchanges of gossip and news, no corner luncheonettes for ready sociability, no street life to speak of." By1957, some 423,000 Jews had made that outer borough their home.[6]

The early postwar years also witnessed an influx of Jewish newcomers; refugees from many lands of oppression and survivors of the Holocaust carved out their own niches in the city. Close to a half of all Jewish immigrants to the United States from the late 1940s to the mid-1960s settled in New York City. The overwhelming majority of these immigrants hailed initially from Russia, Poland, and other East European countries. Arab anger and frustration over the rise of the State of Israel caused endangered Sephardic Jews from Syria, Lebanon, Iraq, and Egypt to flee to America. These new Jewish immigrants helped maintain for a time New York Jewry's thirty-percent share of the city's overall population. More than just replacing those second- and third-generation Jews who opted for suburbia, these

---

5   On Jewish persistence in the city during early suburbanization, see Eli Lederhendler, *New York Jews and the Decline of Urban Ethnicity* (Syracuse: Syracuse University Press, 2001), 34. For population figures of suburban locales, see C. Morris Horowitz and Lawrence J. Kaplan, *The Jewish Population of the New York Area, 1900–1975* (New York: Federation of Jewish Philanthropies, 1959), 17, and Table 1, Appendix to Alvin Chenkin, "Jewish Population in the United States, 1958," *American Jewish Year Book* 60 (1959): 14–15. See also, Simon Glustrom, "Some Aspects of a Suburban Jewish Community," *Conservative Judaism* 11, no. 2 (Winter 1957): 27–28.

6   Marshall Sklare, "Jews, Ethnics, and the American City," *Commentary*, April, 1972, 73; Horowitz and Kaplan, *Jewish Population,* 22, 45, 283, 285, 289, 305.

new arrivals brought new tones and tenors to the neighborhoods in which they settled.[7]

Like so many immigrants before them, these newcomers sought out their own kind. Orthodox Jews from Eastern Europe gravitated to Brooklyn neighborhoods. Cooperative housing complexes—old and new—in the Bronx welcomed those from Eastern Europe with socialist inclinations. German Jews reconnected with earlier refugees in Washington Heights; with some settling on the west side of Manhattan. Sephardim moved into other Brooklyn enclaves, especially in Flatbush and Bensonhurst; a limited number found homes in Forest Hills, Queens. The most noticeable of these newcomers were the varying sects of Hasidic Jews who quickly established themselves in Williamsburg where they perpetuated, when they were not intensifying, the prevailing Orthodoxy of that section.[8]

The influx of Hasidim that changed the neighborhood's appearance and character also hastened the relocation of many non-Hasidic Williamsburg Jews to Queens or Long Island, or in some cases to Borough Park or Crown Heights, just a few miles away in their home borough. Eventually, these Americanized Jews would be on the move again, when in the 1960s varying sects of Hasidim relocated to Borough Park and Crown Heights.[9]

In the early postwar decades, Crown Heights became home to the most renowned Hasidic group, the Lubavitchers, who would in time influence Jewish life well beyond their neighborhood confines. Crown Heights persisted for several additional decades as a prime destination for Jewish visitors, both the faithful and the intrigued, who were attracted to the words and persona of Rabbi Menachem Mendel Schneerson, the Lubavitcher Rebbe. But by the 1960s, there were major problems brewing in the neighborhood that threatened the continuity of the community. For a variety of social, economic, and political reasons, Crown Heights was racially

---

7   William B. Helmreich, *Against All Odds: Holocaust Survivors and the Successful Lives They Made in America* (New York: Simon and Schuster, 1996), 46–48; Victor D. Sanua, "A Study of the Adjustment of Sephardi Jews in the New York Metropolitan Area," *Jewish Journal of Sociology* 9, no. 1 (June 1967): 26–27. See also Joseph A. D. Sutton, *Magic Carpet: Aleppo in Flatbush: The Story of a Unique Ethnic Jewish Community* (New York: Thayer-Jacobi, 1979), 4.

8   George Kranzler, *Williamsburg: A Jewish Community in Transition* (New York: Feldheim, 1961), 40–43; Jerome R. Mintz, *Hasidic People: A Place in the New World* (Cambridge, MA: Harvard University Press, 1992), 30.

9   Egon Mayer, *From Suburb to Shtetl: The Jews of Boro Park* (Philadelphia: Temple University Press, 1979), 31; Kranzler, *Williamsburg,* 40–43.

transformed. As most non-Hasidic Jews left, those who remained would find themselves caught up in the emerging crises of New York urban life that would pit the city's Jews against African Americans.

III.

Until the 1960s, most Jews had little ongoing contact with African Americans, because New York City was still quite segregated by convention and covenant. At least, most Jews experienced it that way. For example, as of 1957, African Americans constituted but 3.5% of the population on the Grand Concourse, even if their real numbers had grown five fold in the previous seven years, from approximately 1,400 to around 6,700. Jews remained two-thirds of the population.[10]

There were a few pockets of geographical tension between some Jews and Blacks, but racial animosities between the groups were not explicitly articulated. The most daunting dynamic surrounded the rapid decline of the East Tremont section of the Bronx when the construction of the Cross Bronx Expressway cut through that neighborhood. During the 1950s, after decades of discussion, municipal official Robert Moses pushed through a plan to link the city with New Jersey and New England through what would become known as the "I-95 corridor." But that endeavor required the destruction of hundreds of apartment buildings. In short order, some 5,000 residents, most of them Jews, lost their homes. As construction of what those affected called "Heartbreak Highway" proceeded, starting with noisy, dirty, and toxic excavation work, some 10,000 additional East Tremont denizens moved out. Those with more money, mostly the younger generation, looked for housing in the suburbs or the suburban-like community of Riverdale, in the north-west corner of the Bronx. This enclave began earning a reputation as an up and coming Jewish neighborhood after the World War II, particularly after Fieldston, its most expensive private home section, dropped its antisemitic restrictions.[11]

---

10 Bureau of Community Statistical Services Research Department, Community Council of Greater New York, *Bronx Communities: Population Characteristics and Neighborhood Social Resources,* typescript (New York: Community Council of Greater New York, 1962), 45–46, 69, 70. See also Horowitz and Kaplan, *Jewish Population,* 175, 217.

11 For a discussion of the long road towards the construction of Cross Bronx Expressway see Ray Bromley, "Not So Simple! Caro, Moses, and the Impact of the Cross-Bronx Expressway," *Bronx County Historical Society Journal* 35, no. 1 (1998): 4–29. On

As Jews vacated East Tremont's apartments, many of the city's poorest of the poor, mostly African Americans, moved into the increasingly dilapidated buildings. Fears and realities of muggings, robberies, break-ins, and violence reverberated through the neighborhood, sparking a chain migration out of the area. As each additional group of Jews left a building, word spread next door and then around the corner. By the mid-1960s, the community's Jewish era had ended. Some of those who did not want, or could not afford, to move to suburbia or pricey Riverdale found refuge in the borough's "decent areas," as one former East Tremont resident put it. But the poor and elderly remained trapped in what would later be described as "ravaged hulks," "barricaded in their freezing apartments." Sadly, the East Tremont experience produced a compelling formula for the next decades of urban crisis as other Jewish sections of the city replicated this template of turmoil—physical deterioration, initial departures, arrival of minorities, fears, and sometimes the reality, of criminality, further evacuations, and intensified deterioration of the neighborhood, leaving behind only the most disadvantaged. Still, for the most part Jews and Blacks lived in different worlds within the same city.[12]

In the summer of 1964, race riots broke out in Harlem and in the Bedford-Stuyvesant section of Brooklyn. Many of the victimized store-owners were Jews, but antisemitism was absent from the rioters' rhetoric. Even the most militant Jewish spokesmen did not see the outbreak as being directed specifically at Jews.[13] It remained for the 1968 battle in Brooklyn over community control of the Ocean Hill-Brownsville public school district for Jews and Blacks to confront one another and for vituperative anti-semitic and racist sentiments to foul relations between the two groups.

The prime combatants in the Ocean Hill-Brownsville conflict were the largely Jewish United Federation of Teachers (UFT) and local Black parents. Both groups found radicalized allies within their respective groups who did much to exacerbate tensions. At prime issue was the sense on the African American street that their youngsters had been long denied a chance at a quality education. It was alleged, furthermore, that UFT

Fieldston antisemitism, see Deborah Dash Moore, *At Home in America: Second Generation New York Jews* (New York: Columbia University Press, 1981), 38.

12   Caro, *Power Broker*, 850–94.

13   On the absence of antisemitism attached to the riots, see Murray Friedman, *What Went Wrong?: The Creation and Collapse of the Black-Jewish Alliance* (New York: Free Press, 1995), 214.

members were complicit in the underachievement of Black children. Thus, the only solution was "community control" of the schools to ensure that the right types of teachers were in the classroom, and that these instructors evinced the proper respect for Black culture. The UFT, led by its outspoken president Albert Shanker, chafed at the charge that union members were insensitive to the needs of their charges. The UFT objected to the removal of senior teachers without due process. Making matters worse, vitriolic antisemitic statements were spread about the "death of the minds and souls of our black children . . . by Middle East Murderers of Colored People . . . Jews who dominate and control the educational bureaucracy of the New York public school system." The UFT turned to the courts for relief, only to have Mayor John V. Lindsay refuse to implement the justices' decision that supported the union. Now at odds both with City Hall and his African American opponents, Shanker called his rank and file out on the first of three strikes that effectively closed down the entire city school system for close to three months. During this time of troubles, additional charges and counter-charges of antisemitism and racism were heard.[14]

Throughout the school ordeal, which only simmered down in the winter of 1969 when the school district came under control of a state trustee, national and international developments intensified local Black-Jewish tensions. Most critical was the impact of the Six Day War on both communities. That reference to "Middle East murderers" reflected a growing African-American identification with the Third World and denigration of Israel as a colonialist state. Bringing their perceptions back home, Blacks projected local Jews as oppressors. For many New York Jews, by contrast, the Israeli victory inspired them to emulate their courageous brethren and to stand tall against all enemies foreign and domestic. Applying that attitude to their own urban realities, they "concluded that they could and must fight like hell for themselves," specifically in the schoolteachers' case for their jobs.[15]

---

14 Jerald E. Podair, *The Strike that Changed New York: Blacks, Whites and the Ocean Hill-Brownsville Crisis* (New Haven: Yale University Press, 2002), 2, 38, 72, 77–78; Jonathan Kaufman, *Broken Alliance: The Turbulent Times between Blacks and Jews in America* (New York: Scribner, 1988), 142–43,148–49. See also Cheryl Greenberg, *Troubling the Waters: Black-Jewish Relations in the American Century* (Princeton: Princeton University Press, 2006), 230; Friedman, *What Went Wrong*, 260; Zeitz, *White Ethnic New York*, 161–63.

15 On the connection between local Black problems with Jews and the international scene, see Zeitz, *White Ethnic New York*, 64–66. On the relationship between the 1967

These late-1960s conflicts also revealed serious fault lines within the Jewish community. There were Jewish teachers who hardly perceived Shanker as a hero. Though their presence was barely noted, UFT opponents of long-standing, erstwhile members of the leftwing Teachers Union, identified with Black aspirations.[16]

More significantly, young Jewish teachers—forty percent of a replacement cohort in the Ocean Hill-Brownsville schools—publicly denied that antisemitism pervaded the district. A twenty-three-year-old recent graduate of Long Island University characterized his group as "nearly all . . . committed to social change." Older strikers were offended by this youthful rhetoric of "social change." As they reviewed their own lives, they contended that they had been drawn back to a neighborhood that was once "theirs" to teach a new group of underprivileged youngsters. They, too, had been poor children of immigrant newcomers. Now, arrogant young colleagues chastised them while Black antisemites pilloried them as racists.[17]

Possessed of a totally different Jewish perspective, Rabbi Meir Kahane, founder and leader of the Jewish Defense League (JDL), believed his people to be under existential attack. From his pulpit as managing editor of the *Jewish Press*, Kahane constantly argued that the antisemitism that emanated from the school conflict was but the latest manifestation of Black antipathy toward Jews. He ridiculed the "establishment" Jew as "a rich Jew who lives in Scarsdale or some other rich suburb" removed from the realities of city life and without any feeling for what the "grass-roots" was facing. Though "Scarsdale" was his metaphor, he did not spare better-off and decidedly liberal Jews who resided in classy places in Manhattan and even in some affluent sections of Brooklyn and Queens either. They too failed to recognize the threats his people faced. All told, Kahane viewed the city as "polarized beyond hope" with "anger, hate, frustration."[18]

Israeli victory and New York Jewish assertiveness, see Freeman, *Working-Class New York*, 223–34.

16   On the history of the Teachers Union and its relationship with the United Federation of Teachers, see Celia Lewis Zitron, *The New York City Teachers Union 1916–1964: A Story of Educational and Social Commitment* (New York: Humanities Press, 1968), 45–52, and Podair, *Strike that Changed New York,* 142.

17   Freeman, *Working-Class New York,* 221; Charles S. Isaacs, "A J.H.S. 271 Teacher Tells It Like He Sees It," *New York Times Magazine,* November 24, 1968, accessed July 18, 2018. On the return of Jewish teachers to their old neighborhood to teach minority youngsters, see Zeitz, *White Ethnic New York,* 167.

18   On the Jewish Defense League and the teachers' strike, see Kaufman, *Broken Alliance,* 157-158, Robert G. Weissbord and Arthur Stein, *Bittersweet Encounter: The*

Kahane's rhetoric and methods did not capture the hearts and minds of the vast majority of the city's Jews. But his articulation of a Brooklyn vs. Scarsdale, or, for that matter, threatened Brooklyn vs. affluent Manhattan, dichotomy reflected real disagreements among Jews. The splits reflected the comfort level of Jewish groups and enclaves within the metropolis. One sociologist has argued that the Brooklyn school events of 1968 transformed "outer-borough Jews" from "optimistic universalism" to "nervous parochialism" while inner-borough cohorts maintained their long-standing personal equanimity and liberal equilibrium. [19] In 1970, this profound sense of alienation among dissatisfied Jews resurfaced in Forest Hills. The controversy arose in reaction to Lindsay's plan to build low-cost housing in the neighborhood. City Hall considered it a "moral imperative" to end tacit racial segregation. But opponents heard "projects" when they contemplated a plan to construct 840 apartment units in three twenty-four-story buildings in their neighborhood. The government's arguments that the new construction would also house deserving elderly did not dampen objections. Many of the protestors saw themselves as "refugees" from Bronx and Brooklyn communities that had "turned" due to governmental tampering. They perceived themselves as victims of an insensitive, if not cynical, Lindsay administration that had taken for granted their supposed unalterable Jewish liberalism. Eventually, lawyer and future governor Mario Cuomo, together with intercession from the federal government, brokered a compromise that stilled the angry voices. But as the new decade began New York Jews walked away from these disputes increasingly of several minds over how comfortable they were in Gotham.[20]

IV.

During the mid-1970s, a confluence of social, economic and political crises brought New York City to the brink of bankruptcy. Under the watch of Mayor Abraham Beame, the first Jew to occupy City Hall, problems on many interconnected fronts undermined Gotham's viability. New York provided the classic city-in-decline scenario: loss of manufacturing jobs,

Afro-American and the American Jew (Westport, CT: Negro Universities Press, 1970), 201–204; Lederhendler, *New York Jews and the Decline of Urban Ethnicity,* 192–94.

19 Greenberg, *Troubling the Waters,* 231; Jonathan Rieder, *Canarsie: The Jews and Italians of Brooklyn against Liberalism* (Cambridge, MA: Harvard University Press, 1985), 73, discussed in Podair, *Strike that Changed New York,* 144.

20 Zeitz, *White Ethnic New York,* 190–92.

financial instability, rent control conundrums, white working-class exodus, drugs, crime, and abandonment of housing.[21]

These years severely tested the faith of New York's Jews in the metropolis. As always there was no singular Jewish voice. Differences in perspectives between optimistic "Manhattan" and pessimistic "Brooklyn" Jews, and their counterparts in other boroughs, appeared in the sharpest relief. Tens of thousands answered the basic question of whether they belonged in New York with an unqualified no. They constituted a significant component in the middle class exodus of the 1970s and the 1980s. Now, for the first time, Jews were as "equally suburbanized" as the general population.[22]

But, at the same time, Jewish refugees from the Soviet Union and Arab countries, along with expatriates from Israel, mitigated the substantial decline of New York Jews. The "Russians" largely settled in the Brighton Beach section of Brooklyn. Israelis and Bukharans concentrated in the Rego Park, Forest Hills, Flushing, and Kew Gardens neighborhoods of Queens, while Syrian, Iranian, and Iraqi Jews in time predominated in the Flatbush and Midwood parts of Brooklyn. Together, they helped to maintain a very substantial Jewish presence in the city. Starting out from their own enclaves, the newcomers began their quests to see what New York, even in decline, had to offer.[23]

Some Jews who stayed in the city shared their suburban compatriots' pessimism about the destiny of New York City. In the 1970s, many Canarsie Jews felt alienated from the metropolis although their Brooklyn enclave had been spared much of the worst of urban blight. Those who worked in service industries among the poor or as city employees, social workers and most notably, teachers, encountered daily the economic and

---

21 Samuel Kaplan, "The Bronx Arrangement," *New York*, December 14, 1970, 10; Herbert E. Meyer, "How Government Helped Ruin the South Bronx," *Fortune*, November 1975, 145; Freeman, *Working Class New York*, 281.

22 Fred Massarik, "Basic Characteristics of the Greater New York Jewish Population," *American Jewish Year Book* 76 (1976): 239, 242; Steven M. Cohen and Paul Ritterband, "The Social Characteristics of the New York Jewish Community, 1981," *American Jewish Year Book* 84 (1984): 129, 140; Frederick M. Binder and David M. Reimers, *All the Nations under Heaven: An Ethnic and Racial History of New York City* (New York: Columbia University Press, 1995), 240–42.

23 Fran Markowitz, *A Community in Spite of Itself: Soviet Jewish Emigres in New York* (Washington: Smithsonian Institution Press, 1993), 1; Aviva Ben-Ur, *Sephardic Jews in America: A Diasporic History* (New York: New York University Press, 2009), 220, n.80; Moshe Shokeid, *Children of Circumstances: Israeli Emigrants in New York* (Ithaca: Cornell University Press, 1988), 15.

social problems just beyond their borders. They decided to protect their community by joining forces with their Italian neighbors to forcefully limit the numbers of Blacks and Latinos around them.[24]

At the same time, Jews in Co-op City hoped that whatever became of their old neighborhoods, they could live securely in new environs in the city. However, that promise was only partially fulfilled. They had been lured away from their stable and affordable communities, most notably from the Grand Concourse, by a gigantic 15,400-unit apartment in a northeastern corner of the Bronx. The dream was to construct a bucolic residential environment "for friendly people living together."[25]

Some older Jewish residents of Parkchester in the East Bronx also moved to Co-op City, even though it represented but a half-step up. While their buildings were well maintained, the prewar structures lacked air conditioning. Sitting outside with friends until late at night during the summer was no substitute for the promises of Co-op City. Some of their adult children who grew up in Parkchester settled in Riverdale. There they discovered an "island entirely of itself . . . in the city yet not of it," a new-era urban bedroom community tucked away from New York's decline. By the 1980s, 30,000 Jews lived in Riverdale.[26]

While middle- and upper-class Jews sank secure roots in Riverdale, poor planning plagued Co-op City. Coop leaders and government officials badly underestimated expenses in building and maintaining the endeavor. Carrying costs became an increasingly onerous burden on residents. By the end of that decade, nay-sayers described this neighborhood as "a dream gone sour."[27]

---

24 Rieder, *Canarsie*, 16, 20, 22, 65, 69–71, 80, 110–11, 128, 129, 172, 184, 193–98, 207–14.

25 Allan M. Siegal, "Rent is Primary Issue for Co-op City," *New York Times* [hereinafter *NYT*], September 6, 1974, 73; James F. Clarity, "Co-op City, Home to 40,000 is Given Tempered Praise," *NYT*, May 27, 1971, 41; Rita Reif, "Some Subsidized Co-ops Far from Pioneers' Ideal," *NYT*, January 25, 1976, 2, 6; Samuel G. Freedman, "Co-op City: A Refuge in Transition," *NYT*, June 25, 1986, B1; Don Terry, "Co-op City: A Haven Marred as Drugs Slip In," *NYT*, August 10, 1989, B1.

26 Robert E. Thompson, "As Change Intrudes, the Concourse Sells," *NYT*, August 13, 1972, R1; Kaplan, "Bronx Arrangement," 10; Jack Luria, "A Pox on You, Riverdale," *NYT*, June 21, 1972, 43. See also for Riverdale population statistics for 1981, *Greater New York Jewish Population Study* (New York: United Jewish Appeal-Federation of Jewish Philanthropies, 1981).

27 Freedman, "Co-op City," B1; David Bird, "Tentative Agreement is Negotiated by State on Co-op Repairs," *NYT*, May 13, 1979, 17; Susan Chira, "Co-op City: Life Begins to Improve," *NYT*, May 8, 1982, 27.

While Riverdalians felt right at home, Co-op City families wondered about their decisions and Canarsie Jews struggled, other New York Jews in the 1970s evinced confidence that the city still possessed, as it always had, so much to offer. These upwardly mobile singles and young couples, with and without children, had soured on suburbia and found both comfort and excitement in the metropolis. Even at the very nadir of New York's decline, the beginnings of an alternate urban dynamic were visible. In some cases, these "trend-setting gentrifiers" started to turn once dismal districts into "delightful neighborhoods." Manhattan's Columbus Avenue, once run-down and dreary, possessed "colorful shops and restaurants." With the right bottom-line bank accounts, and the right pigmentation, they found banks ready and willing to extend to them the necessary lines of credit to assist their initiatives.[28]

Young Jews participated in the emergence of this other optimistic New York scene because so many of them had escaped the occupational downturn in their city. Part of a new generation, no longer working-class, they possessed financial security. They had choices and moved around the city's neighborhoods. They proved the old adage about American Jews, romanticized as early as the 1920s, that East Europeans were "neither the sons nor the fathers of workers," had now come true on a large scale.[29]

This younger generation had taken full advantage of the increasing openness of American society towards Jews. Academic achievers, they contributed to the statistic that by the close of the 1970s more than half of New York Jewish heads of households were college educated. In Manhattan, a borough described as home for over a decade to "an influx of socio-economic 'upscale' individuals," more than one third of Jewish men and twenty-nine percent of women possessed graduate degrees. After graduation, these Jews obtained jobs offering more financial security than their parents had achieved. These second-stage gentrifiers—able to pay ever increasing high rents—often replaced the first less-affluent Jews and gentiles who had taken a chance on neighborhoods that were only beginning to change for the better. "Sadly," lamented one critic of this rapid turnover,

---

28 Andrew Hacker, "The City's Comings, Goings," *NYT,* December 2, 1973, 26; Editorial, "Victims of Urban Revival," *NYT,* November 18, 1978, 20; Blake Fleetwood, "The New Elite and an Urban Renaissance," *NYT,* January 14, 1979, SM 26, 34.

29 On the assumed early periodization for Jews leaving the blue-collar labor force by the 1920s, see Will Herberg, "The Jewish Labor Movement in the United States," *American Jewish Year Book* 53 (1952): 28.

pioneers of neighborhood improvement were being driven "into the arms of the Mayor of Jersey City."[30]

But while young people on the make enthused about their prospects, more than 200,000 needy, elderly Jewish New Yorkers struggled to merely survive in run-down neighborhoods.[31] In many cases, these men and women were remnants of the Jewish laboring class. They were too old to continue working or their jobs had evaporated as the city's manufacturing base shrank. In addition, poverty-plagued Hasidic communities constituted "the third largest poverty group in New York." Their resistance to American mores, highly esteemed in their community, severely limited their economic mobility. However, Hasidic feelings about New York's future directions and their place within the city would be tied not to any city-wide economic renaissance. Rather, their range of sentiments depended on the municipality's ability to keep them safe within their enclaves.[32]

In their own sections of Brooklyn, Syrian Jews also came to terms with the city. With entrepreneurial skills brought from Aleppo or Damascus, they carved out successful business niches and engaged customers of all backgrounds. Often relying on friends and relatives for start-up cash, a time-honored tradition, they achieved prominence in discount store operations. Syrian Jews exploited New York's economic promises but cultivated

---

30 Paul Ritterband and Steven M. Cohen, "The Social Characteristics of the New York Area Jewish Community," typescript report, October 1982, on file in the Brandeis University library, II-6, V-1, V-2; Cohen and Ritterband, "The Social Characteristics of the New York Area Jewish Community, 1981," 132, 156. On the issue of second-stage gentrification, see Leslie Bennets, "If You're Thinking of Living in Chelsea," *NYT*, May 2, 1982, R9; Jan Morris, "The Future Looks Familiar," *NYT*, April 26, 1987, SMA 16; Samuel Freedman, "Real Estate Boom Cited as Peril to the City," *NYT*, April 15, 1986, C 13.

31 Mark Effron, "It Wasn't Supposed to Happen This Way," unpublished manuscript, Columbia University School of Journalism, 1973, noted in Thomas J. Cottle, *Hidden Survivors: Portraits of Poor Jews in America* (Englewood Cliffs, NJ: Prentice-Hall, 1980), 5; Naomi B. Levine and Martin Hochbaum, eds., *Poor Jews: An American Awakening* (New Brunswick, NJ: Transaction Books, 1974), 2–3; Anne G. Wolfe, "The Invisible Jewish Poor," *Journal of Jewish Communal Service* 48, no. 3 (Spring 1972): 259–65. See also Michael Harrington, *The Other America* (New York: Macmillan, 1962), 3.

32 Levine and Hochbaum, *Poor Jews*, 34; Center for New York City Affairs, New School for Social Research, *New York's Jewish Poor and Jewish Working Class: Economic Status and Social Needs*, typescript (New York: Federation of Jewish Philanthropies, 1972), 16, 29. See also, Robert McG. Thomas Jr., "Elderly Cling to Old Neighborhoods despite Growing Fear of Crime," *NYT*, June 17, 1974, 20; Phyllis Franck, "The Hasidic Poor in New York City," in Levine and Hochbaum, *Poor Jews*, 60–61; Mintz, *Hasidic People*, 33.

an "in-group and clannishness syndrome" to limit their engagement with New York's wider cultural scene. Gradually, these patterns changed in the 1970s. Young men and women broadened their social circles by attending colleges and universities. Some aspired to professional careers. By the 1990s, Syrian Jews included a cadre of their own physicians, attorneys, and accountants.[33]

Differences in attitudes among New York's Jews towards their city, and their sense of place within it, grew more striking during the recovery decade of the 1980s. Metropolitan fortunes began to change under the first administration of Mayor Edward I. Koch (1978–1981). The new Jewish incumbent and his constituents rode the crest of an improving national economy and benefited from the energetic efforts of Governor Hugh Carey that started even before Koch took office. Albany marshaled a group of investment bankers to create regulatory agencies like the Municipal Assistance Corporation and the Financial Control Board, which secured the city's finances. The Mayor amplified practically and psychologically the city's renewed cachet. He personified the advertising slogan, "I Love New York."[34]

By the middle of his second term, 1982–1985, Koch's ebullience seemed to have rubbed off on his fellow New Yorkers. While harboring "an acerbic portrait of metropolitan life," they were not "nearly as gloomy about the city's future as in years past. . . . Fewer residents dream[ed] of moving to more placid places."[35]

Indeed, New York was rebounding, with revenue streams flowing in because of "the post-industrial revolution." The city's service industries rather than manufacturing or distributing companies generated the jobs and income. Those with proper training and motivation made their fortunes in these exciting, when not cutthroat, pursuits. Working with clients and customers around the world and around the clock, they transformed New York into a global city. And given the length of their working "shifts" it made sense for high achievers to live near the office even if private car services also flourished in that labor-intensive environment. Gentrification

---

33   Sutton, *Magic Carpet*, 62, 66–67, 96–102; Walter P. Zenner, *A Global Community: The Jews from Aleppo, Syria* (Detroit: Wayne State University Press, 2000), 138–41, 156, 166–62, 166.

34   Chris McNickle, *To Be Mayor of the City of New York: Ethnic Politics in the City* (New York: Columbia University Press, 1993), 272–75.

35   Maureen Dowd, "Poll Finds New Yorkers' Pessimism Subsides," *NYT,* January 19, 1985, 1.

increased as former loft manufacturing space morphed into luxury residences; new neighborhoods arose.[36]

Most young Manhattan Jews fit the profile of those New Yorkers most energized and excited by a revived city who did well for themselves. In the early 1980s, this borough was deemed "the pre-eminent home of the never-married" as "fully one half" of young Jewish singles in the metropolitan area lived there. This generation grasped the chance to enjoy "the proximity to expanding sources of business and professional employment and the cultural richness of the center city." They blended their success story with that of others of diverse ethnic backgrounds to create a new cultural texture to New York Jewish neighborhood life. This new Jewish generation did not sense that its whole world was Jewish or desire that it be that way. They did, however, maintain one long-standing tradition widely observed years ago on the Grand Concourse and on Eastern Parkway. They shunned local synagogues eager to welcome them. Perhaps, as in past eras, some of them could be found promenading around their neighborhood in their holiday finery on Rosh ha-Shanah. But their crowd likely included non-Jewish friends and, increasingly, relatives.[37]

The excitement of the city scene in the 1980s with its new neighborhood dynamics was largely lost upon those who continued to be part of the "other" Jewish New York. The elderly poor, widowed or divorced still struggled, though their numbers gradually declined. Surviving stalwarts witnessed some improvement in their lives due both to the efforts of Jewish community social service agencies as well as the beginnings of a physical revival of their neighborhoods. Still, while a bit more comfortable where they resided, though always wary of their surroundings, with their days numbered, they did not expect to live to carve out new Jewish places for themselves if, and when, gentrification arrived.[38]

---

36   Matthew Drennan, "The Decline and Rise of the New York Economy," in *Dual City: Restructuring New York*, ed. John Mollenkopf and Manuel Castells (New York: Russell Sage Foundation, 1991), 34–37. See also John Hull Mollenkopf, *A Phoenix in the Ashes: The Rise and Fall of the Koch Coalition in New York City Politics* (Princeton: Princeton University Press, 1992), 46–47.

37   *Greater New York Population Study* (New York: United Jewish Appeal-Federation of Jewish Philanthropies, 1981), 9, 10, 29, 40.

38   On the numbers and status of the Jewish poor elderly from 1981–1991, see *Greater New York Population Study*, 10, 36, 37, 40; and *The New York Jewish Population Study: Profiles of Counties, Boroughs and Neighborhoods, 1991* (New York: United Jewish Appeal-Federation of Jewish Philanthropies), 1, 9, 10. On the numbers of elderly assisted and the greater concern with the problems of those poor, see *The 1991 New*

Hasidic communities in Brooklyn scorned the bright lights of a changing Manhattan. Proud of their social insularity, they were heartened by their strength of numbers that contributed to their borough maintaining its reputation as "a virtual demographic heartland of New York's Orthodox community." The faith of the devout in neighborhood continuity expressed itself in investments in educational and cultural institutions that, under the sway of their religious leaders, kept more affluent Hasidim in place, supporting the poor. Still, many families struggled to maintain an adequate standard of living. Committed to maintaining in their enclaves, Hasidim demanded that the municipality secure and enhance their living conditions.[39]

V.

In 1991, a tragedy took place in Crown Heights that led to a violent confrontation between the neighborhood's Blacks and Jews. Amid this conflagration, the persistent fault lines separating "Manhattan" and "Brooklyn" Jews were revealed in sharpest relief. A year earlier, David Dinkins had entered City Hall, succeeding Koch, who had served three terms as Mayor. New York's first African American mayor fashioned his victory over Republican Rudolph Giuliani through capturing the overwhelming majority of Black and Latino voters and garnering the votes of affluent and liberal Jews primarily in Manhattan and Riverdale. His pitch to these Jewish voters was that he would champion a quieter, more egalitarian, and more inclusive city. Unmoved by these appeals, most Jews, most notably in the heavily Hasidic neighborhoods in Brooklyn and in the Queens Jewish sections of Forest Hills and Kew Gardens, voted for Giuliani.[40]

Dinkins's promise to fashion a gorgeous urban mosaic was marred, however, and his reputation for fairness irreparably damaged when Crown Heights erupted. The outbreak began after seven-year-old Gavin Cato, a child of Guyanese immigrants, was killed on August 19 in a traffic accident by a car driven by Yosef Lifsh, a Hasid who was part of an entourage

---

York Jewish Population Study (New York: United Jewish Appeal-Federation of Jewish Philanthropies, 1993), xvi, 116–17.

39   *1991 New York Jewish Population Study*, xvi; *New York Jewish Population Study: Profiles of Counties, Boroughs and Neighborhoods 1991*, 37.

40   John Kifner, "The Mayor-Elect Inspires Pride, but It's Hardly Universal," *NYT,* November 9, 1989, B1; Sam Roberts, "Almost Lost at the Wire," *NYT,* November 9, 1989, A1; Richard Levine, "Koch Confers with Dinkins on Transition," *NYT,* November 9, 1989, A1. See also, Mollenkopf, *Phoenix,* 184, and McNickle, *To Be Mayor of New York,* 313.

escorting the Lubavitcher Rebbe through neighborhood streets. Erroneous rumors quickly spread that Hatzalah, a Jewish-run volunteer ambulance corps, had rushed Lifsh to nearby Methodist Hospital but left the young boy to die. Incited by local demagogues to avenge Cato's "murder," bands of enraged Black youths rampaged through the night attacking Jews and police and destroying property. The mob beat and stabbed twenty-nine-year-old Yankel Rosenbaum, a graduate student in history from Australia, who, though not a Lubavitcher, was identified as an Orthodox Jew by his beard, dark clothing and visible *tsitsit* (the ritual fringed undergarment). He died at Kings County Hospital, the same place where Cato had been pronounced dead. Rosenbaum's death did not restrain the still-outraged bands. The outbreak lasted for three days, as troublemakers from outside the neighborhood joined local rioters.

Not just Cato's death but a number of unmitigated points of tensions fueled the attacks. The Lubavitchers' effective manipulation of the city's political system chafed their neighbors. To help their own poor, the Hasidim had effectively gained control of a local community planning board and directed public funds their way to the exclusion of needy Blacks; many of whom were Afro-Caribbean immigrants. Seeking to expand their presence in Crown Heights, Hasidim had used government money to purchase and rent houses and apartments. Blacks resented when Lubavitchers knocked on their doors asking whether their houses were on the market. Jews, on the other hand, worried about rising crime, blaming first their neighbors, and then the police, for insufficient protection. But their unhappy neighbors thought that Jews engaged in racial-profiling and vigilantism, and resented the apparent special treatment accorded the Lubavitcher Rebbe. Though Koch had removed the police post from outside his international head-quarters at 770 Eastern Parkway, the entourage that followed the Rebbe through the streets on that fateful day in August, 1991 had a police patrol-car escort.

Mayor Dinkins failed as a conciliator in this time of testing. While he distinguished between the youngster's accidental death and the murder of Rosenbaum, and called for restraint, many within the Jewish community falsely believed he intentionally delayed ordering the police to stop the rioting. Dinkins purportedly intimated that he had accorded "a sort of day of grace to the mob" on August 19th, the very day that Rosenbaum fell victim to its criminal intentions. Though the charge was false, Dinkins's lack of strong leadership at that critical juncture left him open to charges that he had coddled perpetrators at the expense of the safety of Jewish constituents. His most virulent critics called him an antisemite.

For the Jews of Crown Heights, the riot and perceived governmental indifference called into question the security of the American diaspora, as safety and security is the most basic promise of New York. They called the attack a "pogrom," because it reminded them of anti-Jewish violence in nineteenth- and early twentieth-century Eastern Europe. It confirmed fears that Jews would eventually be victimized wherever they might live. New York City was no different from Kishinev; America was just like Russia. Possessed of a totally different vocabulary for describing what had transpired, Crown Heights Blacks characterized the violence after Cato's death as a "rebellion" against racism and prejudice in their neighborhood that "resonated with a history of injuries Black communities in the Americas have suffered at the hands of callous and indifferent whites." For them, the young boy's death did not just happen; it was not an "accident."

The Lubavitchers garnered sympathetic expressions from many corners of the New York Jewish community. Some Modern Orthodox activists from Riverdale, who agreed with the Lubavitchers that the riot was a pogrom, rushed to the scene to support their brethren, calling upon the police to bring Rosenbaum's killers to justice.

As the investigations and recriminations proceeded, another fault line appeared, separating these Brooklyn Jews, and their allies, from Jewish Manhattanites, or at least from a segment of influential spokespeople who operated out of midtown headquarters. This establishment group included not only the long-standing American Jewish Committee, the American Jewish Congress and the Anti-Defamation League, but also the Jewish Community Relations Council, an agency established after World War II to advocate for Jewish rights on local fronts. Brooklyn Jews charged that each of these organizations had been either silent or hesitant to address the plight of fellow Jews in Crown Heights. They allegedly constrained themselves because of their overwhelming desire to maintain good relations with the Black community at the expense of their own kind.

For community-observer Jerome Chanes, those powerful "Manhattan" Jews—our term not his—"were generally distant from the Hasidim and ambivalent toward them." Editorialists for the *Forward,* that classic critic of Jewish establishments, went further in pillorying the powerful. For them, such "sluggishness [was] at best an unwillingness to revise sentimental notions about Black-Jewish relations [and] at worst an aversion to the plight of so conspicuous and fervent a population as the Chasidim," these most Jewish of New York's Jews. All told, Crown Heights made abundantly clear the deep divisions among New York Jews over what life in the city had in store for them in the future.[41]

VI.

At the turn of the millennium, Gotham was still a city of varying Jewish neighborhoods, classes and attitudes. Young Jewish professionals participated actively in neighborhood gentrification both in Manhattan and the outer boroughs that revived during the Wall Street boom of the 1990s. Sounding like Jews of earlier eras, those who helped restore "the Brooklyn brownstone belt" of Fort Greene, Cobble Hill, Carroll Gardens, Park Slope, and Boerum Hill, or transformed the factory and warehouse district called "Dumbo" (Down under the Manhattan Bridge Overpass) into residential space, bragged that it took only fifteen minutes to reach their managerial or executive jobs in Manhattan investment banks, law firms or software companies. By 2000, upper-class Jews lived on both east and west sides of Manhattan south of Sixtieth Street and north of the Lower East Side. In Harlem, gentrification fulfilled a 1984 prediction that "affluent whites" would "inevitably" migrate there due to its stock of transformable low cost housing and its "location just a few miles from midtown."[42]

New York Jews had their poor, their aged and Russian immigrants whose needs required communal support. Poverty pockets endured within the Hasidic Williamsburg enclaves and Borough Park.[43] But, generally speaking, stability aptly characterized New York's Jewish enclaves. Those

---

41 On the events in Crown Heights, see Edward S. Shapiro, *Crown Heights: Blacks, Jews and the 1991 Brooklyn Riot* (Waltham, MA: Brandeis University Press, 2006), especially xi–xvi, 5–6, 27, 43, 47–48, 57–62, 75–77, 83–87, 108, 112, 137, n.98; Henry Goldschmidt, *Race and Religion among the Chosen People of Crown Heights* (New Brunswick, NJ: Rutgers University Press, 2006), especially 38–39, 40, 47, 48–50, 59, 61–71.

42 *The Jewish Community Study of New York: 2002 Geographic Profile* (New York: United Jewish Appeal-Federation of Jewish Philanthropies, 2004), 110–11. On the transformation of Harlem, see "Migration of Affluent Whites to Harlem Forecast," *NYT,* May 28, 1984, 23; Sam Roberts, "In Harlem, Blacks Are No Longer a Majority," *NYT,* January 6, 2010, A 16.

43 *Geographic Profile,* 27, 43, 69, 77, 101, 177. See also Deborah Pardo, "Synagogues Fade in the Northeast Bronx," September 1, 2003, http://web.jrn.columbia.edu/studentwork/religion; Jonathan Mark, "A Season's Simple Gifts," *Jewish Week,* September 18, 2009, 23.

who had decided, through the trying times of the 1970s to the early 1990s, to remain in the city ensured that textures of community life continued. If anything, these enduring neighborhoods attracted newcomers to their midst. Riverdale prospered as an affluent preserve. The Upper West Side retained its idiosyncratic character, as "two populations distinct in their levels of Jewish affiliation and practice" lived side by side. One group joined synagogues, visited Israel, and enrolled children in Jewish day school, while the other group rejected religious affiliation and often intermarried. Perhaps their Jewishness was expressed through liberal universalism.[44]

Continuity also characterized Brooklyn's old Orthodox neighborhoods of Williamsburg, Borough Park, and Crown Heights, even as families and leaders coped with poverty. As in the past, significant Jewish movement occurred within the city. Staten Island attracted a culturally diverse crowd that included better-off Orthodox Jews from Brooklyn, Russian immigrants who had prospered, and native-born Jews with little interest in Jewish causes and affiliation. Suburbia also continued to absorb its share of Jews, as it had for more than a half a century. But rates of out-migration slowed during the 1990s. While a 2002 study showed that the total number of Jews in the five boroughs had dropped, for the first time in more than a century, to under one million (972,000) "unlike other East Coast and Midwestern Jewish communities whose suburbanization has resulted in a restructuring of the center of Jewish life," the city remain[ed] the unofficial Jewish capital of the eight-county area, if not the country. Those who left did not move too far as "approximately 70% of the metropolitan area Jewish community resided in New York City." Suburban Jews retained urban connections for both business and cultural activities.[45]

In the first decade of the new millennium, even as New York's Jews continued to be of many minds on who they were and what they wanted from the city, an unexpected and terrifying event would unify them with all other denizens of Gotham. In the aftermath of 9/11, subscribing to a citywide resolve to survive and advance, Jews remained committed to being part of New York's future. Indeed, a new identity was discernible in the Jewish streets, a sense more than ever before that as citizens of this town over the long haul, they possessed a shared destiny with their neighbors.

---

44 *Geographic Profile*, 35, 36, 143, 169, 187.
45 *Jewish Community Study of New York: 2002* (New York: United Jewish Appeal-Federation of Jewish Philanthropies of New York, 2004), 25, 30.

For Further Reading

Ben-Ur, Aviva. *Sephardic Jews in America: A Diasporic History.* New York: New York University Press, 2009.

Binder, Frederick M. and David M. Reimers, *All the Nations under Heaven: An Ethnic and Racial History of New York City.* New York: Columbia University Press, 1995.

Bromley, Ray. "Not So Simple! Caro, Moses, and the Impact of the Cross-Bronx Expressway." *Bronx County Historical Society Journal* 35, no. 1 (1998): 4–29.

Caro, Robert A. *The Power Broker and the Fall of New York.* New York: Knopf, 1974.

Center for New York City Affairs, New School for Social Research. *New York's Jewish Poor and Jewish Working Class: Economic Status and Social Needs,* typescript. New York: Federation of Jewish Philanthropies, 1972.

Cohen, Steven M., and Paul Ritterband. "The Social Characteristics of the New York Jewish Community, 1981." *American Jewish Year Book* 84 (1984): 128–61.

Cottle, Thomas J. *Hidden Survivors: Portraits of Poor Jews in America.* Englewood Cliffs, NJ: Prentice-Hall, 1980.

Drennan, Matthew. "The Decline and Rise of the New York Economy." In *Dual City: Restructuring New York*, edited by John Mollenkopf and Manuel Castells, 25–41. New York: Russell Sage Foundation, 1991.

Freeman, Joshua. *Working Class New York: Life and Labor since World War II.* New York: Free Press, 2000.

Friedman, Murray. *What Went Wrong?: The Creation and Collapse of the Black-Jewish Alliance.* New York: Free Press, 1995.

Glustrom, Simon. "Some Aspects of a Suburban Jewish Community." *Conservative Judaism* 11, no. 2 (Winter 1957): 26–32.

Goldschmidt, Henry. *Race and Religion among the Chosen People of Crown Heights.* New Brunswick, NJ: Rutgers University Press, 2006.

Greenberg, Cheryl. *Troubling the Waters: Black-Jewish Relations in the American Century.* Princeton: Princeton University Press, 2006.

Harrington, Michael. *The Other America.* New York: Macmillan, 1962.

Helmreich, William B. *Against All Odds: Holocaust Survivors and the Successful Lives They Made in America.* New York: Simon and Schuster, 1996.

Herberg, Will. "The Jewish Labor Movement in the United States." *American Jewish Year Book* 53 (1952).

Horowitz, C. Morris, and Lawrence J. Kaplan. *The Jewish Population of the New York Area, 1900–1975*. New York: Federation of Jewish Philanthropies, 1959.

Kaufman, Jonathan. *Broken Alliance: The Turbulent Times between Blacks and Jews in America*. New York: Scribner, 1988.

Kranzler, George. *Williamsburg: A Jewish Community in Transition*. New York: Feldheim, 1961.

Lederhendler, Eli. *New York Jews and the Decline of Urban Ethnicity*. Syracuse: Syracuse University Press, 2001.

Levine, Naomi B. and Martin Hochbaum, eds. *Poor Jews: An American Awakening*. New Brunswick, NJ: Transaction Books, 1974.

Markowitz, Fran. *A Community in Spite of Itself: Soviet Jewish Emigres in New York*. Washington: Smithsonian Institution Press, 1993.

Massarik, Fred. "Basic Characteristics of the Greater New York Jewish Population." *American Jewish Year Book* 76 (1976): 239–48.

Mayer, Egon. *From Suburb to Shtetl: The Jews of Boro Park*. Philadelphia: Temple University Press, 1979.

McNickle, Chris. *To Be Mayor of the City of New York: Ethnic Politics in the City*. New York: Columbia University Press, 1993.

Mintz, Jerome R. *Hasidic People: A Place in the New World*. Cambridge, MA: Harvard University Press, 1992.

Mollenkopf, John Hull. *A Phoenix in the Ashes: The Rise and Fall of the Koch Coalition in New York City Politics*. Princeton: Princeton University Press, 1992.

Moore, Deborah Dash. *At Home in America: Second Generation New York Jews*. New York: Columbia University Press, 1981.

Podair, Jerald. *The Strike that Changed New York: Blacks, Whites and the Ocean Hill-Brownsville Crisis*. New Haven: Yale University Press, 2002.

Rieder, Jonathan. *Canarsie: The Jews and Italians of Brooklyn against Liberalism*. Cambridge, MA: Harvard University Press, 1985.

Shapiro, Edward S. *Crown Heights: Blacks, Jews and the 1991 Brooklyn Riot*. Waltham, MA: Brandeis University Press, 2006.

Shokeid, Moshe. *Children of Circumstances: Israeli Emigrants in New York*. Ithaca: Cornell University Press, 1988.

Sutton, Joseph A. D. *Magic Carpet: Aleppo in Flatbush: The Story of a Unique Ethnic Jewish Community*. New York: Thayer-Jacobi, 1979.

Weissbord, Robert G., and Arthur Stein. *Bittersweet Encounter: The Afro-American and the American Jew.* Westport, CT: Negro Universities Press, 1970.

Wolfe, Anne G. "The Invisible Jewish Poor." *Journal of Jewish Communal Service* 48, no. 3 (Spring 1972): 259–65.

Zeitz, Joshua M. *White Ethnic New York: Jews, Catholics and the Shaping of Postwar Politics.* Chapel Hill: University of North Carolina Press, 2007.

Zenner, Walter P. *A Global Community: The Jews from Aleppo, Syria.* Detroit: Wayne State University Press, 2000.

Zitron, Celia Lewis. *The New York City Teachers Union 1916–1964: A Story of Educational and Social Commitment.* New York: Humanities Press, 1968.

Chapter 11

New York
and American Judaism

Rachel Gordan

"Jewish" has long had an almost synonymous relationship with "New York."
For much of the twentieth century, to call something "very New York," was
a way to euphemistically refer to its Jewish ethnic or cultural quality. But
what about *Judaism*—what kind of place has New York been for Jewish *religion*? Some might argue that, in fact, New York's renown for Jewish life of
all varieties (gastronomic, intellectual, and literary, to name a few) has, at
times, had the effect of overshadowing Jewish religion. As with the state of
Israel—where secular Jews report feeling that there is less of a need to adhere
to religion, because the very air one breathes somehow seems Jewish—so too
is there an ambient Jewishness in New York. What this has meant, in practice, is that a Jewish New Yorker, particularly in the twentieth century, might
refer to certain streets, neighborhoods, or city landmarks, such as Zabar's,
the Ninety-Second Street Y, or Ellis Island, to explain why simply *being in
New York* allows one to feel Jewish, without ever saying a Jewish prayer or
entering a synagogue. Could the same be said for Methodists, Mormons,
Hindus, or followers of other traditions? That Jews move through New York
with an unusual feeling of affiliation with Jewishness has helped make the
city a kind of unofficial Jewish capital of the United States.[1]

---

1   Howard B. Rock, *Haven of Liberty: New York Jews in the New World, 1654–1865* (New
    York: NYU Press, 2012).

New York as Jewish capital was never as much about religion as it was about the entirety of Jewish lives. That a substantial portion of American Jewish literature takes New York as its setting, *and* seems to have little to do with religion, yet plenty to say about Jewishness—has further cemented the equivalence between New York and Jews in the American imagination, while teaching readers that religion is not necessarily part of that equation.[2] By the early twentieth century, surveys showed that more Jews did not affiliate with a synagogue than did.[3] The 2011 Jewish Community Study of New York brought that trend into the present century, showing that "major segments of Jews do not necessarily identify being Jewish with Judaism as a religion. Significant numbers of Jews claim their religion as 'none.'"[4]

Despite the fact that New York as a "capital of Jewishness" never depended solely on formal Jewish religion, Judaism has been uniquely affected by New York. Historian Deborah Dash Moore writes that what we know as American Judaism today "emerged out of Jewish encounters with American cities," particularly in the nineteenth and twentieth centuries.[5] No city has been more consistently involved in that alchemy of Judaism and urbanism than New York. In part, it was the close quarters and geography of Jewish life in New York that put Judaism and Jews in constant touch with other religions and immigrant groups, politics, and new ideas; in part it was the diversity of Jewish religious options, supported by what was believed to be an American tradition of religious freedom, that made for a more vibrant Jewish religious scene; and in part it was the sheer number of Jewish religious virtuosos who resided or passed through New York (Rabbis Solomon Schechter, Leo Jung, Mordecai Kaplan, Milton Steinberg, Abraham Joshua Heschel, Menachem Mendel Schneerson, and Shlomo Carlebach, and Blu Greenberg, Debbie Friedman, and Rebbetzin Esther Jungreis, to name a few). Even in the nineteenth century, there were "almost as many Judaisms as there were individuals," the historian of American Jews, Jacob Rader

---

2   While many well-known writers have established New York as Jewish without making religion central to that Jewishness, Chaim Potok's novels set in New York were conspicuously concerned with Jewish religion.

3   Jonathan Sarna, *American Judaism: A History* (New Haven: Yale University Press, 2004), 154.

4   *Jewish Community Study of New York: 2011*, "Comprehensive Report," 112. http://www. jewishdatabank.org/studies/downloadFile.cfm?FileID=2852.

5   Deborah Dash Moore, *Urban Origins of American Judaism* (Athens: University of Georgia Press, 2014), 12, 15.

Marcus, later observed.[6] That three of the four major American Jewish religious movements (Reform, Conservative, and Orthodox) have, since the mid-twentieth century, housed seminaries in New York, suggests that New York did indeed become the heartland for Jewish religion in America. How did that come to pass?

Late-nineteenth- and twentieth-century events were most influential in creating the New York of many Judaisms that we know today, but New York's earlier history provided a template for how New York would respond to Jews in later years, and, over time, New York provided a feeling of at-homeness that made the city fertile ground for those seeking to cultivate new forms of Jewish religion. To this day, there may be surprise when one hears of a new venture in Judaism initiated in other parts of the country, but efforts to create Jewish religious institutions seem as natural in New York as a new Broadway play or restaurant. Jews' earliest experiences in the new world also demonstrate the kind of religious example that Jews became for other minority religious groups: once persecuted, Jews and their religion became accepted, and even came to seem integral to the city. When Jews first arrived in New Amsterdam in 1654, Peter Stuyvesant, the director-general of New Netherland, sought to exclude them, charging that the Jews were "deceitful," "repugnant," and "hateful enemies and blasphemers of the name of Christ," and arguing that granting religious toleration to Jews would undermine the colony's social harmony. But the directors of the Dutch West India Company in Amsterdam—to whom Stuyvesant reported—overruled the governor, deciding that Jews be allowed to "travel," "trade," "live and remain" in their colony.[7] New Amsterdam's Jews enjoyed a measure of religious toleration that owed more to the Dutch tradition of allowing private religious practice, outside of the Dutch Reformed Church, than to New World innovations.[8] Indeed, Jews were more tolerated than welcome in the Dutch colony, but they did enjoy economic and civic rights.[9]

When New Amsterdam became New York in 1664, the British allowed Jews to keep the rights the Dutch had granted them. As with other religious

---

6   Sarna, *American Judaism*, 46.

7   Sarna, *American Judaism*, 2. Rock, *Haven of Liberty*, 14.

8   "The essence of Dutch tolerance was never to compel anyone to abandon their faith or convert, even though they frequently denied those of other faiths the capacity to practice their faith in any sort of organized, public fashion." Evan Haefeli, *New Netherland and the Dutch Origins of American Religious Liberty* (Philadelphia: University of Pennsylvania Press, 2012), 285.

9   Rock, *Haven of Liberty*, 22.

groups, as long as religious practice was confined to the private sphere, it was tolerated.[10] By the turn of the eighteenth century, New York's Jews were allowed to worship in public and to build a synagogue.[11] Alongside religious edifices built by a range of Protestant denominations, Catholics, and Quakers, eighteenth-century Jews helped to build a religiously diverse New York, although they likely did not realize this shift, or perceive their own progress toward religious freedom as connected with that of other groups.[12] Still, New York's colonial Jews cultivated religious life and expected their children to preserve their religious heritage through endogamy. Death was one of the first motivators of communal religious life, as when in 1655, New Amsterdam's Jews successfully petitioned for their own burial ground, separate from the Christian burial place.[13] Abigail Levy Franks's (1696–1756) distraught reaction to her daughter marrying a non-Jew reveals the value she placed on Judaism—unsurprising, given her efforts as a mother of nine to educate her children in Jewish ritual, and that her husband, businessman Jacob Franks, was the president of Shearith Israel, the city's only Jewish congregation.[14] Even from afar, Franks admonished her grown son, living in England, to uphold *kashrut* and continue his morning prayers: "I Desire you will Never Eat Anything with him Unless it be bread & butter, nor noe where Else where there is the Least doubt of things not done after our Strict Judiacall method."[15] Reform of Judaism, which arose in the next century, would have been understandable to Franks, who wrote to her son that, "I cant help Condemning the Many Supersti[ti]ons wee are Clog'd with & heartly wish a Calvin or Luther would rise amongst Us," explaining that were there such a leader among Jews, "I would be the first of there followers, for I dont think religion Consist in Idle Cerimonies & works of Supperoregations."[16] But she, nevertheless, would not condone the abandonment of Judaism.

---

10   Sarna, *American Judaism*, 11.

11   Deborah Dash Moore, Jeffrey S. Gurock, Annie Polland, Howard B. Rock, Daniel Soyer, *Jewish New York: The Remarkable Story of a City and a People* (New York: NYU Press, 2017), 16.

12   See Hafaeli, *New Netherland*, 137.

13   Sarna, *American Judaism*, 10.

14   Ellen Smith, "Bilah Abigail Levy Franks," Jewish Women's Archive, https://jwa.org/encyclopedia/article/franks-bilhah-abigail-levy.

15   Edith B. Gelles, *The Letters of Abigaill Levy Franks, 1733–1748* (New Haven: Yale University Press, 2004), xxii, 7.

16   Gelles, *Letters of Abigaill Levy Franks,* 68.

Jews built on the rights they had won in New Amsterdam after the British arrived in 1664. They obtained permission to worship in public and to construct a synagogue. Around the turn of the eighteenth century, a house on Mill Street became the first home for Congregation Shearith Israel, which remained the only Jewish congregation in New York City until 1825.

With no established church in New York, unlike in some of the other British colonies in North America, Jews enjoyed religious liberty in the context of a multi-religious, multilingual, and multiethnic society—what Stuyvesant had feared, and what would increasingly characterize New York. The 1740 Plantation Act passed by the British Parliament allowed foreign-born Jews living in the colonies to become naturalized, and confirmed Jewish citizenship. And by the last quarter of the eighteenth century, New York was the first state to formally renounce religious discrimination, in its post-independence constitution.[17] From the beginning, Jews and Christians married each other, signaling Jewish acceptance by the majority culture. Estimates of Jewish intermarriage in the colonial period range from ten to fifteen percent of all marriages. New York was one of the few colonies where Jews were not entirely invisible, for only New York and Newport had synagogue buildings, but even New York's Jewish community was small compared with those of Curacao, Surinam, and Jamaica, during the 1700s.[18]

The Sephardic form of Judaism predominated, as it always had, even though most New York Jews were actually Ashkenazim by the mid-eighteenth century. Shearith Israel thus followed the Sephardic ritual and customs, and used Sephardic Torah trope and melodies.

Enlightenment values of religious toleration combined with Jews' status as merchants to influence observance. New York Jews traded with port cities around the Atlantic, including larger Jewish communities in Surinam and Curacao, London and Amsterdam. In time, the receptivity of New York's marketplace for Jewish business ventures would seem like the reason that many Jews fell away from religion. Hoping to achieve the kind of wealth and status that had seemed impossible in other countries, many Jews prioritized these material aspirations over strict religious observance—observance that Shearith Israel had helped to promote by providing services related to dietary laws, worship, lifecycle events, and the ritual bath.

---

17   Hasia Diner, *The Jews of the United States, 1654 to 2000* (Berkeley: University of California Press, 2004), 48.
18   Sarna, *American Judaism*, 28.

Shearith Israel was able to provide these services because New York Jews adopted the model of a "synagogue community," with the city's Jewish community exerting control over members' behavior through moral suasion. With the city still small, it was not difficult for Jews to live within walking distance of the synagogue. Shearith Israel's commitment to meeting the religious needs of all Jews found expression in its physical structures, which included a *mikveh* (ritual bath), school, caretaker's home, and cemetery, in addition to the synagogue itself.[19]

Architecture of Reform: Synagogues and Clergy of New York

The visibility of Judaism in New York was greatly increased in the nineteenth century. As Hasia Diner notes of this period, Jews "maintained communities with religious, political, cultural, recreational, educational, philanthropic and medical institutions bearing the name 'Jewish' or 'Hebrew.'"[20] These sights would have been unusual in other parts of the country, but in New York, they were a sign of the ubiquitous, and relatively comfortable, presence of Judaism.

Like many other congregations, Shearith Israel did not have a regularly ordained rabbi until the latter half of the nineteenth century. Before that time, without seminaries to ordain American rabbis, it was difficult to convince European rabbis to come to America, where they would lack for rabbinic colleagues. Nonetheless, as cantor of Shearith Israel, Gershom Mendes Seixas, who had received his own Jewish education primarily from his father, and became the hazzan at Shearith Israel at age twenty-three, was at the center of the congregation's community. His friends and associates included many of New York's Protestant elite. One sign of the respect in which Seixas—and Judaism—were held was his appointment as a trustee of Columbia College, from 1787 until 1815.

After Shearith Israel, New York's second synagogue was B'nai Jeshurun, founded in 1825, by a breakaway group of young immigrants and the descendants of immigrants from German and Polish lands.[21] These founders sought more time for explanations of the prayers, less formal services, and fewer distinctions between members (there was also no

19   Moore, et al., *Jewish New York*, 18.
20   Diner, *The Jews of the United States*, 76.
21   Jeffrey Gurock, "The Orthodox Synagogue," in *The American Synagogue: A Sanctuary Transformed*, ed. Jack Wertheimer (New York: Cambridge University Press, 1987), 41.

permanent leader), thus bringing to bear the currents of nineteenth-century American religion as they challenged authority, and promoted revivalism, democratization, and anti-elitism.[22] B'nai Jeshurun's founding marked the beginnings of congregationalism for New York Jewry and the Ashkenazic Jews who sought to lead their own religious congregation.[23] The increasingly Ashkenazic Jewish presence in the city made the direction of B'nai Jeshurun's founders fitting; their intention was to follow the "German and Polish *minhag* [rite]."[24] The congregation dedicated its first building on Elm Street in Manhattan in 1827. The first rabbi, Samuel Isaacs, was appointed in 1839.[25] By 1850, the congregation had grown sufficiently large to require a new building.

A breakaway group from B'nai Jeshurun resulted in the creation of Ansche Chesed, founded in 1828 by German, Dutch, and Polish Jews. By the mid-nineteenth century, Ansche Chesed's membership was dominated by Jews of German origin. Its building was designed by a famous Berlin-born Jewish architect, Alexander Saeltzer, and inspired by the Gothic style of the world-famous medieval Roman Catholic Cathedral in Cologne.[26]

Judaism in New York was now pluralistic, with New Yorkers able to choose between synagogue options, and synagogues increasingly responding to members' needs. The Reform Temple Emanu-El ("God is with us"), was not established until 1845, by German Jewish immigrants, who with the name of their congregation, demonstrated their belief that God was with them, even as they adapted their religion to the spirit of the age. Both Emanu-El, the oldest Reform synagogue, and Shearith Israel, New York's oldest synagogue, exemplify religion's entanglement with social class for New York Jews. The nineteenth-century German Reform Jewish members may have looked down on the Eastern European Jews who immigrated after them, but to the Spanish-Portuguese members of Shearith Israel, it was the German Jews who were the uncouth upstarts.

---

22 Sarna, *American Judaism*, 56.
23 Moore, et al., *Jewish New York*, 43.
24 Sarna, American Judaism, 56.
25 Israel Goldstein, *A Century of Judaism In New York: B'nai Jeshurun, 1825–1925* (New York: Congregation B'nai Jeshurun, 1930), 95.
26 Gerard R. Wolfe, *The Synagogues of New York's Lower East Side: A Retrospective and Contemporary View* (New York: Empire State Editions, 2013), 65, 66.

Emanu-El held its first services in a Lower East Side loft at the corner of Grand and Clinton Streets. With more Jews coming from Germany to New York, the congregation "moved progressively uptown—both physically and spiritually."[27] When the group adapted an old church as their new synagogue building, in 1847, and decided to keep the family pew structure, Emanu-El introduced an innovation in American synagogues that was soon followed by other synagogues.[28] Only twenty-three years after its founding, in 1868, Temple Emanu-El's congregants erected a building at Fifth Avenue and East Forty-Third Street, which was then the country's largest synagogue structure. By this time, Temple Emanu-El had already gained a reputation for its prominent members. The building, designed by the architectural team of Leopold Eidlitz, who had a reputation as an architect of prominent Protestant Churches, and Henry Fernbach, reflected Reform's revisionist ideology, as historian Kathryn Holliday observes, with its mixed-gender seating pews, modeled after Christian family pews.[29]

Temple Emanu-El's first Fifth Avenue building also heralded a new architectural presence for New York's Jews that was reflected in synagogue buildings with Jewish symbols and words. In particular, the Moorish architecture of synagogues such as Emanu-El constituted a distinctive choice among religious edifices that is still apparent in the Eldridge Street Synagogue, the Park East Synagogue and Central Synagogue, the latter's cornerstone having been laid by Reform leader Isaac Mayer Wise in the early 1870s.[30]

As Emanu-El continued to grow, its neighborhood became increasingly commercialized, leading to a decision to relocate in the mid-1920s. Consolidating in 1927 with Temple Beth-El, the congregation built its present structure at Fifth Avenue and East Sixty-Fifth Street. Finally, in December 1960, with its congregation still expanding, Emanu-El purchased adjoining property on East Sixty-Sixth Street.

---

27   See the synagogue's website at http://www.emanuelnyc.org/simple.php/about_history.
28   Karla Goldman, *Beyond the Synagogue Gallery: Finding a Place for Women in American Judaism* (Cambridge: Harvard University Press, 2001), 94.
29   Kathryn E. Holliday, *Leopold Eidlitz: Architecture and Idealism in the Gilded Age* (New York: W. W. Norton & Company, 2008), 71–73.
30   Hasia Diner, *How America Met the Jews* (Providence: Brown University, 2017), 13; Annie Polland, *Landmark of the Spirit: The Eldridge Street Synagogue* (New Haven: Yale University Press, 2009).

Emanu-El was hailed not only for its Moorish architecture, but also as a beacon of reason over blind and bigoted faith.[31] In fact, Reform Judaism, of which Emanu-El was a flagship congregation, had its origins in the European Enlightenment belief that if Jews would only adapt their religion and customs to better align with Protestant norms, they could find acceptance among their Christian neighbors.[32] With these ideas in the air, Reform developed as a result of Emancipation and a Jewish desire to increase decorum so as to better fulfill societal expectations. Reform in Judaism led to new approaches to Jewish theology and ritual practices, with the most radical decision of the reformers being to reject the binding nature of Jewish law. As with most reform movements, its leaders did not intend to create a new religion, or even denomination, but rather to adapt all of Judaism to contemporary needs. But as Jewish reformers took their stand, other leaders emerged to establish what would become the Conservative and Orthodox movements, in response.

Temple Emanu-El was not the country's first Reform synagogue (that first occurred in Charleston, South Carolina, when the Reformed Society of Israelites was organized in 1824), but it did establish New York as a center for Reform, despite the fact that the movement's "headquarters," that is, the Union of American Hebrew Congregations, was ultimately established in Cincinnati.

Beyond the Synagogue, beyond Judaism

Even in the mid-nineteenth century, as some New York Jews were reforming the synagogue, others were already demonstrating a knack for non-synagogue Jewish life. America entered a golden age of fraternal organizations, with 5.4 million Americans, mostly men, belonging to fraternal orders in 1897, a number that almost doubled by 1926.[33] These organizations were distinguished by religion, ethnicity, and race: Catholics, African Americans, and Slavs were among the groups who had their own fraternal organizations. Jews joined in, putting common fraternal culture to their own use. In particular,

---

31 "New Jewish Temple: Consecration of the Temple," *New York Times*, September 12, 1868, 12.

32 Dana Evans Kaplan, *The New Reform Judaism: Challenges and Reflections* (Lincoln: University of Nebraska Press, 2015), 54.

33 Linda Gordon, *The Second Coming of the KKK: The Ku Klux Klan of the 1920s and the American Political Tradition* (New York: W. W. Norton, 2017), 30.

members of B'nai B'rith and other Jewish fraternal orders found ways to affirm their Jewish identity through non-traditional ritual. Initiation ceremonies involving scripts, candles, and pledges by new members combined Jewish heritage with features of freemasonry. Such mutual benefit societies provided for burial expenses, support of widows, and medical expenses, in addition to male friendship opportunities.

B'nai B'rith's founding in 1843 was a reaction to what many felt was an antiquated religion requiring rehabilitation.[34] From the mid-nineteenth century, B'nai B'rith functioned as a "secular synagogue," providing new immigrants with support, and one of the several secular Jewish options available to Jewish New Yorkers. Also on that list of Jewish affiliations that took place outside the synagogue were *landsmanshaftn*, or hometown associations, and women's burial societies, which did more than their name suggests, as they looked after the welfare of Jewish women and children. These communal organizations allowed New York Jews multiple ways of staying true to certain Jewish religious values, as they cared for other Jews.[35]

Other New York Jews took religious innovation a step further, moving beyond Judaism altogether. In addition to mixed seating, Temple Emanu-El, in its first few decades, birthed the New York Society for Ethical Culture. Ethical Culture was the idea of Felix Adler, born into a family with a rich rabbinic tradition, and the son of Emanu-El's Rabbi Samuel Adler, a leading figure in Reform Judaism.[36] Emanu-El's congregation had expected that Felix would follow in his father's footsteps, but in 1874, at age twenty-three, and after receiving his doctorate in Germany, Felix Adler was invited to preach at Emanu-El, where he spoke about "The Judaism of the Future." Without mentioning God, Adler stressed the need for "deed, not creed," and a desire to unite theists, atheists, and agnostics in a movement working toward the advancement of social justice. The resulting Society for Ethical Culture, founded in 1876, worked to improve conditions in tenement houses, and to create libraries, gyms, job programs, and employment bureaus, as well as to provide a platform for speakers, such as John

---

34 Deborah Dash Moore, *B'nai B'rith and the Challenge of Ethnic Leadership* (Waltham: Brandeis University Press, 1981).

35 Hasia Diner, "American Judaism, 1820–1945," in *The Cambridge History of Religions in America*, vol. 2: *1790 to 1945*, ed. Stephen J. Stein (New York: Cambridge University Press, 2012), 288.

36 Benny Kraut, "Felix Adler's Emergence out of Judaism" (PhD diss., Brandeis University, 1975).

Dewey, Booker T. Washington, W.E.B. Du Bois, and Harlem Renaissance writer, James Weldon Johnson, who all broached themes of social justice.[37]

Religious Authority

As some sought to reform Judaism or move beyond it, others attempted to reinvigorate Jewish tradition. Jewish seminaries served to anchor New York as a headquarters for Judaism through difficult times. Even in a city where democracy and diversity seemed to militate against top-down authority, the religious authority that derived from these seminaries provided individuals and congregations with reassurance, guidance, and standards to argue against.

The first was the Jewish Theological Seminary, established in 1886. As was often the case in New York, the direction of JTS was shaped, in part, by reactions to other nearby forms of Judaism. The tradition-minded Jews who started the seminary intended it to train traditionally observant rabbis who would give English-language sermons to congregations in which middle-class American standards of decorum would prevail. These founders of JTS had not expected to create another denomination, but were, rather, responding to what they perceived as nineteenth-century American Judaism shifting toward Reform. When JTS brought Solomon Schechter—then a lecturer at Cambridge University and already famous for having excavated the Cairo Geniza in 1896—to the seminary in 1902, he, too, believed that he was leading a community that represented the future of Judaism, while Reform, with its rejection of tradition, and the more traditionalist Jews, in their unwillingness to accommodate to the American milieu, would fail.[38] To accomplish his goals, Schechter hired world-class faculty members, many of whom he met while touring Europe. As Michael R. Cohen observes, Solomon Schechter became the kind of charismatic religious leader who sparked excitement in his New York orbit, providing another important luminary for Jewish New York.

Though the term "Orthodox" was in use among American Jews for much of the nineteenth century, Orthodoxy's crystallization as a movement distinct from Conservative Judaism would begin around the turn of

---

37   See the Society's website at http://www.nysec.org/history.
38   Michael R. Cohen, *The Birth of Conservative Judaism: Solomon Schechter's Disciples and the Creation of an American Religious Movement* (New York: Columbia University Press, 2012), 24.

the twentieth century.[39] New York Orthodoxy proceeded along two tracks. One, which led in 1898 to the founding of the Union of Orthodox Jewish Congregations of America by Rabbi Henry Pereira Mendes and many of the same rabbis who created the Jewish Theological Seminary, sought an Orthodox accommodation with American culture that would appeal to English-speaking American Jews.

The other Orthodox stream resisted Americanization, finding its base in the burgeoning community of Eastern European Jewish immigrants. Its leaders insisted that New York—the Lower East Side, where they resided, in particular—had the potential to recreate the religious civilization they had cherished in Eastern Europe. With the right leadership, they believed, America could be a center of Torah and traditional Judaism.[40] Feeling that American Jews needed a chief rabbi to unite New York Jewry, as was the norm in parts of Europe, a group of immigrant Orthodox lay leaders raised money to bring Rabbi Jacob Joseph of Vilna to New York in 1888. Although he was able to establish a *beth din* in New York, his attempts at improving New York's *kashrut* standards were less successful. After his support from Jewish communal leaders began to wither, Joseph's health failed, too.[41] He remained in his New York post until his death in 1902, but was not able to reinvigorate Orthodoxy in New York, as his supporters had hoped.[42] Faith in the idea of a chief rabbi for New York had suffered too.

That Rabbi Joseph proved unsuccessful suggested the ill fit of a top-down religious authority, but he did pave the way for more East European rabbis to immigrate to America. That America's first Orthodox yeshiva, Etz Chaim ("Tree of Life"), had been founded in New York, in 1886, with the desire for the more traditional Jewish learning of Eastern Europe—Talmud study in particular—to take root in America, further helped make New York into a more hospitable place for Orthodox Jews.

39 Zev Eleff, *Modern Orthodox Judaism: A Documentary History* (Philadelphia: Jewish Publication Society, 2016), xxx.
40 Jeffrey Gurock and Jacob Schacter, *A Modern Heretic and a Traditional Community: Mordecai M. Kaplan, Orthodoxy and American Judaism* (New York: Columbia University Press, 1997), 7.
41 Moshe D. Sherman, *Orthodox Judaism in America: A Biographical Dictionary and Sourcebook* (Westport, CT: Greenwood, 1996), 110.
42 Eric Goldstein, "The Great Wave: Eastern European Jewish Immigration to the United States, 1880–1924," in *The Columbia History of Jews and Judaism in America*, ed. Marc Lee Raphael (New York: Columbia University Press, 2008), 78.

In 1902, more traditionalist Orthodox rabbis formed the Orthodox Agudath Harabanim ("union of rabbis"). Just as JTS was established in reaction to Reform, the Agudath Harabanim was part of a critical response to Schechter and fear of what would become the Conservative movement. Out of their concern over increasingly lax standards of *kashrut* and religious observance, Agudath Harabanim responded by strengthening their own rabbis' authority. Agudath Harabanim also formed in response to the Orthodox Union, which had a more American-born base, as opposed to its own European-born and Yiddish-speaking members. In promoting the Rabbi Isaac Elchanan Theological Seminary (RIETS), founded in 1897, to serve as an American counterpart of Eastern European yeshivas, the Agudah championed its vision of more traditional Jewish learning in New York.[43]

All of these institutions sought to deal with the flood of Eastern European Jewish immigrants at the end of the nineteenth century and the start of the twentieth century, when signs of declining religiosity were apparent. A report from 1912 revealed that only one-quarter of Jewish workers in New York did not labor on the Sabbath. A year later, in 1913, a second study revealed that nearly sixty percent of the stores in a Jewish neighborhood on the Lower East Side were open on Saturday, although New York's Jews were known to hold on to *kashrut* longer than Sabbath observance.[44] By the 1920s and 1930s, however, an Americanized Orthodoxy came of age in New York, as a religious movement that managed to be modern, American, and traditional.[45]

Religious Innovators in the Twentieth Century

Emanu-El inadvertently contributed to the founding of an important Reform New York landmark when in 1905 it told the leading candidate to take over as its rabbi that "the pulpit of Emanu-El . . . is subject to and under the control of the board of trustees." Rabbi Stephen Samuel Wise, then in Portland, Oregon, refused to accept that condition, and, out of his desire for a more independent pulpit, decided to move to New York to lead

---

43 Sarna, *American Judaism*, 192.
44 Jeffrey Gurock, *Orthodox Jews in America* (Bloomington: Indiana University Press, 2009), 98, 112.
45 Jenna Weissman Joselit, *New York's Jewish Jews: The Orthodox Community in the Interwar Years* (Bloomington: Indiana University Press, 1990).

a new Jewish religious movement.[46] That Wise understood, even from afar, that in New York he could find followers speaks to the reputation of the city as a hub of Jewish religion. Once in New York, Wise became an important social activist, helping to found the NAACP and the American Jewish Congress, and becoming president of the Zionist Organization of America. At his new synagogue, the Free Synagogue, Wise's services were brief and centered around his sermon. By addressing thousands every Sunday morning at Carnegie Hall he became one of America's best known rabbis.[47] New York continued to be fertile ground for Wise to initiate other Jewish ventures, as he opened a new rabbinical seminary called the Jewish Institute of Religion, for students of a variety of theological beliefs and Jewish backgrounds who were united by Wise's three pillars of Zionism, social justice, and service to the Jewish people. (In 1950, JIR merged with Hebrew Union College.)[48] The Stephen Wise Free Synagogue would become the first synagogue with a female ordained rabbi, when Sally Jane Priesand joined the pulpit in 1972.

Mordecai Kaplan (1881–1983) was another New York religious innovator. Reared in an immigrant Orthodox New York home, Kaplan became one of the most outspoken critics of Orthodoxy, yet remained an observant Jew throughout his life.[49] Initially a rabbi at the Orthodox Jewish Center on West Eighty-Sixth Street, Kaplan's innovative views eventually led to a split with other members, and Kaplan left the Jewish Center to found the Society for the Advancement of Judaism, in 1922. Not long after the SAJ's founding, it became the site of the *bat mitzvah* of Judith Kaplan, Mordecai Kaplan's daughter, and the first American girl to have a *bat mitzvah*.

Kaplan's first pulpit, the Jewish Center, was established in 1918, by wealthy Upper West Side Jews. Its tall, neo-classical Eighty-Sixth-Street building was unique at the time, as a synagogue that was built not only to satisfy spiritual needs, but the cultural, social and recreational needs of its members, as well, thus signaling—even from an Orthodox institution— the sprawling, all-encompassing nature of Jewish religious life in New York, and foreshadowing the Jewish movement that Kaplan would later help establish. The multi-storied Jewish Center took its cues from both the

---

46   Melvin I. Urofksy, *A Voice that Spoke for Justice: The Life and Times of Stephen S. Wise* (Albany: State University of New York Press, 1982), 52.
47   Sarna, *American Judaism*, 251.
48   Ibid.
49   Gurock and Schacter, *A Modern Heretic and a Traditional Community*.

requirements of Judaism and the new cultural and recreational needs of an emerging New York Jewish middle class. In the late 1920s, New Yorkers spent more than $12 million on synagogue construction, with a significant portion spent on synagogue centers, which provided social, educational, and recreational facilities.[50]

With Kaplan's influence, synagogue centers became more common by the 1920s, replacing the nineteenth-century setup of worship hall and classrooms.[51] Kaplan's religious contributions also occurred through his teaching of rabbinical students at the Jewish Theological Seminary—a position that he assumed, as Kaplan later recounted, because the Seminary's leader, Solomon Schechter, had heard Kaplan give a talk in which Kaplan "developed the thesis that the future of Judaism demanded that all Jewish teaching and practical activity be based on the proposition that the Jewish religion existed for the Jewish people and not the Jewish people for the Jewish religion."[52] It was, as Kaplan noted, "a Copernican revolution in my understanding of Judaism," and one that resonated with twentieth-century Jewish New Yorkers who felt the pressing nature of Kaplan's question about how Judaism—and religion—could survive modern times, where secular society's acceptance of Jews, ironically, seemed to place the Jewish community at risk

Over time, and in conversation with his New York colleagues, Mordecai Kaplan's viewpoint evolved into what became Reconstructionism, the only one of the four major movements of Judaism truly born in America—and in New York. The Society for the Advancement of Judaism became the leading synagogue of the movement. Kaplan knew that traditional Jewish concepts, such as resurrection of the dead and the chosenness of the Jewish people were difficult for modern Jews to accept, and through his explanations of Judaism for moderns, he showed his congregants how to reconstruct Judaism to better suit their time and place, explaining that Jews had always adapted Judaism.

True to his thesis that Judaism must meet the needs of Jews, rather than the reverse, Kaplan performed an impressive feat in observing and analyzing those needs in his 1934 magnum opus, *Judaism as a Civilization*. He began his book by writing about the prevalence of self-hatred among

---

50 Beth Wenger, *New York Jews and the Great Depression: Uncertain Promise* (New Haven: Yale, 1996), 168.

51 David Kaufman, *Shul with a Pool: The "Synagogue-Center" in American Jewish History* (Waltham: Brandeis University Press, 1999).

52 Mordecai Kaplan, *Judaism as a Civilization* (New York: Macmillan, 1934), xii.

American Jews, and how those feelings of inferiority and self-contempt harmed both Jews and Judaism. The density of New York's Jewish populations had put Kaplan in touch with more "data" than would have been the case anywhere else in America, allowing him—someone who loved Jewish culture, peoplehood, and aspects of its religion—to become both well-acquainted with the problems of modern Jews and attuned to appropriate solutions. One of the most important Jewish thinkers of the twentieth century, Mordecai Kaplan demonstrated that the sheer number of Jews in New York did not prevent antisemitism from being a significant factor in Jewish life. If anything, the conspicuous presence of Jews, by the 1920s, had made antisemitism a potent force in New York, and one that played a role in shaping Jewish religion in that city.

During the 1930s, antisemitism and financial hardship combined to create challenges for Judaism in New York. As historian Beth Wenger notes, "The Depression decade has generally been characterized as a period of stagnation and religious malaise in American synagogues. During the 1930s, synagogues struggled under heavy financial burdens and mortgage debts, watched their memberships shrink, and were often forced to curtail programs and dismiss personnel."[53] New York synagogue staffs regularly went unpaid. Mordecai Kaplan wrote in his journal, during the Depression, "Among those who are bound to suffer most keenly from the demoralizing effect of the present economic depression are the rabbis, the superfluousness of whose calling has become more conspicuous than ever. Most of my colleagues are going through torments of hell."[54] "Mushroom synagogues"—large spaces temporarily converted into houses of worship—became a feature of Depression-era's New York Jewish life, when many Jews chose not to pay synagogue dues, opting, instead, to pay for religious services as the need arose. Meanwhile, the recreational services—if not the religious services—of the synagogue centers built in the preceding decades were popular among underemployed Depression-era Jews with time on their hands.

Postwar New York Judaism

Ironically, the 1950s, an era that is frequently referred to as a golden decade in American Jewish history, was a less vibrant time for Jewish religious

---

53   Wenger, *New York Jews and the Great Depression*, 166.
54   Ibid., 171.

life in Manhattan than would be case by the last decade of the twentieth century and the early twenty-first century, when new interest in urban living, gentrification and safer conditions in New York, particularly on the Upper West Side, led to increased Jewish religious activity.[55] Instead, New York's outer boroughs and suburbs became the site of institutional Jewish religious growth—although according to the mid-century social scientists documenting religious life on the suburban frontiers, it was a superficial Judaism, lacking in piety, and largely for the sake of appearances. When Nathan Glazer, New York-born and bred, wrote about contemporary Judaism for his 1957 book, *American Judaism*, he could only look to the Hasidim of Williamsburg for contemporary signs of what he deemed true piety and observance of Jewish law and ritual. "In Williamsburg, in Brooklyn," Glazer observed, "in a small area containing about twenty thousand people, three-quarters of them Jews, an Orthodox revival took place which, while it will never affect any but the most Orthodox fringes of American Jewry, still has something to tell us about the other variants of Jewish religious life in America."[56] Trained as a sociologist, Glazer reflected that among the Williamsburg Hasidim, something different from the typical postwar Jewish assimilation story was occurring: "We have here, for the first time, something that might become a Jewish equivalent of the Mennonites but with a stronger potential appeal to other Jews than the Mennonites have for other Protestants."[57] Glazer was amazed by the "converts" that Hasidism was winning among the Orthodox, but-not-yet-Hasidic Jews who sampled a service, "drawn by curiosity . . . swept up by the singing and dancing, moved by the personality of the *rebbe,* and impressed by the devotion of his followers; many of them would become followers themselves."[58]

Glazer had reason to be surprised. The history of Judaism in New York had been moving in the opposite direction: Jews moving away from tradition and religious piety, while concerned rabbis and communal leaders scrambled to try to catch them in a net of provisional Judaism. "Whatever works" might well have been a slogan of Rabbi Mordecai Kaplan, whose ideas about which aspects of Jewish ritual and law to uphold were grounded in pragmatism.

55 Arthur Goren labeled the 1950s a "Golden Decade" for Jews. See his "A 'Golden Decade' for American Jews: 1945–1955," in Jeffrey Gurock, *American Jewish Life, 1920-1990* (New York: Routledge, 1998), 17.

56 Nathan Glazer, *American Judaism* (Chicago: University of Chicago Press, 1957), 145.

57 Glazer, *American Judaism*, 147.

58 Glazer, Ibid., 147.

But in 1950s' Williamsburg, Brooklyn, something else (spiritual quests? a search for authenticity?) was at work, and it would be at work for the rest of the twentieth century. By September of 1999, a *New York Times* article titled "Keeping the Faith" chronicled the ways in which the Sabbath had "made a comeback, and the synagogue has become a bustling place year round," for the Jews of New York's greater metropolitan area.[59] By the end of the twentieth century, it still seemed newsworthy for the *New York Times* to emphasize the "surprising fact" that "many of today's Sabbath observers are regular participants in the secular world Sunday through Thursday. It is not just bearded, black-hatted denizens of Crown Heights who are taking Sabbath seriously these days, but Jews who live in regular suburban neighborhoods, wear contemporary clothing and work in law, medicine, on Wall Street and in just about every other field." What Glazer had judged unlikely to spread beyond the Williamsburg Hasidim—renewed interest in traditional Judaism—had become a fact of New York life.

New York Jewish Renewal

In the decades following the mid-twentieth century, renewal of interest in Judaism took shape in various ways. Contrary to Glazer's expectations, Hasidism itself flourished in the late twentieth century, especially in parts of Brooklyn. One important force behind the resurgence of "ultra-Orthodox" Judaism was Rabbi Menachem Mendel Schneerson (1902–1994), the Lubavitcher Rebbe, who became one of the most influential Jewish leaders of the twentieth century. While most Hasidim had given up hope of proselytizing other Jews to their cause by the end of the nineteenth century, Lubavitcher or Chabad (an acronym for the Hebrew words for wisdom, understanding, and knowledge) Hasidism never gave up missionizing.[60] From his home at 770 Eastern Parkway, in Crown Heights, Brooklyn, which was also the headquarters of Chabad, Schneerson led the movement that he began rebuilding in the 1950s, successfully directing its worldwide outreach efforts toward secular Jews. While he was alive, according to some

---

59 Debra Galant, "Keeping the Faith," *New York Times*, September 19, 1999, http://www. nytimes.com/1999/09/19/nyregion/keeping-the-faith.html. The title plays on the title of a popular Ben Stiller film of that year, about a charismatic young Upper West Side rabbi, who reflected the zeitgeist of a New York Judaism that was both fashionable and celebrating tradition.

60 Samuel Heilman and Menachem Friedman, *The Rebbe: The Life and Afterlife of Menachem Mendel Schneerson* (Princeton: Princeton University Press, 2010), 3.

reports, most Lubavitchers believed that Schneerson was the messiah; when he died, a fissure split the movement between the messianists who believed they had to convince as many people as possible that Schneerson was the messiah, and the anti-messianists, who have become the majority.[61] Even critics of Chabad often cannot help but acknowledge the movement's success in building an international presence and a network of classes, camps, holiday programs, and services for Jews in all kinds of need.

The influence of Hasidism on liberal Judaism is most apparent in the Jewish Renewal movement, created by New York Rabbi Zalman Schachter-Shalomi, or "Reb Zalman," as he preferred to be called. Reb Zalman (1924–2014) had grown up in Vienna, and experienced many Jewish movements that took him far from his family's Belzer Hasidic roots. After fleeing the Nazis, the family settled in New York in 1941, where he studied to become an Orthodox rabbi, was ordained by the Lubavitch Hassidic yeshiva in 1947, and became an emissary to college campuses. In the process, Zalman became interested in more liberal and universalist strands of Judaism and meditative practices that encouraged personal connections with God. Christian, Sufi and Eastern mysticism also influenced Reb Zalman in founding a movement that is often considered neo-Hasidic.[62] Renewal Judaism thus emerged from the counterculture of the 1960s and 1970s as a New Age expression of Judaism. Shaul Magid calls Renewal an attempt at "translating Hasidism into an American medium."[63] Reb Zalman is also considered a founder of the Havurah movement throughout North America. The 1972 first *Jewish Catalog* helped to bring Reb Zalman's spiritual and practical teachings to Jews all over the country.

Closer to the centrist mainstream than Schneerson or Schachter-Shalomi was the kind of initiative that began in 1964 in the living room of an apartment in Lincoln Towers, on the Upper West Side of Manhattan, where the Yeshiva University-trained Rabbi Steven (Shlomo) Riskin transformed Lincoln Square Synagogue into what became known as an inviting Orthodox community, even for those new to Orthodoxy. While Riskin might be compared with Schneerson, because of the centrality of outreach

---

61 Jonathan Mahler, "Waiting for the Messiah of Eastern Parkway," *New York Times Magazine,* September 21, 2003, https://www.nytimes.com/2003/09/21/magazine/waiting-for-the-messiah-of-eastern-parkway.html?src=pm&pagewanted=4.

62 "Rabbi Zalman Schachter-Shalomi," Aleph.org, https://aleph.org/reb-zalman.

63 Rachel Delia Benaim and Yitzhak Bronstein, "Can Jewish Renewal Keep Its Groove On?, *Tablet,* January 22, 2016, http://www.tabletmag.com/jewish-life-and-religion/196518/renewal-after-reb-zalman.

in their Judaism, Riskin's message was distinctly Modern Orthodox, as Zev Eleff points out.[64] Since the 1970s, the synagogue's services and classes have been responsive to the needs of *ba'alei t'shuva* and single Jews, with a beginner's service designed to make newcomers feel at home.[65] Lincoln Square Synagogue is celebrated for helping to spark a growing Jewish renaissance on the Upper West Side, which continued into the next century. Nicknamed "Wink-and-stare," as it became a place for single Jewish professionals to meet and socialize, and because the round sanctuary allowed men and women, though seated separately, to see each other, Lincoln Square Synagogue became a model for what synagogues could provide a new generation of New York Jews: a chance to connect to Judaism and each other. Recognizing an interest in Jewish learning, LSS members founded the first full-time Modern Orthodox Religious Zionist Kollel in the New York metropolitan area.[66] LSS had discovered that what was very old in Judaism had become new and exciting to New Yorkers who were uninitiated in Jewish religious life. The founding of the egalitarian, traditional-liturgy, lay-led Kehilat Hadar in 2001, by three twenty-somethings, suggested that, more than a generation after the founding of LSS, the Upper West Side continued to be a neighborhood for reviving traditional forms of Judaism for young Jews.[67]

What many of these late twentieth-century Jewish New York initiatives shared was a focus on bringing new people into Jewish religious life, often by tapping into the counterculture that had emerged in the late 1960s and 1970s. The founding of the Jewish feminist organization Ezrat Nashim in 1971, for example, was a product of the feminist movement and dedication to Judaism. Initially formed as a Jewish women's study group, Ezrat Nashim presented a manifesto, "Jewish Women Call for Change," in 1972, to the Conservative Rabbinical Assembly, demanding that women "be counted in a minyan (prayer quorum), be allowed full participation in religious observances, be allowed to initiate divorce proceedings and be counted

---

64 Zev Eleff, *Modern Orthodox Judaism: A Documentary History* (Philadelphia: Jewish Publication Society, 2016), 245–46.

65 M. Herbert Danzger, *Returning to Tradition: The Contemporary Revival of Orthodox Judaism* (New Haven: Yale University Press, 1989), 36–39.

66 "Lincoln Square Synagogue Inc," Guidestar, https://www.guidestar.org/profile/13-2509155.

67 Elie Kaunfer, *Empowered Judaism: What Independent Minyanim Can Teach Us about Building Vibrant Jewish Communities* (Vermont: Jewish Lights Publishing, 2010). "History and Values," Kehilat Hadar, https://www.kehilathadar.org/history-values.

as witnesses under Jewish law, and admitted to rabbinical and cantorial schools." They also asked that Jewish women "be considered bound equally . . . in the fulfillment of *mitzvot*."[68] Paula Hyman, then a twenty-five-year-old Columbia University graduate student and a spokeswoman for the group, told the *NYT*, "When tradition is incompatible with a sense of self, with some of your basic ethics, then you have to go back and examine the tradition."[69] The Conservative movement did not act on Ezrat Nashim's recommendations immediately, but in 1983 the Jewish Theological Seminary voted to admit women to the rabbinical school. The activism of New York's Jewish women had dramatically changed American Judaism.[70]

The liberatory spirit of the times was also evident in the case of the 1973 founding of Congregation Beit Simchat Torah, New York's first and the world's largest gay and lesbian synagogue, and one of the first New York synagogues to move beyond denominational labels.[71] CBST was founded "by 10 lesbian and gay Jews who sought to create a Jewish community that would accept their sexual identities," as the *Jerusalem Post* reported.[72] A do-it-yourself mentality was evident in CBST's early years, when the synagogue was called the "shopping bag synagogue," as someone was always responsible for bringing a bag with the necessary wine, kiddush cups, candles, and challah for communal Shabbat observance. By 1975, approximately 100 people regularly attended Friday night services, and by 1982, 200 members attended weekly. Some of that DIY style was replaced by more stable leadership, when in 1992, Rabbi Sharon Kleinbaum became the congregation's spiritual leader. [73] In 1993, Kleinbaum told the *New York Times* about her exciting pulpit: "People don't come here to please

---

68 "Ezrat Nashim Presents Manifesto for Women's Equality to Conservative Rabbis," This Week in History, Jewish Women's Archive, https://jwa.org/thisweek/mar/14/1972/ezrat-nashim; Enid Nemy, "Young Women Challenging Their '2d-Class Status' in Judaism," *New York Times*, June 12, 1972, 43; Pamela Nadell, *Women Who Would Be Rabbis* (Boston: Beacon Press, 1998), chap. 5; Joyce Antler, *Jewish Radical Feminism: Voices from the Women's Liberation Movement* (New York: NYU Press, 2018), chap. 5.

69 Nemy, "Young Women Challenging Their '2d-Class Status' in Judaism," 45.

70 Cohen, *The Birth of Conservative Judaism*, 160.

71 Moshe Shokeid, *A Gay Synagogue in New York* (Philadelphia: University of Pennsylvania Press, 1995), 16. Lawrence Grossman, "Jewish Communal Affairs; April 1, 2014 to March 31, 2015," *American Jewish Year Book 2015* (2016): 130.

72 Sue Fishkoff, "A Synagogue of One's Own," *The Jerusalem Post*, September 18, 1992, 1B.

73 "Sharon Kleinbaum," The Feminist Revolution, Jewish Women's Archive, https://jwa.org/feminism/kleinbaum-sharon.

Grandma. They're making Judaism mean something in 1993."[74] Under Kleinbaum's leadership, CBST has played an important role in gay rights and social justice activism.

Some of the biggest changes in the Jewish religious scene in twenty-first-century New York occurred among the Orthodox, particularly with the growth of Orthodox feminism, which had followers for years, but gained momentum with the establishment of the Jewish Orthodox Feminist Alliance (JOFA) in 1997. The organization's website explains their mission as seeking to expand "the spiritual, ritual, intellectual, and political opportunities for Jewish women within the framework of halakha, by advocating meaningful participation and equality for women in family life, synagogues, houses of learning and Jewish communal organizations to the full extent possible within halakha."[75] Feminism had woven its way into the other movements in Judaism, perhaps more quickly in New York than in some parts of the country. Nevertheless, it still caused a stir, as the *New York Times* reported, when in 1998, the Lincoln Square Synagogue was one of two New York Modern Orthodox synagogues to hire female interns to assist their rabbis. Until that time, such interns had been male rabbinical students. The *New York Times* quoted the response of a former president of Lincoln Square Synagogue: "There has been a feeling that if you start here, it could easily slide into other things, to a breakdown of values, the slippery slope thing. . . . But life is a slippery slope. If you're afraid of the slippery slope, you're never going to get up the hill."[76] The *Times* further observed that "nobody involved in this experiment can say what these women are 'interning' to become. There is no clear next step."

Just over a decade later, Rabbi Avi Weiss ordained the first *maharat* (female religious leader) at the Hebrew Institute of Riverdale, one of the two Modern Orthodox synagogues that had hired female interns in 1998. Weiss's ordination of women was part of his founding of a new movement called Open Orthodoxy (a term coined, in 1997, by Weiss, who views halakha as being open to innovation), which emphasizes adherence to halakha, intellectual openness, and inclusivity. This desire for a

---

74 Alex Witchel, "At Work With: Sharon Kleinbaum; 'Luckiest Rabbi in America' Holds Faith amid the Hate," *New York Times*, May 5, 1993, C1.

75 See the informaton at https://www.jofa.org/about-us.

76 Laurie Goodstein, "Unusual, but Not Unorthodox," *Times*, February 6, 1998, http://www.nytimes.com/1998/02/06/nyregion/unusual-but-not-unorthodox-causing-stir-2-synagogues-hire-women-assist-rabbis.html.

more inclusive Judaism led Weiss to found two new institutions, Yeshivat Chovevei Torah Rabbinical School (YCT) and Yeshivat Maharat to train female clergy. YCT has met a clear need, but it has also stirred controversy. In 2006, YCT applied for membership in the Rabbinical Council of America, the rabbinical body affiliated with the Orthodox Union, and then withdrew its application when it became clear that it would be denied. Avi Weiss's challenges to establishment Orthodoxy have changed Orthodoxy in New York, and the graduates of both of his institutions continue to influence Orthodox Judaism in this country.[77]

New York and Judaism in Conclusion

One of the findings of the 2011 New York Community Study that would have surprised an earlier era was the ease with which Jewish New Yorkers at the borders of Jewishness (meaning that they were set apart from what is perceived as conventional Jewish life) opted in and out of Jewishness. They do this, "either by saying they are 'partially Jewish' or by identifying with Christianity or some other non-Jewish religion."[78] Boundaries of Jewish identity are porous and frequently hybrid. The survey also found that even former relationships with Jews were sufficient basis for claiming Jewish identity. "Fully 5% of survey respondents had no Jewish parents and came to identify as Jewish in ways other than formally converting, primarily because of some family connection," the study found.[79] This fluidity of Jewish identity was likely aided by the Jewish culture of New York—that unique feeling that one imbibed Jewishness by simply living in New York. Unlike other religious groups, major segments of Jews do not think about Jewishness as a matter of religion, so the fact that non-Jews or loosely affiliated Jews can feel strongly Jewish in New York is due to the unique nature of both Judaism and New York. At the same time, the 2011 study also found signs of increasing religious intensification among certain segments of New York's Jews, who imposed stronger group boundaries and more exclusivity. Both ends of the spectrum of Judaism, in other words, find expression

---

77 Abigail Pogrebin, "The Rabbi and the Rabba," *New York Magazine*, July 11, 2010. http://nymag.com/news/features/67145/.

78 Steven M. Cohen, Jacob B. Ukeles, and Ron Miller, "Special Study on 'Partly Jewish' Jews," *Jewish Community Study of New York: 2011*, November 2013, https://www.jewishdatabank.org/content/upload/bjdb/597/JCSNY-2011-Special-Study-on-Partly-Jewish-Jews.pdf.

79 *Jewish Community Study of New York: 2011*, 112.

in New York: the not very religious Jews with porous boundaries on their group identity, as well as the more stringently observant and exclusive. One of the reasons New York continues to hold the position of "Jewish capital" is that it accommodates so many varieties of Jewish religious experience. New York is likely the easiest place in the diaspora to be a religious Jew, *and* one of the easiest places not to be a religious Jew—and still feel Jewish.

For many of New York's Jews—and other New Yorkers interested in Jewishness—religion exists as one choice among several possibilities for accessing Jewishness in this city. Judaism as a religion in New York has the voluntary quality that has defined the religious experience in America, a country without a state religion, where Americans prize religious affiliation as a free choice. As a city full of the history of Judaism—most important Jewish religious leaders have spent some time in this city, and many have left their marks, with new institutions, buildings, movements, and religious firsts. The accumulation of these events makes New York a center of Jewish religion. That the city is also a center for Jewish irreligion is no coincidence. Throughout New York Jewish history, Jewish religion and irreligion have frequently been in dialectical relationship, resulting in innovations in Jewish religious and cultural life that have reverberated far outside the city of their birth.

For Further Reading

Antler, Joyce. *Jewish Radical Feminism: Voices from the Women's Liberation Movement.* New York: NYU Press, 2018.

Cohen, Michael R. *The Birth of Conservative Judaism: Solomon Schechter's Disciples and the Creation of an American Religious Movement.* New York: Columbia University Press, 2012.

Danzger, M. Herbert. *Returning to Tradition: The Contemporary Revival of Orthodox Judaism.* New Haven: Yale University Press, 1989.

Diner, Hasia. *The Jews of the United States, 1654 to 2000.* Berkeley: University of California Press, 2004.

———. "American Judaism, 1820–1945." In *The Cambridge History of Religions in America*, vol. 2: *1790 to 1945*, edited by Stephen J. Stein, 273–99. New York: Cambridge University Press, 2012.

———. *How America Met the Jews.* Providence: Brown Judaica Series, 2017.

Eleff, Zev. *Modern Orthodox Judaism: A Documentary History.* Philadelphia: Jewish Publication Society, 2016.

Gelles, Edith B. *The Letters of Abigaill Levy Franks, 1733–1748.* New Haven: Yale University Press, 2004.

Glazer, Nathan. *American Judaism.* Chicago: University of Chicago Press, 1957.

Goldman, Karla. *Beyond the Synagogue Gallery: Finding a Place for Women in American Judaism.* Cambridge: Harvard University Press, 2001.

Goldstein, Eric. "The Great Wave: Eastern European Jewish Immigration to the United States, 1880–1924." In *The Columbia History of Jews and Judaism in America*, edited by Marc Lee Raphael, 70–92. New York: Columbia University Press, 2008.

Goren, Arthur. "A 'Golden Decade' for American Jews: 1945–1955." In Jeffrey Gurock, *American Jewish Life, 1920-1990.* New York: Routledge, 1998.

Gordon, Linda. *The Second Coming of the KKK: The Ku Klux Klan of the 1920s and the American Political Tradition.* New York: W.W. Norton, 2017.

Gurock, Jeffrey. "The Orthodox Synagogue." In Jack Wertheimer, *The American Synagogue: A Sanctuary Transformed*, 37–84. New York: Cambridge University Press, 1987.

———. *Orthodox Jews in America.* Bloomington: Indiana University Press, 2009.

Gurock, Jeffrey, and Jacob Schacter. *A Modern Heretic and a Traditional Community: Mordecai M. Kaplan, Orthodoxy and American Judaism.* New York: Columbia University Press, 1997.

Haefeli, Evan. *New Netherland and the Dutch Origins of American Religious Liberty.* Philadelphia: University of Pennsylvania Press, 2012.

Heilman, Samuel, and Menachem Friedman, *The Rebbe: The Life and Afterlife of Menachem Mendel Schneerson* (Princeton: Princeton University Press, 2010).

Holliday, Kathyrn E. *Leopold Eidlitz: Architecture and Idealism in the Gilded Age.* New York: W. W. Norton & Company, 2008.

Kaplan, Dana Evan. *The New Reform Judaism: Challenges and Reflections.* Lincoln: University of Nebraska Press, 2015.

Kaplan, Mordecai. *Judaism as a Civilization.* New York: Macmillan, 1934.

Kaufman, David. *Shul with a Pool: The "Synagogue-Center" in American Jewish History.* Waltham: Brandeis University Press, 1999.

Kaunfer, Elie. *Empowered Judaism: What Independent Minyanim Can Teach Us about Building Vibrant Jewish Communities.* Vermont: Jewish Lights Publishing, 2010.

Kraut, Benny. "Felix Adler's Emergence out of Judaism." PhD diss., Brandeis University, 1975.

Moore, Deborah Dash. *B'nai B'rith and the Challenge of Ethnic Leadership.* Waltham: Brandeis University Press, 1981.

———. *Urban Origins of American Judaism.* Athens: University of Georgia Press, 2014.

Moore, Deborah Dash, Jeffrey S. Gurock, Annie Polland, Howard B. Rock, and Daniel Soyer. *Jewish New York: The Remarkable Story of a City and a People.* New York: NYU Press, 2017.

Pamela Nadell. *Women Who Would Be Rabbis.* Boston: Beacon Press, 1998.

Polland, Annie. *Landmark of the Spirit: the Eldridge Street Synagogue.* New Haven: Yale University Press, 2009.

Rock, Howard B. *Haven of Liberty: New York Jews in the New World, 1654–1865.* New York: NYU Press, 2012.

Sarna, Jonathan. *American Judaism: A History.* New Haven: Yale University Press, 2004.

Sherman, Moshe D. *Orthodox Judaism in America: A Biographical Dictionary and Sourcebook.* Westport, CT: Greenwood, 1996.

Shokeid, Moshe. *A Gay Synagogue in New York.* Philadelphia: University of Pennsylvania Press, 1995.

Urofksy, Melvin I. *A Voice that Spoke for Justice: The Life and Times of Stephen S. Wise*. Albany: State University of New York Press, 1982.

Weissman, Jenna Joselit. *New York's Jewish Jews: The Orthodox Community in the Interwar Years*. Bloomington: Indiana University Press, 1990.

Wenger, Beth. *New York Jews and the Great Depression: Uncertain Promise*. New Haven: Yale, 1996.

Wolfe, Gerard R. *The Synagogues of New York's Lower East Side: A Retrospective and Contemporary View*. New York: Empire State Editions, 2013.

Chapter 12

Jews and Politics in New York City

Daniel Soyer

Jews' first political activity in what would become New York was lobbying the Dutch West India Company for the right to stay in its colony of New Amsterdam when, in 1654, Governor Peter Stuyvesant sought to expel them. They won, and for the next two centuries Jews enjoyed a degree of political integration in New Amsterdam and New York that was nearly unique in the world. But it was only after the Civil War, and especially with the great wave of immigration of the late nineteenth and early twentieth centuries, that Jews became a significant and distinctive political constituency in the city. They have remained such ever since. The nature of their participation, however, has changed over the last century and a half, demonstrating that "Jewish values" as expressed through political attitudes and activities are historically contingent. For much of the twentieth century, Jews often took the lead in promoting the liberal and social-democratic values that came to characterize New York City politics. But New York Jewish politics shifted in the wake of the racial and fiscal turmoil of the 1960s and 1970s, and many New York Jews came to support a variety of more conservative brands of politics.

It was in the late 1860s that New York political leaders began to take notice of Jews as a distinct constituency that needed to be addressed. The 1868 campaign saw the formation of small and short-lived Jewish

Republican and Democratic clubs, and over the next several years Tammany Hall boss William M. Tweed saw to it that the English-language *Hebrew Leader* and the city's first Yiddish newspaper, *Di yidishe tsaytung,* got both city and Tammany advertising. When Gerson Hermann was nominated for the Board of Supervisors in 1867, he was probably the first candidate placed on a ticket expressly as an inducement to Jewish voters. He later served as coroner, an office that for a time was virtually reserved for Jews. When prominent Tammanyite Albert Cardozo (father of future US Supreme Court Justice Benjamin Cardozo) ran for a seat on the state supreme court, his campaign issued a flyer in Hebrew promising lax enforcement of Sunday blue laws, a perennial problem for Jewish shopkeepers.

Jews were involved in reform politics as well as in the Tammany machine. A number of Jews served on the Committee of Seventy, made up of prominent citizens who helped to bring down the Tweed Ring in 1872. The most prominent was probably Simon Sterne, a lawyer and free-trade Democrat, who served as the committee's secretary. Supporters of civil service expansion and electoral reform, Sterne and others like him were conservative reformers. They supported government by the "best men" and feared that suffrage for too many of the wrong sort of people (immigrants; the poor) would only serve the interests of what Sterne called the "tax eaters."[1]

By defining "good government" as a moral issue and not a political one, Reform movements offered a loophole through which women could enter the political sphere even before they could vote. Jewish women such as Maud Nathan, a vice president of the Women's Municipal League, and Lilian Wald, founder of the Henry Street Settlement, worked to extend reform movements into the burgeoning Jewish immigrant neighborhoods. But reformers like Wald and Nathan differed from conservative good-government activists in that they looked to use the power of government to solve the kinds of social problems that plagued the growing immigrant Jewish working class. Nathan, for example, was a cofounder of the New York section of National Consumers' League, an organization that

---

1   Arthur Silver, "Jews in the Political Life of New York City, 1865–1897" (DHL diss., Yeshiva University, 1954), 27, 30–41, 119; Jacob Rader Marcus, *United States Jewry 1776–1985,* vol. 3 (Detroit: Wayne State University Press, 1993), 205, 217; David Hammack, *Power and Society: Greater New York at the Turn of the Century* (1982; reprint ed., New York: Columbia University Press, 1987), 9.

aimed to harness the power of middle- and upper-class consumers to aid workers.[2]

The influx of Yiddish-speaking immigrants between the 1870s and the 1920s transformed the Jewish profile in New York politics. First, it vastly increased the number, the concentration, and therefore the importance of Jewish voters. By 1920, there were over a million and a half Jews in the city, and as neighborhoods in Manhattan, Brooklyn and the Bronx became predominantly Jewish, so did the electoral districts in which they were located. Political organizations needed to take into account this ethnic constituency, and the Jewish identities of politicians therefore became more salient than they had been before. Thus, when Republican Edwin Einstein ran for Congress in 1878 he did so as a German, but when in 1892 he became the first Jewish nominee of a major party for mayor, he was put forward as a Jew.[3]

Second, New York Jews began to develop a brand of progressive politics that called for government action on the local, state and federal levels to solve social problems in areas such as housing, health care, and industrial relations. It was often internationalist, even cosmopolitan, in outlook, and zealously guarded the secularity of the state. It could take the form of Progressivism, Socialism, or liberalism depending on the period, and acted at various times through the Democratic, Socialist, American Labor, Liberal, and even sometimes the Republican parties. But, in any case, it contributed to the emergence of New York's unusual inclination toward municipal social democracy, with its widespread public and cooperative housing, municipal hospitals and colleges, and trade union power.[4] Jews were certainly not the only supporters of this kind of politics, but they provided its most consistent base.

Tammany Hall certainly remained a powerful presence, especially in the immigrant neighborhoods where Jews lived. By the last decades of the nineteenth century, Irish Americans dominated the Hall. The same was true of the similar Democratic machines that operated separately outside

---

2   S. Sara Monson, "The Lady and the Tiger: Women's Electoral Activism in New York before Suffrage," *Journal of Women's History* 2, no. 2 (Fall 1990): 100–134; Joyce Antler, *The Journey Home: Jewish Women and the American Century* (New York: Free Press, 1997), 54–61; Maud Nathan, *The Story of an Epoch-Making Movement* (Garden City, NY: Doubleday, Page, 1926); Marjorie Feld, *Lillian Wald: A Biography* (Chapel Hill: University of North Carolina Press, 2008).

3   Silver, "Jews in the Political Life of New York City," 75, 112–13.

4   See Joshua Freeman, *Working Class New York: Life and Labor since World War II* (New York: Free Press, 2000).

of Manhattan in the unified city that was created in 1898. Nevertheless, many Jews found a home in Tammany, assimilating into its culture of politics as a business characterized by networks of personal loyalty. The action in Tammany was in party offices, not public ones, and for a time at least, few Jews filled the former. Martin Engel, the flamboyant "Kosher Chicken Czar," was an exception as leader of the predominantly Jewish Eighth Assembly District. But when in 1902, Engel, who also dabbled in prostitution and protection rackets, was purged in one of Tammany's periodic internal house cleanings he was replaced by a more reliable Irish American leader.

As Tammany incorporated more Jews, Jewish public office holders became the norm in Jewish districts. Silver Dollar Smith, whose birth name was probably Charles Solomon, was first elected to the state assembly from the Eighth District in 1888. He was a saloon keeper, a typical occupation for a machine politician, but nevertheless connected with his Jewish immigrant constituents. According to his obituary, he was "one of the few politicians in the district who understood the Hebrew residents and their language." Likewise, Congressman Henry Goldfogle, a higher class of Tammany politician and the first New York congressman to be nominated as a Jew to represent a Jewish district, was eulogized at his funeral as "the typical son of typical Jewish immigrant parents." Portrayed by Tammany as "not *a* Jewish congressman, but *the* Jewish congressman," Goldfogle spoke out on issues such as Russian antisemitism and immigration restriction that were of special concern to his Jewish constituents.[5]

It was perhaps easier for Jews to rise in the Republican Party. When Edward Lauterbach was elected county leader in 1895, he regarded his rise as an indication of a "levelling ... of class and racial distinctions." Lauterbach was followed by Samuel Koenig, an immigrant from Austria-Hungary who headed the Republican Party in Manhattan from 1911 to 1933. Republican politics at

---

5   Edmund James, Oscar Flynn, J. Paulding, Mrs. Simon Patton, Walter Scott Andrews, *The Immigrant Jew in America* (New York: B. Buck, 1906), 258–59; Moses Rischin, *Promised City: New York's Jews, 1870–1914* (Cambridge, MA: Harvard University Press, 1962), 221–24; Irving Howe, *World of Our Fathers* (New York: Harcourt Brace Jovanovich, 1976), 365–77; Timothy Gilfoyle, *City of Eros: New York City, Prostitution, and the Commercialization of Sex, 1790–1920* (New York: Norton, 1992), 261; Oliver Allen, *The Tiger: The Rise and Fall of Tammany Hall* (Reading, MA: Addison-Wesley, 1993), 212–13; Morris Werner, *Tammany Hall* (Garden City, NY: Doubleday, Doran, 1928), 381–82; *New York Times*, December 23, 1999; Louis Eisenstein and Elliot Rosenberg, *A Stripe of Tammany's Tiger* (New York: Robert Speller & Sons, 1966), 29–30; "H. M. Goldfogle," *New York Times*, June 2, 1929; "Eulogies Paid H. M. Goldfogle," *New York Times*, June 15, 1929.

a day-to-day grassroots level was not that different from Democratic politics. As Koenig's friend, the Tammany ward heeler Louis Eisenstein recalled, the Republican leader worked "along the familiar lines cut by Tammany, with some of the coarser edges smoothed out."[6]

Political reform continued to appeal to some Jews, including new immigrants dissatisfied with living and working conditions, or disgruntled over the distribution of political spoils by the party machines. When William Strong was elected mayor in 1894, he received significant support from Jewish districts. And when Seth Low ran an independent campaign for mayor in 1901, his supporters made an all-out effort to win the votes of immigrants on the Lower East Side with Yiddish flyers and speeches. Unfortunately, these coalitions were fragile, and genteel reformers such as Strong and Low often quickly antagonized their immigrant constituencies by strenuously enforcing Sunday blue laws that the reformers considered bulwarks of social propriety and order, and the immigrants considered a nuisance and obstacle to earning a living. Both Strong and Low lost their immigrant votes and their battles for reelection.[7]

To the left of the reformers were the Socialists, who established a considerable presence and, for a short time, electoral control, in the Jewish immigrant neighborhoods. Socialism made inroads among East European Jews in both Europe, where it offered an answer to downward economic mobility and religious and ethnic persecution, and America, where it promised a way out of the exploitative sweatshops and dismal tenements. By 1910, the Socialists had built a considerable organizational infrastructure that eventually included the *Forverts* (*Forward*), the largest Yiddish daily newspaper; the Workmen's Circle, a labor fraternal order; and the garment workers' unions.[8]

---

6 Naomi Cohen, *Encounter with Emancipation: The German Jews in the United States, 1830–1914* (Philadelphia: Jewish Publication Society, 1984), 329; James, *Immigrant Jew,* 260; Eisenstein, *Stripe of Tammany's Tiger,* 56–58; *New York Times,* March 18, 1955.

7 James, *Immigrant Jew,* 257, 261–62; Howe, *World of Our Fathers,* 362; Rischin, *Promised City,* 228; Lawrence Fuchs, *The Political Behavior of American Jews* (Glencoe, IL: Free Press, 1956), 123; Silver, *Jews in the Political Life of New York City,* 120–22; Cohen, *Encounter with Emancipation,* 331–36.

8 Tony Michels, *Fire in their Hearts: Yiddish Socialists in New York* (Cambridge, MA: Harvard University Press, 2005); Melech Epstein, *Jewish Labor in USA,* vol. 1: *1882–1914* (1950; reprint ed., New York: Ktav, 1969); Howe, *World of Our Fathers,* 101–15, 287–304, 522–43; Hadassa Kosak, *Cultures of Opposition: Jewish Immigrant Workers in New York City, 1881–1905* (Albany: SUNY Press, 2000).

The infamous Triangle Shirtwaist Company Fire, in which 146 mostly young female Jewish workers were killed, took place on March 25, 1911. The fire's political impact was twofold. Amidst the memorial meetings, funerals, and protests that took place in the fire's aftermath, some participants called for expanding workers' political power through a Socialist vote. At the same time, the fire shook some Tammany politicians, most notably Assemblyman Al Smith and State Senator Robert F. Wagner, both of whom represented districts in which many of the victims lived. They undertook a major investigation of industrial conditions throughout the state that led to dozens of pieces of legislation regulating working conditions, wages and hours. Smith and Wagner now entered into an alliance with the kinds of social reformers, Jewish and otherwise, who would have looked down on them before. The staff of Smith and Wagner's Factory Investigating Commission even included several radical Jewish labor activists, such as Rose Schneiderman, Clara Lemlich and Pauline Newman. Labor radicals and social reformers alike developed a respect for Smith and Wagner that would make it difficult in the future to reject them out of hand as representatives of the capitalist parties or corrupt Tammany machine.[9]

The 1912 election pitted incumbent Republican William Howard Taft against Democrat Woodrow Wilson and former President Theodore Roosevelt, running under the banner of a new Progressive Party. In New York, the Progressives nominated the Jewish former secretary of commerce Oscar Straus for governor, his nomination seconded by Belle Israels, who would later become better known, under the name Belle Moskowitz, as Governor Al Smith's closest advisor. The Democrats countered by naming Congressman William Sulzer, a non-Jew who had won Jewish admiration for his fiery speeches against Russian antisemitism. Sulzer, in fact, made more blatant ethnic appeals to Jewish voters during the campaign than did Straus. Straus nevertheless carried the Jewish districts, though Sulzer won the election. He was impeached the next year when he double-crossed his Tammany backers by endorsing a number of good government reforms. In the Sulzer affair too, Jews played prominent, if opposing, roles: Assembly

---

9   On the fire and its aftermath, see David Von Drehle, *Triangle: The Fire that Changed America* (New York: Atlantic Monthly Press, 2003); Leon Stein, *The Triangle Fire* (Philadelphia: J. B. Lippincott, 1962); Richard Greenwald, *The Triangle Fire, the Protocols of Peace, and Industrial Democracy in Progressive Era New York* (Philadelphia: Temple University Press, 2005); Annelise Orleck, *Common Sense and a Little Fire: Women and Working-Class Politics in the Unites States, 1900–1965* (Chapel Hill: University of North Carolina Press, 1995), 130–34.

Majority Leader Aaron Jefferson Levy acted as prosecutor, while prominent Jewish communal leader Louis Marshall served as Sulzer's counsel.[10]

Meanwhile, the Socialists were gaining ground. In 1914, the Socialist electoral heyday began, when Meyer London, a saintly immigrant labor lawyer, beat the incumbent and took the Lower East Side's seat in Congress for the first of three terms. Over the next several years, Socialists were elected to the city Board of Aldermen, to the state legislature, and, in one case, as a municipal judge. The most spectacular, though not the most successful, Socialist campaign was that of Morris Hillquit for mayor in 1917. Hillquit, like London, was an immigrant attorney, but though he had also done pro bono work for the garment unions, he had a successful career as a corporate lawyer as well. In 1917, the mayoral election was fought against the backdrop of the United States entry into World War I, which the Socialists opposed, and Hillquit ran on an antiwar platform. He came in a strong third in a four-way race.[11]

The political excitement of 1917 also included a statewide referendum that gave women the right to vote in New York State. All classes of Jewish society supported women's suffrage, from the central body of Reform rabbis to the United Hebrew Trades. Suffrage leaders included middle-class women such as Nathan and working-class activists like Lemlich, Schneiderman, and Theresa Malkiel. Moreover, suffragists found in canvassing the immigrant neighborhoods that Jewish men as well as Jewish women supported extending suffrage. The upsurge in Jewish and Socialist voting brought

10   Rischin, *Promised City,* 231–33; Fuchs, *The Political Behavior of American Jews,* 58–59; Werner, *Tammany Hall,* 529–54; Thomas Henderson, *Tammany Hall and the New Immigrants: The Progressive Years* (New York: Arno, 1976), 114–21; Naomi Cohen, *Encounter with Emancipation,* 144–47; Eisenstein, *Stripe of Tammany's Tiger,* 21–24.

11   Melech Epstein, *Profiles of Eleven* (Detroit: Wayne State University Press, 1965), 159–232; Howe, *World of Our Fathers,* 310–24; Arthur Goren, *The Politics and Public Culture of American Jews* (Bloomington: Indiana University Press, 1999), 83–99; Melvin Dubofsky, "Success and Failure of Socialism in New York City, 1900–1918: A Case Study," *Labor History* 9, no. 3 (Autumn 1968): 361–75; Gil Ribak, "'For Peace, Not Socialism': The 1917 Mayoralty Campaign in New York City and Immigrant Jews in a Global Perspective," *American Jewish History* 101, no. 4 (2017): 465–88. On London, see also Harry Rogoff, *An East Side Epic: The Life and Work of Meyer London* (New York: Vanguard Press, 1930); Gordon Goldberg, *Meyer London: A Biography of the Socialist New York Congressman, 1871–1926* (Jefferson, NC: McFarland, 2013). On Hillquit, see also Norma Fain Pratt, *Morris Hillquit: A Political History of an American Jewish Socialist* (Westport, CT: Greenwood, 1979).

about by the Hillquit campaign that year thus played a role in getting the referendum passed.[12]

Elected governor in 1918, Al Smith attracted Jewish support to the Democratic Party, both on the basis of liberal policy initiatives, and because his urban, working-class persona resonated with first- and second-generation Americans, Jewish and non-Jewish. In eight years as governor (1919–1921, 1923–1929), Smith expanded social legislation and modernized the state's infrastructure and government. All along, he explicitly invited Jews into his coalition. In fact, many of his top advisors were Jewish. Belle Moskowitz was the most remarkable member of Smith's inner circle, not only for her ethnicity and reform pedigree, but for her gender. A Progressive activist, she played a role in Smith's 1918 campaign, and then emerged as the governor's most trusted advisor, responsible for a number of his reform initiatives. Smith garnered the support of Jewish voters in his races for governor, and in 1928 for president. Even some Jewish Socialists, such as ILGWU president David Dubinsky, kept quiet that year, unable to oppose him, but not yet ready to publically endorse a capitalist-party candidate.[13]

Another progressive politician who attracted Jewish attention was the maverick Republican Congressman Fiorello La Guardia. La Guardia was a social reformer who joined the Republican Party out of distaste for Tammany Hall, and perhaps from the calculation that he would not advance in the Irish-dominated machine. He himself had an unusual background: His mother was an Italian-speaking Jew from the Austrian Empire, his

---

12 Elinor Lerner, "Jewish Involvement in the New York City Woman Suffrage Movement," *American Jewish History* 70, no. 4 (June 1981): 442–61; Orleck, *Common Sense and a Little Fire*, 87–113.

13 Joel Schwartz, "The Triumph of Liberalism (1914–1945)," in *The Empire State: A History of New York*, ed. Milton Klein (Ithaca: Cornell University Press, 2001), 545–48, 564–67; Howe, *World of Our Fathers*, 385–91; Fuchs, *Political Behavior of American Jews*, 66–67, 141; Deborah Dash Moore, *At Home in America: Second Generation New York Jews* (New York: Columbia University Press, 1981), 219–220; David Dubinsky and A. H. Raskin, *David Dubinsky: A Life with Labor* (New York: Simon and Schuster, 1977), 263–64; Matthew Josephson and Hannah Josephson, *Al Smith: Hero of the Cities: A Political Portrait Drawing on the Papers of Frances Perkins* (Boston: Houghton Mifflin, 1969), 193–97, 217–20, 237–40, 301–307; John Thomas McGuire, "From Socialism to Social Justice Feminism: Rose Schneiderman and the Quest for Urban Equity, 1911–1933," *Journal of Urban History* 35, no. 7 (November 2009): 998–1019; Robert A. Slayton, *Empire Statesman: The Rise and Redemption of Al Smith* (New York: Free Press, 2001), 175–76, 295–96, 325; Elizabeth Israels Perry, *Belle Moskowitz: Feminine Politics and the Exercise of Power in the Age of Al Smith* (1987; Boston: Northeastern University Press, 1992).

father was a freethinker, and Fiorello had been raised Episcopalian, mostly in Arizona, where his father was stationed as an army bandleader. Despite his maternal background, he never claimed Jewish identity, and his Jewish ancestry was seldom raised by others. La Guardia was capable of delivering a rousing speech in Yiddish, but only because it was one of several languages in which he was fluent. Generally, he was viewed as an Italian, and so he viewed himself.[14]

On the grassroots level, neighborhood and district political clubs played a major role in mobilizing voters and sponsoring political careers. In the Jewish neighborhoods, Democratic clubs predominated, especially as the New York Democratic Party under Smith, and his successors as governor, Franklin Roosevelt and Herbert Lehman, began to espouse liberal ideas more consistently. For the most part, however, the Jewish share of leadership in the clubs and party districts lagged behind the Jewish share of the membership. This was especially true in Manhattan, where Tammany still prevailed, and in the Bronx. In Brooklyn, by contrast, a relatively smooth process of ethnic succession took place, as Irish leaders retired and handed the reins over to Jews.

Two figures, Hymie Schorenstein and Irwin Steingut, exemplified the Jewish rise to prominence in the Brooklyn Democratic Party. Schorenstein, a Yiddish-accented immigrant, took over as Democratic leader in Brownsville in 1919 and successfully reclaimed Brownsville from the Socialists. Illiterate, the colorful Schorenstein held a number of public positions including that of county registrar. In nearby middle-class Crown Heights, Irwin Steingut, the son of a German Jewish immigrant who had been active in Tammany, was first elected to the state assembly and then to the district leadership, succeeding county leader John McCooey. Steingut had founded his own predominantly Jewish club, but also maintained cordial relations with McCooey's Madison Club, which Steingut later headed. In the assembly, he eventually served as speaker.[15]

14   Fiorello LaGuardia, *The Making of an Insurgent* (Philadelphia: JB Lippincott, 1948), especially 30, 101; Thomas Kessner, *Fiorello H. La Guardia and the Making of Modern New York* (1989; 2nd ed., New York: Penguin, 1991), 4–5, 11–12, 20–31, 73–74, 91–93, 103, 117–18; Arthur Mann, *La Guardia: Fighter against His Times, 1882-1933* (Philadelphia: J.B. Lippincott, 1959), 21–32, 50–51, 155–58.

15   Moore, *At Home in America*, 204–10, 217–18; Jeffrey Gerson, "Building the Brooklyn Machine: Irish, Jewish and Black Political Succession in Central Brooklyn, 1919-1964" (PhD diss., City University of New York, 1990), 102–52; Beth Wenger, *New York Jews and the Great Depression: Uncertain Promise* (New Haven: Yale University Press, 1996),

By the onset of the Great Depression, the Socialist Party had ceased to be a significant electoral force, and Jewish radicalism gradually merged with Progressivism and social reformism to form a new urban liberalism with a social-democratic tinge. Jews became enthusiastic backers of the New Deal and President Franklin D. Roosevelt, who by the 1940 election garnered an estimated 90% of the Jewish vote nationwide. Indeed, as one Yiddish witticism put it, the Jews had *dray veltn* ("three worlds"): *di velt* ("this world"), *yene velt* ("the next world"), and *Roosevelt.* The fact that Herbert Lehman succeeded Roosevelt as governor also undoubtedly enhanced the Democratic appeal to Jewish voters. Lehman was a financier and Jewish communal leader who had long dabbled in Democratic politics. Moreover, he had built ties to the garment unions over the years as a mediator and trouble shooter in the industry for Governors Smith and Roosevelt. With a reputation for rectitude, Lehman appealed to Jews not only because of his religious or ethnic ties, but because he represented the New Deal in the state.[16]

At the same time, however, the ascension of Fiorello La Guardia to the mayoralty in 1933 made it impossible to regard the Democratic Party as the unambiguous political vehicle of the New Deal in New York. In 1933, La Guardia was still a nominal Republican, but as head of a local coalition that included most Jews and Italians, he emerged as the city's leading New Dealer, forging close relations with the Roosevelt Administration to carry out a massive program of public works. New York's New Deal coalition thus intersected the two major parties.[17]

127–30; Alter Landesman, *Brownsville: The Birth, Development and Passing of a Jewish Community in New York* (New York: Bloch, 1971), 297–98.

16   Ira Forman, "The Politics of Minority Consciousness," in L. Sandy Maisel and Ira N. Forman, *Jews in American Politics* (Lanham, MD: Rowman and Littlefield, 2001), 153; Howe, *World of Our Fathers*, 393; Allan Nevins, *Herbert H. Lehman and His Era* (New York: Scribner's, 1963), 85–91, 121; Robert Parmet, *Master of Seventh Avenue: David Dubinsky and the American Labor Movement* (New York: NYU Press, 2005), 84, 86, 116; Robert Ingalls, *Herbert H. Lehman and New York's Little New Deal* (New York: NYU Press, 1975), 7, 134–35; Epstein, *Jewish Labor in the USA*, vol. 2, 155, 162; Duane Tananbaum, *Herbert H. Lehman: A Political Biography* (Albany: SUNY Press, 2016), 6, 47–48.

17   Arthur Mann, *La Guardia Comes to Power, 1933* (Philadelphia: J. B. Lippincott, 1965), 112–116, 138–152; Kessner, *Fiorello H. La Guardia*, 240, 399–404, *passim*; Ronald Bayor, *Neighbors in Conflict: The Irish, Germans, Jews, and Italians of New York, 1929–1941* (Baltimore: Johns Hopkins University Press, 1978), 130, 137; Mason Williams, *City of Ambition: FDR, La Guardia, and the Making of Modern New York* (New York: W. W. Norton, 2013).

Socialists and Communists, many of them Jewish, also eventually joined the New Deal coalition in New York. Their chief electoral vehicle was the American Labor Party, formed in 1936. The ALP enabled its founders—independent liberals, moderate Socialists, and union leaders—to back sympathetic candidates of either major party, or to run their own candidates when necessary. With much of its support coming from the garment unions, the ALP inherited many of the old Socialist voters in the Jewish districts, added more, and played an important role in garnering votes for Roosevelt, Lehman, and La Guardia. In some predominantly Jewish areas, the Labor Party became the second party behind the Democrats, and elected several of its members to the city council and other offices. Within the ALP, sharp disagreements between pro- and anti-Soviet factions led to years of internal conflict, however, until the anti-Communists split in 1944 to form the Liberal Party, which played an important role in New York politics for the rest of the twentieth century.[18]

By the end of World War II, Jews were well-represented in the city's political establishment. Manhattan's Jewish Borough President Hugo Rogers even served briefly as leader of Tammany Hall as the storied machine declined. This was the era of the ethnically "balanced ticket," with representation from the "Three I's"—Ireland, Italy, and Israel. Every citywide Democratic ticket from 1945 through 1969 included an Irish American (counting Mayor Robert F. Wagner, who was of partly Irish descent), an Italian American, and a Jew. Only one important city elective office eluded Jews altogether—the mayoralty. The second Jewish major-party candidate (not counting Hillquit as a major-party candidate, or La Guardia as a Jew) was disgruntled Democrat Judge Jonah Goldstein, running in 1945 as a Republican-Liberal, and beaten badly. Republicans Harold Riegelman and Louis Lefkowitz also fell well short in 1953 and 1961, respectively. Comptroller Abraham Beame won the Democratic nomination in 1965, an accomplishment that usually spelled election, but he was defeated in a tough three-way race by liberal Republican John Lindsay, who received significant Jewish support.[19]

---

18 Kenneth Waltzer, "The American Labor Party: Third Party Politics in New Deal/Cold War New York, 1936–1954" (PhD diss., Harvard University, 1977); Daniel Soyer, "The Soviet Union, Jewish Concerns, and the New York Electoral Left, 1939–1944," in *Jews and the Left*, ed. Jack Jacobs (New York: Cambridge University Press, 2017), 291–311; Soyer, "Executed Bundists, Soviet Delegates and the Wartime Jewish Popular Front in New York," *American Communist History* 15, no. 3 (2016): 293–332.

19 Nathan Glazer and Daniel Moynihan, *Beyond the Melting Pot: The Negroes, Puerto Ricans, Jews, Italians, and Irish of New York City* (1963; 2nd ed., Cambridge: MIT Press,

Jewish voters generally voted Democratic, but the Liberal Party continued to play an important role. In addition to providing votes on their line, the Liberals offered a "seal of approval" that many voters looked for in deciding which candidates to support. In statewide races, Liberal support was imperative for Democrats seeking office. In citywide contests, conversely, the Liberal nomination was key to a Republican victory. Although its chair was always a Gentile intellectual—a professor or minister—the Liberal Party's real leaders were Yiddish-accented trade unionists David Dubinsky of the ILGWU and Alex Rose of the hatters. Its base was in the Jewish working-class and lower-middle-class districts.[20]

Emerging from Adlai Stevenson's presidential campaigns of the 1950s, an insurgent reform movement within the Democratic Party also attracted many Jews. Local Reform clubs coalesced in 1958 as the Committee for Democratic Voters, under the leadership of liberal elders Herbert Lehman and Eleanor Roosevelt. Like the old reformers, the new Reform Democrats were for good, clean government, but they also supported the expansion of the New Deal welfare state and the civil rights movement. Socially, they were young, highly educated professionals, and mostly Jewish. In the early 1960s, the Reform Democrats scored a number of primary victories over the "regular" Democratic organizations. But by the late 1960s, now organized as the New Democratic Coalition, the Reformers gained a reputation for fractiousness. Their critics claimed that they were so focused on primary elections that NDC actually stood for "November Doesn't Count."[21]

There were, of course, still Jewish Republicans as well. US Senator Jacob Javits was probably the most prominent individual Jewish politician in New York from the late 1950s until the early 1970s. The son of East European Jewish immigrants, Javits joined the Republican Party out of revulsion to Tammany Hall and the southern white supremacists in the national Democratic Party.

1970), 170–71; Chris McNickle, *To Be Mayor of New York: Ethnic Politics in the City* (New York: Columbia University Press, 1993), 58–64, 68, 88, 95, 106–107, 164–65, 174–75, 198–209; Eli Lederhendler, *New York Jews and the Decline of Urban Ethnicity, 1950–1970* (Syracuse: Syracuse University Press, 2001), 136.

20 Daniel Link, "'Every Day Was a Battle': Liberal Anticommunism in Cold War New York, 1944-1956" (PhD diss., New York University, 2006).

21 McNickle, *To Be Mayor of New York*, 138–44, 244; Glazer and Moynihan, *Beyond the Melting Pot*, 170–71; Martin Shefter, *Political Crisis, Fiscal Crisis: The Collapse and Revival of New York City* (1985; 2nd ed., New York: Columbia University Press, 1992), 44–46; Warren Moscow, *What Have You Done for Me Lately? The Ins and Outs of New York City Politics* (New York: Prentice Hall, 1967), 61–62; Jonathan Soffer, *Ed Koch and the Rebuilding of New York City* (New York: Columbia University Press, 2010), 33.

In congress, however, he proved a cautious liberal, and he remained loyal to the GOP (breaking only with the Goldwater candidacy in 1964). Javits was a popular vote getter in New York City, but he eventually lost the Republican primary in 1980, as the party shifted to the right.[22]

In the 1960s and 1970s, progressive causes such as the civil rights, anti-war and feminist movements intersected with local electoral politics, often through the Reform Democratic movement. Two Jewish politicians who embodied these intersections were Bella Abzug and Elizabeth Holtzman. Abzug, the daughter of an immigrant kosher butcher, was a civil rights and civil liberties attorney and an outspoken feminist. She served three terms in Congress before narrowly losing the Democratic senatorial primary in 1976 to Daniel Patrick Moynihan, who had become a hero to many centrist and conservative Jews for his defense of Israel as US ambassador to the United Nations. Perhaps the last major figure of the old predominantly Jewish New York political left, Abzug also ran for mayor in 1977 as a vocal critic of the austerity regime that emerged after the city's fiscal crisis of 1975. Liz Holtzman, on the other hand, was thirty-one years old in 1972, when as an anti-war and Reform challenger, she defeated fifty-year Brooklyn Congressional incumbent Emanuel Celler in the Democratic primary. Holtzman played a visible role in the Watergate hearings the following year, and seemed destined for higher office. But she was defeated in her try for the senate in 1980, and though she later served as Brooklyn district attorney and New York City comptroller, she never regained a national stage.[23]

The upheavals of the 1960s and 1970s also created deep divisions among New York Jews. In the face of rapid demographic change and rising crime, with the Jewish population in the city dropping, some Jews—often described as working-class, lower-middle-class, or "outer-borough"—adopted a defensive posture and conservative politics. They were more likely than before to identify as "white," and to seek alliances with other white ethnic

---

22   Jacob Javits and Rafael Steinberg, *Javits: The Autobiography of a Republican* (Boston: Haughton Mifflin, 1981).

23   Alan Levy, *The Political Life of Bella Abzug, 1920-1970: Political Passions, Women's Rights, and Congressional Battles* (Lanham, MD: Lexington Books, 2013); Suzanne Braun Levine and Mary Thom, *Bella Abzug* (New York: Farrar, Straus and Giroux, 2007); Eli Lederhendler, "Elizabeth Holtzman," Encyclopedia, Jewish Women's Archive, https://jwa.org/encyclopedia/article/holtzman-elizabeth, accessed July 9, 2017; Elizabeth Holtzman, *Who Said It Would Be Easy? One Woman's Life in the Political Arena* (New York: Arcade, 1996).

groups against the political claims of the growing African American and Puerto Rican communities. New voting patterns could be seen, for example, when a majority of Jews voted against a mixed civilian-police Civilian Complaint Review Board in a 1966 referendum, despite the support it had from most major Jewish communal organizations. Similarly, whereas Jews in places like Brownsville had once *demanded* public housing for their neighborhoods, in 1971–1972, Jews in upper-middle-class Forest Hills, Queens, mobilized to fight the placement of a project there in a struggle that took on strong racial overtones.[24]

The event that most emblematically demonstrated the strains in New York Jewish liberalism was the teachers' strike of 1968. Jews had long had a love affair with the public school system, and by the 1960s, a majority of city public school teachers were Jewish. They were well ensconced in the bureaucracy and in the United Federation of Teachers, which had recently won bargaining rights for its members. In 1968, the union came into conflict with the African American-led board of the experimental Ocean Hill-Brownsville school district in Brooklyn over the abrupt firing of a number of teachers. What followed were a series of on-again, off-again strikes that quickly assumed a racial and ethnic character. A number of antisemitic incidents demonstrated to many Jews that the experiment in community control constituted an attack on both Jewish material interests and cherished values of educational meritocracy. The conflict posed an especially thorny and painful dilemma to progressive Jews who had always supported both workers' rights and racial equality. Many sided with the community board, and many of the teachers hired by the board to replace the strikers were Jewish. But the strike dealt a serious blow to Jewish liberalism, and although Mayor Lindsay, running for reelection the following year, finished

---

24 Michael Flamm, "'Law and Order' at Large: The New York Civilian Review Board Referendum of 1966 and the Crisis of Liberalism," *Historian* 64, nos. 3–4 (Spring/Summer 2002): 643–65; Vincent Cannato, *The Ungovernable City: John Lindsay and his Struggle to Save New York* (New York: Basic, 2001), 155–88, 504–15; Wendell Pritchett, *Brownsville, Brooklyn: Blacks, Jews, and the Changing Face of the Ghetto* (Chicago: University of Chicago Press, 2002), 62–67; Daniel Wishnoff, "The Tolerance Point: Race, Public Housing and the Forest Hills Controversy, 1945–1975" (PhD diss., CUNY, 2005), especially 192–237; Soffer, *Ed Koch and the Rebuilding of New York City*, 108–11; Joshua Zeitz, *White Ethnic New York: Jews, Catholics, and the Shaping of Postwar Politics* (Chapel Hill: University of North Carolina Press, 2007), 141–95.

in a virtual tie with his Democratic rival among Jewish voters, a significant share of the Jewish community now saw liberalism as a threat.[25]

Elected in 1973, the first Jewish mayor of New York, Abraham Beame, was a middle-of-the-road product of the Brooklyn machine. Having served as city budget director and comptroller, Beame ran on an image of fiscal competence and integrity. It was ironic, then, that New York endured its most crippling fiscal crisis on his watch. As the crisis unfolded, a number of Jews played prominent roles in seeking a way to avoid municipal default. In addition to Beame, there were union leaders such as the teachers' Albert Shanker and municipal workers' Victor Gotbaum, as well as investment banker Felix Rohatyn, appointed by the governor to head the Municipal Assistance Corporation, an agency charged with selling the city's bonds while taking control of some tax revenues. The new regime saved the city from bankruptcy, but shifted power to banks and corporations, and spelled the end to the local experiment in social democracy that had been the legacy (partly) of earlier Jewish political involvement.[26]

On the heels of the crisis, the second Jewish mayor of New York defeated the first in a wild seven-way 1977 Democratic primary. Congressman Ed Koch had made a name for himself as a Greenwich Village Reform Democrat. But in the 1970s, he began to break with liberal orthodoxy, at first over the Forest Hills housing controversy and then over crime and policing. Styling himself a "liberal with sanity," Koch positioned himself as the candidate with fiscal common sense. But he also appealed to angry white backlash voters who associated high crime with the growing minority presence in the city. As mayor, Koch was credited with putting the city on a solid fiscal footing. But his in-your-face ethnic style and often belligerent

---

25   Ruth Jacknow Markowitz, *My Daughter, the Teacher: Jewish Teachers in the New York City Schools* (New Brunswick: Rutgers University Press, 1993), 2; Jerald Podair, *The Strike that Changed New York: Blacks, Whites and the Ocean Hill-Brownsville Crisis* (New Haven: Yale University Press, 2002); Jacob Dorman, "Dreams Defended and Deferred: The Brooklyn Schools Crisis of 1968 and Black Power's Influence on Rabbi Meir Kahane," *American Jewish History* 100, no. 3 (July 2016): 411–37; Cannato, *Ungovernable City,* 424–26, 438–39; Jeffrey Taffet, "The Snubs and the 'Sukkah': John Lindsay and Jewish Voters in New York City," *American Jewish History* 97, no. 4 (October 2013): 413–38; Jonathan Rieder, *Canarsie: The Jews and Italians of Brooklyn against Liberalism* (Cambridge, MA: Harvard University Press, 1985).

26   McNickle, *To Be Mayor of New York,* 245–46, 252–56; Freeman, *Working Class New York,* 256–87; Kim Phillips-Fein, *Fear City: New York's Fiscal Crisis and the Rise of Austerity Politics* (New York: Metropolitan and Henry Holt, 2017).

rhetoric alienated many minority voters, and his vision of a revived city catered to the interests and sensibilities of the well off.[27]

After cruising to reelection twice, Koch overreached for an unprecedented fourth term, and was defeated in the 1989 Democratic primary by David Dinkins, the African American Manhattan borough president. Dinkins's campaign put together what had been an elusive coalition of African Americans, Latinos, and progressive whites, including about a third of Jewish voters. Two thirds of Jewish voters, however, pulled the lever for Dinkins's opponent, Republican Rudolph Giuliani, running with Liberal Party support as the law-and-order candidate. Dinkins's tenure was a tumultuous one. One low point came in the summer of 1991. When a car in the motorcade of the Lubavitcher Rebbe accidentally struck and killed a Black child, several days of rioting ensued in which angry mobs attacked Hasidic Jews in Crown Heights, Brooklyn. A visiting Jewish graduate student was stabbed to death. Many Orthodox Jews believed, incorrectly, that the mayor had ordered the police not to intervene, but the city's response was unquestionably weak. The Crown Heights riots not only exacerbated tensions between Blacks and Orthodox Jews, but also revealed the deep chasm between the political sensibilities of Orthodox and non-Orthodox Jews. In the 1993 elections, Dinkins's Jewish support slid only slightly, but he lost a close rematch to Giuliani.[28]

At the turn of the twenty-first century, Jews continued to play an important role in New York City politics, but the nature of that role was shifting. Jews could still be found in leadership positions in progressive movements. And the 2001 mayoral election pitted the left-liberal Democrat Mark Green against cosmopolitan billionaire Democrat-turned-Republican Michael Bloomberg. Neither made much of their Jewish backgrounds, and neither was particularly "ethnic" in manner or speech. But Jews no longer constituted the chief electoral constituency of liberal and leftwing causes or candidates. This is partly explained by demographic changes: With the Jewish population of slightly over a million growing for the first time in half a century, a third of New York Jews identified themselves as

---

27 McNickle, *To Be Mayor of New York*, 257–92; Soffer, *Ed Koch and the Rebuilding of New York City*, 96, *passim*.

28 McNickle, *To Be Mayor of New York*, 293–314; Soffer, *Ed Koch and the Rebuilding of New York City*, 374–87; Edward Shapiro, *Crown Heights: Blacks, Jews, and the 1991 Brooklyn Riot* (Waltham/Hannover: Brandeis University Press / University Press of New England, 2006); "A Portrait of New York City Voters," *New York Times*, November 4, 1993, B6, accessed July 10, 2017.

Orthodox by 2011. Together with the many Soviet Jewish immigrants and their children (the so-called "Russians"), these Jews expressed generally conservative political beliefs. Especially in Brooklyn, these two sub-groups began to wield political clout, electing members of the city council and state legislature. Often these local political leaders were nominal Democrats, but at least one, State Senator Simcha Felder, caucused with the legislature's Republicans. Many supported the candidacy of Donald Trump in the 2016 presidential elections, putting them at odds not only with most of their fellow New Yorkers, but also with most American Jews. In the new century, then, New York Jews were likely to become a conservative, rather than liberal, force.[29]

29 *Jewish Community Study of New York: 2011* (New York: UJA-Federation, 2012), 19, 45, 54, 122–23, 214–17, 226–27; *A Portrait of Jewish Americans* (Washington: Pew Research Center, 2013), 95, 97; Vivian Yee, "Simcha Felder, Rogue Democratic Senator, Will Remain Loyal to G.O.P.," *New York Times,* November 21, 2016, https://www. nytimes.com/2016/11/21/nyregion/simcha-felder-rogue-democratic-senator-will-remain-loyal-to-gop.html, accessed July 10, 2017; "Jewish Caucus," https://council. nyc.gov/caucuses/jewish-caucus/, accessed July 10, 2017; Michelle Young, "Did Your Neighborhood Go Clinton or Trump in the 2016 Presidential Elections," Untapped Cities, November 10, 2016, https://untappedcities.com/2016/11/10/did-your-nyc-neighborhood-vote-for-clinton-or-trump/, accessed July 19, 2018.

For Further Reading

Allen, Oliver. *The Tiger: The Rise and Fall of Tammany Hall*. Reading, MA: Addison-Wesley, 1993.

Antler, Joyce. *The Journey Home: Jewish Women and the American Century*. New York: Free Press, 1997.

Bayor, Ronald. *Neighbors in Conflict: The Irish, Germans, Jews, and Italians of New York, 1929–1941*. Baltimore: Johns Hopkins University Press, 1978.

Cannato, Vincent. *The Ungovernable City: John Lindsay and his Struggle to Save New York*. New York: Basic, 2001.

Cohen, Naomi. *Encounter with Emancipation: The German Jews in the United States, 1830–1914*. Philadelphia: Jewish Publication Society, 1984.

Dorman, Jacob. "Dreams Defended and Deferred: The Brooklyn Schools Crisis of 1968 and Black Power's Influence on Rabbi Meir Kahane." *American Jewish History* 100, no.3 (July 2016): 411–37.

Dubinsky, David, and A. H. Raskin, *David Dubinsky: A Life with Labor*. New York: Simon and Schuster, 1977.

Dubofsky, Melvin. "Success and Failure of Socialism in New York City, 1900–1918: A Case Study." *Labor History* 9, no. 3 (Autumn 1968): 361–75.

Eisenstein, Louis, and Elliot Rosenberg. *A Stripe of Tammany's Tiger*. New York: Robert Speller & Sons, 1966.

Epstein, Melech. *Jewish Labor in USA*, vol. 1: *1882–1914*, reprint ed. New York: Ktav, 1969. Original edition, 1950.

Epstein, Melech. *Profiles of Eleven*. Detroit: Wayne State University Press, 1965.

Feld, Marjorie. *Lillian Wald: A Biography*. Chapel Hill: University of North Carolina Press, 2008.

Forman, Ira. "The Politics of Minority Consciousness." In *Jews in American Politics*, edited by L. Sandy Maisel and Ira N. Forman, 141–60. Lanham, MD: Rowman and Littlefield, 2001.

Flamm, Michael. "'Law and Order' at Large: The New York Civilian Review Board Referendum of 1966 and the Crisis of Liberalism," *Historian* 64, nos. 3–4 (Spring/Summer 2002): 643–65.

Freeman, Joshua. *Working Class New York: Life and Labor since World War II*. New York: Free Press, 2000.

Fuchs, Lawrence, *The Political Behavior of American Jews*. Glencoe, IL: Free Press, 1956.

Gerson, Jeffrey. "Building the Brooklyn Machine: Irish, Jewish and Black Political Succession in Central Brooklyn, 1919–1964." PhD diss., City University of New York, 1990.

Gilfoyle, Timothy. *City of Eros: New York City, Prostitution, and the Commercialization of Sex, 1790–1920.* New York: Norton, 1992.

Glazer, Nathan, and Daniel Moynihan. *Beyond the Melting Pot: The Negroes, Puerto Ricans, Jews, Italians, and Irish of New York City,* 2nd ed. Cambridge: MIT Press, 1970. Original edition, 1963.

Greenwald, Richard. *The Triangle Fire, the Protocols of Peace, and Industrial Democracy in Progressive Era New York.* Philadelphia: Temple University Press, 2005.

Goldberg, Gordon. *Meyer London: A Biography of the Socialist New York Congressman, 1871–1926.* Jefferson, NC: McFarland, 2013.

Goren, Arthur. *The Politics and Public Culture of American Jews.* Bloomington: Indiana University Press, 1999.

Hammack, David. *Power and Society: Greater New York at the Turn of the Century,* reprint ed. New York: Columbia University Press, 1987. Original edition, 1982.

Henderson, Thomas. *Tammany Hall and the New Immigrants: The Progressive Years.* New York: Arno, 1976.

Holtzman, Elizabeth. *Who Said It Would Be Easy? One Woman's Life in the Political Arena.* New York: Arcade, 1996.

Howe, Irving. *World of Our Fathers.* New York: Harcourt Brace Jovanovich, 1976.

Ingalls, Robert. *Herbert H. Lehman and New York's Little New Deal.* New York: NYU Press, 1975.

Josephson, Matthew, and Hannah Josephson. *Al Smith: Hero of the Cities: A Political Portrait Drawing on the Papers of Frances Perkins.* Boston: Houghton Mifflin, 1969.

Kessner, Thomas. *Fiorello H. La Guardia and the Making of Modern New York,* 2nd ed. New York: Penguin, 1991. Original edition, 1989.

Kosak, Hadassa. *Cultures of Opposition: Jewish Immigrant Workers in New York City, 1881-1905.* Albany: SUNY Press, 2000.

Landesman, Alter. *Brownsville: The Birth, Development and Passing of a Jewish Community in New York.* New York: Bloch, 1971.

Lederhendler, Eli. *New York Jews and the Decline of Urban Ethnicity, 1950-1970.* Syracuse: Syracuse University Press, 2001.

Lerner, Elinor. "Jewish Involvement in the New York City Woman Suffrage Movement." *American Jewish History* 70, no. 4 (June 1981): 442–61.

Levine, Suzanne Braun, and Mary Thom. *Bella Abzug.* New York: Farrar, Straus and Giroux, 2007.

Levy, Alan. *The Political Life of Bella Abzug, 1920-1970: Political Passions, Women's Rights, and Congressional Battles.* Lanham, MD: Lexington Books, 2013.

Link, Daniel. "'Every Day Was a Battle': Liberal Anticommunism in Cold War New York, 1944–1956." PhD diss., New York University, 2006.

Maisel, L. Sandy, and Ira N. Forman. *Jews in American Politics.* Lanham, MD: Rowman and Littlefield, 2001.

Mann, Arthur. *La Guardia: Fighter against His Times, 1882–1933.* Philadelphia: J. B. Lippincott, 1959.

———. *La Guardia Comes to Power, 1933.* Philadelphia: J. B. Lippincott, 1965.

Markowitz, Ruth Jacknow. *My Daughter, the Teacher: Jewish Teachers in the New York City Schools.* New Brunswick: Rutgers University Press, 1993.

Marcus, Jacob Rader. *United States Jewry 1776–1985*, vol. 3. Detroit: Wayne State University Press, 1993.

McGuire, Thomas John. "From Socialism to Social Justice Feminism: Rose Schneiderman and the Quest for Urban Equity, 1911–1933." *Journal of Urban History* 35, no. 7 (November 2009): 998–1019.

McNickle, Chris. *To Be Mayor of New York: Ethnic Politics in the City.* New York: Columbia University Press, 1993.

Michaels, Tony. *Fire in their Hearts: Yiddish Socialists in New York.* Cambridge, MA: Harvard University Press, 2005.

Monson, Sara S. "The Lady and the Tiger: Women's Electoral Activism in New York before Suffrage." *Journal of Women's History* 2, no. 2 (Fall 1990): 100–134.

Moore, Deborah Dash. *At Home in America: Second Generation New York Jews.* New York: Columbia University Press, 1981.

Moscow, Warren. *What Have You Done for Me Lately? The Ins and Outs of New York City Politics.* New York: Prentice Hall, 1967.

Nevins, Allan. *Herbert H. Lehman and His Era.* New York: Scribner's, 1963.

Orleck, Annelise. *Common Sense and a Little Fire: Women and Working-Class Politics in the Unites States, 1900–1965.* Chapel Hill: University of North Carolina Press, 1995.

Parmet, Robert. *Master of Seventh Avenue: David Dubinsky and the American Labor Movement.* New York: NYU Press, 2005.

Perry, Elizabeth Israels. *Belle Moskowitz: Feminine Politics and the Exercise of Power in the Age of Al Smith*, 2nd ed. Boston: Northeastern University Press, 1992. Original edition, 1987.

Phillips-Fein, Kim. *Fear City: New York's Fiscal Crisis and the Rise of Austerity Politics.* New York: Metropolitan and Henry Holt, 2017.

Podair, Jerald. *The Strike that Changed New York: Blacks, Whites and the Ocean Hill-Brownsville Crisis.* New Haven: Yale University Press, 2002.

Pratt, Norma Fain. *Morris Hillquit: A Political History of an American Jewish Socialist.* Westport, CT: Greenwood, 1979.

Pritchett, Wendell. *Brownsville, Brooklyn: Blacks, Jews, and the Changing Face of the Ghetto.* Chicago: University of Chicago Press, 2002.

Ribak, Gil. "'For Peace, Not Socialism': The 1917 Mayoralty Campaign in New York City and Immigrant Jews in a Global Perspective." *American Jewish History* 101, no. 4 (2017): 465–88.

Rieder, Jonathan. *Canarsie: The Jews and Italians of Brooklyn against Liberalism.* Cambridge, MA: Harvard University Press, 1985.

Rischin, Moses. *Promised City: New York's Jews, 1870–1914.* Cambridge, MA: Harvard University Press, 1962.

Rogoff, Harry. *An East Side Epic: The Life and Work of Meyer London.* New York: Vanguard Press, 1930.

Schwartz, Joel. "The Triumph of Liberalism (1914–1945)." In *The Empire State: A History of New York*, edited by Milton Klein, 517–620. Ithaca: Cornell University Press, 2001.

Shapiro, Edward. *Crown Heights: Blacks, Jews, and the 1991 Brooklyn Riot.* Waltham/Hannover: Brandeis University Press / University Press of New England, 2006.

Shefter, Martin. *Political Crisis, Fiscal Crisis: The Collapse and Revival of New York City*, 2nd ed. New York: Columbia University Press, 1992. Original edition, 1985.

Silver, Arthur. "Jews in the Political Life of New York City, 1865–1897." DHL diss., Yeshiva University, 1954.

Slayton, Robert A. *Empire Statesman: The Rise and Redemption of Al Smith.* New York: Free Press, 2001.

Soffer, Jonathan. *Ed Koch and the Rebuilding of New York City.* New York: Columbia University Press, 2010.

Stein, Leon. *The Triangle Fire.* Philadelphia: J. B. Lippincott, 1962.

Taffet, Jeffrey. "The Snubs and the 'Sukkah': John Lindsay and Jewish Voters in New York City." *American Jewish History* 97, no. 4 (October 2013): 413–38.

Tananbaum, Duane. *Herbert H. Lehman: A Political Biography.* Albany: SUNY Press, 2016.

Von Drehle, David. *Triangle: The Fire that Changed America.* New York: Atlantic Monthly Press, 2003.

Waltzer, Kenneth. "The American Labor Party: Third Party Politics in New Deal/Cold War New York, 1936–1954." PhD diss., Harvard University, 1977.

Wenger, Beth. *New York Jews and the Great Depression: Uncertain Promise.* New Haven: Yale University Press, 1996.

Werner, Morris. *Tammany Hall.* Garden City, NY: Doubleday, Doran, 1928.

Williams, Mason. *City of Ambition: FDR, La Guardia, and the Making of Modern New York.* New York: W. W. Norton, 2013.

Wishnoff, Daniel. "The Tolerance Point: Race, Public Housing and the Forest Hills Controversy, 1945–1975." PhD diss., CUNY, 2005.

Zeitz, Joshua. *White Ethnic New York: Jews, Catholics, and the Shaping of Postwar Politics.* Chapel Hill: University of North Carolina Press, 2007.

Chapter 13

How Are New York City Jews Different from Other American Jews?

Steven M. Cohen

New York City Jewry: Numerous and Diverse

For over a century, the City of New York has been home to the largest Jewish population of any city in the world. With a Jewish population estimated in at 1.1 million in 2011,[1] up from 970,000 in 2002,[2] the city is home to enormous numbers of Jews of various social identities. For New York City, the data set from the Jewish Community Study of 2011 puts the number of Orthodox adults and children at 440,000, of whom 320,000 were Haredi (so-called "ultra-Orthodox"). The Conservative and Reform Jewish populations in the City totaled 150,000 each. It also found over 170,000 Jews living in Russian-speaking households, along with almost 100,000 in households where at least one adult is Israeli-born. The same study also

---

1   Steven Cohen, Jacob Ukeles, Ron Miller, "Comprehensive Report," *Jewish Community Study of New York: 2011* (New York: UJA-Federation of New York, 2012), https://www.bjpa.org/search-results/publication/14186. Calculations reported here refer to the five boroughs of New York City, while the published report generally encompasses Westchester, Nassau, and Suffolk counties as well.
2   Jacob Ukeles and Ron Miller, *The Jewish Community Study of New York: 2002* (UJA-Federation of New York, 2004), https://www.bjpa.org/search-results/publication/671.

found that over 120,000 Jews lived in homes where at least one member was bi-racial, Hispanic or non-white. Over 160,000 Jews live in Sephardi households in the five boroughs, and over 30,000 of these are in Syrian households. Clearly the Jewish population of Bronx, Brooklyn, Manhattan, Queens and Staten Island is not only large, but in these and so many other ways, highly diverse.

While the diversity of the City's Jewish population has been thoroughly established and well-appreciated in a number of Jewish population studies dating back decades (most recently in 1981, 1991, 2002, and 2011),[3] we have yet to see a systematic comparison of New York area Jews with those in other parts of the nation—the objective of this chapter. More specifically, how does New York City Jewry differ from American Jewry as a whole in terms of socio-demographic and Jewish identity characteristics? Since distinctions can best be understand and appreciated in context, comparing NYC Jews with an appropriate US comparison group can help illuminate the features that set NYC Jewry apart from others.

The Data: Pew "Portrait of Jewish Americans"

To undertake this task, we turn to the data set assembled by the Pew Research Center in its 2013 study entitled, "Portrait of Jewish Americans."[4] The data set holds numerous advantages for the comparative enterprise. First, it consists of 3,475 respondents from across the country. Of these are 926 residents of New York's five boroughs, of whom 726 are non-Haredi, comprising the key New York group for comparison purposes.

Unweighted number of Pew survey respondents in New York City and elsewhere, Haredi and others

	United States, not New York City	New York City	Total
Haredi	130	190	320
Others	2429	726	3155
Total	2559	916	3475

---

3   See the Berman Jewish Data Bank, http://www.jewishdatabank.org/.
4   *A Portrait of Jewish Americans: Findings from a Pew Research Center Survey of U.S. Jews* (Washington, DC: Pew Research Center, 2013), http://assets.pewresearch.org/wp-content/uploads/sites/11/2013/10/jewish-american-full-report-for-web.pdf.

Number of adult Jews in New York City and elsewhere, Haredi and others			
	United States, not New York City	New York City	Total
Haredi	164,000	146,000	310,000
Others	4,411,000	519,000	4,930,000
Total	4,575,000	665,000	5,240,000

Another advantage of the Pew survey is its uniformity. Quite simply, the same team of interviewers asked the same questions of all respondents, and used the same methodology to sample Jews in New York as in the rest of the country. The uniformity of questions and sampling overcomes a key drawback entailed in another quite valid approach to comparative research—using several recent Jewish community studies to compare New York with other communities. While undoubtedly of value, such an enterprise is complicated by variations in questionnaires, sampling, researchers, interviewing teams, and time.

Comparing New York City with US Jews—No Haredim, Not the West

One way to make the comparisons would be (or would have been) to simply divide between NYC residents and those everywhere else. The comparison would show fairly large gaps in Jewish engagement between the more Jewishly committed New Yorkers and the more assimilated (may we still use that term?) American Jewish population everywhere else. For example, NYC Jews differ widely from other American Jews on such items as identifying as Orthodox (32% vs. 6%), having mostly Jewish friends (61% vs. 29%), fasting on Yom Kippur (73% vs. 53%), and usually lighting Shabbat candles (45% vs. 20%).

But such a comparison would be, in some ways, misleading, or at least not as interesting or informative as it could be. One reason is that, among adults, the NYC population contains over five times more Haredi Jews, proportionately, than the rest of the United States: 22% in New York vs. 4% of those elsewhere (including the children and not just the adults, these numbers would be higher). Hence any comparisons of NYC Jewry with those in the rest of America would provoke the question: Well, how much of those gaps are due to the Haredim? What would happen if we set aside the many Haredim in New York City and the few everywhere else?

As for the comparison group—Jews in the United States outside of New York City—the regional variation poses another complication. Of the four major regions of the country, the West (mountain and Pacific states) displays far lower levels of Jewish engagement than the other three (East, South, Midwest). Hence the more interesting comparisons are between Jews in New York and Jews in the rest of the United States, excluding the West, a region which so clearly differs from all the rest and New York as well. Hence, the comparison tables below present the West as a separate column.

The specific question most centrally addressed in the analysis below is this: Setting aside the Haredim, be they in New York or the rest of America, how do NYC area Jews compare with other American Jews, in all regions combined, excluding the West?

In the tables below, we compare these two groups on key socio-demographic and Jewish identity characteristics, but also present results for the West, the Haredim throughout the country, and totals for the country as a whole. (On Jewish identity variables in the Pew study, Haredim in New York City and else report very similar results.)

By way of preliminary background, the following table presents the distribution of Jewish adults in the relevant areas:

Number of Jewish Adults by Area and Haredi Status

	Frequency	Percent
New York City, non-Haredi	518,880	10%
East, South, and Midwest, non-Haredi	3,227,566	62%
West, non-Haredi	1,183,338	23%
US Haredi	310,063	6%
Total	5,239,846	100%

Findings: NYC Jews vs. US Jews

Socio-demographic Characteristics

More Seniors in New York City:

New York Jewry is distinguished by a larger number of older adults than elsewhere. 28% of non-Haredi NY Jewish adults are over the age of sixty-five as opposed to 23% elsewhere. (In the course of reporting on comparisons, where the narrative says "elsewhere" or "the United States" it generally refers to non-Haredi Jews living in the Midwest, South and East, but not the five boroughs of New York; "New York" should be read as "New

York City.") The older New York population may well reflect the long-term out-migration of younger adults from New York to other parts of the country, particularly the West.

Age distributions for New York City and elsewhere

Age	New York City, non-Haredi	East, South, and Midwest, non-Haredi	West, non-Haredi	US Haredi	Total
65+	28%	23%	17%	5%	21%
50–64	24%	31%	35%	17%	31%
40–49	12%	12%	19%	16%	14%
30–39	18%	13%	11%	31%	14%
18–29	19%	21%	19%	32%	21%
Total	100%	100%	100%	100%	100%

Notably, the Haredim are much younger than the Jews of the United States generally. Of Haredi adults, 62% are 18–39 vs. 35% of all American Jews including Haredim. The inclusion of Haredim in the New York population would have projected a much younger profile, and obscured the higher number of seniors relative to other parts of the country.

Large FSU Population in NY:

New York Jewry is distinguished by the very large presence of emigres from the Former Soviet Union. Of non-Haredi NY Jewry, over a fifth (22%) are FSU-born vs. just 4% elsewhere, and 5% among all American Jews, including New York and the Haredim.

Geographic region in which respondent was born, New York City and elsewhere

	New York City, non-Haredi	East, South, and Midwest, non-Haredi	West, non-Haredi	US Haredi	Total
United States (native born)	71%	88%	88%	85%	86%
Americas (excluding United States)	2%	2%	2%	3%	2%
Asia/Pacific (except FSU)	1%	1%	2%	0%	1%

Contd.

Europe (except FSU)	3%	3%	3%	5%	3%
Middle East / North Africa (except Israel/ Palestine)	0%	0%	0%	0%	0%
Sub-Saharan Africa	0%	0%	1%	1%	0%
Former Soviet Union (FSU)	22%	4%	2%	3%	5%
Israel/Palestine	1%	2%	2%	4%	2%
Total	100%	100%	100%	100%	100%

Note that all numbers in a random sample survey are subject to sampling variation and small numbers are especially prone to appear inaccurate. The Jewish Community Study of New York 2013 reports that 3% of adults in Jewish households were born in Israel and 0.4% were born in other Middle Eastern countries.

Equally Educated:

Jewish New Yorkers' educational attainment is remarkably similar to that of Jews elsewhere, with almost a third reporting a post-graduate degree and almost two thirds having earned a BA or more. Their educational attainment do slightly exceed that of Jews in the West.

Again, the Haredim look very different. As compared with New York area Jews, only a third as many have a post-graduate degree and more than twice as many never went beyond high school. Their inclusion in the New York distributions would add significantly those with lower levels of educational attainment.

Educational attainment for New York and elsewhere

	New York City, non-Haredi	East, South, and Midwest, non-Haredi	West, non-Haredi	US Haredi	Total
Post-grad degree	31%	30%	26%	10%	28%
BA/BS	34%	32%	28%	15%	30%
Some college	20%	24%	29%	36%	25%
HS or less	16%	15%	17%	38%	17%
Total	100%	100%	100%	100%	100%

More Poor New Yorkers:

In large measure, the income distribution of New Yorkers largely resembles that of other non-Haredi American Jews. The one noticeable deviation is with respect to the number earning under $30,000 annually. In New York City, we find 28% as compared with 19% elsewhere. The Poverty Report of the Jewish Community Study of New York detailed significant number of New York area Jews living at or near poverty, and that poverty was not only the province of the Haredim—as is widely believed—but afflicts a variety of New York area Jews, among them older Russian-speaking Jews. The bump in very low-income Jews here should be seen as consistent with the extent of financially hard-pressed Jews reported in earlier research.[5]

Income distribution for New York and elsewhere

LT	New York City, non-Haredi	East, South, and Midwest, non-Haredi	West, non-Haredi	US Haredi	Total
$150,000+	23%	26%	25%	24%	25%
$100–$150,000	17%	18%	16%	14%	17%
$75–$100,000	9%	14%	16%	7%	14%
$50–$75,000	14%	13%	9%	13%	12%
$30–$50,000	10%	10%	15%	17%	12%
$30,000	28%	19%	20%	26%	20%
Total	100%	100%	100%	100%	100%

Fewer Are Married:

As compared with American Jews elsewhere, fewer New York City Jews are married (44% vs. 52% in regions other than the West). Proportionately more New Yorkers are widowed, in line with their more numerous seniors, and more have never been married. The inclusion of the Haredim

5   Jacob Ukeles, Ron Miller, and Steven Cohen, "Special Report on Poverty," *Jewish Community Study of New York: 2011* (New York: UJA-Federation of New York, 2013), https://www.bjpa.org/search-results/publication/16652. See also idem, "3. People in Need and Access to Support," *Jewish Community Study of New York: 2011* (New York: UJA-Federation of New York, 2012), https://www.bjpa.org/search-results/publication/14210; and Jacob Ukeles, *Economic Vulnerability and Jewish Continuity in New York's Jewish Community* (New York: Hebrew Free Loan Society, 1998), 1-15, https://www.bjpa.org/search-results/publication/21460.

in the comparisons would have obscured the marriage gap between New York City and elsewhere as a very large number of Haredi adults (80%) are married.

Marital status for New Yorkers and Jews elsewhere

	New York City, non-Haredi	East, South, and Midwest, non-Haredi	West, non-Haredi	US Haredi	Total
Married	44%	52%	43%	80%	51%
Living with a partner	8%	6%	11%	1%	7%
Divorced	6%	9%	15%	3%	9%
Separated	2%	1%	2%		1%
Widowed	11%	7%	4%	1%	7%
Never been married	29%	25%	25%	15%	25%
Total	100%	100%	100%	100%	100%

Politically Liberal and Democratic, in New York City and the United States:

Surveys have repeatedly demonstrated the liberal and Democratic party inclinations of American Jews.[6] Like their counterparts elsewhere, non-Haredi New York City Jews are far more liberal than conservative, and they are far more Democratic than Republican in terms of party identification. In fact, the ratio of politically left to politically right identification is almost three to one. The difference between New Yorkers and the others, if there is any, is in a very slightly rightward direction among the New Yorkers, although the political gap is far greater with the Jews of the West than those elsewhere in the United States.

As one might expect, the Haredim are far more right-wing, with large numbers of Republicans (41% vs. 16% among other NY Jews). Their presence in the NY population, then, makes New York City the most Republican and most politically conservative large Jewish community in the United States, even as non-Haredi NY Jews are only slightly to the right of other American Jews.

---

6   See, for example, *A Portrait of Jewish Americans*, chap. 6: "Social and Political Views," Pew Research Center, October 1, 2013, http://www.pewforum.org/2013/10/01/chapter-6-social-and-political-views/.

Party identification in New York and elsewhere

	New York City, non-Haredi	East, South, and Midwest, non-Haredi	West, non-Haredi	US Haredi	Total
Republican	16%	11%	11%	40%	13%
Democrat	49%	57%	61%	17%	55%
Independent	28%	29%	23%	35%	28%
(VOL) No preference	3%	1%	2%	4%	2%
(VOL) Other party	0%	1%	1%	0%	1%
(VOL) Don't Know / Refused	3%	1%	2%	3%	2%
Total	100%	100%	100%	100%	100%

"In general, would you describe your political views as . . ." for New York City and elsewhere

	New York City, non-Haredi	East, South, and Midwest, non-Haredi	West, non-Haredi	US Haredi	Total
Very conservative	2%	3%	4%	13%	4%
Conservative	17%	14%	11%	57%	16%
Moderate	30%	31%	27%	24%	30%
Liberal	34%	35%	28%	6%	32%
Very liberal	17%	17%	29%	0%	19%
Total	100%	100%	100%	100%	100%

Jewish Engagement

Very High Parental In-Marriage among the New Yorkers:

The survey asked respondents whether each of their parents regarded themselves as Jewish, allowing the analysis to differentiate the number of respondents' parents who were Jewish. Since all the respondents are currently Jewish, those with no Jewish parents effectively converted to Judaism, either with a rabbi or by personal choice, that is, deciding to identify as Jewish without rabbinic ceremony.[7] Those with one Jewish parent are the

---

7   Steven M. Cohen. "Rabbinical vs. Personal Converts to Judaism: What's the Difference?," *Jerusalem Post*, November 16, 2016, https://www.jpost.com/Opinion/Rabbinical-vs-personal-converts-to-Judaism-Whats-the-difference-472829.

Jewish-identifying adult children of intermarried couples, and those with two Jewish parents are the adult children of in-married couples.

In terms of the number of converts, rabbinic or otherwise, the small proportions in New York and elsewhere are roughly equivalent. While the numbers of converts are very small, the small differences between regions are consistent with the much larger rates of intermarriage. Both rates of intermarriage and converts in the population are lowest in New York, highest in the West, and in between New York and the West for the rest of the country. To be sure, the statistical basis for inference for the following claim here is weak—very weak. But the data do suggest that at least ecologically, more intermarriage is associated with more conversion.

The major—and almost stunning—difference in these data centers on the balance between inmarried and intermarried parents. For New York, the inmarried out-number the intermarried by almost 8:1; elsewhere in America, the ratio stands at roughly 5:2. In other words, at least in the last generation, inmarriage was far more frequent in New York than elsewhere—and this is without including the Haredi population who report near universal inmarriage among their parents.

Number of parents who were Jewish in New York and elsewhere				
	East, South,			
New York City,	and Midwest,	West,	US	
non-Haredi	non-Haredi	non-Haredi	Haredi	Total
Both parents were 86%	69%	65%	99%	71%
Jewish				
One parent was Jewish 11%	28%	30%	0%	25%
Neither was Jewish 3%	4%	5%	1%	4%
Total 100%	100%	100%	100%	100%

More New Yorkers Went to Day Schools or No Schools:

The Jewish schooling patterns display some intriguing differences between New York and rest of America, aside from the West. On the one hand, more New York area Jews than elsewhere report having received no Jewish schooling. At the same time, somewhat more New Yorkers attended Jewish day schools for three years or more (and to underscore, these figures exclude the Haredim).

Different reasons, undoubtedly, account for the relatively large number of Jewish New Yorkers at both ends of the Jewish schooling spectrum (day schools and no schools). Underlying the large number with no Jewish schooling is the large number who were born in the Former Soviet Union, where Jewish schooling was largely unavailable.

The relatively large day-school population (about a third of New York Jews who went to a Jewish school vs. about a fifth elsewhere) can be attributed both to the higher rates of parental inmarriage seen above as well as to the larger presence of Orthodoxy in New York (see immediately below), even after we have set aside Haredim from the calculations.

	New York City, non-Haredi	East, South, and Midwest, non-Haredi	West, non-Haredi	US Haredi	Total
Day school 3+ years	21%	15%	17%	82%	21%
Religious school 7+ years	17%	31%	19%	3%	25%
Religious school 1–6 years	25%	33%	34%	2%	30%
None	38%	22%	29%	13%	25%
Total	100%	100%	100%	100%	100%

Jewish schooling in childhood for New York and elsewhere

Denominational Upbringing:

Consistent with the schooling patterns, we observe two ways in which New York non-Haredi Jews differ with their counterparts in the East, South, and Midwest. On the one hand, about twice as many New Yorkers were raised Orthodox. On the other, far more than elsewhere, New Yorkers report having had no denominational upbringing or, as we saw, any Jewish schooling. Again, as with schooling, the same considerations apply to the relatively larger number of people located in the most and least traditional ends of the spectrum.

In New York City, Much More Orthodox, Much Less Reform:

New York Jews, even when we exclude the Haredim, look denominationally much different from those in the United States, excluding the Western states. In particular, about five times as many New Yorkers as those in the East, Midwest and South are Orthodox; far fewer New Yorkers are Reform; and somewhat fewer of them are Conservative; with the no denomination group among New Yorkers exceeding the level found elsewhere (but not the West).

Denomination raised for New York and elsewhere

	New York City, non-Haredi	East, South, and Midwest, non-Haredi	West, non-Haredi	US Haredi	Total
Orthodox raised, parents inmarried*	16%	8%	10%	80%	14%
Conservative raised, some Jewish schooling	20%	31%	24%	14%	27%
Reform raised, some Jewish schooling	21%	33%	28%	1%	28%
Other or no denomination, or no Jewish schooling	43%	29%	39%	5%	31%
Total	100%	100%	100%	100%	100%

* Qualifying criteria were applied to the answers on denomination raised. Those who called their upbringing Orthodox and yet reported that only one parent was Jewish—an intermarriage—were re-classified as "other denomination." So too were those raised Conservative or Reform who reported having received no Jewish schooling.

Denomination now for New York and elsewhere

	New York City, non-Haredi	East, South, and Midwest, non-Haredi	West, non-Haredi	US Haredi	Total
Orthodox	13%	3%	1%	100%	9%
Conservative	16%	22%	15%	0%	18%
Reform	28%	42%	36%	0%	37%
Other	42%	34%	48%	0%	36%
Total	100%	100%	100%	100%	100%

More Jewish Spouses and Friends:

Far more than other American Jews, New York City Jews are married to other Jews and report that more of their close friends are Jewish. Of those who are married, 28% of New York non-Haredi Jews are intermarried vs. 45% in the East, Midwest and South, and 60% of Jews in the West. No Haredim are intermarried.

Not only do more New Yorkers report Jewish spouses, more also report Jewish friends. Half report having mostly Jewish close friends, almost double the number reported in the East, South and Midwest, and triple the number in the West. In contrast, almost all Haredim report having mostly Jewish friends and almost half say that all of their close friends are Jewish.

The strong Jewish social networks in New York reflect both the size of the Jewish population and its concomitant residential density, as well as its character, in particular, the large number of Orthodox and FSU Jews. In addition, the large extent to which New York City Jews maintain marital and friendship ties with other Jews undergirds the several ways in which the Jews of New York City surpass Jews in other parts of America in terms of many indicators of Jewish engagement, as we shall see presently.

Intermarriage rates for New York and elsewhere

New York City, non-Haredi	East, South, and Midwest, non-Haredi	West, non-Haredi	US Haredi	Total
28%	45%	60%	0%	42%

Number of close friends who are Jewish, New York and elsewhere

	New York City, non-Haredi	East, South, and Midwest, non-Haredi	West, non-Haredi	US Haredi	Total
All of them	8%	2%	2%	45%	6%
Most of them	42%	26%	15%	53%	27%
Some of them	44%	49%	50%	2%	46%
Hardly any of them	5%	19%	31%	0%	20%
(VOL) None of them	1%	3%	1%	0%	2%
Total	100%	100%	100%	100%	100%

More Jewishly Engaged, in All Ways:

To compare the Jewish engagement of New Yorkers with Jews elsewhere, I selected sixteen of the many Jewish engagement indicators for tabulation. In all but two of the cases, the levels for New York City Jews (without Haredim) exceed their counterpart in the East, Midwest and South. The differences are even larger with Jews in the West.

In comparison with the non-West Jews in the United States, the leads of New York Jews are the largest with respect to lighting Shabbat candles (30% vs. 16%), and for maintaining a kosher home (30% vs. 19%). In these areas, the gaps are in part due to the larger Orthodox population in New York.

The very sizeable gaps in abstaining from having a Christmas tree (80% vs. 66%) should also be seen as deriving from an aspect of population composition reported earlier: far fewer intermarried Jews in New York than elsewhere.

We find other substantial gaps with respect to feeling that being Jewish is very important (53% vs. 44%), and fasting Yom Kippur (65% vs. 54%). Only with respect to synagogue and Jewish organizational belonging do we find the New Yorkers slightly trailing the non-West United States (28% vs. 30% and 26% vs. 29% respectively), possibly reflecting the lesser need to formally affiliate with Jewish institutions in an environment with higher Jewish residential density and stronger Jewish social networks.

Indicators of Jewish engagement, New York and elsewhere

	New York City, non-Haredi	East, South, and Midwest, non-Haredi	West, non-Haredi	US Haredi	Total
Feels proud to be Jewish	94%	94%	92%	100%	94%
Jewish people belonging	80%	74%	70%	99%	75%
Jews in need	67%	63%	52%	96%	63%
Important being Jewish	53%	44%	38%	89%	46%
God belief	71%	71%	67%	99%	72%
Seder attended	79%	69%	59%	99%	70%
Fasted Yom Kippur	65%	54%	43%	100%	55%
Attend High Holiday services	62%	58%	48%	99%	59%
No Christmas tree	80%	66%	58%	100%	68%
Shabbat candles lit usually	30%	16%	17%	100%	23%
Kosher home	30%	19%	14%	99%	24%
Attends syn monthly	26%	21%	15%	72%	23%
Synagogue member	28%	30%	24%	68%	31%
Jewish organization member	26%	29%	20%	52%	28%
Donor to a Jewish charity	65%	57%	42%	97%	57%
Israel, very attached	36%	29%	24%	56%	31%

* Question wording (basic stems):

I am proud to be Jewish.

I have a strong sense of belonging to the Jewish people.

I have a special responsibility to take care of Jews in need around the world.

How important is being Jewish in your life—very important, somewhat
important, not too important, or not at all important?

Do you believe in God or a universal spirit, or not?

Last Passover, did you hold or attend a seder, or not?

During the last Yom Kippur, did you fast?

Aside from special occasions like weddings, funerals and bar mitzvahs, how
often do you attend Jewish religious services at a synagogue, temple, minyan,
or havurah?

Last Christmas, did your household have a Christmas tree, or not?

How often, if at all, does anyone in your household light Sabbath candles on
Friday night?

Do you keep kosher in your home, or not?

Ask if someone is member of synagogue/temple: And is that you or someone
else in your household?

In 2012, did you make a financial donation to any Jewish charity or cause,
such as a synagogue, Jewish school, or a group supporting Israel?

How emotionally attached are you to Israel?

More Israel Travel:

In addition to being more emotionally attached to Israel, New York Jews
are more likely to have traveled to Israel—54% have done so vs. 42% among
non-Haredi Jews in the East, Midwest and South, and as few as 34% in the
West. The contrasts in the number who have visited twice or more or have
lived there among the non-Israeli born are perhaps even more impressive:
30% for the New Yorkers, 20% in the non-West United States, and 17% in
the West. As we would expect, Haredi visits to Israel are even more extensive and frequent that among non-Haredi New York Jews.

	Number of Israel visits, New York and elsewhere				
	New York City, non-Haredi	East, South, and Midwest, non-Haredi	West, non-Haredi	US Haredi	Total
Israel-born	1%	2%	2%	4%	2%
Twice or more or lived there	30%	20%	17%	58%	22%
Once	23%	20%	15%	14%	19%
Never visited Israel	46%	58%	67%	25%	57%
Total	100%	100%	100%	100%	100%

Children in New York More Often Raised as Jews:

Children of New York Jews are far more often raised as Jews. The Pew survey asked respondents with children to choose from among a variety of options to express how their children are being raised. The option associated with the highest levels of Jewish engagement in the home is, "Jewish by religion." For the oldest child, we find very large gaps when comparing New York City Jews, with those from the East, South and Midwest and with those from the West: 77%, 51%, 40% respectively. Correlatively, outside New York, about four times as many firstborn children are being raised as non-Jews (24%) as in New York (6%). The major driver here is the far lower intermarriage rate in the New York City area.

Childrearing as Jewish or not for New York and elsewhere

	New York City, non-Haredi	East, South, and Midwest, non-Haredi	West, non-Haredi	US Haredi	Total
Jewish by religion	77%	51%	40%	100%	59%
Partly Jewish by religion	12%	16%	25%	0%	15%
Jewish but NOT by religion	5%	9%	9%	0%	8%
Not Jewish	6%	24%	26%	0%	19%
Total	100%	100%	100%	100%	100%

In addition to raising their children as Jewish-by-religion more often than elsewhere, New York Jewish parents are far more likely to send their children to day school. Almost a third of non-Haredi children of Jewish parents in New York had enrolled in Jewish day schools as compared with far fewer (13%) in the East, South, and Midwest.

Child(ren)'s Jewish school, for children age 6–17 in New York City and elsewhere

	New York City, non-Haredi	East, South, and Midwest, non-Haredi	West, non-Haredi	US Haredi	Total
Day school	32%	13%	16%	97%	27%
Religious school	21%	29%	16%	1%	22%
None	47%	58%	68%	3%	51%
Total	100%	100%	100%	100%	100%

Conclusion

The Jews of New York City—even when we set aside the Haredim for comparison purposes—both resemble and depart from Jews elsewhere. When compared with Jews in the United States, excluding the West with its far lower levels of Jewish engagement, the Jews of New York display fairly similar socio-demographic patterns. We do see slight differences, though. They're a bit older, poorer, and single. Probably the most notable variation is with respect to the large number of FSU-origin Jews in New York.

New York Jews, again even with the Haredim excluded, tilt a little to the right of the rest of largely liberal and Democratic American Jewry.

Driving a good number of the other findings, with respect to Jewish identity indicators, is the much higher rate of inmarriage among New York Jewry—both in the parents' and the current generation. Jews in New York are surrounded by large numbers of fellow Jews, influencing their family circles and friendship networks. New York is also distinguished by its large concentrations of Modern Orthodox Jews who complement and interact with the even larger numbers of Haredi Orthodox Jews.

The inmarriage and the Orthodox segments serve to support higher levels of Jewish engagement in New York relative to the rest of the country, and especially so with regard to the Western United States with its far lower levels of Jewish engagement. Commensurate with all this, New Yorkers exhibit greater attachment to and travel to Israel. And they are far more likely to raise their children as Jews and send them to day school as well.

Of course, all of these observations pertain to the 1.1 million Jews of New York in their entirety. At the same time, we need to recall the huge variations across several dimensions of social differentiation, particularly religio-ethnic ideology, geography, and social class.

For Further Reading

Cohen, Steven, Jacob Ukeles, and Ron Miller. "Comprehensive Report." *Jewish Community Study of New York: 2011*. New York: UJA-Federation of New York, 2012. https://www.bjpa.org/search-results/publication/14186.

Miller, Ron, Jacob Ukeles, and Steven Cohen. "3. People in Need and Access to Support." *Jewish Community Study of New York: 2011*. New York: UJA-Federation of New York, 2012. https://www.bjpa.org/search-results/publication/14210.

Portrait of Jewish Americans Findings from a Pew Research Center Survey of U.S. Jews. Washington, DC: Pew Research Center, 2013. http://assets.pewresearch.org/wp-content/uploads/sites/11/2013/10/jewish-american-full-report-for-web.pdf.

Ukeles, Jacob, and Ron Miller. *The Jewish Community Study of New York: 2002*. UJA-Federation of New York, 2004. https://www.bjpa.org/search-results/publication/671.

Ukeles, Jacob. *Economic Vulnerability and Jewish Continuity in New York's Jewish Community*. New York: Hebrew Free Loan Society, 1998. https://www.bjpa.org/search-results/publication/21460.

Ukeles, Jacob, Ron Miller, and Steven Cohen. "Special Report on Poverty." *Jewish Community Study of New York: 2011*. New York: UJA-Federation of New York, 2013. https://www.bjpa.org/search-results/publication/16652.

Contributors

Gur Alroey is professor in the Department of Israel studies at the University of Haifa. He is also the author of *Bread to Eat and Clothes to Wear: Letters from Jewish Migrants in the Early Twentieth Century* (Detroit: Wayne State University Press, 2011); *An Unpromising Land: Jewish Migration to Palestine in the Early Twentieth Century* (Stanford: Stanford University Press, 2014); and *Zionism without Zion: Jewish Territorial Organization and Its Conflict with the Zionist Organization* (Detroit: Wayne State University Press, 2016).

Tobias Brinkmann is the Malvin and Lea Bank associate professor of Jewish studies and history at Penn State University. He is completing a monograph about Jewish migration from Eastern Europe after 1860. He is the author of *Sundays at Sinai: A Jewish Congregation in Chicago* (Chicago: University of Chicago Press, 2012).

Ayelet Brinn received her PhD in history in 2019 from the University of Pennsylvania. She is currently a fellow at the Katz Center for Advanced Judaic Studies at the University of Pennsylvania, and is working on a book manuscript about gender politics and the American Yiddish press.

Steven M. Cohen was research professor of Jewish social policy at Hebrew Union College-Jewish Institute of Religion, and the director of the Berman Jewish Policy Archive at Stanford University.

John Dixon is associate professor of history at the College of Staten Island and the Graduate Center, City University of New York. A historian of colonial New York and the Atlantic world, and a former fellow of the Goldstein-Goren Center for American Jewish History, New York University, he is currently completing a history of Jews in the early modern Americas.

Rachel Gordan is an assistant professor of religion and Jewish studies at the University of Florida, where she is the Shorstein Fellow in American Jewish Culture.

Jeffrey S. Gurock is the Libby M. Klaperman professor of Jewish history at Yeshiva University.

Diana L. Linden is a historian of American art. Her *Ben Shahn's New Deal Murals: Jewish Identity in the American Scene* (Detroit: Wayne State University Press, 2015) was a finalist for a National Jewish Book Award. She was part of the team behind the award-winning *City of Promises: A History of the Jews of New York* (New York: NYU Press, 2012). In 2019, the journal *Smithsonian Studies in America Art* awarded her the Frost Prize for excellence in scholarship.

David Mikics is John and Rebecca Moores professor of English and honors at the University of Houston, as well as a columnist for *Salmagundi* and *Tablet* (www.tabletmag.com). His most recent books are *Stanley Kubrick* (New Haven: Yale University Press, 2020), *Bellow's People* (New York: Norton, 2016) and *Slow Reading in a Hurried Age* (Cambridge, MA: Harvard University Press, 2013). He lives in Brooklyn and Houston.

Deborah Dash Moore is Frederick G. L. Huetwell professor of history and professor of Judaic studies at the University of Michigan. An historian of American Jews, she specializes in twentieth-century urban history. She currently serves as editor in chief of The Posen Library of Jewish Culture and Civilization.

Devin Naar is the Isaac Alhadeff professor in Sephardic studies, associate professor of history, and faculty at the Stroum Center for Jewish Studies in the Jackson School of International Studies at the University of Washington. His book, Jewish Salonica: Between the Ottoman Empire and Modern Greece (Stanford: Stanford University Press, 2016), won a National Jewish Book Award and the Edmund Keeley Prize for best book in modern Greek studies.

Eddy Portnoy is the academic advisor and director of exhibitions at the YIVO Institute for Jewish Research. He is also the author of *Bad Rabbi and Other Strange but True Stories from the Yiddish Press* (Stanford: Stanford University Press, 2017).

Howard B. Rock is emeritus professor of history at Florida International University. His most recent books are *Cityscapes: A History of New York in Images* (with Deborah Dash Moore, New York: Columbia University Press, 2001) and *Haven of Liberty: New York Jews in the New World, 1654–1865* (New York: NYU Press, 2012).

Daniel Soyer is professor of history at Fordham University, in New York, where he has lived all his life. He is author, with Annie Polland, of *The Emerging Metropolis: New York Jews in the Age of Migration, 1840–1920* (New York: NYU Press, 2012), and coeditor of the journal *American Jewish History.*

Index

CPSIA information can be obtained
at www.ICGtesting.com
Printed in the USA
JSHW032012060421
13290JS00008B/51